OFFICIAL TOURIST BOARD GUIDE

Britain's Camping, Caravan & Holiday Parks
2008

visit**Britain**™

Contents

FURTHER INFORMATION

USEFUL INDEXES
A full list of indexes, including David Bellamy
Conservation Award winners and place indexes,

KEY TO SYMBOLS
Inside back-cover flap

Whinstone Lee Tor,
Peak District, Derbyshire

VisitBritain

VisitBritain is the organisation created to
market Britain to the rest of the world, and
England to the British.

Formed by the merger of the British Tourist
Authority and the English Tourism Council,
its mission is to build the value of tourism
by creating world-class destination brands
and marketing campaigns.

It will also build partnerships with – and
provide insights to – other organisations
which have a stake in British and English
tourism.

Constantine Bay, Cornwall

The guide that gives you more

This official VisitBritain guide is packed with information from where to stay, to how to get there and what to see and do. In fact, everything you need to know to enjoy Britain.

Quality accommodation

Choose from a wide range of quality-assessed accommodation to suit all budgets and tastes. This guide contains a comprehensive listing of touring, camping and ho;iday parks plus holiday villages in England, Scotland and Wales participating in The British Graded Holiday Parks Scheme.

Regional information

Every region has its own unique attractions – in each section we highlight a selection of interesting ideas for memorable days out. Regional maps show their location as well as National Trails and sections of the National Cycle Network. You'll also find a selection of great events and regional tourism contact details. For even more ideas go online at visitbritain.com.

Useful indexes

Indexes at the back make it easy to find sites that match your requirements – and if you know the name of the site use the park index.

Tourist information centres

For local information phone or call in to a Tourist Information Centre. Location and contact details can be found at the beginning of each regional section. Alternatively, you can text **INFO** to 62233 to find your nearest Official Partner Tourist Information Centre.

How to use this guide

In this invaluable camping and caravan parks guide, you'll find a great choice of touring, camping and holiday parks plus holiday villages in England, Scotland and Wales.

Each site has been visited annually by national tourist board assessors under The British Graded Holiday Parks Scheme so that you can book with confidence knowing all parks in the guide have been checked and rated for quality.

Detailed entries include descriptions, prices and facilities. You'll also find special offers and themed breaks to suit your tastes, interests and budget.

Finding accommodation is easy

Regional entries
The guide is divided into eleven regional sections and entries are listed alphabetically by place name within each region. Start your search for accommodation in the regional sections of this guide. For an even wider choice, turn to the listing section, starting on page 272, where you will find ALL parks/holiday villages in England participating in The British Graded Holiday Parks Scheme, including those that have not taken a paid entry.

Colour maps
Use the colour maps, starting on page 28, to pinpoint the location of all sites featured in the regional sections. Then refer to the place index at the back of the guide to find the page number. The index also includes tourism areas such as the New Forest and the Cotswolds.

Indexes
The indexes, listed on page 309, will help you find the right place to stay. If you require a swimming pool, for example, there is an index that lists all parks with this facility with disabilities or those that welcome cyclists.

Kids and weather. They change mood from one moment to the next. Fortunately, that's also one of the most striking things about Britain's great outdoors and attractions: you just step across the threshold and its landscapes and entertainment venues offer all the varied play potential you need to fill holidays, sunny afternoons or rainy weekends.

So, there you are on the beach building sandcastles, paddling, eating ice cream and basking in the warm memory that you'll take home. You watch the teenagers hanging out with their surfboards, part of the family outing but doing their own thing. There's something for all ages and that's priceless in every sense of the word. Next time, maybe picnicking in woods, leaping through treetops on an aerial adventure, or getting your hands on heritage - whatever makes everyone happy.

Then it rains and you want to stay indoors. London's Science Museum is free, like a good number of England's top attractions, and that pleases Money Bags. Everyone immediately vanishes into one of the galleries: in Who Am I? you're morphing your face older and younger, in another you're discovering how to forecast weather and learning about climate change, which could be useful for planning your next trip!

Anticipate the family's next mood. Animal magic at Chester Zoo, following Harry Potter to Alnwick Castle, or screaming your heads off at Drayton Manor Theme Park in Staffordshire? There's always another boredom-buster just around the corner.

For lots more great ideas visit
visitbritain.com

Seaside fun,
Brighton & Hove

Make fun of Britain, it runs in the family

Take one of the hundreds of footpaths along the eastern end of Hope Valley in the Peak District and you'll find yourself at Stanage Edge, a bold outcrop of gritstone worshipped throughout the climbing world.

The wind whips the flap of your rucksack, the material snapping like a spinnaker in a force 9, as you pedal up the last few yards of muddy track to where the rock emerges from the stunted bracken. It's only a five-minute walk from the road side car park and an easy drive to find this spot. But make this small effort and you're rewarded with one of the most astounding views in the country.

Out here you feel the full primitive energy of nature. And whether you've packed the crampons and ropes, a pair of hiking boots and a flask or you've brought the Rover and simply come to stretch your legs, it's one of those precious places where you can escape the crowds, taste true freedom and find inner peace.

England boasts an astonishing diversity of natural wonders, from the flat waterscapes of the Norfolk Broads to the jutting peaks of the Lake District, from the ancient woodlands of the New Forest to Dorset's fossil-jewelled Jurassic Coast.

This is our natural heritage, shaped by primeval forces and just waiting to be explored. Do so and you'll return with weary legs, a ravenous appetite and that wonderful tingling sensation you get on your face after a day in the fresh air.

For lots more ideas visit visitbritain.com

Whinstone Lee Tor, Peak District, Derbyshire

The edge of the world – just a short stroll away

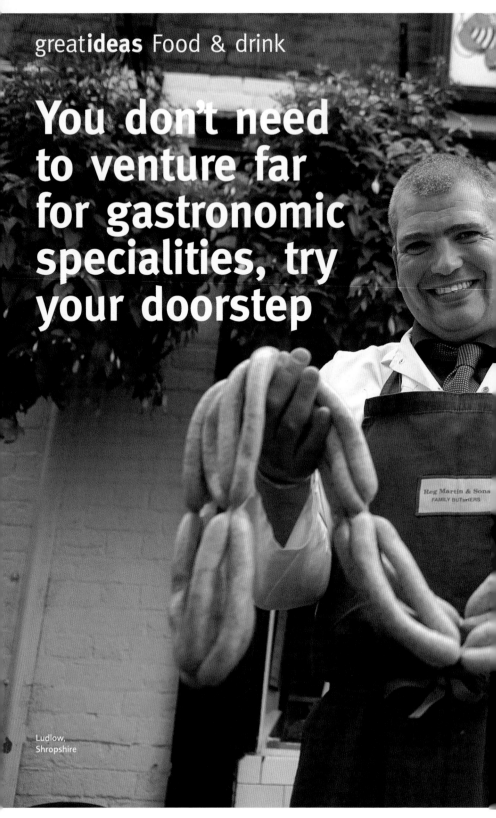

You don't need to venture far for gastronomic specialities, try your doorstep

Ludlow,
Shropshire

A quiet revolution has been simmering away in Britain. Fresh, locally-sourced and organic ingredients have become the order of the day. From bustling farmers' markets to family kitchens turning out hand-made puddings, jams and breads, Dining in or out, you'll more than likely be presented with fresh wholesome food cooked with passion.

Start with the famous Ludlow Food Festival and follow the little-known Sausage Trail, an event in which the town's five independent butchers create new sausage varieties and vie for the crown of People's Choice. You'll find everything from organic rare breeds sausages to the Shropshire Sizzler - a rich blend of local pork, peaches and blue cheese. Take some back to base and spark up the barbie for a fantastic feast.

Fancy lunch while out exploring? Three cheers for the gastropub where high quality cooked-from-scratch bistro meals are served at bar room prices. As you tuck into a crisp salad and garlic mayo (made with free range eggs, of course) you begin to wonder if Chicken in a Basket wasn't just a bad dream.

At the charming Waffle House in St Alban's you can't help but admire the blend of inventiveness, quality produce and sheer dedication that goes into the cooking. Here you'll find waffles of every conceivable shape and size, served with freshly made toppings such as chick pea curry and mango chutney as well as an endless choice of sweet varieties.

The good news is, you'll find places like this all over Britain: it's a foodies' heaven.

For lots more ideas visit
visitbritain.com

It's the kids who first spot them, those surfers with kites. You pull over and stare open-mouthed from the safety of the promenade. For hours on end they skip over waves like a shoal of exotic flying fish, the wind's power made visible by the taught cables yanking them through the air.

Watergate Bay,
Cornwall

Just 24 hours of pestering later, and you and the kids are lining up at the peeling door of the Kite Surf Shack for your first lesson. They (in sleek new wetsuits) take to it like ducks to water; you (in baggy Hawaiian shorts) don't. The rest of that day is a tumble of memories - pounding waves, stinging eyes, blistered palms and a feeling of sheer, utter exhilaration. And the best bit is this: that glorious afternoon is something you'll always share.

Kite surfing is one of the new breed of adrenalin sports to hit these shores, coming (rather fast) to a coastline near you. It's not something most of us have seen before. But give it a go and you'll be hooked.

Of course, you could simply dust off the old bat and ball, take the kids to the beach and show them just why you were captain of the school cricket team. But discover the world of emerging sports, leave your comfort zone where it belongs (at home) and we guarantee you'll experience the great outdoors like you've never experienced it before. And you don't even have to own a dayglo wetsuit.

For lots more ideas visit
visitbritain.com

lying kites –
what could be
nore relaxing?

Ratings and awards at a glance

Reliable, rigorous, easy to use – look out for the following ratings and awards to help you choose with confidence:

Ratings made easy

★	Acceptable quality
★★	Good quality
★★★	Very good quality
★★★★	Excellent quality
★★★★★	Exceptional quality

See overleaf for holiday villages.

Star ratings

Parks are awarded a rating of one to five stars following an assessment of the quality, cleanliness, maintenance and condition of the various facilities provided. It is not necessary to provide a wide range of facilities in order to achieve a high rating, as the emphasis is on the quality of what is actually provided rather than a rating restricted by a lack of facilities. Holiday Villages are rated under a separate scheme. See overleaf for an explanation of what you can expect.

Enjoy England Awards for Excellence

The prestigious and coveted Enjoy England Awards for Excellence showcase the very best in English tourism. Run by VisitBritain in association with England's regions, they include a Caravan Holiday Park of the Year category (see page 25).

National Accessible Scheme

Sites with a National Accessible Scheme rating have been thoroughly assessed to set criteria and provide access to facilities and services for guests with visual, hearing or mobility impairment (see page 22).

Welcome schemes

VisitBritain runs four special Welcome schemes: Cyclists Welcome, Walkers Welcome, Welcome Pets! and Families Welcome. Scheme participants actively encourage these types of visitors and in many instances make special provision to ensure a welcoming, comfortable stay (see page 20).

David Bellamy Conservation Award

This special award is a signpost to parks that are making real achievements in protecting our environment (see page 26).

Visitor Attraction Quality Assurance

Attractions achieving high standards in all aspects of the visitor experience, from initial telephone enquiry to departure, receive this Enjoy England award and are visited every year by professional assessors.

Caravan Holiday Home Award Scheme

VisitBritain, VisitScotland and Visit Wales run award schemes for individual holiday caravan homes on highly graded caravan parks. In addition to complying with standards for Holiday Parks, these exceptional caravans must have a shower or bath, toilet, mains electricity and water heating (at no extra charge) and a fridge (many also have a colour TV).

Award-winning parks listed in this guide show the relevant logo by their entry.

What to expect

Star ratings

Parks are required to meet progressively higher standards of quality as they move up the scale from one to five stars:

ONE STAR Acceptable
To achieve this grade, the park must be clean with good standards of maintenance and customer care.

TWO STAR Good
All the above points plus an improved level of landscaping, lighting, refuse disposal and maintenance. May be less expensive than more highly rated parks.

THREE STAR Very good
Most parks fall within this category; three stars represent the industry standard. The range of facilities provided may vary from park to park, but they will be of a very good standard and will be well maintained.

FOUR STAR Excellent
You can expect careful attention to detail in the provision of all services and facilities. Four star parks rank among the industry's best.

FIVE STAR Exceptional
Highest levels of customer care will be provided. All facilities will be maintained in pristine condition in attractive surroundings.

Holiday Villages

Holiday Villages are assessed under a separate rating scheme and are awarded one to five stars based on both the quality of facilities **and** the range of services provided. The option to include breakfast and dinner is normally available. A variety of accommodation if offered, mostly in custom-built rooms such as chalets.

★ Simple, practical, no frills

★★ Well presented and well run

★★★ Good level of quality and comfort

★★★★ Excellent standard throughout

★★★★★ Exceptional with a degree of luxury

Classifications explained

Parks vary greatly in style and in the facilities they offer. The following will help you decide which is right for you whether you are looking for an overnight caravan stop or an open-air family holiday with all the extras.

Camping Park

These sites only have pitches available for tents.

Touring Park

If you are planning to travel with your own caravan, motor home or tent, then look for a Touring Park.

Holiday Park

If you want to hire a caravan holiday home for a short break or longer holiday, or are looking to buy your own holiday home, a Holiday Park is the right choice. They range from small, rural sites to larger parks with all the added extras, such as a swimming pool.

Many parks will offer a combination of these classifications.

Holiday Village

Holiday villages usually comprise a variety of types of accommodation, with the majority in custom-built rooms, chalets for example. The option to book on a bed and breakfast, or dinner, bed and breakfast basis is normally available. A range of facilities, entertainment and activities are also provided which may, or may not, be included in the tariff.

Holiday Villages must meet a minimum entry requirement for both the provision and quality of facilities and services, including fixtures, fittings, furnishings, decor and any other extra facilities. Progressively higher levels of quality and customer care are provided at each star level.

Forest Holiday Village

A holiday village which is situated in a forest setting with conservation and sustainable tourism being a key feature. It will usually comprise a variety of accommodation, often purpose built; and with a range of entertainment, activities and facilities available on site free of charge or at extra cost.

A special welcome

To help make your selection of accommodation easier there are four special Welcome schemes which accommodation can be assessed to. Owners participating in these schemes go the extra mile to welcome walkers, cyclists, families or pet owners and provide additional facilities and services to make your stay even more comfortable.

Families Welcome

If you are searching for a great family break look out for the Families Welcome sign. The sign indicates that the proprietor offers additional facilities and services catering for a range of ages and family units. For families with young children, the accommodation will have special facilities such as cots and highchairs, storage for push-chairs and somewhere to heat baby food or milk. Where meals are provided, children's choices will be clearly indicated, with healthy options available. They'll also have information on local walks, attractions, activities or events suitable for children, as well as local child-friendly pubs and restaurants. Not all accommodation is able to cater for all ages or combinations of family units, so do check when you book.

Welcome Pets!

Want to travel with your faithful companion? Look out for accommodation displaying the Welcome Pets! sign. Participants in this scheme go out of their way to meet the needs of guests bringing dogs, cats and/or small birds. In addition to providing water and food bowls, torches or nightlights, spare leads and pet washing facilities, they'll buy in food on request, and offer toys, treats and bedding. They'll also have information on pet-friendly attractions, pubs, restaurants and recreation. Of course, not everyone is able to offer suitable facilities for every pet, so do check if there are any restrictions on the type, size and number of animals when you book.

Walkers Welcome

If walking is your passion seek out accommodation participating in the Walkers Welcome scheme. Facilities include a place for drying clothes and boots, maps and books for reference and a first-aid kit. Packed breakfasts and lunch are available on request in hotels and guesthouses, and you have the option to pre-order basic groceries in self-catering accommodation. A wide range of information is provided including public transport, weather, local restaurants and attractions, details of the nearest bank and all night chemists.

Cyclists Welcome

If you like to explore by bike seek out accommodation displaying the Cyclists Welcome symbol. Facilities include a lockable undercover area and a place to dry outdoor clothing and footwear, an evening meal if there are no eating facilities available within one mile, and a packed breakfast or lunch on request. Information is also provided on cycle hire and cycle repair shops, maps and books for reference, weather and details of the nearest bank and all night chemists and more.

For further information go online at enjoyengland.com/quality.

Entries explained

Each entry contains detailed information to help you decide if it is right for you. This has been provided by proprietors and our aim is to ensure that it is as objective and factual as possible.

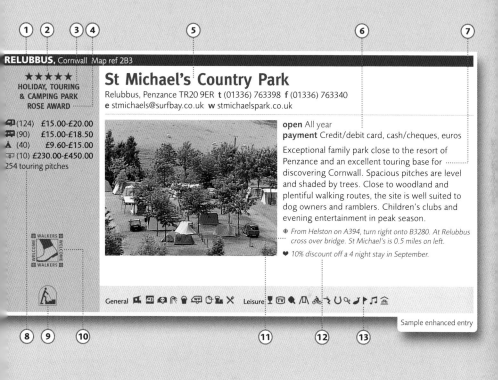

RELUBBUS, Cornwall Map ref 2B3

★★★★★
HOLIDAY, TOURING
& CAMPING PARK
ROSE AWARD

(124) £15.00-£20.00
(90) £15.00-£18.50
(40) £9.60-£15.00
(10) £230.00-£450.00
254 touring pitches

St Michael's Country Park

Relubbus, Penzance TR20 9ER t (01336) 763398 f (01336) 763340
e stmichaels@surfbay.co.uk w stmichaelspark.co.uk

open All year
payment Credit/debit card, cash/cheques, euros

Exceptional family park close to the resort of Penzance and an excellent touring base for discovering Cornwall. Spacious pitches are level and shaded by trees. Close to woodland and plentiful walking routes, the site is well suited to dog owners and ramblers. Children's clubs and evening entertainment in peak season.

⊕ From Helston on A394, turn right onto B3280. At Relubbus cross over bridge. St Michael's is 0.5 miles on left.

♥ 10% discount off a 4 night stay in September.

General Leisure

Sample enhanced entry

1 Listing under town or village with map reference

2 Star rating

3 Classification

4 Award (if applicable)

5 Site name, address, telephone and fax numbers, email and website address

6 Indicates when the site is open and payment accepted.

7 Description

8 Prices per pitch per night for touring pitches; per unit per week for caravan holiday homes

9 Accessible rating where applicable

10 Walkers, cyclists, pets and families welcome, where applicable

11 Travel directions

12 Special promotions

13 At-a-glance facility symbols

**A key to symbols can be found on the back-cover flap.
Keep it open for easy reference.**

National Accessible Scheme

Finding suitable accommodation is not always easy, especially if you have to seek out rooms with level entry or large print menus. Use the National Accessible Scheme to help you make your choice.

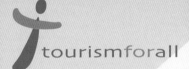

The National Accessible Scheme forms part of the Tourism for All Campaign that is being promoted by VisitBritain and national/ regional tourism organisations. Additional help and guidance on finding suitable holiday accommodation can be obtained from:

Tourism for All
c/o Vitalise, Shap Road Industrial
Estate, Kendal LA9 6NZ

information helpline 0845 124 9971
reservations 0845 124 9973
(lines open 9-5 Mon-Fri)

f (01539) 735567

e info@tourismforall.org.uk

w tourismforall.org.uk

The criteria VisitBritain and national/regional tourism organisations have adopted do not necessarily conform to British Standards or to Building Regulations. They reflect what the organisations understand to be acceptable to meet the practical needs of guests with mobility or sensory impairments and encourage the industry to increase access to all.

Proprietors of parks taking part in the National Accessible Scheme provide facilities and services to ensure a comfortable stay for guests with special hearing, visual or mobility needs. Look at the logos to find out the rating awarded to these exceptional places which provide specific items to make your stay easier and more comfortable, from handrails to tactile markings and level-access showers. Members of the staff may have attended a disability awareness course and will know what assistance will really be appreciated.

Appropriate National Accessible symbols are included in the guide entries for English and Scottish sites (for differences, see below). If you have additional needs or special requirements we strongly recommend that you make sure your chosen site can meet these before you confirm your reservation. The index at the back of the guide gives a list of sites that have received a National Accessible rating.

For a wider selection of accessible accommodation, order a copy of the Easy Access Britain guide featuring almost 500 places to stay. Available from Tourism for All for £9.99 (plus P&P).

Scotland

Category 1
Accessible to a wheelchair user travelling independently.

Category 2
Accessible to a wheelchair user travelling with assistance.

Category 3
Accessible to a wheelchair user able to walk a few paces and up a maximum of three steps.

Wales

Caravan holiday homes and parks in Wales should have an Access Statement available to visitors. Sites have been invited to join the National Accessible Scheme from autumn 2006.

England
Mobility Impairment Symbols

Typically suitable for a person with sufficient mobility to climb a flight of steps but who would benefit from fixtures and fittings to aid balance.

Typically suitable for a person with restricted walking ability and for those who may need to use a wheelchair some of the time and can negotiate a maximum of three steps.

Typically suitable for a person who depends on the use of a wheelchair and transfers unaided to and from the wheelchair in a seated position. This person may be an independent traveller.

Typically suitable for a person who depends on the use of a wheelchair in a seated position. This person also requires personal/mechanical assistance to aid transfer (eg carer, hoist).

Access Exceptional is awarded to establishments that meet the requirements of independent wheelchair users or assisted wheelchair users shown above and also fulfil more demanding requirements with reference to the British Standards BS8300:2001.

Visual Impairment Symbols

Typically provides key additional services and facilities to meet the needs of visually impaired guests.

Typically provides a higher level of additional services and facilities to meet the needs of visually impaired guests.

Hearing Impairment Symbols

Typically provides key additional services and facilities to meet the needs of guests with hearing impairment.

Typically provides a higher level of additional services and facilities to meet the needs of guests with hearing impairment.

Camp for less
on sites with more

Damage Barton Club Site

£5 off your stay on one of our award-winning UK Club Sites

If you love camping as much as we do, you'll love staying on one of The Camping and Caravanning Club's 101 UK Club Sites. And with this £5 voucher, you can stay for less. If you're already a member, feel free to use this voucher on your next holiday. If you're not a member, use the voucher to try a Club Site and experience life as a Club member.

There's just one thing: once you've discovered the friendly welcome, the excellent facilities and clean, safe surroundings, you'll probably want to join anyway!

To book your adventure or to join The Club

call **0845 130 7633**

quoting code **0926** or visit

www.campingandcaravanningclub.co.uk

- More choice of highly maintained, regularly inspected sites
- Friendly sites that are clean and safe, so great for families
- Preferential rates – recoup your membership fee in just 6 nights' stay
- Reduced site fees for 55's and over and special deals for families
- Exclusive Member Services including specialist insurance and advice.

£5 off voucher · £5 off voucher · £5 off voucher · £5 off voucher · £5 off voucher

£5 off your site fee with this voucher. Simply present this voucher when you arrive on any Camping and Caravanning Club UK Club Site. Ref **0926**

Awards
for Excellence

enjoy**England**
Awards for
Excellence
—— 2008 ——

Enjoy England Awards for Excellence are all about telling the world what a fantastic place England is to visit, whether it's for a day trip, a weekend break or a fortnight's holiday.

The Awards, now in their 19th year, are run by VisitBritain in association with England's regional tourism organisations. This year there are 12 categories, including Caravan Holiday Park of the Year, Tourist Information Centre of the Year and awards for the best tourism website and the best tourism experience.

Winners of the 2007 Caravan Holiday Park of the Year Award

- **GOLD WINNER**
  Skelwith Fold Caravan Park, Ambleside, *Cumbria*

- **SILVER WINNER**
  Oakdown Touring and Holiday Home Park, Sidmouth, *Devon*
  Pearl Lake Leisure Park, Leominster, *Herefordshire*

Winners of the 2008 awards will receive their trophies at a ceremony in April 2008. The day will celebrate excellence in tourism in England.
For more information about the awards visit enjoyengland.com.

Above: Skelwith Fold Caravan Park, Ambleside, Cumbria

David Bellamy Conservation Award

'These well-deserved awards are a signpost to parks which are making real achievements in protecting our environment. Go there and experience wrap-around nature...you could be amazed at what you find!'** says Professor David Bellamy.

More than 600 gold, silver and bronze parks were named this year in the David Bellamy Conservation Awards, organised in conjunction with the British Holiday and Home Parks Association.
These parks are recognised for their commitment to conservation and the environment through their management of landscaping, recycling policies, waste management, the cultivation of flora and fauna and the creation of habitats designed to encourage a variety of wildlife onto the park. Links with the local community and the use of local materials are also important considerations.

Parks participating in the scheme are assessed for the awards by holidaymakers who complete postcards to be returned to David Bellamy, an inspection by a local, independent Environmental Consultant and David Bellamy's own study of the parks environmental audit completed when joining the scheme.

An index of award-winning parks featured in the regional pages of this guide can be found on page 325.

enjoyEngland ™

official tourist board guides

Hotels, including country house and town house hotels, metro and budget hotels in England 2008

Guest accommodation, B&Bs, guest houses, farmhouses, inns, restaurants with rooms, campus and hostel accommodation in England 2008

Self-catering holiday homes, including serviced apartments and approved caravan holiday homes, boat accommodation and holiday cottage agencies in England 2008

Touring parks, camping holidays and holiday parks and villages in Britain 2008

£10.99

£11.99

£11.99

£8.99

informative, easy to use and great value for money

Pet-friendly hotels, B&Bs and self-catering accommodation in England 2008

Great ideas for places to visit, eat and stay in England

Places to stay and visit in South West England

Places to stay and visit in Northern England

Accessible places to stay in Britain

£9.99

£10.99

£9.99

£9.99

£9.99

Now available in good bookshops.
For special offers on VisitBritain publications,
please visit **visitbritaindirect.com**

Map 1

Location Maps

Every place name featured in the regional accommodation sections of this guide has a map reference to help you locate it on the maps which follow. For example, to find Swanage, which has 'Map ref 2B3', turn to Map 2 and refer to grid square B3.

All place names appearing in the regional sections are shown in black type on the maps. This enables you to find other places in your chosen area which may have suitable accommodation – the place index (at the back of this guide) gives page numbers.

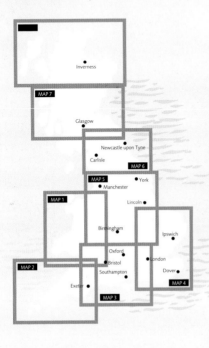

Inverness

MAP 7

Glasgow

Newcastle upon Tyne
Carlisle
MAP 6
MAP 5   York
Manchester
MAP 1
Lincoln
Birmingham
Ipswich
Oxford   London
Bristol
MAP 2   Southampton   Dover
Exeter   MAP 4
MAP 3

Tintagel

Padstow
St Merryn
Newquay Cornwall
International
Newquay   CORNWALL
Lanivet

St Agnes   St Austell   Fowey
Blackwater   Po
Porthtowan   by-
Portreath   Truro
Mevagissey
St Ives   Redruth
Connor Downs   St Just in Roseland
Penzance   Hayle
St Just in Penwith
Land's End   Penzance   Helston
(St Just)   Rosudgeon
Land's End

Tresco Isles of Scilly
St Mary's

Ruan Minor

Key to regions: South West England

28

Map 1

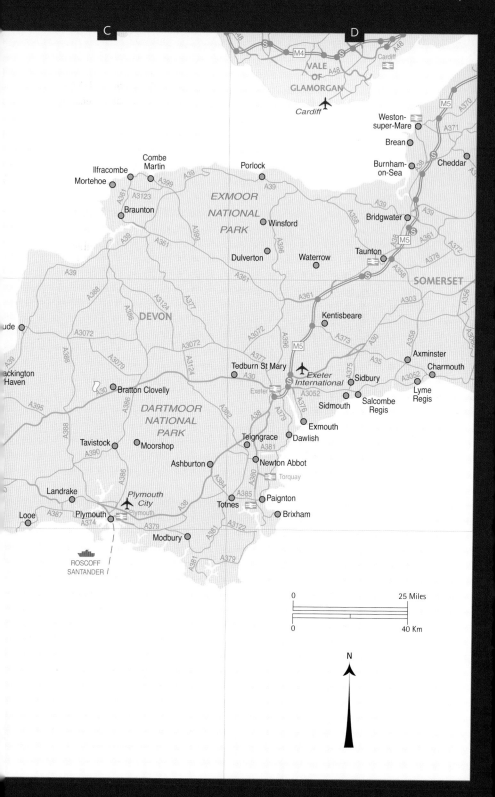

Map 2

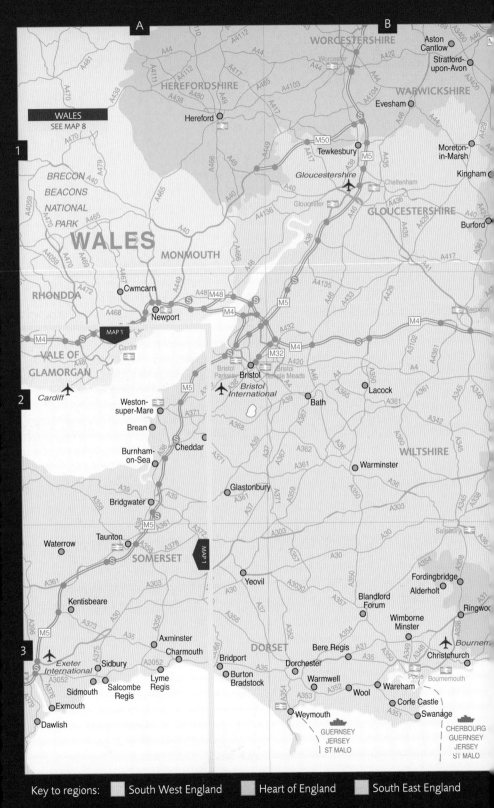

Key to regions: South West England Heart of England South East England

Map 2

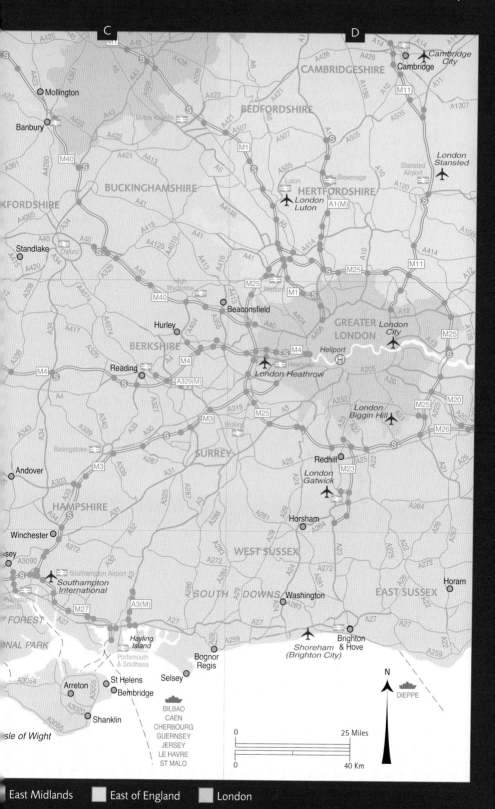

East Midlands   East of England   London

All place names in black offer parks in this guide

Map 3

Key to regions: █ East Midlands █ South East England █ East of England █ London

Map 3

Map 4

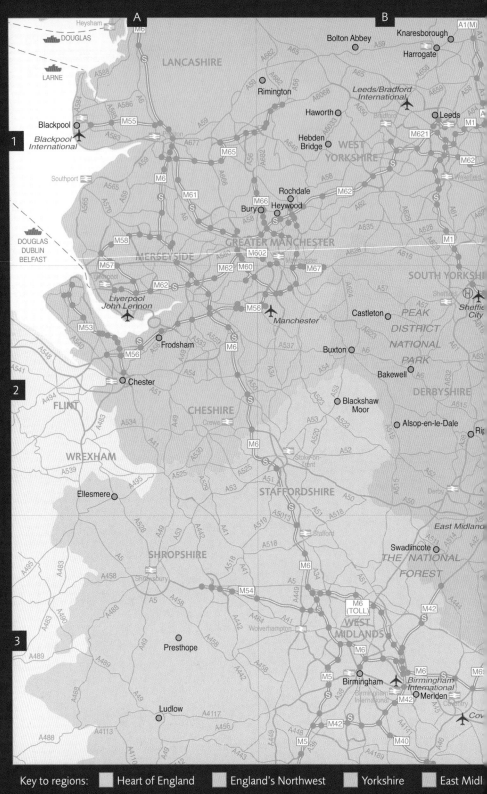

Key to regions: ▢ Heart of England ▢ England's Northwest ▢ Yorkshire ▢ East Midl

Map 4

East of England

All place names in black offer parks in this guide

Map 5

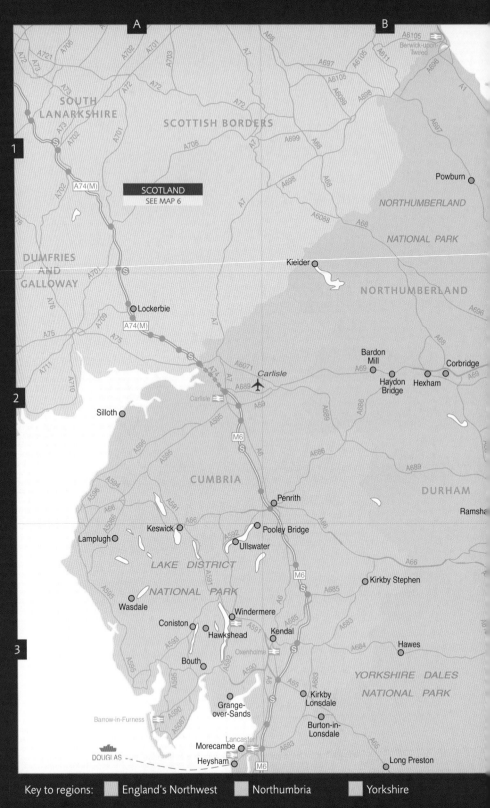

Key to regions: England's Northwest · Northumbria · Yorkshire

Map 5

C   D

0   25 Miles
0   40 Km

N

Bamburgh
Seahouses

Newcastle
International

Newcastle

Sunderland

Durham

A1(M)

Stockton-
on-Tees

Middlesbrough

Darlington

Durham
Tees Valley

Whitby

BERGEN
STAVANGER
KRISTIANSAND
HAUGESUND
GOTHENBERG
AMSTERDAM (Ijmuiden)

NORTH YORK MOORS
NATIONAL PARK

Bedale

Helmsley
Wombleton   Pickering

Scarborough

Filey

NORTH
YORKSHIRE

Ripon

Slingsby

A1(M)

Bridlington

All place names in black offer parks in this guide   37

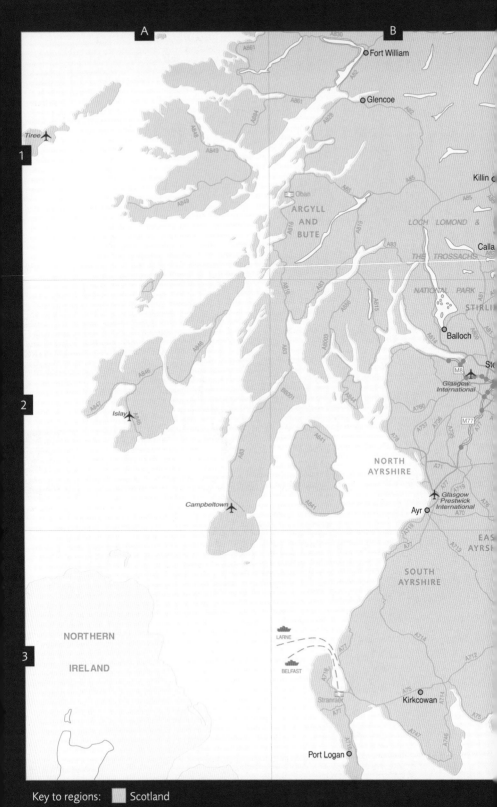

Map 6

A B

1

Fort William

Glencoe

Tiree ✈

Oban

ARGYLL
AND
BUTE

Killin

LOCH LOMOND &

Calla

THE TROSSACHS

NATIONAL PARK

STIRLI

Balloch

STIRLIN

2

Islay ✈

M8

Ste

Glasgow
International

M77

NORTH
AYRSHIRE

Campbeltown ✈

Glasgow
Prestwick
International

Ayr

EAS
AYRSH

SOUTH
AYRSHIRE

3

NORTHERN

IRELAND

LARNE

BELFAST

Stranraer

Kirkcowan

Port Logan

Key to regions: Scotland

Map 6

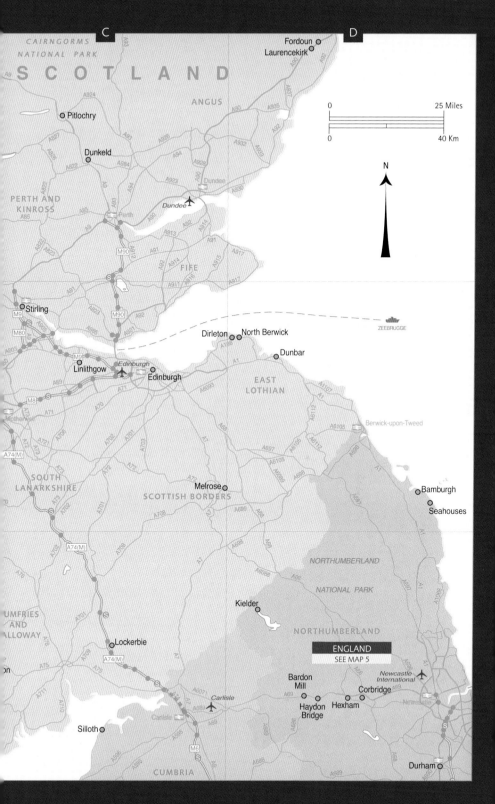

All place names in black offer parks in this guide

Map 7

A   B

1

2

WESTERN ISLES

Stornoway

Benbecula

3

Barra

Kyle of Lochalsh

Balmacara

Shiel Bridge

HIGHLAND

Key to regions: Scotland

Map 7

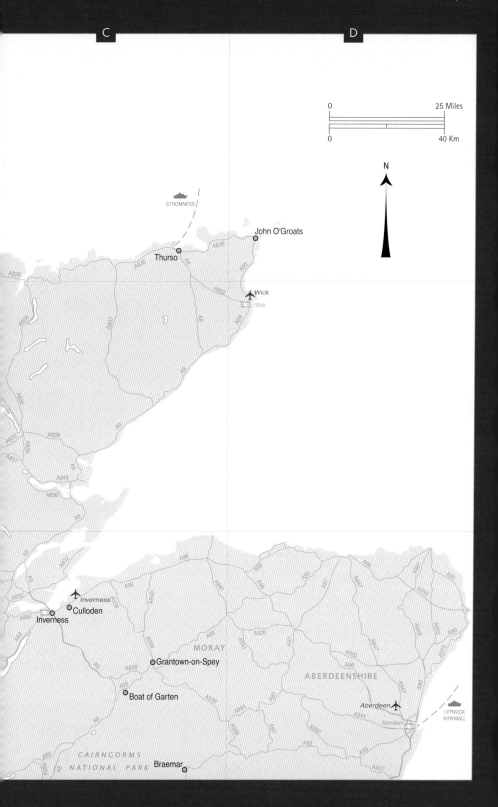

C
D

0   25 Miles

0   40 Km

N

STROMNESS

John O'Groats

A836

Thurso

A836

A838

A897

A99

✈ Wick
Wick

A9

A839

A9

A949

A838

A9

A862

A96

A96

A98

A981

A950

✈ Inverness

A96

A940

A941

A96

A947

A948

A952

A90

A832

Culloden

Inverness

A862

A95

A920

A97

A920

A947

A90

MORAY

A938

Grantown-on-Spey

A944

ABERDEENSHIRE

A96

A9

Boat of Garten

A939

A944

A97

Aberdeen ✈
Aberdeen

A944

A90

A98

LERWICK
KIRKWALL

A86

CAIRNGORMS
NATIONAL PARK

A93

Braemar

A980

A93

A957

Map 8

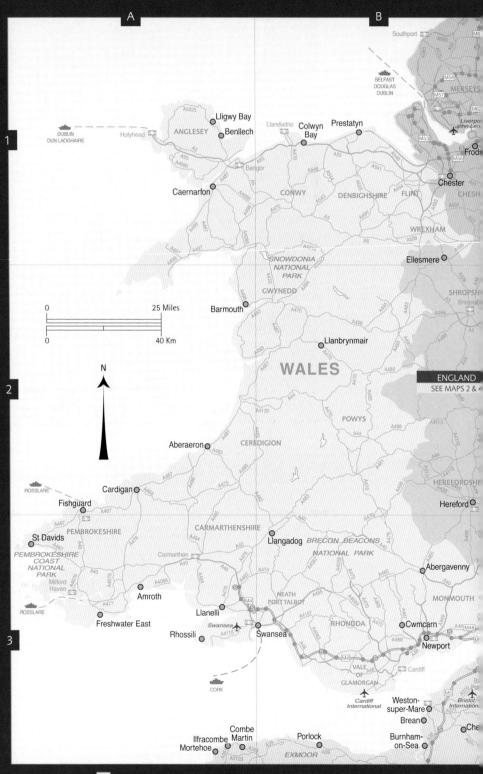

Key to regions: ⬜ Wales

All place names in black offer parks in this guide

Finding a park
is easy

Britain's Camping, Caravan & Holiday Parks guide makes it quick and easy to find a place to stay. There are several ways to use this guide.

PARK INDEX

If you know the name of the site you wish to book, turn to the park index at the back where the relevant page number is shown.

PLACE INDEX

The place index at the back lists all locations with parks featured in the regional sections. A page number is shown where you can find full accommodation and contact details.

COLOUR MAPS

All the place names in black on the colour maps at the front have an entry in the regional sections. Refer to the place index for the page number where you will find one or more parks in your chosen town or village.

ALL ASSESSED ACCOMMODATION

Contact details for all British Graded Holiday Parks Scheme participants throughout England, together with their quality rating, are given in the back section of this guide. Parks with a full entry in the regional sections are shown in bold. Look in the park index for the page number where their full entry appears.

England's Northwest

Blackpool and Lancashire, Chester and
Cheshire, Cumbria – The Lake District,
Liverpool and Merseyside, Manchester

Constant
variety and
continual
delights

England's Northwest is a
region of astonishing
contrasts. Where else can
you travel to four different
worlds – from peak to plain,
from coast to city – in one
short day?

England's Northwest
visitenglandsnorthwest.com

Overlooking Ullswater, Cumbria

Albert Dock, Liverpool   Tatton Park, Cheshire

The Lowry, Manchester

From the Cumbrian peaks to the Cheshire plain, from the seaside thrills of Blackpool to the buzzing energy of Manchester, England's Northwest is bursting with choice for the holidaymaker. Liverpool celebrated its 800th anniversary in 2007 and is an exciting place to be. Fancy a little R&R? Head for Cumbria. This place is a natural wonderland where plunging lakes and swooshing mountains collide in a perfect marriage. Prefer the bright lights to starry skies? Make Manchester your next stop. This glamorous city is a magnet for every designer label and trendy club out there. Or for a peaceful family break, hire a narrow boat in leafy Cheshire and drift along the waterways of the Cheshire Ring.

Experience a sense of déjà vu at Lyme Park in Cheshire – the setting for BBC's Pride and Prejudice. Another must is a visit to Arley Hall, a magnificent Victorian Jacobean stately home with magical gardens. If you find yourself in Chester, book into The Grosvenor Spa – it's the perfect place to escape the hustle and bustle. And no trip to Manchester would be complete without seeing Imperial War Museum North, a powerful exploration of the impact of war on ordinary lives.

If you love mystical places, you'll adore Alderly Edge in Cheshire. Legend has it that this strange place is linked to King Arthur and Merlin. It's also the setting for the classic children's story The Weirdstone of Brisingamen. If you prefer bargain-hunting to wizard-hunting, there's no more colourful and fascinating market than Affleck's Palace in Manchester. And if you want to experience the great outdoors, it doesn't get much grander that in Cumbria – The Lake District.

Whether it's for a night out, day trip or weekend away with the family, England's Northwest has a wealth of attractions to inspire you.

Destinations

Blackpool

Britain's favourite holiday resort. Feel the thrill on the Pepsi Max Big One at the Pleasure Beach, take high tea in the magnificent Tower Ballroom, or stroll the seven miles of sandy beaches. Blackpool offers you world-class shows, cosmopolitan restaurants, vibrant nightlife, an active sports scene and breathtakingly beautiful scenery on the doorstep – every ingredient, in fact, for an unforgettable, carefree break.

Chester

Experience one of Europe's top heritage cities. Walk the unique city walls, complete with surviving Roman sections, then visit the famous Rows, unique two-tiered galleries in black and white 'magpie' style, to shop for everything from antiques to high fashion. Stroll along the banks of the beautiful River Dee, explore the Roman amphitheatre, and don't miss the Grosvenor and Cheshire Military Museums, the beautiful Grosvenor Park and Chester's famous Roodee Racecourse.

Chester

The Cavern Club, Liverpool

Cumbria – The Lake District

Imperial War Museum North, Manchester

Blackpool

Cumbria – The Lake District

With breathtaking mountains and 16 sparkling lakes, the unsurpassed scenery of Cumbria – The Lake District has inspired writers and poets across the ages. Explore the best walking and climbing routes that England has to offer. Only five peaks in England are over 900m and they are all in Cumbria. Visit the magnificent World Heritage Site at Hadrian's Wall, the most important Roman monument in Britain. Pull off your hiking boots and relax in high-quality accommodation – you'll be thoroughly spoilt for choice.

Liverpool

Experience the unique atmosphere of Liverpool. The birthplace of the Beatles and European Capital of Culture 2008 offers you more theatres, museums and galleries than any UK city outside London. Its history as one of the world's great ports has left a remarkable legacy of art and architecture for you to explore, not forgetting, of course, the city's famous sporting pedigree. So if it's Strawberry Fields, Premiership football or Europe's finest culture you're looking for, it has to be Liverpool.

Manchester

If you haven't been to Manchester, there's never been a better time to visit. Explore a city that has come a long way from its industrial roots and reinvented itself as a truly contemporary metropolis. You'll find modern landmark buildings, a wealth of art and culture, great bars and world-class hospitality. Here there's every experience imaginable, from fine dining and top-class theatre, to major sporting events and year-round festivals. It's a shopping destination in its own right, rivalling that of the capital, with top stores and chic boutiques.

Places to visit

Anderton Boat Lift
Northwich, Cheshire
(01606) 786777
andertonboatlift.co.uk
*Sail through the magnificent
Victorian boat lift*

Arley Hall and Gardens
Northwich, Cheshire
(01565) 777353
arleyhallandgardens.com
*Victorian country house with
splendid gardens*

Beatles Story
Liverpool, Merseyside
(0151) 709 1963
beatlesstory.com
The history of the Fab Four

**Blackwell, The Arts & Crafts
House**
Windermere, Cumbria
(015394) 46139
blackwell.org.uk
*Elegant Arts and Crafts house and
gardens*

Bowland Wild Boar Park
Preston, Lancashire
(01995) 61554
wildboarpark.co.uk
*Hand-feed animals in a beautiful
wooded park*

Chester Zoo
Cheshire
(01244) 380280
chesterzoo.org.uk
*Black Rhinos and 7,000 other
animals in natural enclosures*

**Go Ape! High Wire
Forest Adventure**
Delamere, Cheshire
0870 444 5562
goape.co.uk
Rope bridges, swings and zip slides

**Imperial War
Museum North**
Large Visitor
Attraction of the Year
– Silver Winner
Manchester
(0161) 836 4000
iwm.org.uk/north
*Spectacular museum with
innovative display techniques*

**Jodrell Bank
Visitor Centre**
near Macclesfield,
Cheshire
(01477) 571339
jb.man.ac.uk
*Home of the Lovell radio
telescope*

Lady Lever Art Gallery
Wirral, Merseyside
(0151) 478 4136
ladyleverartgallery.org.uk
*Magnificent collection of fine and
decorative arts*

The Lowry
Salford, Greater
Manchester
(0161) 876 2000
thelowry.com
*Art and entertainment in stunning
21st century landmark*

**The Manchester
Museum**
(0161) 275 2634

manchester.ac.uk/museum
*Displays and exhibitions from
around the world*

**Manchester United
Museum & Tour**
0870 442 1994
manutd.com
*Delve behind the scenes at the
Theatre of Dreams*

Mirehouse Historic House
Keswick, Cumbria
(017687) 72287
mirehouse.com
*Historic house with literary
connections*

Muncaster Experience
Lake District National Park,
Cumbria
(01229) 717614
muncaster.co.uk
*Historic castle with ghostly
goings-on*

**The Museum of
Science and Industry**
Manchester
(0161) 832 2244
msim.org.uk
*Historic buildings packed with
fascinating exhibits*

The National Football Museum
Preston, Lancashire
(01772) 908442
nationalfootballmuseum.com
*Amazing journey through football
history*

**National Wildflower
Centre**
Liverpool, Merseyside
(0151) 738 1913
nwc.org.uk
*Wild flowers in a family-friendly
environment*

Pleasure Beach, Blackpool
Lancashire
0870 444 5566
blackpoolpleasurebeach.co.uk
*Thrills and spills featuring Valhalla
and the Pepsi Max Big One*

The Rum Story
Whitehaven, Cumbria
(01946) 592933
rumstory.co.uk
Story of the rum trade

Diary dates 2008

South Lakes Wild Animal Park
Dalton-in-Furness, Cumbria
(01229) 466086
wildanimalpark.co.uk
The ultimate interactive animal experience

Tate Liverpool
Merseyside
(0151) 702 7400
tate.org.uk/liverpool
Modern and contemporary art in historic setting

Tatton Park (NT)
Knutsford, Cheshire
(01625) 534400
tattonpark.org.uk
Historic mansion set in deer park

Urbis
Manchester
(0161) 605 8200
urbis.org.uk
Multi-media exhibitions of city life

Wildfowl & Wetland Trust Martin Mere
Nr Ormskirk, Lancashire
(01704) 895181
wwt.org.uk
Feed endangered species straight from your hand

World Museum Liverpool
Merseyside
(0151) 478 4393
worldmuseumliverpool.org.uk
Treasures from across the world

The World of Glass
St Helens, Merseyside
0870 011 4466
worldofglass.com
Live glass-blowing and multi-media shows

John Smiths Grand National
Aintree, Merseyside
aintree.co.uk
3 – 5 Apr

Ullswater Walking Festival
ullswater.visitor-centre.co.uk
10 – 18 May

Chester Mystery Plays
Cathedral Green, Chester
chestermysteryplays.com
28 Jun – 19 Jul

The British Open (Golf)
Royal Birkdale, Merseyside
opengolf.com
17 – 20 Jul

RHS Flower Show at Tatton Park
Knutsford, Cheshire
rhs.org.uk
23 – 26 Jul*

Pennine Lancashire Food and Drink Festival
Various locations, Lancashire
penninelancashirefood.co.uk
4 – 7 Sep*

Westmorland County Show
Crooklands, Cumbria
westmorland-county-show.co.uk
11 Sep

Blackpool Illuminations
visitblackpool.com
Sep – Nov*

Manchester Food and Drink Festival
Various locations, Manchester
foodanddrinkfestival.com
10 – 20 Oct*

Muncaster Halloween Week
muncaster.co.uk
27 – 31 Oct

* provisional date at time of going to press

Tourist Information Centres

When you arrive at your destination, visit an Official Partner Tourist Information Centre for quality assured help with accommodation and information about local attractions and events, or email your request before you go. To search for attractions and Tourist Information Centres on the move just text INFO to 62233, and a web link will be sent to your mobile phone.

Accrington	Blackburn Road	(01254) 872595	tourism@hyndburnbc.gov.uk
Altrincham	20 Stamford New Road	(0161) 912 5931	tourist.information@trafford.gov.uk
Ashton-under-Lyne	Wellington Road	(0161) 343 4343	tourist.information@tameside.gov.uk
Barnoldswick	Fernlea Avenue	(01282) 666704	tourist.info@pendle.gov.uk
Barrow-in-Furness	Duke Street	(01229) 876505	touristinfo@barrowbc.gov.uk
Blackburn	50-54 Church Street	(01254) 53277	visit@blackburn.gov.uk
Blackpool	1 Clifton Street	(01253) 478222	tic@blackpool.gov.uk
Bolton	Le Mans Crescent	(01204) 334321	tourist.info@bolton.gov.uk
Bowness	Glebe Road	(015394) 42895	bownesstic@lake-district.gov.uk
Burnley	Croft Street	(01282) 664421	tic@burnley.gov.uk
Bury	Market Street	(0161) 253 5111	touristinformation@bury.gov.uk
Carlisle	Greenmarket	(01228) 625600	tourism@carlisle-city.gov.uk
Chester (Town Hall)	Northgate Street	(01244) 402111	tis@chester.gov.uk
Chester Visitor Centre	Vicars Lane	(01244) 351609	tis@chester.gov.uk
Cleveleys	Victoria Square	(01253) 853378	cleveleystic@wyrebc.gov.uk
Clitheroe	12-14 Market Place	(01200) 425566	tourism@ribblevalley.gov.uk
Congleton	High Street	(01260) 271095	tourism@congleton.gov.uk
Coniston	Ruskin Avenue	(015394) 41533	Conistontic@lake-district.gov.uk
Ellesmere Port	Kinsey Road	(0151) 356 7879	
Fleetwood	The Esplanade	(01253) 773953	fleetwoodtic@btopenworld.com
Garstang	High Street	(01995) 602125	garstangtic@wyrebc.gov.uk
Kendal	Highgate	(01539) 725758	kendaltic@southlakeland.gov.uk
Keswick	Market Square	(017687) 72645	keswicktic@lake-district.gov.uk
Knutsford	Toft Road	(01565) 632611	ktic@macclesfield.gov.uk
Lancaster	29 Castle Hill	(01524) 32878	lancastertic@lancaster.gov.uk
Liverpool 08 Place	Whitechapel	(0151) 233 2459	contact@liverpool.08.com
Liverpool John Lennon Airport	Speke Hall Avenue	0906 680 6886**	info@visitliverpool.com
Lytham St Annes	67 St Annes Road West	(01253) 725610	touristinformation@fylde.gov.uk
Macclesfield	Town Hall	(01625) 504114	informationcentre@macclesfield.gov.uk
Manchester Visitor Information Centre	Lloyd Street	0871 222 8223	touristinformation@ marketing-manchester.co.uk
Morecambe	Marine Road Central	(01524) 582808	morecambetic@lancaster.gov.uk
Nantwich	Market Street	(01270) 537359	touristi@crewe-nantwich.gov.uk
Northwich	1 The Arcade	(01606) 353534	tourism@valeroyal.gov.uk
Oldham	12 Albion Street	(0161) 627 1024	ecs.tourist@oldham.gov.uk
Pendle Heritage Centre	Park Hill	(01282) 661701	heritage.centre@pendle.gov.uk

Penrith	Middlegate	(01768) 867466	pen.tic@eden.gov.uk
Preston	Lancaster Road	(01772) 253731	tourism@preston.gov.uk
Rochdale	The Esplanade	(01706) 864928	tic@link4life.org
Saddleworth	High Street	(01457) 870336	ecs.saddleworthtic@oldham.gov.uk
St Helens	Chalon Way East	(01744) 755150	info@sthelenstic.com
Salford	Salford Quays	(0161) 848 8601	tic@salford.gov.uk
Southport	112 Lord Street	(01704) 533333	info@visitsouthport.com
Stockport	30 Market Place	(0161) 474 4444	tourist.information@stockport.gov.uk
Warrington	Horsemarket Street	(01925) 428585	informationcentre@warrington.gov.uk
Whitehaven	Market Place	(01946) 598914	tic@copelandbc.gov.uk
Wigan	62 Wallgate	(01942) 825677	tic@wlct.org
Wilmslow	Rectory Fields	(01625) 522275	i.hillaby@macclesfield.gov.uk
Windermere	Victoria Street	(015394) 46499	windermeretic@southlakeland.gov.uk

** calls to this number are charged at premium rate

River Mersey and Liverpool

Travel info

By road:
Motorways intersect within the region which has the best road network in the country. Travelling north or south use the M6, and east or west the M62.

By rail:
Most Northwest coastal resorts are connected to InterCity routes with trains from many parts of the country, and there are through trains to major cities and towns.

By air:
Fly into Liverpool John Lennon, Manchester or Blackpool airports.

Find out more

Windermere, Cumbria

There are various publications and guides about England's Northwest available from the following Tourist Boards or by logging on to visitenglandsnorthwest.com or calling 0845 600 6040:

Visit Chester and Cheshire
Chester Railway Station, 1st Floor, West Wing Offices, Station Road, Chester CH1 3NT
t (01244) 405600
e info@visitchesterandcheshire.co.uk
w visitchester.com or visitcheshire.com

Cumbria Tourism
Windermere Road, Staveley, Kendal LA8 9PL
t (015398) 22222
e info@cumbriatourism.org
w golakes.co.uk

The Lancashire and Blackpool Tourist Board
St George's House, St George's Street Chorley PR7 2AA
t (01257) 226600 (Brochure request)
e info@visitlancashire.com
w visitlancashire.com

Marketing Manchester – The Tourist Board for Greater Manchester
Churchgate House, 56 Oxford Street Manchester M1 6EU
t (0161) 237 1010
 Brochure request: 0870 609 3013
e touristinformation@marketing-manchester.co.uk
w visitmanchester.com

The Mersey Partnership – The Tourist Board for Liverpool and Merseyside
12 Princes Parade, Liverpool L3 1BG
t (0151) 233 2008 (information enquiries)
t 0844 870 0123 (accommodation booking)
e info@visitliverpool.com (accommodation enquiries)
e 08place@liverpool.gov.uk (information enquiries)
w visitliverpool.com

Ratings you can trust

enjoyEngland.com

★ ★ ★
HOLIDAY PARK

When you're looking for a place to stay, you need a rating system you can trust. The British Graded Holiday Parks Scheme, operated jointly by VisitBritain, VisitScotland and Visit Wales, gives you a clear guide as to what to expect.

Based on the internationally recognised rating of one to five stars, the system puts great emphasis on quality and reflects customer expectations.

Parks are visited annually by professional assessors who award a rating based on cleanliness, environment and the quality of services and facilities provided.

Ratings made easy

★　　　　　Simple, practical, no frills
★★　　　　Well presented and well run
★★★　　　Good level of quality and comfort
★★★★　　Excellent standard throughout
★★★★★　Exceptional with a degree of luxury

For full details of VisitBritains's Quality Rose assessment schemes, go online at enjoyengland.com/quality

where to stay in
England's Northwest

All place names in the blue bands are shown on the maps at the front of this guide.

A complete listing of all VisitBritain assessed parks in England appears at the back.

Accommodation symbols
Symbols give useful information about services and facilities. Inside the back-cover flap you can find a key to these symbols. Keep it open for easy reference.

BLACKPOOL, Lancashire Map ref 4A1

★★★★
HOLIDAY PARK
⊞ (18) £150.00–£490.00

Newton Hall Holiday Park

Staining Road, Blackpool FY3 0AX **t** (01253) 882512 **f** (01253) 893101 **e** reception@newtonhall.net **w** partingtons.com

Family park ideally situated in open country, 2.5 miles from Blackpool town centre. Caravans and flats for hire. New leisure complex. Regular live entertainment. No pets. Loads to do. Open 1 March to 15 November.

payment Credit/debit cards, cash/cheques

General 🔌 🖭 P 🕐 📷 🖪 🔊 ✕ ☼   Leisure 🎣 📺 🍴 🎵 ♦ 🎿 🎵

BOUTH, Cumbria Map ref 5A3

★★★★★
HOLIDAY &
TOURING PARK
ROSE AWARD

🚐 (26)   £12.50–£20.00
🚉 (4)   £12.50–£20.00
⊞ (3) £195.00–£495.00
30 touring pitches

Black Beck Caravan Park

Bouth, Ulverston LA12 8JN **t** (01229) 861274 **f** (01229) 861041 **e** reception@blackbeck.com

Black Beck is situated within the Lake District National Park, nestled in the beautiful Rusland Valley between the southern tips of Lake Windermere and Coniston. Surrounded by spectacular woodland scenery.

payment Credit/debit cards, cash/cheques

General 🔌 P 🕐 🛢 📷 🗻 ⊙ 📷 🖪 🔊 🐾 ☼   Leisure 🎿 U 🎵 🚲

Get on the road

Take yourself on a journey through England's historic towns and villages, past stunning coastlines and beautiful countryside with VisitBritain's series of inspirational touring guides. You can purchase the guides from good bookshops and online at visitbritaindirect.com.

BURY, Greater Manchester Map ref 4B1

★★★★★
TOURING PARK
(85) £13.60–£25.60
(85) £13.60–£25.60
85 touring pitches

See Ad on inside front cover

THE CARAVAN CLUB

Burrs Country Park Caravan Club Site

Woodhill Road, Bury BL8 1BN **t** (0161) 761 0489 **w** caravanclub.co.uk

open All year
payment Credit/debit cards, cash/cheques

On a historic mill site, Burrs has much to offer, including relaxing river and countryside walks as well as easy access into Manchester.

From A676 (signposted Ramsbottom), follow signs for Burrs Country Park.

Special member rates mean you can save your membership subscription in less than a week. Visit our website to find out more.

General P

CHESTER, Cheshire Map ref 4A2

★★★★★
TOURING & CAMPING PARK
(100) £14.30–£27.70
(100) £14.30–£27.70
on application
100 touring pitches

See Ad on inside front cover

THE CARAVAN CLUB

Chester Fairoaks Caravan Club Site

Rake Lane, Little Stanney, Chester CH2 4HS **t** (0151) 355 1600 **w** caravanclub.co.uk

open All year
payment Credit/debit cards, cash/cheques

A tranquil site only six miles from the walled city of Chester with its famous zoo, historic sites, top-class entertainment and excellent shopping. Take an open-top bus or walk around the walls to absorb the colourful atmosphere.

From M53 take jct 10 and join A5117. Travel towards Queensferry, follow brown signs. Turn left in Little Stanney at signpost Chorlton. Site 0.25 miles on left.

Special member rates mean you can save your membership subscription in less than a week. Visit our website to find out more.

General P Leisure

CHESTER, Cheshire Map ref 4A2

★★★★★
HOLIDAY, TOURING & CAMPING PARK
(45) £15.00–£17.00
(15) £15.00–£17.00
(15) £15.00–£17.00
(6) £250.00–£450.00
45 touring pitches

Manor Wood Country Caravan Park

Manor Wood, Coddington, Chester CH3 9EN **t** (01829) 782990 & 07762 817827 **f** (01829) 782990
e info@manorwoodcaravans.co.uk **w** cheshire-caravan-sites.co.uk

Touring caravan park for 45 units in the Cheshire countryside. Enjoying spectacular views, fishing, swimming, play area and a tennis court on site. Accessible to all.

open All year
payment Credit/debit cards, cash/cheques

General P Leisure

CONISTON, Cumbria Map ref 5A3

★★★★★
HOLIDAY PARK
ROSE AWARD
(6) Min £15.00
(15) £205.00–£545.00

Crake Valley Holiday Park

Lake Bank, Water Yeat, Ulverston LA12 8DL **t** (01229) 885203 **f** (01229) 885203
e crakevalley@coniston1.fslife.co.uk **w** crakevalley.co.uk

Small, top-graded holiday park. Caravans and lodges for hire in secluded setting opposite Coniston Water. Ideal base for touring the Lakes. Open March to January.

payment Cash/cheques

General P

CONISTON, Cumbria Map ref 5A3

★★★★
TOURING &
CAMPING PARK

🚐 (280) £12.10–£24.90
🚙 (280) £12.10–£24.90
Å on application
280 touring pitches

See Ad on inside front cover

THE
CARAVAN
CLUB

Park Coppice Caravan Club Site

Park Gate, Coniston LA21 8LA t (015394) 41555 w caravanclub.co.uk

payment Credit/debit cards, cash/cheques

Landscaped site set in 63 acres of National Trust woodland. Lake for watersports, on-site play areas, orienteering courses and Red Squirrel Nature Trail. Open March to November.

⊕ Follow A593, 1.5 miles south of Coniston village. Final approach from the north or south is narrow in places.

♥ Special member rates mean you can save your membership subscription in less than a week. Visit our website to find out more.

General ▣ P 🔌 🕒 🚽 🌐 🌡 ☉ 📷 🔳 🐾 ☼ Leisure ⛺ 🎣

FRODSHAM, Cheshire Map ref 4A2

★★★★
HOLIDAY PARK

🏠 (10) £209.00–£563.00

Ridgeway Country Holiday Park

The Ridgeway, Frodsham WA6 6XQ t (01928) 734981 f (01928) 734981 e sue@ridgewaypark.com w ridgewaypark.com

payment Credit/debit cards, cash/cheques

An ideal base for exploring the scenic Cheshire countryside, yet within close proximity to Liverpool and Chester. Prices weekly for the lodges and caravans. Open 1 March to 2 January. Short-break prices available.

⊕ Ten minutes from jct 12 M56. A56 towards Frodsham. Pas through town then left onto B5393. Pass Foxhill Conference Centre then immediately left onto The Ridgeway. Up hill on left.

General ⚡ P 🕒 📷 🔳 🐾 Leisure ∪ 🎣 ⮕ 🚲

GRANGE-OVER-SANDS, Cumbria Map ref 5A3

★★★★
HOLIDAY &
TOURING PARK
ROSE AWARD

🚐 (3) £11.00–£14.00
🚙 (3) £11.00–£14.00
Å (5) £9.00–£12.00
🏠 (2) £250.00–£350.00
8 touring pitches

Greaves Farm Caravan Park

Field Broughton, Grange-over-Sands LA11 6HR t (015395) 36329 & (015395) 36587

Small, quiet site two miles north of Cartmel. A convenient base for Lake District touring, and under personal supervision of the owner. Directions given with booking confirmation. Open March to October.

payment Cash/cheques

General P 🔌 🕒 🚽 🌡 ☉ 📷 🐾 ☼

GRANGE-OVER-SANDS, Cumbria Map ref 5A3

★★★★★
TOURING PARK
🚐(131) £13.60–£25.60
🚎(131) £13.60–£25.60
131 touring pitches

See Ad on inside front cover

THE
CARAVAN
CLUB

Meathop Fell Caravan Club Site

Meathop, Grange-over-Sands LA11 6RB t (015395) 32912 w caravanclub.co.uk

payment Credit/debit cards, cash/cheques

Peaceful site, ideal for exploring the southern Lake District. Kendal, famous for its mint cake, is within easy reach; Grange-over-Sands and Ulverston are close by.

⊕ M6 jct 36, A590 to Barrow. After about 3.25 miles take slip road and follow A590 to Barrow. At 1st roundabout follow International Camping signs. Steep approach.

♥ Special member rates mean you can save your membership subscription in less than a week. Visit our website to find out more.

General P 🚐 🏕 🚻 🚾 🅿 ☉ 🔌 🐕 ☼ Leisure 🎣 ♪ ▶

HAWKSHEAD, Cumbria Map ref 5A3

★★★★
HOLIDAY, TOURING
& CAMPING PARK
🚐(25) £17.00–£20.50
🚎   £14.00–£16.75
⛺ (75) £14.00–£16.75
🏠(20) £264.00–£520.00
100 touring pitches

The Croft Caravan and Camp Site

North Lonsdale Road, Hawkshead, Ambleside LA22 0NX t (015394) 36374 f (015394) 36544
e enquiries@hawkshead-croft.com w hawkshead-croft.com

Quiet family site at Hawkshead village, close to shops and pubs. Flat, grassy and well sheltered holiday homes for hire. Open mid-March to mid-November.

payment Credit/debit cards, cash/cheques

General P 🚐 🏕 🚻 🚾 🅿 ☉ 🔌 🐕 ☼ Leisure 📺 ♦ ♪

HEYSHAM, Lancashire Map ref 5A3

★★★
HOLIDAY, TOURING
& CAMPING PARK
🚐   £14.00–£18.00
🚎   £14.00–£18.00
⛺ (6) £10.00–£14.00
🏠(26) £122.00–£474.00
91 touring pitches

Ocean Edge Leisure Park

Moneyclose Lane, Morecambe LA3 2XA t 0870 774 4024 f (015395) 69839
e enquiries@southlakelandparks.co.uk w southlakelandparks.co.uk

A scenic park situated on the shores of Morecambe Bay. The park facilities are unrivalled including indoor heated swimming pool, family cabaret lounge with themed weekends, children's indoor play area and amusement arcade.

open All year except Christmas and New Year
payment Credit/debit cards, cash/cheques

General 🖥 🛏 P 🚐 🏕 🚻 🚾 🅿 ☉ 🔌 🛒 ✕ 🐕 🏇 ☼ Leisure ♒ 📺 🍽 ♫ ♦ 🎣 ∪ ♪ ▶ ♿

HEYWOOD, Greater Manchester Map ref 4B1

★★★★★
TOURING &
CAMPING PARK
🚐   £14.00–£18.00
🚎 (6) £14.00–£18.00
⛺ (4) £14.00–£18.00
24 touring pitches

Gelder Wood Country Park

Oak Leigh Cottage, Ashworth Road, Rochdale OL11 5UP t (01706) 364858 f (01706) 364858
e gelderwood@aol.com

The country park comprises ten acres of well-maintained grounds and 15 acres of mature woodland. Within walking distance of several restaurants to suit all tastes.

open All year except Christmas and New Year
payment Cash/cheques

General P 🚐 🏕 🚻 🅿 🛒 🐕 ☼ Leisure ∪

KENDAL, Cumbria Map ref 5B3

★★★★
TOURING PARK
🚐(141) £10.40–£22.40
🚍(141) £10.40–£22.40
141 touring pitches

See Ad on inside front cover

THE
CARAVAN
CLUB

Low Park Wood Caravan Club Site

Sedgwick, Kendal LA8 0JZ **t** (015395) 60186 **w** caravanclub.co.uk

payment Credit/debit cards, cash/cheques

This peaceful country site is a haven for birdwatchers, freshwater fishermen and wild-flower enthusiasts. A dog-friendly site with extensive woodland to walk them in. Open April to November

⊕ *Leave M6 at jct 36 and go onto A590 signed South Lakes. After approximately 3.25 miles leave via slip road (signed Milnthorpe, Barrow) at roundabout and follow caravan signs.*

♥ *Special member rates mean you can save your membership subscription in less than a week. Visit our website to find out more.*

General 🖵 P 🚐 🗘 🎈 🚐 🌾 ☉ 📖 🔅 ⛺ ☀ Leisure ⛰ ♪ ⚑

KENDAL, Cumbria Map ref 5B3

★★★★
HOLIDAY, TOURING & CAMPING PARK
🚐(26) £11.50–£20.00
🚍(26) £11.50–£20.00
⛺(5) £6.50–£20.00
26 touring pitches

Waters Edge Caravan Park

Crooklands, Milnthorpe LA7 7NN **t** (015395) 67708 **w** watersedgecaravanpark.co.uk

payment Credit/debit cards, cash/cheques

Small, friendly site set in open countryside close to M6. Lake District, Morecambe, Yorkshire Dales within easy reach. All hardstanding pitches. Reception area with small shop. Lounge, bar, pool room, patio area. Modern shower block with laundry and washing-up facilities. Local pub/restaurant within 300yds. Open 1 March to 14 November.

⊕ *Leave M6 at jct 36, take A65 to Kirkby Lonsdale, then A65 to Crooklands. Site approx 0.75 miles on the right.*

General 🖵 🏠 P 🚐 🗘 🎈 🌾 ☉ 🔅 🔅 ⛺ ☀ Leisure 📺 ♟ ♦ ∪ ♪

KESWICK, Cumbria Map ref 5A3

★★★★
TOURING & CAMPING PARK
🚐 £10.00–£15.50
🚍(3) £10.00–£15.50
⛺(30) £9.50–£11.50
3 touring pitches

Castlerigg Farm Camping and Caravan Site

Castlerigg, Keswick CA12 4TE **t** (017687) 72479 **e** info@castleriggfarm.com **w** castleriggfarm.com

A quiet, family-run site with exceptional panoramic views. Ideal base for walking. Approximately 20 minutes' walk to Keswick. Open March to November. Site located on left of lane.

payment Cash/cheques

General P 🚐 🗘 🎈 🚐 🌾 ☉ 📖 🔅 🔅 ✕ 🐾 Leisure ♪ ⚑ 🚲 🏞

Don't forget www.

Web addresses throughout this guide are shown without the prefix www. Please include www. in the address line of your browser.
If a web address does not follow this style it is shown in full.

KESWICK, Cumbria Map ref 5A3

★★★★
HOLIDAY, TOURING
& CAMPING PARK

🚐(53)   £14.20–£16.50
🚐(53)   £13.00–£15.00
▲ (120) £11.50–£14.20
🛖(7)   £195.00–£450.00

Castlerigg Hall Caravan & Camping Park

Castlerigg Hall, Keswick CA12 4TE   t (017687) 74499   e info@castlerigg.co.uk   w castlerigg.co.uk

payment Credit/debit cards, cash/cheques

Situated 1.5 miles south east of the pretty market town of Keswick, our elevated position commands wonderful panoramic views of Derwentwater and the surrounding fells. Formerly a Lakeland hill farm, Castlerigg Hall has been sympathetically developed into a quality touring park. Many scenic walks are available directly from the park. Open April to October.

General P 🚐 🔌 🚻 🛒 🅿 ⊙ 📭 🗑 🐾 🐎   Leisure 📺 🔍 🏠

KIRKBY LONSDALE, Cumbria Map ref 5B3

★★★★★
HOLIDAY, TOURING
& CAMPING PARK

🚐(17)   £10.00–£23.00
🚐(17)   £10.00–£23.00
▲ (12)   £10.00–£16.00
17 touring pitches

Woodclose Caravan Park

Kirkby Lonsdale LA6 2SE   t (01524) 271597   f (01524) 272301   e info@woodclosepark.com
w woodclosepark.com

payment Credit/debit cards, cash/cheques

A quiet, picturesque, exclusive site situated between the Lakes and the Dales, a short walk from Kirkby Lonsdale. All pitches are supplied with electric and TV hook-up points. The camping field is sheltered and secluded. Children's play area and shop. David Bellamy Gold Conservation Award. Open March to November.

⊕ *M6 jct 36, follow A65 for approx 6 miles. The park entrance can be found just past Kirkby Lonsdale on the left-hand side, up the hill.*

General P 🚐 🔌 🚻 🅿 ⊙ 📭 🗑 🐾 ☼   Leisure ⛰ ∪ ♪ ⛵ 🚴

KIRKBY STEPHEN, Cumbria Map ref 5B3

★★★★★
TOURING &
CAMPING PARK

🚐(43)   £14.50–£16.50
🚐(43)
▲ (15)
58 touring pitches

Pennine View Caravan Park

Station Road, Kirkby Stephen CA17 4SZ   t (017683) 71717

Family-run caravan park on edge of small market town of Kirkby Stephen, just off A685. Easy reach of Lake District and Yorkshire Dales. Open March to October.

payment Credit/debit cards, cash/cheques

General 🖴 P 🚐 🔌 🚻 🅿 ⊙ 📭 🗑 🐎   Leisure ⛰ 🚴

visit**Britain**.com

Get in the know – log on for a wealth of information and inspiration. All the latest news on places to visit, events and quality-assessed accommodation is literally at your fingertips. Explore all that Britain has to offer.

LAMPLUGH, Cumbria Map ref 5A3

★★★★
TOURING PARK
🚐 (53)   £9.10–£20.20
🚐 (53)   £9.10–£20.20
53 touring pitches

See Ad on inside front cover

Dockray Meadow Caravan Club Site

Lamplugh CA14 4SH   **t** (01946) 861357   **w** caravanclub.co.uk

payment Credit/debit cards, cash/cheques

Site close to lesser-known lake beauties including Cogra Moss and Ennerdale. Within easy reach of Keswick. Open March to November.

⊕ *From A66 turn onto A5086. In 6.5 miles turn left at signpost for Lamplugh Green. Turn right at signpost for Croasdale. Site on left.*

♥ *Special member rates mean you can save your membership subscription in less than a week. Visit our website to find out more.*

General P 🚗 🅿 🚐 🐕   Leisure ✈

MORECAMBE, Lancashire Map ref 5A3

★★★★
HOLIDAY PARK
🚐 (33) £119.00–£552.00

Regent Leisure Park

Westgate, Morecambe LA3 3DF   **t** 0870 774 4024   **f** (015395) 69839
e enquiries@southlakelandparks.co.uk   **w** southlakelandparks.co.uk

Regent's excellent facilities include family cabaret lounge, indoor children's play area, an indoor leisure centre with heated pool and an outdoor weather pitch. Caravans fully equipped with two and three bedrooms available. Open 1 March to 15 January.

payment Credit/debit cards, cash/cheques

General 🖵 🅿 🍴 📁 🛒 ✕ 🐕   Leisure ♪ 📺 ♨ 🎵 🎯 ⛰ ✈ ⛷ 🚴

PENRITH, Cumbria Map ref 5B2

★★★★★
TOURING PARK
🚐 (151)   £14.30–£27.70
🚐 (151)   £14.30–£27.70
151 touring pitches

See Ad on inside front cover

Troutbeck Head Caravan Club Site

Troutbeck, Penrith CA11 0SS   **t** (01768) 483521   **w** caravanclub.co.uk

payment Credit/debit cards, cash/cheques

Classic Lakeland country. Attractive site sitting in a valley with spectacular views of Blencathra. Numerous attractions and activities within ten-mile radius. Open March to January 2009.

⊕ *Leave M6 at jct 40 onto A66 signposted Keswick. In about 7.25 miles turn left onto A5091, signposted Dockray/ Ullswater, site on right after 1.5 miles.*

♥ *Special member rates mean you can save your membership subscription in less than a week. Visit our website to find out more.*

General P 🚗 🅿 🚐 🍴 ☺ 📁 🐕 ☼   Leisure ♣ ⛰ ∪ ✈ ⛷

POOLEY BRIDGE, Cumbria Map ref 5A3

★★★★
CAMPING PARK
🚐   £12.00–£22.00
⛺ (90)   £12.00–£22.00

Waterside House Campsite

Waterside House, Howtown, Penrith CA10 2NA   **t** (017684) 86332   **f** (017684) 86332
e enquire@watersidefarm-campsite.co.uk   **w** watersidefarm-campsite.co.uk

Beautiful lakeside location on working farm with excellent toilet, shower and laundry facilities. Mountain bike, Canadian canoe and boat hire. Boat storage available. Open March to October inclusive.

payment Cash/cheques

General 🚐 P 🅿 🍴 🐕 ☺ 📁 🛒 🐕 ☼   Leisure ⛰ ∪ ✈ 🚴

RIBBLE VALLEY

See under Rimington

RIMINGTON, Lancashire Map ref 4B1

★★★★★
**HOLIDAY &
TOURING PARK**

🚐 (4)   £16.00
🚐 (4)   £16.00
39 touring pitches

Rimington Caravan Park

Hardacre Lane, Gisburn, Nr Clitheroe BB7 4EE   **t** (01200) 445355
e rimingtoncaravanpark@btinternet.com   **w** rimingtoncaravanpark.co.uk

Quiet, family-run site with clean, modern facilities.   **payment** Cash/cheques
Set in picturesque countryside, just off the beaten
track. Open March to October.

General 🛗 🚐 🖰 🚿 🛉 🕅 ☉ 🗑 🖥 🐾 ☼   Leisure ⛴ 🔍 ∪ 🎣 🏡

ROCHDALE, Greater Manchester Map ref 4B1

★★★
**HOLIDAY, TOURING
& CAMPING PARK**

🚐 (30)   £10.00–£14.00
🚐 (10)   £10.00–£14.00
▲ (10)   £8.00–£14.00
50 touring pitches

Hollingworth Lake Caravan Park

Roundhouse Farm, Hollingworth Lake, Littleborough OL15 0AT   **t** (01706) 378661

open All year
payment Cash/cheques

A popular, five-acre park adjacent to Hollingworth
Lake, at the foot of the Pennines, within easy reach
of many local attractions. Backpackers walking the
Pennine Way are welcome at this family-run park.

⊕ *From M62. Jct 21 Milnrow. Follow Hollingworth Lake
Country Park signs to the Fishermans Inn/The Wine Press.
Take Rakewood Road then 2nd on right.*

General 🖽 **P** 🚐 🖰 🛉 🖵 🕅 ☉ 🗑 🖥 🐾 ☼   Leisure ∪ 🎣

SILLOTH, Cumbria Map ref 5A2

★★★★
**HOLIDAY &
TOURING PARK**

🚐 (16)   £15.00
🚐 (16)   £15.00
16 touring pitches

Seacote Caravan Park

Skinburness Road, Silloth CA7 4QJ   **t** (01697) 331121   **f** (01697) 331031   **e** seacote@bfcltd.co.uk

Peaceful, carefree and tranquil. Well sheltered.   **payment** Cash/cheques
Touring pitches are hardstanding with electric
hook-up. Site is fully illuminated, less than two
minutes from the sea. Open 1 March to
15 November.

General 🛗 **P** 🚐 🖰 🛉 🕅 ☉ 🗑 🖥 🐾   Leisure ⛰ 🎣 🏌

ULLSWATER, Cumbria Map ref 5A3

★★★★★
**HOLIDAY &
TOURING PARK**

🚐   £15.00–£22.50
🚐 (34)   £15.00–£22.50
34 touring pitches

Waterfoot Caravan Park

Pooley Bridge, Penrith CA11 0JF   **t** (017684) 86302   **f** (017684) 86728
e enquiries@waterfootpark.co.uk   **w** waterfootpark.co.uk

payment Cash/cheques

Situated in the grounds of a Georgian mansion
overlooking Ullswater. The park has an excellent
touring area with a mix of hardstanding and lawned
areas. The reception and shop are open daily.
Licensed bar and games room with pool table.
Children's play area. David Bellamy Conservation
Gold Award. Open 1 March to 14 November.

⊕ *M6 jct 40, follow signs marked Ullswater Steamers. West
on A66 1 mile. Left at roundabout onto A592 (Ullswater).
Pass Dalemain; Waterfoot 2 miles on right.*

General **P** 🖰 🛉 🖵 🕅 ☉ 🗑 🖥 🐾 🐾 🏌 ☼   Leisure ⛴ 🔍 ⛰ ∪ 🎣

WASDALE, Cumbria Map ref 5A3

★ ★ ★ ★
**HOLIDAY, TOURING
& CAMPING PARK**
🚐 (9)   £12.00–£14.00
⛺ (41)   £12.00–£14.00
50 touring pitches

Church Stile Holiday Park

Church Stile Farm, Wasdale CA20 1ET **t** (01946) 726252 **f** (01946) 726028
e church-knight@btconnect.com **w** churchstile.com

payment Credit/debit cards, cash/cheques

Small family-run park in woodland clearing. Nature, woodland walk with viewing point. Magnificent scenery and plenty of walks. Families, couples and walkers welcome. Considerate campers only. Open mid-March to 31 October.

General P 🅿 🍴 💧 ☀ 🐕 ☀   Leisure 🏔 🎣 ⛵

WINDERMERE, Cumbria Map ref 5A3

★ ★ ★ ★
TOURING PARK
🚐 (66)   £13.60–£25.60
🚐 (66)   £13.60–£25.60
66 touring pitches

See Ad on inside front cover

Braithwaite Fold Caravan Club Site

Glebe Road, Bowness-on-Windermere, Windermere LA23 3GZ **t** (015394) 42177
w caravanclub.co.uk

payment Credit/debit cards, cash/cheques

Managed by The Club on behalf of South Lakeland District Council, this is an attractively laid out site, close to the shores of Windermere and within easy walking distance of the town. Open March to November.

⊕ From A592 follow signs for Bowness Bay, in 300yds turn right into Glebe Road. Site on right.

♥ Special member rates mean you can save your membership subscription in less than a week. Visit our website to find out more.

THE
CARAVAN
CLUB

General 🚐 P 🅿 🍴 💧 ☀ 🐕   Leisure 🎣

WINDERMERE, Cumbria Map ref 5A3

★ ★ ★ ★ ★
**HOLIDAY &
TOURING PARK**
🚐   £18.00–£26.00
🚐   £18.00–£26.00
🏠 (57) £214.00–£672.00
38 touring pitches

Fallbarrow Park

Rayrigg Road, Bowness-on-Windermere, Windermere LA23 3DL **t** 0870 774 4024 **f** (015395) 69839
w southlakelandparks.co.uk

In the heart of the Lake District, Fallbarrow Park extends a warm welcome to tourers, motorhomes and those looking to hire a static caravan or lodge. The park boasts an unrivalled setting in a natural environment covering 32 acres of wooded parkland. Open 1 March to 14 November.

payment Credit/debit cards, cash/cheques

General 🚐 P 🅿 🍴 💧 ☀ 🐕 ✕ 🐕 ☀   Leisure 📺 🍺 🔍 🏔 ♨ 🎣 ⛳

Check the maps

Colour maps at the front pinpoint all the places you will find accommodation entries in the regional sections. Pick your location and then refer to the place index at the back to find the page number.

WINDERMERE, Cumbria Map ref 5A3

★★★★★
HOLIDAY &
TOURING PARK

🚐 (43)   £10.00–£27.00
🚏   £10.00–£27.00
43 touring pitches

Hill of Oaks and Blakeholme Caravans

Newby Bridge, Nr Ulverston LA12 8NR t (015395) 31578 f (015395) 30431
e enquiries@hillofoaks.co.uk w hillofoaks.co.uk

payment Credit/debit cards, cash/cheques

Award-winning caravan park situated on the shores of Windermere. Very much family orientated, the park has a play area and nature walks through the woodland. The site has six jetties, boat launching and access to watersport activities. Shop and disabled facilities. Children's play area. David Bellamy Gold Conservation Award. Open March to November.

⊕ M6 jct 36, head west on A590 towards Barrow and Newby Bridge. At roundabout turn right, onto A592. Park is approx 3 miles on the left-hand side.

General 🖼 P 🚙 🕒 🦽 🆠 🦪 ☺ 📟 🔋 🐾 🏕 ☼ Leisure ⋀ ∪ 🦌

WINDERMERE, Cumbria Map ref 5A3

★★★★★
HOLIDAY, TOURING
& CAMPING PARK
ROSE AWARD

🚐 (12)   £16.00–£26.00
🚏 (12)   £18.00–£26.00
⛺ (11)   £18.00–£26.00
🛖 (5)   £214.00–£672.00
35 touring pitches

Limefitt Park

Patterdale Road, Windermere LA23 1PA t 0870 774 4024 f (015395) 69839
e enquiries@southlakelandparks.co.uk w southlakelandparks.co.uk

Spectacularly situated in one of Lakeland's most beautiful valleys capturing the very essence of the Lake District National Park. Limefitt offers unrivalled facilities. Open 1 March to 14 January.

payment Credit/debit cards, cash/cheques

General 🖼 P 🚙 🕒 🦽 🆠 🦪 📟 🔋 ✕ ☼ Leisure 📺 🍷 🎵 🦪 ⋀ ∪ 🦌 🚵

WINDERMERE, Cumbria Map ref 5A3

★★★★
HOLIDAY &
TOURING PARK

🚐 (19)   £16.00–£22.00
🚏 (9)   £16.00–£22.00
🛖 (46)   £250.00–£640.00
18 touring pitches

White Cross Bay Holiday Park and Marina

Ambleside Road, Troutbeck Bridge, Windermere LA23 1LF t 0870 774 4024 f (015395) 69839
e enquiries@southlakelandparks.co.uk w southlakelandparks.co.uk

Framed by woodland and inspiring fells, the park nestles on the shores of Lake Windermere. A superb centre in one of the Lake District's most exclusive locations. Open 1 March to 14 November.

payment Credit/debit cards, cash/cheques

General 🖼 P 🚙 🕒 🦽 🆠 🦪 📟 🔋 ✕ 🐾 ☼ Leisure 🔱 📺 🍷 🎵 🦪 ⋀ 🔍 ∪ 🏴 🚵

The great outdoors

Discover Britain's green heart with this easy-to-use guide. Featuring a selection of the most stunning gardens in the country, The Gardens Explorer is complete with a handy fold-out map and illustrated guide. You can purchase the Explorer series from good bookshops and online at visitbritaindirect.com.

North East England

County Durham, NewcastleGateshead,
South Tyneside & North Tyneside,
Sunderland, Tees Valley

Natural treasures and a rich history

If dramatic coastlines and
wild countryscapes are your
thing, you'll be in your
element in North East
England. Add a turbulent
history and warm welcome,
and this region has it all.

One NorthEast Tourism Team
visitnortheastengland.com
0870 160 1781

Lindisfarne Castle, Northumberland

High Force, Middleton-in-Teesdale

The Alnwick Garden, Northumberland

NewcastleGateshead

Few regions can compare with North East England for its natural attractions. Ramblers will have a field day in the glorious wilds of the North Pennines, whilst the rolling heather-blue Cheviot Hills in the Northumberland National Park are a picnickers' paradise. The Northumberland coast is another must-see, with its miles of clean sandy beaches such as Spittal and St Aidans. You can't miss the magnificent coastal castles like Bamburgh, but make sure you catch historic Durham Castle and the town's epic cathedral. But it's not all magical landscapes and colourful history. NewcastleGateshead is a vital, modern city with cutting-edge architecture like the Baltic Centre for Contemporary Art and The Sage Gateshead, along with some of the most glamorous shopping in England and vibrant culture.

No visit to the region would be complete without a trip to the Holy Island of Lindisfarne to admire the Castle and Priory. Cut off twice a day by racing tides, you can now visit the heritage centre and 'turn the pages' of the priceless Lindisfarne Gospels on computer. Or try seal spotting around the Farne Islands – just hop on a boat at Seahouses and you'll be enchanted by these wonderful creatures.

While you're in the North East, take a walk to see Hadrian's Wall and explore the Housesteads outpost with its evocative remains including a Roman barracks. In complete contrast, the latest attraction is the Middlesbrough Institute of Modern Art (mima), a gallery of national importance housing works by Emin, Hockney, Frink and many others. Or discover the twin Anglo-Saxon monastery of Wearmouth-Jarrow. It's the UK's nomination for World Heritage Site status in 2009 because of its links to celebrated Christian scholar the Venerable Bede.

Destinations

Berwick-upon-Tweed

England's northernmost town guards the mouth of the River Tweed. Marvel at some of the finest 16th century city walls in Europe, built by Elizabeth I to protect a town that changed hands between England and Scotland 14 times in the medieval era. Nowadays the town is more than part Scottish. Visit the great edifice of Bamburgh Castle and the beautiful gardens at Alnwick. Roam the magnificent Heritage coastline and see Holy Island and the fairytale Lindisfarne Castle.

Durham

Described by Bill Bryson as 'a perfect little city.' Its history shows in every cobble. Explore majestic Durham Cathedral, a World Heritage Site, and thought by many to be the finest Norman church architecture in England. Visit the tombs of St Cuthbert and the Venerable Bede. Stroll around a relaxed city centre mainly closed to traffic, take a coffee in the cobbled Market Place and enjoy the stunning floral displays. Take a path to the riverbank and take in the stunning views from the River Wear.

Darlington

Gateway to the North East and pioneering railway town. Darlington's Railway Centre and Museum displays Stephenson's Locomotion, which opened the Stockton and Darlington Railway in 1825. Discover a civilised town with a pedestrian heart, where medieval 'yards and wynds' link the main streets. Explore the designer Imperial Quarter with over 400 shops to choose from. Culture-lovers will find plenty to occupy them at the Arts Centre and the superb facilities at the Forum Music Centre.

Saltburn-by-the-Sea, Cleveland coast

Darlington Railway Centre and Museum

NewcastleGateshead Quayside

Durham Cathedral

Bamburgh Castle, Northumberland

Stockton-on-Tees

Middlesbrough

Visit the heart of the North East. Middlesbrough was home to Captain Cook whose life is celebrated at the award-winning Captain Cook Birthplace Museum. Learn about the region at The Dorman, the superb museum of local life. Let the historic, floodlit Transporter Bridge convey you across the River Tees. Sports fans can enjoy Premier League football at Middlesbrough, while walkers can explore the North York Moors and the Cleveland coast.

NewcastleGateshead

In the North East of England, Newcastle and Gateshead face each other across the River Tyne coming together at the dazzling Quayside. Must-see attractions including the award-winning Gateshead Millennium Bridge, the Baltic Centre for Contemporary Art and the magnificent new Sage Gateshead, a stunning Sir Norman Foster building, with billowing curves of glass and steel catering for every genre of music. Rich in culture, architecture and history and with a great reputation for style, shopping and nightlife, the variety of life in NewcastleGateshead surprises even the most well travelled visitor.

Stockton-on-Tees

Most famous for its associations with the Stockton & Darlington railway. Discover this friendly town, situated in the heart of the Tees Valley, and surrounded by smaller towns and villages including the charming Georgian town of Yarm. For lovers of outdoor activity, Stockton-on-Tees is fast becoming an impressive international watersports destination, from fishing to white water rafting to river cruising. You'll also find an impressive network of town and country parks.

Places to visit

Alnwick Castle
Large Visitor Attraction
of the Year - Gold Winner
Northumberland
(01665) 510777
alnwickcastle.com
Magnificent medieval
castle often used as a
film location

The Alnwick Garden
Northumberland
(01665) 511350
alnwickgarden.com
Exciting contemporary garden

BALTIC Centre for Contemporary Art
Gateshead,
Tyne and Wear
(0191) 478 1810
balticmill.com
Diverse international art

Bamburgh Castle
Northumberland
(01668) 214515
bamburghcastle.com
Magnificent coastal castle

Beamish, The North of England Open Air Museum
County Durham
(0191) 370 4000
beamish.org.uk
Let the past come to life

Bede's World
Jarrow, Tyne and Wear
(0191) 489 2106
bedesworld.co.uk
Discover the extraordinary life of
the Venerable Bede

Belsay Hall, Castle and Gardens
Newcastle upon Tyne,
Northumberland
(01661) 881636
english-heritage.org.uk
Medieval castle, 17th-century
manor and gardens

Blue Reef Aquarium
Tynemouth, Tyne and Wear
(0191) 258 1031
bluereefaquarium.co.uk
Giant tanks with spectacular
underwater walkthrough tunnels

The Bowes Museum
Barnard Castle,
County Durham
(01833) 690606
bowesmuseum.org.uk
Outstanding fine and decorative
arts

Captain Cook Birthplace Museum
Middlesbrough
(01642) 311211
captcook-ne.co.uk
Explore Cook's early life and
seafaring career

Centre for Life
Newcastle upon Tyne,
Tyne and Wear
(0191) 243 8210
life.org.uk
Hands-on science for all

Cragside House, Gardens and Estate
Morpeth, Northumberland
(01669) 620333
nationaltrust.org.uk
Woodland estate and adventure
playground

Discovery Museum
Newcastle upon Tyne,
Tyne and Wear
(0191) 232 6789
twmuseums.org.uk/discovery
Explore world-changing
inventions

Dunstanburgh Castle
Craster, Northumberland
(01665) 576231
english-heritage.org.uk
Dramatic ruins of 14th-century
castle

Durham Castle
(0191) 334 4106
durhamcastle.com
Fine example of motte
and bailey

Durham Cathedral
(0191) 386 4266
durhamcathedral.co.uk
Magnificent Norman architecture

Hadrian's Wall Path National Trail
Hexham, Northumberland
(01434) 322002
nationaltrail.co.uk/hadrianswall
An unmissable, historic 84-mile trail

Hartlepool's Maritime Experience
County Durham
(01429) 860077
hartlepoolsmaritimeexperience.com
Authentic reconstruction of an
18th-century seaport

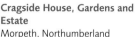

Housesteads Roman Fort (Vercovicium) Hadrian's Wall
near Haydon Bridge,
Northumberland
(01434) 344363
english-heritage.org.uk
Best preserved Roman Fort

Laing Art Gallery
Newcastle upon Tyne,
Tyne and Wear
(0191) 232 7734
twmuseums.org.uk
An important collection of
18th- and 19th-century art

Locomotion The National Railway Museum at Shildon
Shildon, County Durham
(01388) 777999
locomotion.uk.com
Over 100 locomotives

mima, Middlesbrough Institute of Modern Art
(01642) 726720
visitmima.com
Internationally significant fine and applied art

National Glass Centre
Sunderland, Tyne and Wear
(0191) 515 5555
nationalglasscentre.com
Glass exhibitions and live glass-blowing

Nature's World
Middlesbrough
(01642) 594895
naturesworld.org.uk
A pioneering eco-experience

Raby Castle
Darlington,
County Durham
(01833) 660202
rabycastle.com
Medieval castle with deer park and gardens

The Sage Gateshead
Tyne and Wear
(0191) 443 4666
thesagegateshead.org
Pioneering centre for musical discovery

Vindolanda
(Chesterholm)
Hadrian's Wall
near Haydon Bridge,
Northumberland
(01434) 344277
vindolanda.com
Remains of a Roman fort and settlement

Diary dates 2008

Northern Rocks: The North Pennines Festival of Geology and Landscape
Weardale
northpennines.org.uk
17 May – 1 Jun*

South Tyneside Summer Festival
southtyneside.info
1 Jun – 31 Aug*

Durham Regatta
River Wear
durham-regatta.org.uk
Jun*

Alnwick Fair
Market Square
northumberland.gov.uk
9 – 13 Jul*

Sunderland International Friendship Festival featuring the Kite Festival
Northern Area Playing Fields, Washington
sunderland-kites.co.uk
5 – 6 Jul

Whitley Bay International Jazz Festival
whitleybayjazzfest.org
11 – 13 Jul

Sunderland International Air Show
The promenade
sunderland-airshow.com
26 – 27 Jul

Stockton International Riverside Festival
sirf.co.uk
30 Jul – 3 Aug

Hexham Abbey Festival
hexhamabbey.org.uk/festival
25 Sep – 4 Oct

City of Durham Christmas Festival
Various locations, Durham
1 – 2 Dec*

* provisional date at time of going to press

Tourist Information Centres

When you arrive at your destination, visit an Official Partner Tourist Information Centre for quality assured help with accommodation and information about local attractions and events, or email your request before you go. To search for attractions and Tourist Information Centres on the move just text INFO to 62233, and a web link will be sent to your mobile phone.

Alnwick	2 The Shambles	(01665) 511333	alnwicktic@alnwick.gov.uk
Barnard Castle	Flatts Road	(01833) 690909	tourism@teesdale.gov.uk
Darlington	13 Horsemarket	(01325) 388666	tic@darlington.gov.uk
Durham	2 Millennium Place	(0191) 384 3720	touristinfo@durhamcity.gov.uk
Hartlepool	Church Square	(01429) 869706	hpooltic@hartlepool.gov.uk
Hexham	Wentworth Car Park	(01434) 652220	hexham.tic@tynedale.gov.uk
Morpeth	Bridge Street	(01670) 500700	tourism@castlemorpeth.gov.uk
Newcastle upon Tyne	8-9 Central Arcade	(0191) 277 8000	tourist.info@newcastle.gov.uk
Once Brewed*	Military Road	(01434) 344396	tic.oncebrewed@nnpa.org.uk
Sunderland	50 Fawcett Street	(0191) 553 2000	tourist.info@sunderland.gov.uk

* seasonal opening

Travel info

By road:
There is excellent motorway access via the A1(M), and the A69 and A66 connect directly to the M6 from the west. North East England is just two hours from Edinburgh, two-and-a-half hours from Manchester and four-and-a-half hours from London by road.

By rail:
Take the train and you're free to unwind all the way, with a tasty meal, your favourite read or just enjoying the view. North East England is easily reached on the East Coast Main Line from the north and south and via many direct connections from the west. Trains between London and Newcastle take just three hours, Birmingham to Darlington in just under three hours and Sheffield to Newcastle in just over three hours.

By air:
North East England has two international airports enabling easy access from UK, Europe and worldwide. Low cost flights fly into the region from a number of UK and European locations. Fly into Durham Tees Valley or Newcastle International airports.

Berwick-upon-Tweed

Hadrian's Wall, Northumberland

Find out more

Log onto the North East England website at
visitnortheastengland.com for further information on
accommodation, attractions, events and special offers
throughout the region. A range of free guides are
available for you to order online or by calling
0870 160 1781:

- **Holiday and Short Breaks Guide**
  Information on North East England, including hotels,
  bed and breakfast, self-catering, caravan and camping
  parks and accessible accommodation as well as events
  and attractions throughout the region.

- **Cycling Guide**
  A guide to day rides, traffic-free trails and challenging
  cycling routes.

- **Gardens Guide**
  A guide to the region's most inspirational gardens.

- **Walking Guide**
  Circular trails and long distance routes through
  breathtaking countryside.

where to stay in
North East England

All place names in the blue bands are shown on the maps at the front of this guide.

A complete listing of all VisitBritain assessed parks in England appears at the back.

Accommodation symbols
Symbols give useful information about services and facilities. Inside the back-cover flap you can find a key to these symbols. Keep it open for easy reference.

BAMBURGH, Northumberland Map ref 5C1

★★★
HOLIDAY, TOURING
& CAMPING PARK

🚐 (80)   £12.00–£15.00
🚍 (80)   £12.00–£15.00
⛺ (80)   £12.00–£15.00
80 touring pitches

Bradford Kaims Caravan Park

Bradford House, Bamburgh NE70 7JT **t** (01668) 213432 **f** (01668) 213891 **e** lwrob@tiscali.co.uk **w** bradford-leisure.co.uk

Beautiful walking country. Close to Bamburgh, Seahouses, Wooler and Cheviot Hills. Pre-booking advised during school holidays. Open March to November. Bradford Kaims Caravan Park is signposted from the B1341.

payment Credit/debit cards, cash/cheques

General 🚐 🕐 🍴 ☎ 😊 📧 🖥 🔌 ♒ ☼   Leisure ♠ ⛰

BAMBURGH, Northumberland Map ref 5C1

★★★
HOLIDAY &
TOURING PARK

🚐 (34)   £17.00–£18.00
🚍 (34)   £17.00–£18.00
34 touring pitches

Glororum Caravan Park

Glororum, Bamburgh NE69 7AW **t** (01668) 214457 **f** (01668) 214622 **e** info@glororum-caravanpark.co.uk **w** glororum-caravanpark.co.uk

Situated one mile from Bamburgh in peaceful surroundings within easy reach of many historic castles including Alnwick with its magnificent gardens. Endless walks on award-winning beaches only a mile away. No tents. Open April to October.

payment Credit/debit cards, cash/cheques

General 🖥 🛗 P 🚐 🕐 🍴 ☎ 😊 📧 🖥 🔌 ♒ ♒ ☼   Leisure ⛰ ☚ ∪ ♪ ⤳ 🚴

Take a break

Look out for special promotions and themed breaks. It's a golden opportunity to indulge an interest, find a new one, or just relax and enjoy exceptional value. Offers and promotions are highlighted in colour (and are subject to availability).

BAMBURGH, Northumberland Map ref 5C1

★★★★
HOLIDAY, TOURING
& CAMPING PARK
ROSE AWARD

(150) £11.50–£20.00
(150) £11.50–£20.00
(30) £7.50–£20.00
(27) £245.00–£560.00
150 touring pitches

Meadowhead's Waren Caravan and Camping Park

Waren Mill, Belford NE70 7EE t (01668) 214366 f (01668) 214224 e waren@meadowhead.co.uk
w meadowhead.co.uk

payment Credit/debit cards, cash/cheques, euros

Nestled in coastal countryside with great views to Holy Island and Bamburgh Castle. Waren offers restaurant-bar, splash-pool and play facilities. Our happy environment is great if you wish to stay on-site but we also make a great base from which to explore Northumberland's coast and castles, from Alnwick to Berwick. Open 1 March to 7 January.

⊕ Follow B1342 from A1 to Waren Mill towards Bamburgh. By Budle turn right, follow Meadowhead's Waren Caravan and Camping Park signs.

♥ Please see website for promotions and details of our new wigwams too!

General P 🔌 ⬆ ☂ 🖨 📻 ☉ ▣▣ 🛁 ✕ 🐾 ☼   Leisure ⚓ 📺 ⬤ 🔍 ⌂

BARDON MILL, Northumberland Map ref 5B2

★★★
CAMPING PARK

(60) £10.00–£15.00

Winshields Camp Site

Bardon Mill, Hexham NE47 7AN t (01434) 344243 w winshields.co.uk

Set in the heart of beautiful Northumberland. Within a short walk of the highest point of Hadrian's wall, Housesteads and Vindolanda. Campsite located on a working farm. Open April to November.

payment Cash/cheques

General ▣ P ☂ 📻 🛁 🐾   Leisure ⌒ 🎿

CORBRIDGE, Northumberland Map ref 5B2

★★★
TOURING &
CAMPING PARK

(40) £10.00–£14.00
(40) £10.00–£14.00
(40) £4.00–£10.00
40 touring pitches

Well House Farm – Corbridge

Newton, Stocksfield NE43 7UY t (01661) 842193 e info@wellhousefarm.co.uk
w wellhousefarm.co.uk

Peaceful family-run site on a farm near Corbridge one mile south of Hadrian's Wall. Ideal for exploring Northumberland and surrounding areas. Open April to October.

payment Cash/cheques

General ⚏ P 🔌 ☂ 📻 ☉ ▣ 🛁 🐾 🦮 ☼   Leisure 🎿 ▶ ⌂

DURHAM, County Durham Map ref 5C2

★★★★
TOURING PARK

(20) Max £16.00
(20) Max £16.00
(2) £400.00–£600.00
50 touring pitches

Finchale Abbey Caravan Park

Finchale Abbey Farm, Finchale Abbey, Durham DH1 5SH t (0191) 386 6528 & 07989 854704
f (0191) 386 1571 e godricawatson@hotmail.com w finchaleabbey.co.uk

Finchdale Abbey (Priory) touring park is set in beautiful countryside overlooking the ruins, surrounded by the River Wear. Fishing, golf, riverside walks and the local bar are a short distance away. Durham is 2.75 miles away by bike along scenic bridle paths.

open All year
payment Credit/debit cards, cash/cheques

General ⛽ ⚏ P 🔌 ⬆ ☂ 📻 ☉ ▣ 🛁 ✕ 🐾 🦮 ☼   Leisure ⌂ 🎿 ▶

DURHAM, County Durham Map ref 5C2

★★★★★
TOURING &
CAMPING PARK

🚐 (77) £13.60–£25.60
🚎 (77) £13.60–£25.60
⛺ on application
77 touring pitches

See Ad on inside front cover

THE CARAVAN CLUB

Grange Caravan Club Site

Meadow Lane, Durham DH1 1TL t (0191) 384 4778 w caravanclub.co.uk

open All year
payment Credit/debit cards, cash/cheques

An open, level site, this is a lovely location for a short break and an ideal stopover en route to or from Scotland.

⊕ A1(M) jct 62, A690 towards Durham. Turn right after 50m. Signposted Maureen Terrace and brown caravan sign.

♥ Special member rates mean you can save your membership subscription in less than a week. Visit our website to find out more.

General 🚐 P 🔌 🅿 🚿 📶 ☉ 🛒 🐕 ☀ Leisure ⛰ ♪ ⚓

DURHAM, County Durham Map ref 5C2

★★★★
HOLIDAY, TOURING
& CAMPING PARK
ROSE AWARD

🚐 (35) £13.50–£16.50
🚎 (35) £13.50–£16.50
⛺ (10) £13.50–£16.50
🏠 (3) £295.00–£350.00
45 touring pitches

Strawberry Hill Farm Camping & Caravanning Park

Running Waters, Old Cassop, Durham DH6 4QA t (0191) 372 3457 f (0191) 372 2512
e info@strawberryhf.co.uk w strawberry-hill-farm.co.uk

Situated in open countryside with magnificent, panoramic views. Ideally situated to explore the World Heritage site of the castle and cathedral. For further details please see website. Open 1 March to 31 December.

payment Credit/debit cards, cash, euros

General 🚐 🎣 P 🔌 🅿 🚿 📶 📶 ☉ 🛒 🐕 ☀ Leisure ♨ ♪

HAYDON BRIDGE, Northumberland Map ref 5B2

★★★★
HOLIDAY, TOURING
& CAMPING PARK

🚐 (8) £14.00
🚎 (8) £14.00
⛺ (3) £8.00–£14.00

Poplars Riverside Caravan Park

East Lands Ends, Haydon Bridge, Hexham NE47 6BY t (01434) 684427

A secluded riverside site at Haydon Bridge with 550yds to fishing. Near to shops and convenient for Hadrian's Wall. Open 1 March to 31 October.

payment Cash/cheques

General 🚐 P 🔌 🅿 🚿 📶 ☉ 🛒 🐕 Leisure ♨ ♪

HEXHAM, Northumberland Map ref 5B2

★★★★
TOURING &
CAMPING PARK

🚐 (32) £13.50–£14.50
🚎 (6) £13.50–£14.50
⛺ (10) £9.50–£12.00
42 touring pitches

Fallowfield Dene Caravan and Camping Park

Acomb, Hexham NE46 4RP t (01434) 603553 f (01434) 603553 e den@fallowfielddene.co.uk
w fallowfielddene.co.uk

In unspoilt countryside, 1.5 miles from the village of Acomb. The site is within easy reach of Hadrian's Wall and many places of interest. Open March to November.

payment Credit/debit cards, cash/cheques

General 🚐 P 🅿 🚿 📶 📶 ☉ 🛒 🐕 🐾 ☀ Leisure ♨

Place index

If you know where you want to stay, the index at the back of the guide will give you the page number listing accommodation in your chosen town, city or village. Check out the other useful indexes too.

HEXHAM, Northumberland Map ref 5B2

★★★
TOURING &
CAMPING PARK

🏕(40)   £12.00–£15.00
🚐(30)   £12.00–£15.00
⛺ (16)   Min £8.00
40 touring pitches

Hexham Racecourse Caravan Site

Yarridge Road, High Yarridge, Hexham NE46 2JP   t (01434) 606847   f (01434) 605814
e hexrace@aol.com   w hexham-racecourse.co.uk

Set in beautiful open countryside with panoramic views. Close to Hadrian's Wall, and within travelling distance of Northumberland, County Durham, Cumbria and Tyneside. Open May to September.

payment Cash/cheques

General 🍴 P 🔌 🚰 💧 🅿 ☉ 🛒 📶 🐕 ♿   Leisure 🔍 ⛰ ▶

KIELDER, Northumberland Map ref 5B1

TOURING &
CAMPING PARK

🏕(83)   £9.10–£20.20
🚐(83)   £9.10–£20.20
⛺   on application
83 touring pitches

See Ad on inside front cover

Kielder Water Caravan Club Site

Leaplish Waterside Park, Falstone, Hexham NE48 1AX   t (01434) 250278   w caravanclub.co.uk

payment Credit/debit cards, cash/cheques

This is a gently sloping site, with some pitches overlooking the beautiful Kielder Water – Britain's largest man-made lake. A fabulous site for an active holiday. Open March to November.

⊕ *From east on A69. Past Hexham, right onto A6079. Approx 3 miles, left onto B6320. In Bellingham, left to Kielder Water. Right, signposted Leaplish Waterside Park. Site on right.*

♥ *Special member rates mean you can save your membership subscription in less than a week. Visit our website to find out more.*

THE
CARAVAN
CLUB

General 🔌 🚰 💧 🆑 🅿 ☉ 🗑 🐕 ☼

KIELDER FOREST

See under Kielder

POWBURN, Northumberland Map ref 5B1

★★★★★
TOURING &
CAMPING PARK

🏕(74)   £10.40–£22.40
🚐(74)   £10.40–£22.40
⛺   on application
74 touring pitches

See Ad on inside front cover

River Breamish Caravan Club Site

Powburn, Alnwick NE66 4HY   t (01665) 578320   w caravanclub.co.uk

payment Credit/debit cards, cash/cheques

This site is set amid the Cheviot Hills, with excellent walking and cycling in the immediate area. A footbridge in Branton takes you over the river to the delightful Breamish Valley.

⊕ *Turn off A1 onto A697; in about 20 miles (0.25 miles past Powburn) turn left immediately past service station on right. Site on right.*

♥ *Special member rates mean you can save your membership subscription in less than a week. Visit our website to find out more.*

THE
CARAVAN
CLUB

General P 🔌 🚰 💧 🆑 🅿 ☉ 🗑 🐕 ♿ ☼

RAMSHAW, County Durham Map ref 5B2

★★★
HOLIDAY, TOURING
& CAMPING PARK

🏕(40)   £12.00–£15.00
🚐(40)   £12.00–£15.00
40 touring pitches

Craggwood Caravan Park

Gordon Lane, Ramshaw, Bishop Auckland DL14 0NS   t (01388) 835866   f (01388) 835866
e billy6482@btopenworld.com   w craggwoodcaravanpark.co.uk

Craggwood Caravan Park is set in approximately 60 acres with lovely views, woodland and a river running through the park. Open 1 March to 31 October.

payment Credit/debit cards, cash/cheques

General 🍴 P 🔌 🚰 💧 🅿 📶 🗑 🛒 ✕ 🐕 ♿ ☼   Leisure ⛰ ∪ 🎣

SEAHOUSES, Northumberland Map ref 5C1

★ ★ ★ ★ ★
**HOLIDAY &
TOURING PARK**
ROSE AWARD

(18)   £20.00–£40.00
(18)   £20.00–£40.00
(37) £295.00–£620.00
18 touring pitches

Seafield Caravan Park

Seafield Road, Seahouses NE68 7SP **t** (01665) 720628 **f** (01665) 720088 **e** info@seafieldpark.co.uk
w seafieldpark.co.uk

payment Credit/debit cards, cash/cheques

Luxurious holiday homes for hire on Northumberland's premier park. Fully appointed caravans. Superior, fully serviced touring pitches. Prices include full use of Ocean Club facilities (www.ocean-club.co.uk). Gold Award Winner Enjoy England Awards for Excellence 2006.

⊕ *Take the B1340 from Alnwick for 14 miles. East to coast.*

♥ *Seasonal discounts available on 3-, 4- and 7-day breaks.*

General ⊞ P ⊕ ⓒ ☏ ⓡ ⊙ ⓑ ✕ ⌂ ⌖ ☼ Leisure ⌇ ⓨ ⋀ ∪ ♪ ♭

STOCKTON-ON-TEES, Tees Valley Map ref 5C3

★ ★ ★ ★ ★
TOURING PARK
(115) £10.40–£22.40
(115) £10.40–£22.40
▲   on application
115 touring pitches

See Ad on inside front cover

THE
CARAVAN
CLUB

White Water Caravan Club Park

Tees Barrage, Stockton-on-Tees TS18 2QW **t** (01642) 634880 **w** caravanclub.co.uk

open All year
payment Credit/debit cards, cash/cheques

Pleasantly landscaped site, part of the largest white-water canoeing and rafting course built to an international standard in Britain. Nearby Teesside Park for shopping, restaurants etc.

⊕ *Come off the A66 Teesside Park. Follow Teesdale sign, go over Tees Barrage Bridge, turn right. Site 200yds on the left.*

♥ *Special member rates mean you can save your membership subscription in less than a week. Visit our website to find out more.*

General ⊞ P ⊕ ⓒ ☏ ⓪ ⓡ ⊙ ⓑⓑ ⌂ ☼ Leisure ⧆ ⋀ ♪ ♭

Help before you go

When it comes to your next British break, the first stage of your journey could be closer than you think.

You've probably got a Tourist Information Centre nearby which is there to serve the local community – as well as visitors. Knowledgeable staff will be happy to help you, wherever you're heading.

Many Tourist Information Centres can provide you with maps and guides, and it's often possible to book accommodation and travel tickets too.

You'll find the address of your nearest centre in your local phone book, or look at the beginning of each regional section in this guide for a list of Official Partner Tourist Information Centres.

Help before you go

When it comes to your next British break, the first stage of your journey could be closer than you think.

You've probably got a Tourist Information Centre nearby which is there to serve the local community – as well as visitors. Knowledgeable staff will be happy to help you, wherever you're heading.

Many Tourist Information Centres can provide you with maps and guides, and it's often possible to book accommodation and travel tickets too.

You'll find the address of your nearest centre in your local phone book, or look at the beginning of each regional section in this guide for a list of Official Partner Tourist Information Centres.

Yorkshire

East Yorkshire, North Yorkshire,
South Yorkshire, West Yorkshire

The land of romantic moors and vibrant cities

Yorkshire is the country's largest region, and it packs plenty in. From its three national parks brimming with breathtaking countryside to its stylish cosmopolitan cities, Yorkshire is big, beautiful and welcoming.

Yorkshire Tourist Board
yorkshire.com
0870 609 0000

Cow and Calf Rock, Ilkley

Boulby Cliffs   Millennium Galleries, Sheffield

York Minster

Yorkshire is blessed with some of England's wildest, most rugged countryside, including the vast expanse of the North York Moors and the dramatic carved valleys of the Peak District. Prefer your landscape a little lusher? Take a relaxing stroll across the rolling Yorkshire Dales or pretty Herriot Country. And you'll fall in love with the Yorkshire seaside whether it's lively resorts or the fossil-filled Heritage Coast. You'll also be in your element if you are into the urban scene. Vibrant cities like Leeds, Bradford, Hull and Sheffield offer designer shopping, Michelin-starred eateries and a buzzing cultural life. And then there's York. It may boast world-famous Viking roots and masses of medieval appeal, but today it also oozes contemporary chic with its continental café bar culture.

One place you won't want to miss is Fountains Abbey and Studley Royal Water Garden. This World Heritage Site features the impressive remains of a Cistercian abbey and elegant ornamental lakes. Or discover the Forbidden Corner, a unique labyrinth of tunnels, chambers and follies in the Dales. It's an unforgettable day out for the whole family. And you can while away a pleasant afternoon exploring the antique shops of historic Harrogate or the Victorian village of Saltaire. Don't miss York Minster, one of Europe's greatest gothic cathedrals, and while you're in York why not stop off at the National Railway Museum?

Yorkshire is a unique mix of influences and inspirational places. It's restful and zestful, forward looking yet founded on a bedrock of traditional values. The people are a friendly, straight-talking lot and take great pride in introducing visitors to Yorkshire's many and varied faces. Plain speaking may be part of Yorkshire's character, but there's nothing plain about this captivating part of Britain. Country or city, trendy or traditional, ancient history or cutting-edge – Yorkshire has it all.

Destinations

Barnsley

Barnsley, gateway to Pennine Yorkshire, boasts a rich industrial heritage. You'll also find an exciting mix of entertainment to suit all tastes. Shop for bargains at the 700-year-old indoor/outdoor market, then sample the famous 'Barnsley Chop'. Close by is the RSPB Old Moor, a 250-acre wetlands nature reserve and a superb place to watch wildlife. The surrounding rural villages offer quiet, cosy restaurants and pubs.

Halifax

If you appreciate outstanding architecture and a thriving cultural life, Halifax is for you. Visit the superb Borough Market, the galleried Piece Hall, and Eureka! the fascinating Museum for Children. Take in a series of exciting galleries including the Henry Moore Studio and the Dean Clough and find a full programme of great acts at the Victoria Theatre.

Hull

Enjoy the invigorating yet relaxing atmosphere that only a waterfront city can offer. Visit the Museum Quarter linking four of Hull's eight free museums including the interactive Streetlife Museum. Don't miss the £40 million aquarium, 'The Deep', home to 40 sharks and one of the most spectacular sea-life attractions in the world. Marvel at the engineering of the Humber Bridge and, after dark, experience Hull's very own café bar culture and take in a show at Hull Truck or Hull New Theatre.

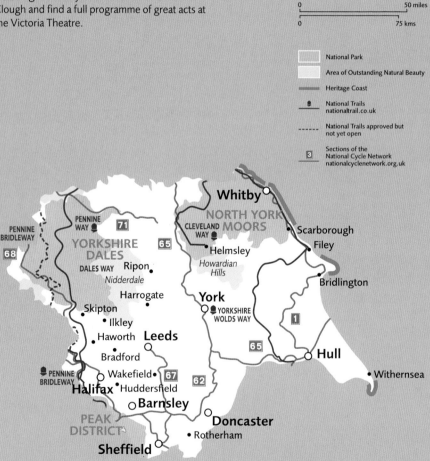

| | 0 | | 50 miles |
| | 0 | | 75 kms |

National Park

Area of Outstanding Natural Beauty

Heritage Coast

National Trails
nationaltrail.co.uk

National Trails approved but not yet open

Sections of the National Cycle Network
nationalcyclenetwork.org.uk

The Deep, Hull

Leeds

Eureka! Museum for Children, Halifax

Village in the Pennines

The Shambles, York

Whitby Abbey

Leeds

Experience a combination of fast-paced, buzzing city centre with the serenity of the Yorkshire Dales on the doorstep. Rich local history, world-class sport and diverse year-round entertainment make Leeds a great place for everyone to enjoy. You'll find a shopaholic's dream, from the elegant Corn Exchange to the exquisite Victoria Quarter, not to mention the only Harvey Nichols outside London. See opera and dance at the internationally acclaimed Opera North and Northern Ballet, jousting at the Royal Armouries and outstanding collections in the many museums and galleries.

Whitby

Visit one of Britain's finest stretches of coastline with cliffs, bays, sandy beaches and attractive villages. Follow Whitby's quaint cobbled streets and climb the steps to the parish church of St Mary, whose churchyard inspired Bram Stocker's 'Dracula'. Then down to the historic quayside of this 1,000-year-old port and celebrate the town's seafaring tradition at the Captain Cook Festival, named in honour of Whitby's most famous son.

York

The history of York is the history of England. Visit award-winning attractions including the magnificent York Minster, and the world's biggest and best railway museum. Let 21st-century technology transport you back to the Viking age at Jorvik, and wander through the terrifying York Dungeon. Pedestrianised streets make York an ideal city to explore on foot. Follow the city's specialist shopping trails '5 Routes to Shopping Heaven', or browse the specialist antique and book dealers. Then take the weight off your feet in one of the many quaint teashops.

Places to visit

Bolton Abbey Estate
Skipton, North Yorkshire
(01756) 718009
boltonabbey.com
Priory ruins in beautiful setting

Brodsworth Hall and Gardens

Doncaster, South Yorkshire
(01302) 722598
english-heritage.org.uk
Country home of Victorian gentry

Brontë Parsonage Museum
Haworth, West Yorkshire
(01535) 642323
bronte.org.uk
Home of the famous literary sisters

Castle Howard
York, North Yorkshire
(01653) 648444
castlehoward.co.uk
Majestic 18th century house in breathtaking parkland

The Deep
Hull, East Yorkshire
(01482) 381000
thedeep.co.uk
One of the most spectacular aquariums in the world

Eureka! The Museum for Children
Halifax, West Yorkshire
(01422) 330069
eureka.org.uk
Britain's leading interactive museum for children

Fountains Abbey and Studley Royal
Ripon, North Yorkshire
(01765) 608888
fountainsabbey.org.uk
Outstanding 800-acre World Heritage Site

Go Ape! High Wire Forest Adventure
near Pickering, North Yorkshire
0870 444 5562
goape.co.uk
Rope bridges, swings and zip slides

Harewood House
West Yorkshire
(0113) 218 1010
harewood.org
Exquisite Adams interiors and Chippendale furniture

The Henry Moore Institute
Leeds, West Yorkshire
(0113) 246 7467
henry-moore-fdn.co.uk
Beautiful exhibition space housing four sculpture galleries

Jorvik - The Viking City
York, North Yorkshire
(01904) 543400
vikingjorvik.com
Viking history comes to life

Magna Science Adventure Centre

Rotherham, South Yorkshire
(01709) 720002
visitmagna.co.uk
Extraordinary science adventure

National Coal Mining Museum for England
Wakefield, West Yorkshire
(01924) 844560
ncm.org.uk
Unique museum of coalfields

National Media Museum
Bradford, West Yorkshire
0870 701 0200
nmpft.org.uk
With spectacular 3D IMAX cinema and interactive television gallery

National Railway Museum
York, North Yorkshire
0870 421 4001
nrm.org.uk
See the Flying Scotsman at the world's largest railway museum

North Yorkshire Moors Railway

Pickering
(01751) 472508
nymr.co.uk
Heritage railway steaming through stunning scenery

The Norwich Union Yorkshire Wheel
York, North Yorkshire
(01904) 686263
nrm.org.uk
York's new landmark aerial attraction

RHS Garden Harlow Carr

Harrogate, North Yorkshire
(01423) 565418
rhs.org.uk
Stunning garden with year-round events

Royal Armouries Museum
Leeds, West Yorkshire
(0113) 220 1916
armouries.org.uk
Jousting tournaments and fabulous exhibitions

Sewerby Hall and Gardens

Bridlington, East Yorkshire
(01262) 673769
eastriding.gov.uk/sewerby
Country house in dramatic cliff-top location

Skipton Castle
North Yorkshire
(01756) 792442
skiptoncastle.co.uk
Fine preserved medieval castle

Thackray Museum
Leeds, West Yorkshire
(0113) 244 4343
thackraymuseum.org
*Interactive museum telling the
story of medicine*

Whitby Abbey
North Yorkshire
(01904) 601974
english-heritage.org.uk
Moody and magnificent ruins

**The World of
James Herriot**
Thirsk, North Yorkshire
(01845) 524234
worldofjamesherriot.org
*Restored home of the famous vet
and author*

Xscape Castleford
West Yorkshire
0871 200 3221
xscape.co.uk
*Ice-climbing, assault course and
real snow slope*

York Castle Museum
North Yorkshire
(01904) 687687
yorkcastlemuseum.org.uk
*England's most popular museum
of everyday life*

York Minster
North Yorkshire
(01904) 557216
yorkminster.org
*One of the great cathedrals
of the world*

Yorkshire Sculpture Park
Wakefield, West Yorkshire
(01924) 832631
ysp.co.uk
*Open-air gallery in beautiful
grounds*

Diary dates 2008

Family History Festival
Kings Hall & Winter Gardens, Ilkley
familyhistoryfestival.co.uk
13 January

Jorvik Viking Festival
Various locations, York
jorvik-viking-centre.co.uk
13 – 17 Feb

**Wakefield Festival of Food, Drink and
Rhubarb**
Various locations, Wakefield
wakefield.gov.uk
29 Feb – 1 Mar

Dales Festival of Food and Drink
Leyburn
dalesfestivaloffood.org
3 – 5 May

The Great Yorkshire Show
Harrogate
greatyorkshireshow.com
8 – 10 Jul

Kettlewell Scarecrow Festival
kettlewell.info
9 – 17 Aug

York Festival of Food and Drink
Various locations, York
yorkfestivaloffoodanddrink.com
19 – 28 Sep

Hull Fair
Walton Street, Hull
hullfair.net
10 – 18 Oct

Dickensian Christmas Fayre
Various locations, Grassington
grassington.net
First three Saturdays in Dec

Tourist Information Centres

When you arrive at your destination, visit an Official Partner Tourist Information Centre for quality assured help with accommodation and information about local attractions and events, or email your request before you go. To search for attractions and Tourist Information Centres on the move just text INFO to 62233, and a web link will be sent to your mobile phone.

Aysgarth Falls	Aysgarth Falls National Park	(01969) 662910	aysgarth@ytbtic.co.uk
Beverley	34 Butcher Row	(01482) 391672	beverley.tic@eastriding .gov.uk
Bradford	Centenary Square	(01274) 433678	tourist.information@bradford.gov.uk
Bridlington	25 Prince Street	(01262) 673474	bridlington.tic@eastriding.gov.uk
Brigg	Market Place	(01652) 657053	brigg.tic@northlincs.gov.uk
Cleethorpes	42-43 Alexandra Road	(01472) 323111	cleetic@nelincs.gov.uk
Danby*	Lodge Lane	(01439) 772737	moorscentre@northyorkmoors-npa.gov.uk
Filey*	John Street	(01723) 383637	fileytic@scarborough.gov.uk
Grassington	Hebden Road	(01756) 751690	grassington@ytbtic.co.uk
Guisborough	Church Street	(01287) 633801	guisborough_tic@redcar-cleveland.gov.uk
Halifax	Piece Hall	(01422) 368725	halifax@ytbtic.co.uk
Harrogate	Crescent Road	(01423) 537300	tic@harrogate.gov.uk
Haworth	2/4 West Lane	(01535) 642329	haworth@ytbtic.co.uk
Hebden Bridge	New Road	(01422) 843831	hebdenbridge@ytbtic.co.uk
Holmfirth	49-51 Huddersfield Road	(01484) 222444	holmfirth.tic@kirklees.gov.uk
Hornsea*	120 Newbegin	(01964) 536404	hornsea.tic@eastriding.gov.uk
Huddersfield	3 Albion Street	(01484) 223200	huddersfield.tic@kirklees.gov.uk
Hull	1 Paragon Street	(01482) 223559	tourist.information@hullcc.gov.uk
Humber Bridge	Ferriby Road	(01482) 640852	humberbridge.tic@eastriding.gov.uk
Ilkley	Station Rd	(01943) 602319	ilkley@ytbtic.co.uk
Knaresborough	Market Place	0845 389 0177	kntic@harrogate.gov.uk
Leeds	The Arcade, City Station	(0113) 242 5242	touristinfo@leeds.gov.uk
Leyburn	Railway Street	(01969) 623069	leyburn@ytbtic.co.uk
Malham	National Park Centre	(01969) 652380	malham@ytbtic.co.uk
Malton	Malton Museum	(01653) 600048	maltontic@btconnect.com
Pateley Bridge*	18 High Street	0845 389 0177	pbtic@harrogate.gov.uk
Pickering	The Ropery	(01751) 473791	pickering@ytbtic.co.uk
Redcar	Esplanade	(01642) 471921	redcar_tic@redcar-cleveland.gov.uk
Reeth	The Green	(01748) 884059	reeth@ytbtic.co.uk
Richmond	Victoria Road	(01748) 850252	richmond@ytbtic.co.uk
Ripon	Minster Road	(01765) 604625	ripontic@harrogate.gov.uk
Rotherham	40 Bridgegate	(01709) 835904	tic@rotherham.gov.uk
Scarborough	Brunswick Shopping Centre	(01723) 383636	tourismbureau@scarborough.gov.uk
Scarborough (Harbourside)	Sandside	(01723) 383636	harboursidetic@scarborough.gov.uk

Selby	52 Micklegate	(01757) 212181	selby@ytbtic.co.uk
Settle	Cheapside	(01729) 825192	settle@ytbtic.co.uk
Sheffield	14 Norfolk Row	(0114) 221 1900	visitor@sheffield.gov.uk
Skipton	35 Coach Street	(01756) 792809	skipton@ytbtic.co.uk
Sutton Bank	Sutton Bank	(01845) 597426	suttonbank@ytbtic.co.uk
Thirsk	49 Market Place	(01845) 522755	thirsktic@hambleton.gov.uk
Wakefield	9 The Bull Ring	0845 601 8353	tic@wakefield.gov.uk
Whitby	Langborne Road	(01723) 383637	whitbytic@scarborough.gov.uk
Withernsea*	131 Queen Street	(01964) 615683	withernsea.tic@eastriding.gov.uk
York (De Grey Rooms)	Exhibition Square	(01904) 550099	tic@visityork.org
York (Railway Station)	Station Road	(01904) 550099	kg@visityork.org

* seasonal opening

Semer Water, near Bainbridge

Find out more

The following publications are available from Yorkshire Tourist Board by logging on to yorkshire.com or calling 0870 609 0000:

- **Yorkshire Accommodation Guide 2008**
  Information on Yorkshire, including hotels, self catering, camping and caravan parks.

- **Make Yorkshire Yours Magazine**
  This entertaining magazine is full of articles and features about what's happening in Yorkshire, including where to go and what to do.

Travel info

By road:
Motorways: M1, M62, M606, M621, M18, M180, M181, A1(M).
Trunk roads: A1, A19, A57, A58, A59, A61, A62, A64, A65, A66.

By rail:
InterCity services to Bradford, Doncaster, Harrogate, Kingston upon Hull, Leeds, Sheffield, Wakefield and York. Frequent regional railway services city centre to city centre, including Manchester Airport service to Scarborough, York and Leeds.

By air:
Fly into Durham Tees Valley, Humberside, Leeds/Bradford International or Robin Hood, Doncaster, Sheffield.

North York Moors

Never has a rose meant so much

Everyone has a trusted friend, someone who tells it straight. Well, that's what the Enjoy England Quality Rose does: reassures you before you check into your holiday accommodation that it will be just what you want, because it's been checked out by independent assessors. Which means you can book with confidence and get on with the real business of having a fantastic break.

The **Quality Rose** is the mark of England's *official*, nationwide quality assessment scheme and covers just about every place you might want to stay, using a clear star rating system: from caravan parks to stylish boutique hotels, farmhouse B&Bs to country house retreats, self-catering cottages by the sea to comfy narrowboats perfect for getting away from it all. Think of the Quality Rose as your personal guarantee that your expectations will be met.

enjoy**England**.com

★ ★ ★

HOLIDAY PARK

Our ratings made easy

★	Simple, practical, no frills
★★	Well presented and well run
★★★	Good level of quality and comfort
★★★★	Excellent standard throughout
★★★★★	Exceptional with a degree of luxury

Look no further. Just look out for the Quality Rose.
Find out more at enjoy**England**.com/quality

where to stay in
Yorkshire

All place names in the blue bands are shown on the maps at the front of this guide.

A complete listing of all VisitBritain assessed parks in England appears at the back.

Accommodation symbols
Symbols give useful information about services and facilities. Inside the back-cover flap you can find a key to these symbols. Keep it open for easy reference.

BEDALE, North Yorkshire Map ref 5C3

★★★★
TOURING &
CAMPING PARK

🚐 (25)	Min £10.00
🚐 (25)	Min £10.00
⛺ (25)	Min £9.00
🏠 (3)	Min £120.00

25 touring pitches

Pembroke Caravan Park
19 Low Street, Leeming Bar, Northallerton DL7 9BW t (01677) 422652

Small sheltered site catering for touring vans, including motor caravans and tents. Excellent A1 night halt. Open March to October.

payment Cash/cheques

General 🖃 🚿 P 🚗 🖰 🚽 🕅 ☺ 📵 🛒 🛌 ☼ Leisure ∪ ⏚ ▸

BEVERLEY, East Riding of Yorkshire Map ref 4C1

★★★★★
HOLIDAY PARK

🏠 (5)	Min £170.00

Barmston Farm Caravan Park
Barmston Farm, Barmston Lane, Woodmansey, Beverley HU17 0TP t (01482) 863566 &
07970 042587 e enquiry@barmstonfarm.co.uk w barmstonfarm.co.uk

open All year
payment Cash/cheques

Small, quiet, friendly site. Caravans positioned around a pond with open countryside views. In an adjacent field there is a well-stocked, two-acre fishing lake.

⊕ Follow A1174 from Beverley, 3 miles to Woodmansey. Church on sharp bend, site at bottom of lane, next to church.

General P 🕅 📵 ☼ Leisure ∪ ⏚

Place index
If you know where you want to stay, the index at the back of the guide will give you the page number listing accommodation in your chosen town, city or village. Check out the other useful indexes too.

BOLTON ABBEY, North Yorkshire Map ref 4B1

★★★★★
TOURING PARK
(57) £13.60–£25.60
(57) £13.60–£25.60
57 touring pitches

See Ad on inside front cover

THE CARAVAN CLUB

Strid Wood Caravan Club Site

Skipton BD23 6AN **t** (01756) 710433 **w** caravanclub.co.uk

payment Credit/debit cards, cash/cheques

One of the prettiest sites on our network and part of the Bolton Abbey Estate in open glades surrounded by woodland and the glorious Yorkshire Dales. Within the boundaries of the estate are some 75 miles of footpaths through moors, woods and farmland. Open March to January 2009.

Special member rates mean you can save your membership subscription in less than a week. Visit our website to find out more.

General P

BRIDLINGTON, East Riding of Yorkshire Map ref 5D3

★★★★
HOLIDAY, TOURING & CAMPING PARK
£17.00–£20.00
£17.00–£20.00
(20) £17.00–£20.00
(10)
175 touring pitches

South Cliff Caravan Park

Wilsthorpe, Bridlington YO15 3QN **t** (01262) 671051 **f** (01262) 605639
e southcliff@eastriding.gov.uk **w** southcliff.co.uk

Situated 300yds from clean, safe, sandy beaches, one mile south of Bridlington. Bus service to Bridlington, also a shop, takeaway and leisure complex including bars, children's lounge and restaurant. Open March to November.

payment Credit/debit cards, cash/cheques

General P Leisure

BURTON-IN-LONSDALE, North Yorkshire Map ref 5B3

★★★★
HOLIDAY, TOURING & CAMPING PARK
(15) £8.50–£10.00
(15) £8.50–£10.00
Min £8.50
(2) £150.00–£250.00
15 touring pitches

Gallaber Farm Caravan Park

Gallaber Farm, Burton in Lonsdale, Carnforth LA6 3LU **t** (01524) 261361
e gallaber@btopenworld.com **w** gallaber.btinternet.co.uk

payment Cash/cheques

A small secluded caravan park set in wonderful countryside with stunning views. Gallaber is a working beef and sheep farm and many of the animals can be seen from the park. Child-friendly, with small play area. Pets welcome. Excellent base for walking and touring. Open March to October.

M6 jct 34 left onto A683. After 10 miles right on A687 through Burton. Join Ireby Road – 1st farm lane on left.

General P Leisure

FILEY, North Yorkshire Map ref 5D3

★★★★★
HOLIDAY PARK
£10.00–£18.00
£10.00–£18.00
(25) £10.00–£18.00
50 touring pitches

Orchard Farm Holiday Village

Stonegate, Hunmanby, Filey YO14 0PU **t** (01723) 891582 **f** (01723) 891582

Family park in edge of village location with easy access to resorts of Filey, Scarborough and Bridlington. Amenities include children's play area, fishing lake and entertainment during peak season. Open March to October.

payment Cash/cheques

General P Leisure

HARROGATE, North Yorkshire Map ref 4B1

★★★★★
HOLIDAY &
TOURING PARK

(200) £16.00–£18.00
(57) £16.00–£18.00
200 touring pitches

High Moor Farm Park

Skipton Road, Felliscliffe, Harrogate HG3 2LT **t** (01423) 563637 **f** (01423) 529449
e highmoorfarmpark@btconnect.com

Secluded site surrounded by trees on the edge of the Yorkshire Dales. Open 1 April to 31 October.

payment Credit/debit cards, cash/cheques

General Leisure

HARROGATE, North Yorkshire Map ref 4B1

★★★★★
HOLIDAY, TOURING
& CAMPING PARK
ROSE AWARD

£15.50–£30.00
£15.50–£30.00
£15.50–£30.00
141 touring pitches

Rudding Holiday Park

Follifoot, Harrogate HG3 1JH **t** (01423) 870439 **f** (01423) 870859 **e** holiday-park@ruddingpark.com
w ruddingpark.com

payment Credit/debit cards, cash/cheques, euros

Award-winning campsite just three miles south of Harrogate, in peaceful setting, offering Deer House pub, swimming pool, golf course, driving range and shop. Closed February. Self-catering timber lodges also available.

⊕ Three miles south of Harrogate, to the north of the A65, between its junction with the A61 to Leeds and the A661 Wetherby.

♥ Peak season: 7 nights for the price of 6. Off-peak season 4 nights for the price of 3.

General Leisure

HAWES, North Yorkshire Map ref 5B3

★★
HOLIDAY, TOURING
& CAMPING PARK

(25) Min £11.00
(5) Min £10.50
(40) Min £10.50
(2) £165.00–£210.00
70 touring pitches

Bainbridge Ings Caravan and Camping Site

Hawes DL8 3NU **t** (01969) 667354 **e** janet@bainbridge-ings.co.uk **w** bainbridge-ings.co.uk

Quiet, clean, well-organised, family-run site. Pitches situated around the edge of open fields with magnificent views. Ten-minute walk into Hawes. Excellent centre for walking and touring the Dales.

payment Cash/cheques

General Leisure

HAWORTH, West Yorkshire Map ref 4B1

★★★★
HOLIDAY, TOURING
& CAMPING PARK

£11.00–£19.50
(2) Min £10.00
(15) Min £9.50
(2) £100.00–£295.00
60 touring pitches

Upwood Holiday Park

Blackmoor Road, Oxenhope, Haworth, Keighley BD22 9SS **t** (01535) 644242 **f** (01535) 647913
e info@upwoodpark.co.uk **w** upwoodpark.co.uk

payment Credit/debit cards, cash/cheques

A family-owned park pleasantly situated close to the Yorkshire Dales National Park – an ideal base from which to explore the area by car or on foot. Large modern toilet facilities, comfortable lounge bar serving snacks, games room with pool and table tennis, small shop for essential items.

General Leisure

HEBDEN BRIDGE, West Yorkshire Map ref 4B1

★★★★★
TOURING PARK

🚐 (45) £9.10–£20.20
🚎 (45) £9.10–£20.20
45 touring pitches

See Ad on inside front cover

Lower Clough Foot Caravan Club Site

Cragg Vale, Hebden Bridge HX7 5RU t (01422) 882531 w caravanclub.co.uk

payment Credit/debit cards, cash/cheques

Pretty site, set in a grassy enclave, well screened by mature trees and bordered by a stream. Good for walkers. Open March to November.

⊕ Turn off A646 onto B6138. Site on right in 1 mile.

♥ Special member rates mean you can save your membership subscription in less than a week. Visit our website to find out more.

General P 🔌 🛱 📶 🛠 Leisure 🏊 🏕

HELMSLEY, North Yorkshire Map ref 5C3

★★★★★
TOURING &
CAMPING PARK

🚐 (60) £12.50–£16.50
🚎 (60) £12.50–£16.50
⛺ (60) £12.50–£16.50
60 touring pitches

Foxholme Touring Caravan Park

Harome, Helmsley YO62 5JG t (01439) 771241 f (01439) 771744

Adults-only park. **payment** Cash/cheques

General 🖵 🛱 P 🔌 🛱 🍴 📶 🎡 ☉ 📠 🛠 🐾

HELMSLEY, North Yorkshire Map ref 5C3

★★★★★
TOURING &
CAMPING PARK

🚐   £13.00–£17.00
🚎   £13.00–£17.00
⛺   £13.00–£17.00
🏠 (1) £155.00–£200.00
129 touring pitches

Golden Square Caravan and Camping Park

Oswaldkirk, Helmsley, York YO62 5YQ t (01439) 788269 f (01439) 788236
e barbara@goldensquarecaravanpark.freeserve.co.uk w goldensquarecaravanpark.com

Secluded site with magnificent view of North York Moors. Award-winning, heated toilet block (refurbished 2006), bathroom, disabled room, shop. Indoor/outdoor play areas. Sports centre nearby. De luxe and seasonal pitches. Storage compound.

payment Cash/cheques, euros

General 🖵 🖵 🛱 P 🔌 🛱 🍴 📶 🎡 ☉ 📠 🛠 🐾 Leisure 🎯 ⛰ ∪ 🏊 🏕 ⚙

KNARESBOROUGH, North Yorkshire Map ref 4B1

★★★★★
TOURING PARK

🚐 (65) £13.60–£25.60
🚎 (65) £13.60–£25.60
⛺   on application
65 touring pitches

See Ad on inside front cover

Knaresborough Caravan Club Site

New Road, Scotton, Knaresborough HG5 9HH t (01342) 336732 w caravanclub.co.uk

payment Credit/debit cards, cash/cheques

Popular family destination located in Lower Nidderdale, gateway to the Yorkshire Dales. Knaresborough and the city of Harrogate are within easy reach. Open March to January 2009.

⊕ Turn right off A59 onto B6165. After approximately 1.5 miles turn right immediately after petrol station into New Road. Site is on right-hand side after 50yds.

♥ Special member rates mean you can save your membership subscription in less than a week. Visit our website to find out more.

General P 🔌 🛱 📶 🎡 ☉ 📠 🛠 ☼ Leisure ⛰ 🏊 🏕

LEEDS, West Yorkshire Map ref 4B1

St Helena's Caravan Site

★★★★
HOLIDAY, TOURING
& CAMPING PARK

🚐 (30) £12.50–£15.00
🚐 (15) £12.50–£15.00
⛺ (15) £10.00–£15.00
60 touring pitches

Otley Old Road, Leeds LS18 5HZ **t** (0113) 284 1142

Secluded site with showers, WCs and washing facilities. Local amenities include golf, fishing, walking. Ten minutes' drive to Otley and the Yorkshire Dales. Note: over 18s only. Open April to October.

payment Cash/cheques

General P 🖭 🛉 📶 ☺ 📠 🖥 🎁 🎯 ☼ Leisure ⫨

LEEDS BRADFORD INTERNATIONAL AIRPORT

See under Leeds

LONG PRESTON, North Yorkshire Map ref 5B3

Gallaber Park

★★★★
HOLIDAY &
TOURING PARK

🚐 £17.50–£25.00
🚐 £17.50–£25.00
⛺ £17.50–£21.50
65 touring pitches

Skipton BD23 4QF **t** (01729) 851397 **f** (01729) 851398 **e** info@gallaberpark.com
w gallaberpark.com

Situated on the edge of the beautiful Yorkshire Dales National Park. Open mid-March to 31 October for touring caravans, March to January for holiday home.

payment Credit/debit cards, cash/cheques

General P 🖭 🕻 🛉 🚐 📶 📠 🖥 🎁 ☼ Leisure 🏔

PICKERING, North Yorkshire Map ref 5D3

Wayside Caravan Park

★★★★
HOLIDAY, TOURING
& CAMPING PARK

🚐 (55) £14.50
🚐 (55) £14.50
⛺ (20) £11.00
55 touring pitches

Pickering YO18 8PG **t** (01751) 472608 **f** (01751) 472608 **e** waysideparks@freenet.co.uk
w waysideparks.co.uk

Sheltered, quiet, south-facing park, delightfully located with lovely country views. A walker's paradise. Steam railway. Castle Howard nearby. Whitby, Scarborough and York within a 45-minute drive. Open March to October.

payment Credit/debit cards, cash/cheques

General 🖵 🚲 P 🖭 🕻 🛉 📶 ☺ 📠 🖥 🎁 🎯 ☼ Leisure 🏔 U ⫨ ▸ 🚴 🛶

RIPON, North Yorkshire Map ref 5C3

Sleningford Watermill Caravan & Camping Park

★★★★★
TOURING &
CAMPING PARK

🚐 (30) £10.00–£17.00
🚐 (20) £10.00–£17.00
⛺ (40) £8.50–£15.00
90 touring pitches

North Stainley, Ripon HG4 3HQ **t** (01765) 635201 **e** sleningford@hotmail.co.uk
w ukparks.co.uk/sleningford

payment Credit/debit cards, cash/cheques

A beautiful, tranquil and friendly riverside park set in semi-wooded parkland, between Ripon and Masham. On-site fly-fishing and white-water canoeing available. Ideal for families, bird watchers and nature lovers. Open April to October. (Access available for canoeing all year).

⊕ *A1 South–A61 to Ripon, then north for 5 miles. A1 North B6267 to West Tanfield, then left on A6108 for 0.5 mile.*

♥ *Special rates Tues-Thu at certain times during season.*

General 🖫 🖵 🚲 P 🖭 🕻 🛉 📶 ☺ 📠 🖥 🎁 🎯 ☼ Leisure ✿ 🏔 ⚲ U ⫨ ▸ 🛶

Key to symbols
Open the back flap for a key to symbols.

RIPON, North Yorkshire Map ref 5C3

★★★★
HOLIDAY, TOURING & CAMPING PARK

(60) £10.50–£15.50
(5) £10.50–£15.50
(40) £9.50–£13.50
100 touring pitches

Woodhouse Farm Caravan & Camping Park

Winksley, Ripon HG4 3PG **t** (01765) 658309 **e** woodhouse.farm@talk21.com
w woodhousewinksley.com

Spacious family park with two coarse-fishing lakes, restaurant/bar, new amenity block, shop and play areas. Open March to October.

payment Credit/debit cards, cash/cheques

General P Leisure TV

SCARBOROUGH, North Yorkshire Map ref 5D3

★★★★★
TOURING & CAMPING PARK

£11.50–£24.00
£11.50–£24.00
£9.00–£19.00
200 touring pitches

Cayton Village Caravan Park

Mill Lane, Cayton Bay, Scarborough YO11 3NN **t** (01723) 583171 **e** info@caytontouring.co.uk
w caytontouring.co.uk

The very best of coast and country. Luxurious facilities, adventure playground, site shop, dog walk. Beach half a mile. Next to village with pubs, chip shop, post office and bus service. Open March to October.

payment Credit/debit cards, cash/cheques

General P Leisure

SCARBOROUGH, North Yorkshire Map ref 5D3

★★★★
HOLIDAY PARK
ROSE AWARD

(50) £14.00–£22.00
(50) £10.00–£22.00
(100) £10.00–£18.00
(40) £120.00–£475.00
150 touring pitches

Crows Nest Caravan Park

Gristhorpe, Filey YO14 9PS **t** (01723) 582206 **f** (01723) 582206
e enquiries@crowsnestcaravanpark.com **w** crowsnestcaravanpark.com

This family-owned, rose-award-winning park is situated between the attractions of Scarborough and the tranquillity of Filey. Full facilities. Holidays and short breaks for families and couples.

payment Credit/debit cards, cash/cheques

General P Leisure TV

SCARBOROUGH, North Yorkshire Map ref 5D3

★★★★★
HOLIDAY, TOURING & CAMPING PARK
ROSE AWARD

(220) £15.00–£20.00
(30) £15.00–£20.00
(50) £12.00–£20.00
(20) £220.00–£450.00
300 touring pitches

Flower of May Holiday Parks Ltd

Lebberston, Scarborough YO11 3NU **t** (01723) 584311 **f** (01723) 581361 **e** info@flowerofmay.com
w flowerofmay.com

payment Credit/debit cards, cash/cheques

Excellent facilities on family-run park. Luxury indoor pool, adventure playground, golf course. Ideal for coast and country. Prices based per pitch, per night, for four people with car. Open April to October.

From A64 take the A165 Scarborough/Filey coast road. Well signposted at Lebberston.

Early-booking discount: £25 off full week's hire. 10% discount off full week's pitch fees, booked by post in advance.

General P Leisure TV

It's all quality-assessed accommodation

Our commitment to quality involves wide-ranging accommodation assessment. Rating and awards were correct at the time of going to press but may change following a new assessment. Please check at time of booking.

SCARBOROUGH, North Yorkshire Map ref 5D3

★★★★★
HOLIDAY, TOURING
& CAMPING PARK

🚐 (74)   £14.00–£20.00
🚐 (74)   £14.00–£20.00
⛺ (20)   £14.00–£20.00
🏠 (1)   £220.00–£370.00
94 touring pitches

Jasmine Park

Cross Lane, Snainton, Scarborough YO13 9BE **t** (01723) 859240 **f** (01723) 859240
e info@jasminepark.co.uk **w** jasminepark.co.uk

payment Credit/debit cards, cash/cheques

Picturesque and peaceful park between Pickering and Scarborough. Family-owned. Flat pitches. Winner of Yorkshire Caravan Park of the Year and Yorkshire in Bloom. National Silver winner of Excellence in England Caravan Park of the Year. Gold David Bellamy Conservation Award. Seasonal pitches available. Open March to October.

⊕ *Turn south off the A170 in Snainton opposite the junior school at traffic lights. Signposted.*

General 🚲 P ♨ 🕒 🍴 🚐 🅵 ☉ 🔌 📷 🐕 🌣 Leisure ∪ 🏊 🏌 🚴

SCARBOROUGH, North Yorkshire Map ref 5D3

★★★★★
TOURING PARK

🚐 (125)   £12.50–£15.00
🚐 (40)   £12.50–£15.00
125 touring pitches

Lebberston Touring Park

Lebberston, Scarborough YO11 3PE **t** (01723) 585723 **e** info@lebberstontouring.co.uk
w lebberstontouring.co.uk

Quiet country location. Well-spaced pitches. Extensive south-facing views. Ideal park for a peaceful, relaxing break. Fully modernised amenity blocks. Dogs on lead. Open March to October.

payment Credit/debit cards, cash/cheques

General 📺 🚲 P ♨ 🕒 🍴 🚐 🅵 ☉ 🔌 📷 🐕 🌣

SLINGSBY, North Yorkshire Map ref 5C3

★★★★★
HOLIDAY, TOURING
& CAMPING PARK
ROSE AWARD

🚐 (32)   £10.00–£18.00
🚐 (32)   £10.00–£18.00
⛺ (32)   £10.00–£18.00
🏠 (20) £140.00–£455.00
32 touring pitches

Robin Hood Caravan & Camping Park

Green Dyke Lane, Slingsby, York YO62 4AP **t** (01653) 628391 **f** (01653) 628392
e info@robinhoodcaravanpark.co.uk **w** robinhoodcaravanpark.co.uk

A privately owned park set in the heart of picturesque Ryedale. Peaceful and tranquil, but within easy reach of York, North Yorkshire Moors, Flamingo Land and the coast.

payment Credit/debit cards, cash/cheques

General 📺 P ♨ 🕒 🍴 🅵 🔌 📷 🐕 🌣 Leisure ⌂ ∪ 🏊

WHITBY, North Yorkshire Map ref 5D3

★★★★
HOLIDAY PARK
ROSE AWARD

🏠 (10) £210.00–£395.00

Flask Holiday Home Park

Robin Hood's Bay, Fylingdales, Whitby YO22 4QH **t** (01947) 880592 **f** (01947) 880592
e flaskinn@aol.com **w** flaskinn.com

payment Credit/debit cards, cash/cheques

Small, family-run site between Whitby and Scarborough, in the North York Moors. All super-luxury caravans have central heating and double glazing. Also TV, DVD, fridge/freezer and microwave.

⊕ *Situated on the A171, 7 miles to Whitby, 12 miles to Scarborough and 4 miles to Robin Hood's Bay.*

General P 🕒 🔌 📷 🐕 ✕ 🌣 Leisure ▼ ⌂ ∪

WHITBY, North Yorkshire Map ref 5D3

★★★★★
TOURING & CAMPING PARK
£14.00–£17.00
(6) £14.00–£17.00
100 touring pitches

Ladycross Plantation Caravan Park

Whitby YO21 1UA **t** (01947) 895502 **e** enquiries@ladycrossplantation.co.uk
w ladycrossplantation.co.uk

Natural woodland site in the National Park. Caravans are pitched in groups of about ten within clearings in the trees. Central amenity block and five service points. Open 23 March to 21 October.

payment Credit/debit cards, cash/cheques

General

WHITBY, North Yorkshire Map ref 5D3

★★★★★
HOLIDAY, TOURING & CAMPING PARK
ROSE AWARD
(20) £12.50–£20.00
(20) £12.50–£20.00
(80) £8.00–£20.00
(30) £150.00–£565.00
100 touring pitches

Middlewood Farm Holiday Park

Middlewood Lane, Fylingthorpe, Robin Hood's Bay, Whitby YO22 4UF **t** (01947) 880414
f (01947) 880871 **e** info@middlewoodfarm.com **w** middlewoodfarm.com

payment Credit/debit cards, cash/cheques

Peaceful, award-winning family park. A walker's paradise with magnificent, panoramic coastal and moorland views! Level, sheltered hardstandings, luxury heated facilities, private bathroom, children's play area. Ten-minute walk to pub/shops/beach and Robin Hood's Bay. Superb caravans for hire. Open 1 March to 4 January. A friendly welcome awaits!

⊕ *Follow A171 Scarborough to Whitby road signposted from Fylingthorpe junction. In Fylingthorpe turn onto Middlewood Lane. Park is 500yds. Follow brown tourist signs.*

General Leisure

WITHERNSEA, East Riding of Yorkshire Map ref 4D1

★★★★
HOLIDAY, TOURING & CAMPING PARK
(20) £15.00–£17.00
(10) £15.00–£17.00
(1) £160.00–£360.00
30 touring pitches

Willows Holiday Park

Hollym Road, Withernsea HU19 2PN **t** (01964) 612233 **f** (01964) 612957
e info@highfield-caravans.co.uk **w** highfield-caravans.co.uk

Set in attractive countryside, within easy reach of sea and town centre. Licensed club with family room, fishing lake, play area, mini-golf, laundry. Supermarket nearby, beach ten minutes. Open March to December (tourers 31 October).

payment Cash/cheques

General Leisure

WOMBLETON, North Yorkshire Map ref 5C3

★★★★★
TOURING & CAMPING PARK
(100) £15.00–£19.00
(8) £15.00–£19.00
(10) £8.00–£17.00
118 touring pitches

Wombleton Caravan Park

Moorfield Lane, York YO62 7RY **t** (01751) 431684 **e** info@wombletoncaravanpark.co.uk
w wombletoncaravanpark.co.uk

A flat level site with electric hook-ups. A small shop for general enquiries, touring and seasonal pitches, tents welcome. Open 1 March to 31 October.

payment Cash/cheques

General Leisure

★★★★★
TOURING &
CAMPING PARK

⊕	£12.00–£13.50
⊞	£12.00
Å	£12.00

40 touring pitches

Alders Caravan Park

Home Farm, Monk Green, Alne, York YO61 1RY **t** (01347) 838722 **f** (01347) 838722
e enquiries@homefarmalne.co.uk **w** alderscaravanpark.co.uk

payment Cash/cheques

On a working farm in historic parkland where visitors may enjoy peace and tranquillity. York (on bus route), moors, dales and coast nearby. Level, dry site, tastefully landscaped, adjoins village cricket ground. Woodland walk. Close to A19 and A1. Luxury toilet and shower facilities. Open March to October inclusive.

⊕ From A19 exit at Alne sign, in 1.5 miles turn left at T-junction, 0.5 miles park on left in village centre.

General ▨ ♨ P ⊙ ◖ ▥ ⦿ ⊙ ▥ ♘ ⊼ ☼ Leisure ♪ ►

★★★★
HOLIDAY, TOURING
& CAMPING PARK

ROSE AWARD

⊕	(20)	£12.00–£14.00
⊞	(20)	£12.00–£14.00
Å	(20)	£12.00–£14.00
▭	(5)	£210.00–£640.00

20 touring pitches

Allerton Park Caravan Park

Allerton Park, Knaresborough HG5 0SE **t** (01423) 330569 **f** (01759) 371377
e enquiries@yorkshireholidayparks.co.uk **w** yorkshireholidayparks.co.uk

A peaceful camping and caravan park 0.5 miles east of the A1 leading from the A59 York to Harrogate road. An ideal touring base for the York area. Timber lodges to hire/buy. Open February to December.

payment Credit/debit cards, cash/cheques

General ▨ P ⊙ ◖ ▥ ⦿ ⊙ ▥ ♘ ⊼ ☼ Leisure ∪

★★★★
TOURING PARK

⊕	(117)	£13.60–£25.60
⊞	(117)	£13.60–£25.60

117 touring pitches

See Ad on inside front cover

CARAVAN
CLUB

Beechwood Grange Caravan Club Site

Malton Road, York YO32 9TH **t** (01904) 424637 **w** caravanclub.co.uk

payment Credit/debit cards, cash/cheques

Situated just outside York in countryside. Plenty of space for children to play. Ideal for families. Within close range of historic York and Yorkshire's varied attractions. Open March to November.

⊕ From A64 on junction of A1237 York ring road and A103 leading to A64, north of York. 3rd roundabout turn right onto road signed local traffic only. Site at end of drive.

♥ Special member rates mean you can save your membership subscription in less than a week. Visit our website to find out more.

General ▨ P ⊙ ◖ ▥ ⊞ ⦿ ⊙ ▥ ♘ ☼ Leisure ⋀ ♪ ►

★★★★★
**TOURING &
CAMPING PARK**

🚐 (102) £14.30–£27.70
🚐 (102) £14.30–£27.70
⛺ on application
102 touring pitches

See Ad on inside front cover

THE
**CARAVAN
CLUB**

Rowntree Park Caravan Club Site

Terry Avenue, York YO23 1JQ **t** (01904) 658997 **w** caravanclub.co.uk

open All year
payment Credit/debit cards, cash/cheques

On the banks of the river Ouse in the heart of York, this popular site is just a few minutes' walk from the city centre. York is a feast, there's so much to see and do – visit the lovely Minster with its dazzling stained glass windows and walk the city walls.

⊕ *A64 onto A19 signposted York centre. After 2 miles join one-way system. Keep left over bridge. Left at International Caravan Club site. Right onto Terry Avenue. Site on right in 0.25 miles.*

♥ *Special member rates mean you can save your membership subscription in less than a week. Visit our website to find out more.*

General 🅿️ ... Leisure ♪ ▶

★★★★
**HOLIDAY, TOURING
& CAMPING PARK**
ROSE AWARD

🚐 (20) £12.00–£14.00
🚐 (20) £12.00–£14.00
⛺ (10) £12.00–£14.00
🚐 (6) £225.00–£410.00
20 touring pitches

Weir Caravan Park

Buttercrambe Road, Stamford Bridge, York YO41 1AN **t** (01759) 371377 **f** (01759) 371377
e enquiries@yorkshireholidayparks.co.uk **w** yorkshireholidayparks.co.uk

On level grassland seven miles east of York on the A166. Near the river where fishing is available. Village, pubs, restaurants etc are within a five-minute walk. Open March to October.

payment Credit/debit cards, cash/cheques

General 🅿️ ... Leisure ∪ ♪

★★★★
**TOURING &
CAMPING PARK**

🚐 (20) £10.00–£18.50
🚐 (20) £10.00–£18.50
⛺ (10) £10.00–£18.50
40 touring pitches

York Touring Caravan Site

Towthorpe Lane, Towthorpe, York YO32 9ST **t** (01904) 499275 **f** (01904) 499271
e info@yorkcaravansite.co.uk **w** yorkcaravansite.co.uk

open All year
payment Credit/debit cards, cash/cheques

Small, family-run, secluded park in an idyllic countryside setting, only five miles from York centre. Spacious pitches and superior facilities. New shower and toilet facilities. Bar open Friday and Saturday nights.

⊕ *Travelling on the A64 towards Scarborough/Malton take the turn-off to the left signposted Strensall/Haxby. We are 1 mile down that road on the left.*

♥ *Book 7 nights in advance and only pay for 6 (excl Bank Holidays).*

General 🅿️ ... Leisure 📺 ...

It's all in the detail

Please remember that all information in this guide has been supplied by the proprietors well in advance of publication. Since changes do sometimes occur it's a good idea to check details at the time of booking.

Heart of England

Herefordshire, Shropshire, Staffordshire, Warwickshire, West Midlands, Worcestershire

Wholesome fun and a whole lot more

When it comes to good food and simple pleasures, people make a bee-line for the Heart of England. Whether it's dining out, gliding along a canal or catching a nerve-jangling rollercoaster, there's nowhere better.

visittheheart.com

Wrekin Reservoir, Shropshire

Malvern Hills, Worcestershire

Charlecote Park, Warwickshire

Symonds Yat, Herefordshire

From Vale of Evesham asparagus to Herefordshire Beef, this region's rich soil and lush pastureland produces some of the UK's finest ingredients. Small wonder that from village pubs to Michelin-starred restaurants, your eating experience will be a highlight of your stay. Great family days out are a speciality, too. Whether it's throwing pots at the famous Wedgwood factory, braving the rides at Drayton Manor Theme Park or unwinding on a narrow boat, there are simply attractions galore. And if you like picnics, take a spread along to Symond's Yat RSPB Nature Reserve overlooking the gorgeous Wye Valley.

Want to get the most from your stay? Pick up a Thrill Hopper ticket that gives you great value access to four top theme park attractions – Drayton Manor Theme Park, Alton Towers, SnowDome and Waterworld. And don't miss Trentham's splendid Italian Garden and the Eastern Pleasure Garden restoration at one of the 19th century's most celebrated gardens. Then there's the National Cold War Exhibition at RAF Museum Cosford, an illuminating and exciting look at the tensions that tormented the superpowers during the 20th century (prepare to be amazed by Britain's three V-Bombers – Vulcan, Valiant and Victor). And Walsall Illuminations transform the town's arboretum into an enchanting wonderland of lakeside lights, laser shows and floodlit gardens.

The region is also famous as the cradle of the Industrial Revolution, so make a pilgrimage to Ironbridge Gorge World Heritage Site and catch ten fantastic museums in one truly spectacular setting.

The Heart of England's appeal lies in both its timelessness and modernity. The cultural diversity and vibrancy of Birmingham reflects a very different England to the one of Shakespeare's Stratford-upon-Avon, the sleepy villages of Warwickshire and Herefordshire and beauty of the Cotswolds.

Destinations

Birmingham

Birmingham is a dynamic city combining a fascinating history with a world-class cultural scene. Lose yourself in shopping heaven in the stunningly remodelled Bullring, wander through the historic Jewellery Quarter then sit back and enjoy the Symphony Orchestra in the magnificent Symphony Hall. Indulge your sweet tooth at Cadbury World, or take in a major event at the NEC or NIA. You'll also find yourself at the heart of a region full of history and heritage, beautiful quaint villages and access to lush rolling countryside – Birmingham really is a gateway to the heart of England!

Hereford

Visit this ancient city on the banks of the River Wye. You'll find historic buildings housing modern shops and modern buildings holding historic treasures. Don't miss Hereford Cathedral with its priceless Mappa Mundi and Chained Library. Wander through the spacious High Town and intriguing side streets. The ancient and modern grace the banks of the beautiful River Wye – including the new Left Bank Village, while the Cider Museum tells a fascinating story and bolsters Hereford's claim to be 'The Apple of England's Eye'.

Coventry

Discover the city that is re-inventing itself. Coventry, the setting for myth and legend, famous for Lady Godiva and St George the dragon-slayer, is now an ideal visitor destination building on its rich heritage with up-to-the-minute shopping, bars and restaurants. Browse one of the oldest indoor markets in Europe, gaze at the beauty of St Mary's Guildhall, visit the late 20th century cathedral standing amid the ruins of its predecessor, and don't miss the Transport Museum for the largest collection of British road transport in the world.

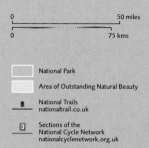

0	50 miles
0	75 kms

National Park

Area of Outstanding Natural Beauty

National Trails
nationaltrail.co.uk

Sections of the
National Cycle Network
nationalcyclenetwork.org.uk

Bullring Shopping Centre, Birmingham

Hereford Cider Museum

Wedgewood Visitor Centre, Stoke-on-Trent

Coventry Cathedral

Bancroft Gardens, Stratford-upon-Avon

River Severn, Shrewsbury

Ludlow

Ludlow

Discover the place Betjemen described as 'the loveliest town in England.' With over 500 listed buildings, Ludlow is a feast for the eyes. Britain's first 'slow' town is also a gastronomic capital and host to the renowned Ludlow Marches Food & Drink Festival. You'll find a host of speciality food shops, and more restaurants and inns than you can shake a cocktail stick at. To walk off lunch, stroll in the enchanting Angel Gardens, or take in a performance at the open-air theatre in the stunning medieval ruin of Ludlow Castle.

Shrewsbury

This charming county town boasts over 660 listed buildings. Wander the Shuts and Passages – a medieval maze of narrow alleys criss-crossing the town, and admire the Norman abbey, medieval castle, and Shrewsbury Museum and Art Gallery housed in Rowley's House. Interesting, independent shops are plentiful, with food a speciality. Track the evolution of Charles Darwin, Shrewsbury's famous son, and, for a summer treat, breathe the scent of more than three million blooms at the internationally famous Shrewsbury Flower Show in August.

Stoke-on-Trent

Visit the UK's capital of china, 'The Potteries'. Award-winning museums tell the full story and the opportunity to throw your own pot. Take in a show at the magnificent Regent Theatre and Victoria Hall with their star-studded programmes of West End shows. Given its close proximity to Alton Towers and its excellent shopping and leisure facilities, Stoke-on-Trent is sure to fire your imagination.

Stratford-upon-Avon

Unearth a magical blend of heritage and drama in and around Shakespeare's home town. Explore five houses with Shakespeare connections including Anne Hathaway's Cottage and Shakespeare's Birthplace. Visit one of England's most beautiful parish churches at Holy Trinity to see Shakespeare's grave and enjoy some of his great works performed by the world's largest classical theatre company, the RSC. Take a boat out on the River Avon, wander the boutiques, specialist stores and gift shops, and discover some of Britain's finest historic houses and gardens.

Places to visit

**Birmingham Museum
& Art Gallery**
(0121) 303 2834
bmag.org.uk
*Fine and applied art, archaeology
and local history collections*

**Black Country
Living Museum**
Dudley, West Midlands
(0121) 557 9643
bclm.co.uk
*Twenty-six acres of fascinating
living history*

**Brockhampton Estate
National Trust**
near Bromyard, Herefordshire
(01885) 482077
nationaltrust.org.uk
*14th-century moated manor
house*

Cadbury World
Bournville, West Midlands
0845 450 3599
cadburyworld.co.uk
*Chocolate-making
demonstrations and samples*

**Cider Museum and
King Offa Distillery**
Hereford
(01432) 354207
cidermuseum.co.uk
*Be sure to sample a free tasting of
distillery products*

The Commandery
Worcester
(01905) 361821
worcestercity-
museums.org.uk
*Exciting stories of power, greed,
war, wealth and romance*

**The Complete
Working Historic Estate
of Shugborough
(The National Trust)**
Milford, Staffordshire
(01889) 881388
shugborough.org.uk
*Explore 900 acres of historic
parkland with working Georgian
buildings*

Compton Verney House
Stratford-upon-Avon,
Warwickshire
(01926) 645500
comptonverney.org.uk
Art collection in a listed building

Coventry Cathedral
West Midlands
(024) 7652 1200
coventrycathedral.org.uk
*Unique 20th-century architecture
to both inspire and enthral*

Coventry Transport Museum
West Midlands
(024) 7623 4270
transport-museum.com
*Fascinating collection of vehicles
spanning all the ages*

Drayton Manor Theme Park
near Tamworth, Staffordshire
0870 872 5252
draytonmanor.co.uk
*Great rides and attractions set in
280 acres of parkland*

Hampton Court Gardens
Leominster, Herefordshire
(01568) 797777
hamptoncourt.org.uk
Stunning organic gardens

**Ironbridge Gorge
Museums**
Ironbridge, Shropshire
(01952) 432405
ironbridge.org.uk
*Revolutionary inventions in
inspiring museums*

Kenilworth Castle
Warwickshire
(01926) 852078
english-heritage.org.uk
*A vast complex of ruined
fortifications and palatial apartments*

**The Museum of the Jewellery
Quarter**
Hockley, Birmingham
(0121) 554 3598
bmag.org.uk
*The story of jewellery making in
Birmingham*

National Motorcycle Museum
Solihull, West Midlands
(01675) 443311
nationalmotorcyclemuseum.co.uk
Largest of its kind in the world

National Sea Life Centre
Birmingham, West Midlands
(0121) 643 6777
sealifeeurope.com
*Features tubular underwater walk-
though tunnel*

Royal Air Force Museum
Cosford, Shropshire
(01902) 376200
rafmuseum.org
*One of the largest aviation
collections in the UK*

Royal Worcester Visitor Centre
(01905) 746000
royalworcester.co.uk
See craftmanship at work

Severn Valley Railway
Bewdley, Worcestershire
(01299) 403816
svr.co.uk
*Steam trains running along the
beautiful Severn Valley*

Shakespeare's Birthplace
Stratford-upon-Avon,
Warwickshire
(01789) 204016
shakespeare.org.uk
The bard's inspiring dwelling place

Shakespearience
Stratford-upon-Avon,
Warwickshire
(01789) 290111
shakespearience.co.uk
*Thrilling show of Shakespeare's
lifestory*

The Snowdome Leisure Island
Tamworth, Staffordshire
0870 500 0011
snowdome.co.uk
UK's premier real snow centre

Thinktank – Birmingham Science Museum
(0121) 202 2222
thinktank.ac
Hands on exhibits and interactive fun

Trentham Leisure Ltd
Stoke-on-Trent, Staffordshire
(01782) 657341
trenthamleisure.co.uk
England's largest garden restoration project

The Wedgwood Visitor Centre
Stoke-on-Trent, Staffordshire
0870 606 1759
thewedgwoodvisitorcentre.com
Displays, factory tours and sweeping parkland

West Midland Safari & Leisure Park
Bewdley, Worcestershire
(01299) 402114
wmsp.co.uk
Observe rare white lions

Weston Park
near Shifnal, Staffordshire
(01952) 852100
weston-park.com
One thousand acres of natural beauty with three centuries of garden design

Diary dates 2008

The National Boat, Caravan & Outdoor Show
NEC, Birmingham
boatandcaravan.co.uk
19 – 24 Feb

Crufts
NEC, Birmingham
thekennelclub.org.uk
6 – 9 Mar

The Ordnance Survey Outdoors Show
NEC, Birmingham
theoutdoorsshow.co.uk
14 – 16 Mar

The Cosford Air Show
cosfordairshow.co.uk
1 Jun

Three Counties Countryside Show
The Malvern Showground, Worcestershire
threecounties.co.uk
13 – 15 Jun

Godiva Festival
Memorial Park, Coventry
godivafestival.co.uk
11 – 13 Jul*

The Big Chill
Eastnor Castle, Ledbury
bigchill.net
1 – 3 Aug

Ludlow Marches Food and Drink Festival
foodfestival.co.uk
12 – 14 Sep

Worcester Christmas Fayre
worcestershire.gov.uk
27 – 30 Nov

Frankfurt Christmas Market
Victoria Square/New Street, Birmingham
birmingham.gov.uk
13 Nov – 23 Dec*

* provisional date at time of going to press

Tourist Information Centres

When you arrive at your destination, visit an Official Partner Tourist Information Centre for quality assured help with accommodation and information about local attractions and events, or email your request before you go.

Bewdley	Load Street	(01299) 404740	bewdleytic@wyreforestdc.gov.uk
Birmingham Rotunda	150 New Street	0870 225 0127	callcentre@marketingbirmingham.com
Bridgnorth	Listley Street	(01746) 763257	bridgnorth.tourism@shropshire-cc.gov.uk
Burton upon Trent	Coors Visitor Centre	(01283) 508111	tic@eaststaffsbc.gov.uk
Coventry Airport	Coventry Airport South	(024) 7622 7264	tic@cvone.co.uk
Coventry Cathedral	Cathedral Ruins	(024) 7622 7264	tic@cvone.co.uk
Coventry Ricoh Arena	Phoenix Way	0870 111 6397	tic@cvone.co.uk
Coventry Transport Museum	Hales Street	(024) 7622 7264	tic@cvone.co.uk
Hereford	1 King Street	(01432) 268430	tic-hereford@herefordshire.gov.uk
Ironbridge	Ironbridge Gorge Museum Trust	(01952) 884391	tic@ironbridge.org.uk
Leamington Spa	The Parade	0870 160 7930	info@shakespeare-country.co.uk
Leek	1 Market Place	(01538) 483741	tourism.services@staffsmoorlands.gov.uk
Lichfield	Lichfield Garrick	(01543) 412112	info@visitlichfield.com
Ludlow	Castle Street	(01584) 875053	ludlow.tourism@shropshire-cc.gov.uk
Malvern	21 Church Street	(01684) 892289	malvern.tic@malvernhills.gov.uk
Oswestry	Mile End	(01691) 662488	tic@oswestry-bc.gov.uk
Ross-on-Wye	Edde Cross Street	(01989) 562768	tic-ross@herefordshire.gov.uk
Rugby	Little Elborow Street	(01788) 534970	visitor.centre@rugby.gov.uk
Shrewsbury	The Square	(01743) 281200	visitorinfo@shrewsbury.gov.uk
Stafford	Market Street	(01785) 619619	tic@staffordbc.gov.uk
Stoke-on-Trent	Victoria Hall	(01782) 236000	stoke.tic@stoke.gov.uk
Stratford-upon-Avon	Bridgefoot	0870 160 7930	info@shakespeare-country.co.uk
Tamworth	29 Market Street	(01827) 709581	tic@tamworth.gov.uk
Warwick	Jury Street	(01926) 492212	touristinfo@warwick-uk.co.uk
Worcester	High Street	(01905) 726311	touristinfo@cityofworcester.gov.uk

Travel info

By road:
Britain's main motorways (M1/M6/M5) meet in the Heart of England; the M40 links with the M42 south of Birmingham while the M4 provides fast access from London to the south of the region. These road links ensure that the Heart of England is more accessible by road than any other region in the UK.

By rail:
The Heart of England is served by an excellent rail network. InterCity rail services are fast and frequent from London and other major cities into the region. Trains run from Euston to Birmingham, Coventry and Rugby; from Paddington to the Cotswolds, Stratford-upon-Avon and Worcester; and from Marylebone to Birmingham and Stourbridge. From the main stations a network of regional routes take you around the Heart of England.

By air:
Fly into Birmingham, Coventry or Nottingham East Midlands.

Brindleyplace, Birmingham

Find out more

Further information is available from the following organisations:

Marketing Birmingham
(0121) 202 5115
visitbirmingham.com

Black Country Tourism
blackcountrytourism.co.uk

Visit Coventry & Warwickshire
(024) 7622 7264
visitcoventryandwarwickshire.co.uk

Visit Herefordshire
(01432) 260621
visitherefordshire.co.uk

Shakespeare Country
0870 160 7930
shakespeare-country.co.uk

Shropshire Tourism
(01743) 462462
shropshiretourism.info

Destination Staffordshire
0870 500 4444
enjoystaffordshire.com

Stoke-on-Trent
(01782) 236000
visitstoke.co.uk

Destination Worcestershire
(01905) 728787
visitworcestershire.org

Help before you go

To search for attractions and Tourist Information Centres on the move just text INFO to 62233, and a web link will be sent to your mobile phone.

where to stay in
Heart of England

All place names in the blue bands are shown on the maps at the front of this guide.

A complete listing of all VisitBritain assessed parks in England appears at the back.

Accommodation symbols
Symbols give useful information about services and facilities. Inside the back-cover flap you can find a key to these symbols. Keep it open for easy reference.

ASTON CANTLOW, Warwickshire Map ref 2B1

★★★
HOLIDAY, TOURING
& CAMPING PARK

🚐 (24)   £16.00
🚍 (24)   £16.00
⛺ (10)   £13.00
🚐 (5) £295.00–£395.00
24 touring pitches

Island Meadow Caravan Park

The Mill House, Aston Cantlow B95 6JP **t** (01789) 488273 **f** (01789) 488273
e holiday@islandmeadowcaravanpark.co.uk **w** islandmeadowcaravanpark.co.uk

A quiet, peaceful riverside park just outside the historic village of Aston Cantlow and within six miles of Stratford. An ideal centre for Warwick, Evesham, Birmingham and the Cotswolds. Open March to October.

payment Cash/cheques, euros

General P 🚭 🕭 🍴 🚐 🈂 ☺ 📱 🔟 🔌 🐕 🏕 ☼ Leisure ✍

BIRMINGHAM, West Midlands Map ref 4B3

★★★★★
TOURING PARK

🚐 (99) £13.60–£25.60
🚍 (99) £13.60–£25.60
99 touring pitches

See Ad on inside front cover

Chapel Lane Caravan Club Site

Chapel Lane, Wythall, Birmingham B47 6JX **t** (01564) 826483 **w** caravanclub.co.uk

open All year
payment Credit/debit cards, cash/cheques

Wythall is a quiet, rural area yet convenient for Birmingham (nine miles) and the NEC (13 miles). Visit Cadbury's World or explore the surrounding countryside and local canals.

⊕ From M1 jct 23a, jct 3 off M42 then A435 to Birmingham. After 1 mile at roundabout take 1st exit, Middle Lane. Turn right at church then immediately right into site.

♥ Special member rates mean you can save your membership subscription in less than a week. Visit our website to find out more.

General 🚐 P 🚭 🕭 🍴 🚐 🈂 ☺ 📱 🔟 🐕 ☼ Leisure ⛰ ✍ ▶

BIRMINGHAM INTERNATIONAL AIRPORT

See under Birmingham, Meriden

Place index

If you know where you want to stay, the index at the back of the guide will give you the page number listing accommodation in your chosen town, city or village. Check out the other useful indexes too.

BLACKSHAW MOOR, Staffordshire Map ref 4B2

★★★★★
TOURING PARK

(89)   £12.10–£24.90
(89)   £12.10–£24.90
89 touring pitches

See Ad on inside front cover

THE
CARAVAN
CLUB

Blackshaw Moor Caravan Club Site

Blackshaw Moor, Leek ST13 8TW t (01538) 300203 w caravanclub.co.uk

payment Credit/debit cards, cash/cheques

A most attractive level and terraced site with spacious pitches on the quieter, southern edge of the Peak District with some of the best views and walks in the region. Open March to January 2009.

General P 🕮 🗘 🕯 🖼 🅿 ☉ 🖩🗑 🛏 🐾 Leisure ✦

ELLESMERE, Shropshire Map ref 4A2

★★★★★
HOLIDAY &
TOURING PARK

        £16.50–£21.00
        £16.50–£21.00
(1) £285.00–£425.00
60 touring pitches

Fernwood Caravan Park

Lyneal, Ellesmere SY12 0QF t (01948) 710221 f (01948) 710324 e enquiries@fernwoodpark.co.uk
w fernwoodpark.co.uk

Picturesque, 25-acre country park for static holiday homes, tourers and motor homes. Forty acres' adjacent woodland and lake for coarse fishing. Shop and launderette. Pets welcome.

payment Credit/debit cards, cash/cheques

General 🖼 P 🕮 🗘 🕯 🖼 🅿 ☉ 🖩🗑 🛒 🛏 ☼ Leisure 🗻 ✦

EVESHAM, Worcestershire Map ref 2B1

★★★★★
HOLIDAY &
TOURING PARK

        £17.50–£22.50
        £17.50–£22.50
(4) £290.00–£430.00
120 touring pitches

The Ranch Caravan Park

Station Road, Honeybourne, Evesham WR11 7PR t (01386) 830744 f (01386) 833503
e enquiries@ranch.co.uk w ranch.co.uk

An established family-run holiday park located in Honeybourne, six miles from Evesham. Level pitches in a landscaped setting. Well situated for visiting the Cotswolds and Shakespeare Country. Open March to November.

payment Credit/debit cards, cash/cheques

General 🖼 P 🕮 🗘 🕯 🖼 🅿 ☉ 🖩🗑 🛒 ✗ 🛏 🐾 ☼ Leisure ⚲ 📺 ▼ 🎵 ● 🗻

HEREFORD, Herefordshire Map ref 2A1

★★★★★
HOLIDAY &
TOURING PARK

(80) £11.50–£15.00
(80) £11.50–£15.00
▲ (40)   £7.00–£15.00
80 touring pitches

Lucksall Caravan and Camping Park

Mordiford, Hereford HR1 4LP t (01432) 870213 f (01432) 870213 e karen@lucksallpark.co.uk
w lucksallpark.co.uk

Non-commercialised, immaculately kept park situated on the banks of the River Wye. Seventeen acres of level ground, 16-amp hook-up. Excellent for walking, canoe hire, fishing. Disabled facilities, shop. Open 1 March to 30 November.

payment Credit/debit cards

General 🖼 🛱 P 🕮 🗘 🕯 🖼 🅿 ☉ 🖩🗑 🛒 🛏 🐾 ☼ Leisure 🗻 ✦ 🚲

It's all quality-assessed accommodation

Our commitment to quality involves wide-ranging accommodation assessment. Rating and awards were correct at the time of going to press but may change following a new assessment. Please check at time of booking.

LUDLOW, Shropshire Map ref 4A3

★★★★★
HOLIDAY &
TOURING PARK
🚐(16) £14.00–£15.00
🚎(16) £14.00–£15.00
⛺ £14.00–£15.00
16 touring pitches

Orleton Rise Holiday Home Park

Green Lane, Orleton, Ludlow SY8 4JE **t** (01584) 831617 **f** (01584) 831617
e enquiries@orletonrisepark.co.uk

Small, quiet, hardstanding touring area. Situated in our ten-acre immaculately kept park. Many mature trees, large colourful shrubberies, surrounded by open countryside – ideal for walking and cycling. Open 1 March to 31 January.

payment Cash/cheques

General **P 🔌 🅿 🎯 🏧 ⊙ 📱🗑 ⅋ ☼**

MERIDEN, West Midlands Map ref 4B3

★★★★★
TOURING PARK
🚐(48) £18.00
🚎(48) £18.00
48 touring pitches

Somers Wood Caravan Park

Somers Road, Meriden CV7 7PL **t** (01676) 522978 **f** (01676) 522978 **e** somerswoodcpk@aol.com
w somerswood.co.uk

A quality touring park, set in woodland, exclusively for adults. Adjacent golf course, club house and coarse fishery. Three miles from the National Exhibition Centre. Open 1 February to 15 December.

payment Credit/debit cards, cash/cheques

General **P 🔌 🅿 🎯 🏧 ⊙ 📱⅋** Leisure **ᑐ 🅙 ▸**

PRESTHOPE, Shropshire Map ref 4A3

★★★
TOURING PARK
🚐(73) £6.00–£13.00
🚎(73) £6.00–£13.00
73 touring pitches

See Ad on inside front cover

Presthope Caravan Club Site

Stretton Road, Much Wenlock TF13 6DQ **t** (01746) 785234 **w** caravanclub.co.uk

payment Credit/debit cards, cash/cheques

Peaceful site on the southern slope of Wenlock Edge. Winner of the 2004 Sites in Bloom Award. An interesting site for the naturalist with abundant wildlife. Beautiful countryside surrounds the site. Open April to September.

⊕ From A458 (signposted Shrewsbury) in 0.25 miles turn left onto B4371. Site on left.

♥ Simply Six: all-inclusive fee for a standard pitch, including electricity, will be £6 per night. A supplement for non-members applies.

THE
CARAVAN
CLUB

General **P 🔌 🅿 🎯 🚰 ⅋ 🗑** Leisure **🅙**

STRATFORD-UPON-AVON, Warwickshire Map ref 2B1

★★★
TOURING &
CAMPING PARK
🚐(50) £14.50–£17.00
🚎(50) £14.50–£17.00
⛺(50) £13.00–£15.50
50 touring pitches

Dodwell Park

Evesham Rd, Stratford-upon-Avon CV37 9SR **t** (01789) 204957 **f** (01926) 620199
e enquiries@dodwellpark.co.uk **w** dodwellpark.co.uk

Small, family-run touring park two miles south west of Stratford-upon-Avon on the B439. Country walks to River Avon and Luddington village. Ideal for visiting Warwick Castle, Shakespeare's birthplace and the Cotswolds.

open All year
payment Credit/debit cards, cash/cheques

General **🍴 P 🔌 🅿 🎯 🏧 ⊙ 📱🗑 ⅋ 🗑 ☼** Leisure **🅙 ♿**

WYE VALLEY

See under Hereford

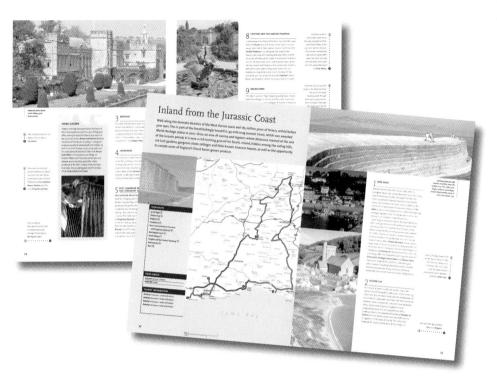

Take a tour of England

VisitBritain presents a series of **three** inspirational touring guides to the regions of England: South and South West, Northern England and Central England.

Each guide takes you on a fascinating journey through stunning countryside and coastlines, picturesque villages and lively market towns, historic houses and gardens.

● Easy-to-use maps
● Clear directions to follow the route
● Lively descriptions of all the places for you to discover
● Stunning photographs bring each area to life

Touring Central England – £14.99
Touring Northern England – £14.99
Touring South and South West England – £14.99
plus postage and handling

East Midlands

Leicestershire & Rutland, Lincolnshire,
Northamptonshire, Nottinghamshire,
Peak District & Derbyshire

Fresh air, fabulous countryside and festivals galore

If you love getting out into
the open air, you'll adore the
East Midlands. Whether
you're the sporty type or
just a fresh air addict, the
East Midlands has lots in
store for the whole family.

East Midlands Tourism
discovereastmidlands.com

Salcey Forest, Northampton

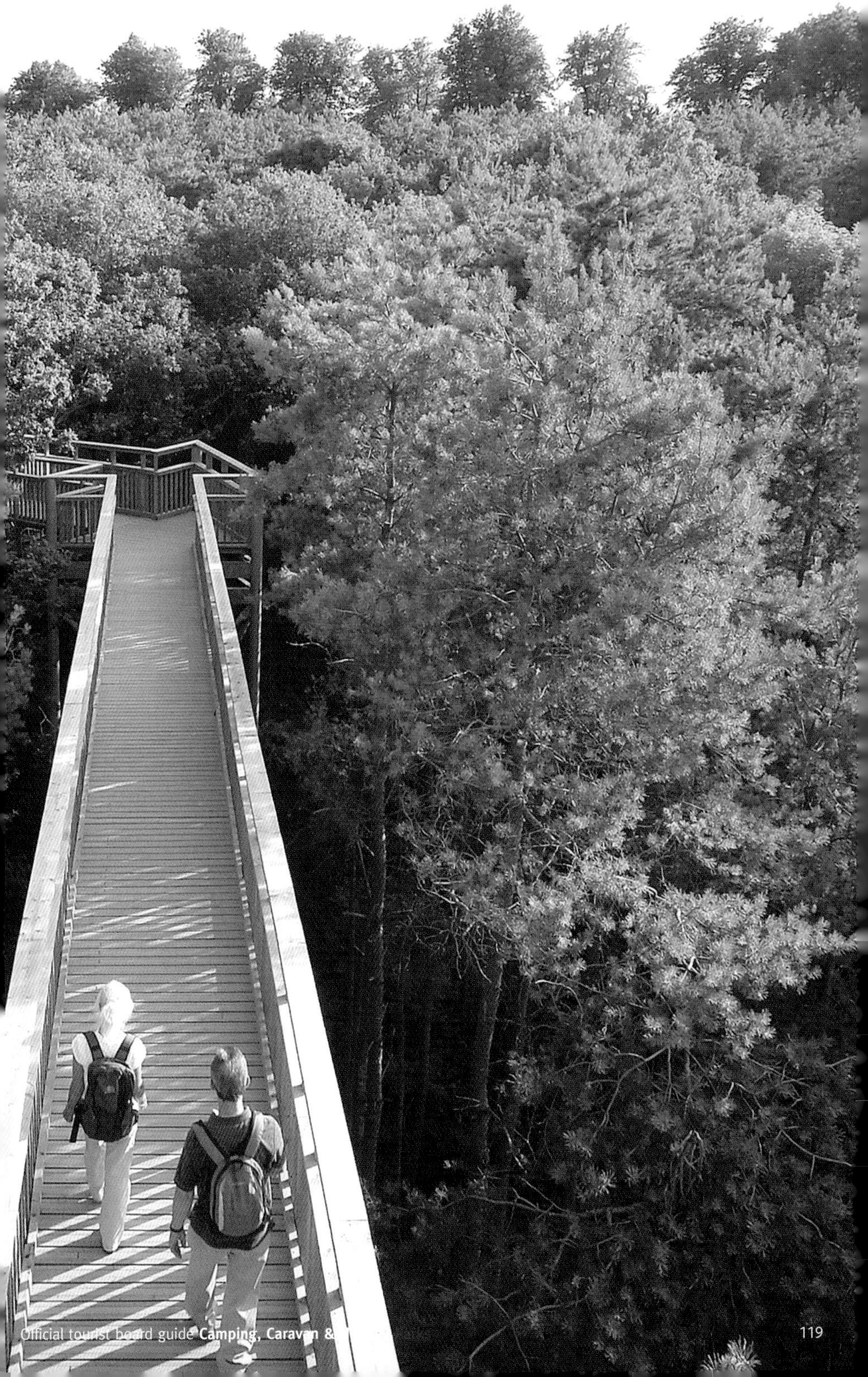

National Space Centre, Leicester

Sherwood Forest Country Park

Chatsworth House, Derbyshire

Walkers be warned: you'll never want to leave. The idyllic River Dove is surrounded by the remains of ancient coral reefs which form Dovedale, and it's reckoned to be the ultimate ramble. Then there's the Pennine Way with its towering mountain plateau of Kinder Scout, not to mention the wild High Peak Trail. Cycling's big in these parts too. Take on the 'Black Death Challenge' and spin into seven medieval plague villages; or tackle the terrifying slalom descent at Sherwood Pines. Feeling adventurous? Try your hand at dragon boat racing at Carsington Water, or water-skiing at the National Watersports Centre. And then there are golf courses galore, the British Grand Prix at Silverstone, the famous Burghley Horse Trials...not forgetting the World Conker Championship in Ashton.

The East Midlands is home to many arts festivals, so be sure to keep an eye out for the Stamford Shakespeare Festival at Tolethorpe Hall and Buxton's Gilbert and Sullivan Festival. With heritage in mind, there are a whole host of dramatic castles such as Bosworth and Peveril to explore. And if you want to be swept off your feet, you won't want to miss the National Space Centre where you can test your ability to survive a perilous voyage into deep space by taking the interactive Human Spaceflight.

Discover Creswell Crags, a limestone gorge honeycombed with caves that were home to Ice Age man. Or lose yourself in the maze at Chatsworth House. And don't miss Snibston Discovery Park in the heart the National Forest, an award-winning family attraction exploring the impact of technology on our everyday lives.

Prefer to live it up? Make for historic Lincoln, Nottingham, Derby or Leicester where fine Asian cuisine is spicily sumptuous. Seek out traditional local fare too – delicious cheeses, gingerbread and the famous Melton Mowbray pork pies.

Destinations

Derby

This multi-cultural city bursts with entertainment venues, attractions, shopping experiences and open green spaces. The compact city centre makes exploring easy. Visit the indoor market housed in the wonderful Victorian Market Hall and take advantage of free attractions including the Museum and Art Gallery where you'll find work by famous local artist, Joseph Wright. Don't miss the cathedral, which has the second highest church tower in England, Royal Crown Derby and Pride Park football stadium.

Leicester

A cosmopolitan and cultured city, Leicester offers unusual shops, fine restaurants, a vibrant nightlife and a strong cultural diversity. Discover designer labels in the Leicester Lanes, and exquisitely embroidered silks along the Golden Mile. Travel to infinity and beyond at the National Space Centre and experience live music at De Montfort Hall. Witness top class action from Leicester's sporting teams and savour a glass of champagne at one of the city's stylish café bars.

Lincoln

Possessing magnificent architectural heritage, Lincoln is a blend of history, cultural variety, shopping and lively entertainment. Approach the city from any direction and you are drawn to the magnificent outline of the cathedral, one of the finest Gothic buildings in Europe. From the cobbled streets and antiques to the modern art scattered throughout the city, the past and present is all around. Events throughout the year make Lincoln irresistible -- the famous Christmas Market, the Brayford Waterfront Festival, and the weekend that most attractions open for free -- Lincoln weekend.

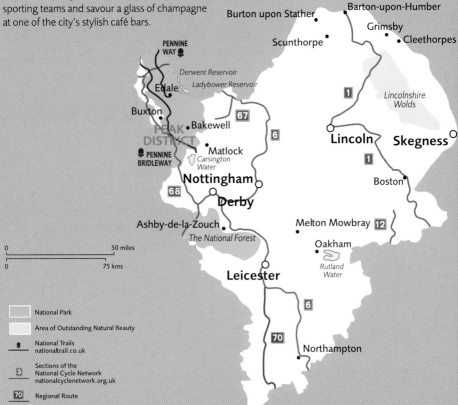

National Park	
Area of Outstanding Natural Beauty	
National Trails nationaltrail.co.uk	
Sections of the National Cycle Network nationalcyclenetwork.org.uk	
Regional Route	

Lincoln Castle

Gibralter Point, near Skegness

The National Forest, near Derby

Peak District

Rutland Water

Leicester

Nottingham

Nottingham

Nottingham is the undisputed capital of the East Midlands, boasting a sophisticated urban environment with an enviable reputation for clubs, theatres, cinemas and galleries, not to mention a deserved reputation as one of the top retail centres in the country. History is never far away, though, with reminders of Nottingham's legendary hero Robin Hood and his adversary the Sheriff of Nottingham. Explore the Castle Museum and Art Gallery, and Wollaton Hall, one of the most ornate Tudor buildings in Britain, complete with 500-acre deer park.

Peak District

The Peak District is Britain's first and most popular National Park. Roam on open moorland to the north and take in the magnificent views over the Derwent Dams. Further south, stroll alongside sparkling rivers in wildlife-rich valleys far from the hustle and bustle of town. The Peak Park Rangers lead regular guided walks – choose from long hikes to village tours. Take in the grandeur of Chatsworth House or Haddon Hall, and sample the local oatcakes with Hartington Stilton, followed by a delicious Bakewell pudding.

Rutland

Tiny Rutland, less than 20 miles across, may be the smallest county in England, but it's packed with hidden treasures. Explore the castle in the historic county town of Oakham, browse the antiquarian bookshops of Uppingham and choose from more than 50 picturesque villages of thatched stone-built cottages. Rutland Water is a must – a giant reservoir where you can fish, walk, cycle and sail. Enjoy Shakespeare at Rutland Open Air Theatre or ride the locomotives at the Rutland Railway Museum. Discover the natural beauty of Rutland – England's best-kept secret!

Skegness

Take time to explore some of the UK's finest seaside resorts. The Lincolnshire coastline, stretching from Skegness to Mablethorpe offers you sun, fun, excitement and laughter, but also tranquillity, clean beaches, and glorious fresh air. Skegness, Lincolnshire's premier resort, features an award-winning six-mile-long beach. Enjoy the seafront illuminations from mid-summer, indulge in family fun at the Pleasure Beach, and visit the seals at the Natureland Sanctuary.

Places to visit

78 Derngate
Northampton
(01604) 603407
78derngate.org.uk
*Terraced house transformed by
Charles Rennie Mackintosh*

Alford Manor House
Alford, Lincolnshire
(01507) 463073
alfordmanorhouse.co.uk
Large thatched manor house

Althorp
Northampton
(01604) 770107
althorp.com
Spencer family home since 1508

**Belton House,
Park and Gardens**
Grantham, Lincolnshire
(01476) 566116
nationaltrust.org.uk
Restoration-period country house

Bolsover Castle
Bolsover, Derbyshire
(01246) 822844
english-heritage.org.uk
*17th-century house on the site of
a Norman fortress*

Burghley House
Stamford, Lincolnshire
(01780) 752451
burghley.co.uk
*The largest and grandest
Elizabethan house*

Castle Ashby Gardens
near Northampton
(01604) 696187
castleashby.co.uk
*Capability Brown landscaped
gardens and parkland*

**Chatsworth House, Garden,
Farmyard & Adventure
Playground**
Bakewell, Derbyshire
(01246) 582204
chatsworth.org
*Beautiful house, garden and
fountains*

Clumber Park
Worksop, Nottinghamshire
(01909) 476592
nationaltrust.org.uk
Year-round colour and interest

**Creswell Crags Museum and
Education Centre, Picnic site,
Caves & Gorge**
Worksop, Derbyshire
(01909) 720378
creswell-crags.org.uk
Limestone gorge, caves and lake

Doddington Hall
Lincoln
(01522) 694308
doddingtonhall.com
*Superb Elizabethan mansion and
gardens*

**Gainsborough
Old Hall**
Gainsborough,
Lincolnshire
(01427) 612669
lincolnshire.gov.uk
Medieval manor house

**Go Ape! High Wire
Forest Adventure**
near Edwinstowe,
Nottinghamshire
0870 444 5562
goape.co.uk
*Rope bridges, swings and zip
slides*

**Grimsthorpe Castle,
Park and Gardens**
near Bourne, Lincolnshire
(01778) 591205
grimsthorpe.co.uk
*Castle covering four periods of
architecture*

Haddon Hall
Bakewell, Derbyshire
(01629) 812855
haddonhall.co.uk
Medieval and Tudor manor house

Hardwick Hall
Chesterfield, Derbyshire
(01246) 850430
nationaltrust.org.uk
*Elizabethan country house and
parkland*

Kirby Hall
Corby, Northamptonshire
(01536) 203230
english-heritage.org.uk
*Elizabethan and 17th-century
house*

Lincoln Castle
(01522) 511068
lincolnshire.gov.uk/
lincolncastle
Historic former court and prison

Lincoln Cathedral
(01522) 561600
lincolncathedral.com
*One of the finest gothic
buildings in Europe*

National Space Centre
Leicester
0870 607 7223
spacecentre.co.uk
The UK's largest space attraction

Newark Castle and Conflict
Nottinghamshire
(01636) 655765
newark-sherwood.gov.uk
Fortress, museum and exhibition

Newstead Abbey
near Nottingham
(01623) 455900
newsteadabbey.org.uk
*800-year-old remains of a priory
church*

Nottingham Castle Museum and Gallery
(0115) 915 3700
nottinghamcity.gov.uk/museums
*17th-century mansion on
medieval-castle site*

Peveril Castle
Castleton, Derbyshire
(01433) 620613
english-heritage.org.uk
Ruined Norman castle

Rockingham Castle
Corby, Northamptonshire
(01536) 770240
rockinghamcastle.com
Rose gardens and exquisite art

Sherwood Forest Country Park
near Mansfield, Nottinghamshire
(01623) 823202
sherwood-forest.org.uk
*Native woodland packed with
adventure*

Silverstone Circuit
Northamptonshire
0870 458 8260
silverstone-circuits.co.uk
The home of British motor racing

Tattershall Castle
Lincoln
(01526) 342543
nationaltrust.org.uk
*Dramatic 15th-century red-brick
tower*

Diary dates 2008

Peak District Walking Festival
Various locations, Peak District
visitpeakdistrict.com
Apr – May*

Lincolnshire Wolds Walking Festival
Various locations, Lincolnshire
visitlincolnshire.com
17 May – 1 Jun

Stamford Shakespeare Festival
Rutland Open Air Theatre, Stamford
stamfordshakespeare.co.uk
Jun – Aug*

Althorp Literary Festival
Althorp House, Northamptonshire
althorp.com/literaryfestival
14 – 15 Jun

Buxton Festival
Various locations, Buxton
buxtonfestival.co.uk
4 – 20 Jul*

Robin Hood Festival
Sherwood Forest Visitor Centre, Edwinstowe
sherwoodforest.org.uk
First week in Aug*

Festival of History
Kelmarsh Hall, Northamptonshire
kelmarsh.com
9 – 10 Aug

DH Lawrence Festival
Eastwood, Nottinghamshire
broxtowe.gov.uk/festival
Mid-Aug – mid-Sep*

East Midlands Food Festival
Melton Mowbray, Leicestershire
eastmidlandsfoodfestival.co.uk
4 – 5 Oct

Lincoln Christmas Market
lincoln.gov.uk
4 – 7 Dec

* provisional date at time of going to press

Tourist Information Centres

When you arrive at your destination, visit an Official Partner Tourist Information Centre for quality assured help with accommodation and information about local attractions and events, or email your request before you go. To search for attractions and Tourist Information Centres on the move just text INFO to 62233, and a web link will be sent to your mobile phone.

Ashbourne	13 Market Place	(01335) 343666	ashbourneinfo@derbyshiredales.gov.uk
Bakewell	Bridge Street	(01629) 816558	bakewell@peakdistrict-npa.gov.uk
Buxton	The Crescent	(01298) 25106	tourism@highpeak.gov.uk
Castleton	Buxton Road	(01433) 620679	castleton@peakdistrict-npa.gov.uk
Chesterfield	Rykneld Square	(01246) 345777	tourism@chesterfield.gov.uk
Derby	Market Place	(01332) 255802	tourism@derby.gov.uk
Leicester	7/9 Every Street	0906 294 1113**	info@goleicestershire.com
Lincoln Castle Hill	9 Castle Hill	(01522) 873213	tourism@lincoln.gov.uk
Matlock	Crown Square	(01629) 583388	matlockinfo@derbyshiredales.gov.uk
Matlock Bath	The Pavillion	(01629) 55082	matlockbathinfo@derbyshiredales.gov.uk
Ripley	Market Place	(01773) 841488	touristinformation@ambervalley.gov.uk
Sleaford	Carre Street	(01529) 414294	tic@n-kesteven.gov.uk
Swadlincote	West Street	(01283) 222848	tic@sharpespotterymuseum.org.uk

** calls to this number are charged at premium rate

Travel info

The central location of the East Midlands makes it easily accessible from all parts of the UK.

By road:
From the north and south, the M1 bisects the East Midlands with access to the region from junctions 14 through to 31. The A1 offers better access to the eastern part of the region, particularly Lincolnshire and Rutland. From the west, the M69, M/A42 and A50 provide easy access.

By rail:
The region is well served by InterCity services, offering direct routes from London, the north of England and Scotland to the East Midlands' major cities and towns. East/west links offer not only access to the region but also travel within it.

By air:
East Midlands Airport (Nottingham, Leicester, Derby) is located centrally in the region, with scheduled domestic flights from Aberdeen, Belfast, Edinburgh, Glasgow, Isle of Man and the Channel Islands. Manchester, Birmingham, Luton, Stansted and Humberside airports also offer domestic scheduled routes, with easy access to the region by road and rail.

Find out more

Further publications are available from the following organisations:

East Midlands Tourism
w discovereastmidlands.com
• Discover East Midlands

Experience Nottinghamshire
t (0115) 915 5330
w visitnotts.com
• Nottinghamshire Essential Guide,
  Where to Stay Guide, Stay Somewhere Different,
  City Breaks, Attractions – A Family Day Out
• Robin Hood Breaks
• Pilgrim Fathers

Peak District and Derbyshire
t 0870 444 7275
w visitpeakdistrict.com
• Peak District Visitor Guide
• Savour the Flavour of the Peak District
• Derbyshire – the Peak District Visitor Guide
• Derbyshire – the Peak District Attractions Guide
• Camping and Caravanning Guide
• What's on Guide

Lincolnshire
t (01522) 873213
w visitlincolnshire.com
• Visit Lincolnshire – Destination Guide,
  Great days out, Gardens & Nurseries,
  Aviation Heritage, Good Taste
• Go with the flow

Explore Northamptonshire
t (01604) 838800
w explorenorthamptonshire.co.uk
• Explore Northamptonshire Visitor Guide,
  County Map, Food and Drink

Leicestershire and Rutland
t 0906 294 1113
w goleicestershire.com
• Rutland Visitor Guide
• Market Harborough & Lutterworth Guide
• Ashby de la Zouch and The National Forest Guide
• Melton Mowbray and the Vale of Belvoir
• Loughborough and Charnwood Forest
• GoLeicestershire
• Must See 3

Whinstone Lee Tor, Peak District

Whinstone Lee Tor, Peak District

where to stay in
East Midlands

All place names in the blue bands are shown on the maps at the front of this guide.

A complete listing of all VisitBritain assessed parks in England appears at the back.

Accommodation symbols
Symbols give useful information about services and facilities. Inside the back-cover flap you can find a key to these symbols. Keep it open for easy reference.

ALSOP-EN-LE-DALE, Derbyshire Map ref 4B2

★★★★
HOLIDAY, TOURING
& CAMPING PARK

🚐(81) £10.50–£21.70
🚐(81) £10.50–£21.70
⛺(30) £10.50–£21.70
111 touring pitches

Rivendale Caravan and Leisure Park

Buxton Road, Alsop en le Dale, Ashbourne DE6 1QU t (01335) 310311 f (01332) 842311
e greg@rivendalecaravanpark.co.uk w rivendalecaravanpark.co.uk

payment Credit/debit cards, cash/cheques

Surrounded by spectacular Peak District scenery, convenient for Alton Towers, Chatsworth, Dove Dale and Carsington Water. Ideal for cyclists and ramblers with a network of footpaths and trails accessible directly from site. Choice of all-grass, hardstanding or 50/50 pitches. Closed 7 January to 1 February.

⊕ From A515, Rivendale is situated 6.5 miles north of Ashbourne, directly off the A515 Buxton road on the right hand side, travelling north.

♥ Receive £15 discount for every 7-night stay (includes multiples of 7-night stays).

General 🚐 P 🚿 🖰 🍴 🚰 ⟲ ⊙ 🗓 🍳 ✕ 🐕 ⛺ ☼ Leisure 📺 🍷 🔦 ⚲ ∪ 🚣 ⛭

BAKEWELL, Derbyshire Map ref 4B2

★★★★★
TOURING PARK

🚐(120) £14.30–£27.70
🚐(120) £14.30–£27.70
120 touring pitches

See Ad on inside front cover

THE
CARAVAN
CLUB

Chatsworth Park Caravan Club Site

Chatsworth, Bakewell DE45 1PN t (01246) 582226 w caravanclub.co.uk

payment Credit/debit cards, cash/cheques

Breathtaking setting in walled garden on the Estate. Farmyard and adventure playground for children. The Peak District National Park's towns are nearby. Open March to January 2009.

⊕ From Bakewell on A619. In 3.75 miles on the outskirts of Baslow turn right at roundabout (signposted Sheffield). Site entrance on right in 150yds.

♥ Special member rates mean you can save your membership subscription in less than a week. Visit our website to find out more.

General P 🚿 🖰 🍴 🚰 ⟲ 🗓 🐕 ☼ Leisure ⚲

Check it out
Please check prices, quality ratings and other details when you book.

BURGH-LE-MARSH, Lincolnshire Map ref 4D2

★★★★
TOURING &
CAMPING PARK

🚐 £14.00–£16.00
🚏 £14.00–£16.00
⛺ £12.00–£16.00
🏠 (9) £335.00–£425.00
54 touring pitches

Sycamore Lakes Touring Site

Skegness Road, Burgh le Marsh PE24 5LN **t** (01754) 811411 **f** (01754) 811411
w sycamorelakes.co.uk

payment Cash/cheques

Set in 16 acres of landscaped grounds with four fishing lakes (well stocked with carp, tench, rudd, roach and perch). Spacious, level pitches with hook-ups. Nine lakeside cottages and cabins. Superb amenity block. Lakeside cafeteria/Sunday lunch carvery. Tackle shop, dog walk and footpaths. Plenty of space to relax and unwind. Open March to October.

⊕ Situated on the A158 between Burgh-le-Marsh and Skegness.

General 🛋 🖵 🍴 P 🔌 🚿 🏧 🚻 ⊙ 🗑 🧺 ✕ 🐕 🎣 ☼ Leisure 🏔 🏊 ⚓

BUXTON, Derbyshire Map ref 4B2

★★★
TOURING &
CAMPING PARK

🚐 (30) £12.00
🚏 (30) £12.00
⛺ (30) £10.00–£12.00
30 touring pitches

Cottage Farm Caravan Park

Beech Croft, Blackwell, Buxton SK17 9TQ **t** (01298) 85330 **e** mail@cottagefarmsite.co.uk
w cottagefarmsite.co.uk

We are a family-run site, southerly facing with easy access from the A6. We can boast a beautiful walk along the River Wye at nearby Cheedale. Limited facilities Nov-Mar.

open All year
payment Cash/cheques

General P 🔌 🚿 🍴 🏧 ⊙ 🗑 🧺 🐕

BUXTON, Derbyshire Map ref 4B2

★★★★★
TOURING &
CAMPING PARK

🚐 (117) £12.10–£24.90
🚏 (117) £12.10–£24.90
⛺ on application
117 touring pitches

See Ad on inside front cover

CARAVAN CLUB

Grin Low Caravan Club Site

Grin Low Road, Ladmanlow, Buxton SK17 6UJ **t** (01298) 77735 **w** caravanclub.co.uk

payment Credit/debit cards, cash/cheques

Attractively landscaped site ideally situated for Buxton, at the centre of the Peak District National Park, and for visiting Chatsworth and Haddon Hall. Open March to November.

⊕ From Buxton left off A53 Buxton to Leek road. Within 1.5 miles at Grin Low signpost, in 300yds turn left into site approach road; site entrance 0.25 miles.

♥ Special member rates mean you can save your membership subscription in less than a week. Visit our website to find out more..

General 🖵 P 🔌 🚿 🍴 🏧 ⊙ 📻 🗑 🐕 ☼ Leisure 🏔 ►

BUXTON, Derbyshire Map ref 4B2

★★★★
HOLIDAY, TOURING
& CAMPING PARK
ROSE AWARD

🚐 (65) £12.00–£20.00
🚏 (15) £12.00–£20.00
⛺ (70) £6.50–£20.00
🏠 (12) £190.00–£450.00
65 touring pitches

Lime Tree Park

Dukes Drive, Buxton SK17 9RP **t** (01298) 22988 **f** (01298) 22988 **e** info@limetreeparkbuxton.co.uk
w limetreeparkbuxton.co.uk

A convenient site in a gently sloping valley on the southern outskirts of Buxton. Facilities for touring and camping. From the town centre, travel south for 0.75 miles on A515, then turn left after Buxton hospital. Closed January.

payment Credit/debit cards, cash/cheques

General 🛋 🖵 P 🔌 🚿 🍴 🏧 ⊙ 📻 🗑 🧺 🐕 ☼ Leisure 📺 ⚡ 🏔 ∪ 🚴

BUXTON, Derbyshire Map ref 4B2

★★★
HOLIDAY, TOURING
& CAMPING PARK

🚐 (95)　£10.00–£11.75
🚎 (14)　£10.00–£11.75
⛺ (30)　£10.00–£11.75
125 touring pitches

Newhaven Caravan and Camping Park

Newhaven, Nr Buxton SK17 0DT　t (01298) 84300　f (01332) 726027　e bobmacara@ntlworld.com
w newhavencaravanpark.co.uk

Halfway between Ashbourne and Buxton in the Peak National Park. Well-established park with modern facilities, close to the Tessington and High Peak trails, historic houses and Derbyshire Dales. Open March to October.

payment Credit/debit cards, cash/cheques

General 🖵 P 🅿 🕒 🚻 🛱 🕓 📵 🔋 🛒 🐕 ☼　Leisure 🎣 ⛰

CASTLETON, Derbyshire Map ref 4B2

★★★★★
TOURING &
CAMPING PARK

🚐 (78)　£13.60–£25.60
🚎 (78)　£13.60–£25.60
78 touring pitches

See Ad on inside front cover

Losehill Caravan Club Site

Castleton, Hope Valley S33 8WB　t (01433) 620636　w caravanclub.co.uk

open All year
payment Credit/debit cards, cash/cheques

This popular site, set in the north of the Peak District National Park, is an excellent base for outdoor activities, including rock-climbing, potholing, biking and horse-riding.

🚾 *From Hathersage on the B6001. In about 2.5 miles, turn left onto the A6187 (signposted Castleton). Site on right in 5 miles.*

♥ *Special member rates mean you can save your membership subscription in less than a week. Visit our website to find out more.*

General 🖵 P 🅿 🕒 🚻 🚐 🛱 🕓 📵 🐕 🛒 ☼　Leisure ⛰ 🎵 ►

FINESHADE, Northamptonshire Map ref 3A1

★★★★
TOURING PARK

🚐 (83)　£9.10–£20.20
🚎 (83)　£9.10–£20.20
83 touring pitches

See Ad on inside front cover

Top Lodge Caravan Club Site

Fineshade, Duddington, Corby NN17 3BB　t (01780) 444617　w caravanclub.co.uk

payment Credit/debit cards, cash/cheques

Tranquil, open meadowland site surrounded by woodland where you can walk freely, watch birds and deer and enjoy a profusion of wild flowers. Open March to November. Own sanitation required

♥ *Special member rates mean you can save your membership subscription in less than a week. Visit our website to find out more.*

General P 🅿 🕒 🚻 🚐 🐕　Leisure 🎵

Our quality rating schemes

For a detailed explanation of the quality and facilities represented by the stars, please refer to the information pages at the back of this guide.

HORNCASTLE, Lincolnshire Map ref 4D2

★★★★
HOLIDAY, TOURING
& CAMPING PARK

(70) £11.00–£19.50
(10) £11.00–£19.50
(10) £11.00–£14.50
90 touring pitches

Ashby Park

Horncastle, West Ashby LN9 5PP   t (01507) 527966   e ashsbyparklakes@aol.com
w ukparks.co.uk/ashby

payment Credit/debit cards, cash/cheques

David Bellamy Gold Conservation Award park offering a friendly and informal atmosphere, peace and tranquillity, good walks, seven fishing lakes and a diversity of wildlife. Set in 70 acres of unspoilt countryside. Open for statics 1 March to 6 January, touring 1 March to 1 December.

⊕ 1.5 miles north of Horncastle between the A153 and the A158.

General ▨ ⇱ P ⊕ ⏶ ☗ ⛽ ⍣ ☉ ⊡⊙ ☘ ⚲ ☼   Leisure ∪ ♪ ⅂

LINCOLN, Lincolnshire Map ref 4C2

★★★
TOURING PARK

  £10.30–£17.90
  £10.30–£17.90
(14) £6.20–£14.60
26 touring pitches

Hartsholme Country Park

Skellingthorpe Road, Lincoln LN6 0EY   t (01522) 873578   e hartsholmecp@lincoln.gov.uk
w lincoln.gov.uk

Flat, level grassy site set in mature wooded park. Ideal for a relaxing family holiday or when visiting friends and relatives. Easy access to city centre and tourist sites. Open March to October.

payment Credit/debit cards, cash/cheques

General P ⏶ ☗ ⍣ ☉ ⊾ ✕ ☘   Leisure ⌂ ♪

PEAK DISTRICT

See under Alsop-En-le-Dale, Bakewell, Buxton, Castleton

RIPLEY, Derbyshire Map ref 4B2

★★★★
TOURING &
CAMPING PARK

  £20.00–£25.00
  £20.00–£25.00
  £15.00–£20.00
24 touring pitches

Golden Valley Caravan & Camping

The Tanyard, Coach Road, Golden Valley, Ripley DE55 4ES   t (01773) 513881
e enquiries@goldenvalleycaravanpark.co.uk   w goldenvalleycaravanpark.co.uk

payment Credit/debit cards, cash/cheques

Secluded woodland hideaway. All-weather children's play facilities. Electric hook-ups on individual landscaped sites. Jacuzzi, gymnasium, pool table, bar, cafe and takeaway. Fishing on site. Next to Butterley Railway. Function room. New Fort Adventure facility. Gold David Bellamy Conservation Award. Open March to October.

⊕ M1 jct 26 onto A610. Follow signs to Alfreton. Turn right at lights at Codnor. Then right.

General ⇱ P ⏶ ⏶ ☗ ⛽ ⍣ ☉ ⊡⊙ ⊾ ☘ ⚲   Leisure ⏲ ♫ ⚲ ⌂ ♪ ⅂ ⌾

SCUNTHORPE, Lincolnshire Map ref 4C1

★★★★★
TOURING PARK

(15) £13.00
(15) £13.00
(5) £10.00
35 touring pitches

Brookside Caravan Park

Stather Road, Burton upon Stather, Scunthorpe DN15 9DH   t (01724) 721369
e brooksidecp@aol.com   w brooksidecaravanpark.co.uk

Quiet, family-run park that will meet all your requirements, with views over the River Trent and woodland.

open All year
payment Cash/cheques

General ▨ ⇱ P ⏶ ☗ ⛽ ⍣ ☉ ⊡⊙ ☘ ⚲ ☼   Leisure ⌂ ∪ ♪ ⅂ ⌾

SHERWOOD FOREST

See under Worksop

SKEGNESS, Lincolnshire Map ref 4D2

★★★
HOLIDAY &
TOURING PARK

🚐(67) £15.00–£21.00
🚍(67) £15.00–£21.00
⛺(120) £190.00–
£480.00
67 touring pitches

Richmond Holiday Centre

Richmond Drive, Skegness PE25 3TQ t (01754) 762097 f (01754) 765631
e sales@richmondholidays.com w richmondholidays.com

The ideal holiday base, a gentle stroll from the bustling resort of Skegness with its funfairs, sandy beaches and donkey rides. Nightly entertainment during the peak weeks. Open March to October.

payment Credit/debit cards, cash/cheques

General P 🚐 🕆 🛢 🅿 ⊙ 🛢 🛢 ⚡ ✕ 🐕 ☼   Leisure ⚡ 🍽 🎵 🔍 ⚠

SKEGNESS, Lincolnshire Map ref 4D2

★★★
HOLIDAY, TOURING
& CAMPING PARK

🚐 £14.00
🚍 £18.00
⛺ £14.00
250 touring pitches

Skegness Water Leisure Park

Walls Lane, Ingoldmells, Skegness PE25 1JF t (01754) 899400 f (01754) 897867
e enquiries@skegnesswaterleisurepark.co.uk w skegnesswaterleisurepark.co.uk

Family-orientated caravan and camping site 'where the coast meets the countryside'. Ten-minute walk to award-winning beaches with scenic, rural views. Open March to November.

payment Credit/debit cards, cash/cheques

General 🔌 P 🚐 🕆 🛢 🅿 ⊙ 🛢 🛢 ⚡ ✕ 🐕 🏠 ☼   Leisure 🍽 🎵 ∪ 🛶

SWADLINCOTE, Derbyshire Map ref 4B3

★★★
TOURING &
CAMPING PARK

🚐(25) £13.00–£15.00
🚍(5) £13.00–£15.00
⛺(60) £10.00–£20.00
30 touring pitches

Beehive Farm Woodland Lakes

Rosliston, Swadlincote DE12 8HZ t (01283) 763981 e info@beehivefarm-woodlandlakes.co.uk
w beehivefarm-woodlandlakes.co.uk

In the heart of the National Forest and within easy reach of the Derbyshire Dales and many great local attractions, Beehive Farm Woodland Lakes is a great place to stay over.

open All year except Christmas and New Year
payment Cash/cheques

General 🖵 P 🚐 🛢 🅿 ⊙ ⚡ 🐕 ☼   Leisure ⚠ 🛶

WORKSOP, Nottinghamshire Map ref 4C2

★★★★
TOURING PARK

🚐(183) £14.30–£27.70
🚍(183) £14.30–£27.70
183 touring pitches

See Ad on inside front cover

Clumber Park Caravan Club Site

Lime Tree Avenue, Clumber Park, Worksop S80 3AE t (01909) 484758 w caravanclub.co.uk

open All year
payment Credit/debit cards, cash/cheques

There's a great feeling of spaciousness here, for th site is on 20 acres within 4,000 acres of parkland. S in the heart of Sherwood Forest and redeveloped a high standard in 2002. Visit Nottingham Castle ar the watersports centre at Holme Pierrepont.

⊕ *From the junction of the A1 and A57, take the A614 signposted to Nottingham for 0.5 miles. Turn right into Clumber Park site. The club is signposted thereafter.*

♥ *Midweek discount: pitch fee for standard pitches for sta on any Tue, Wed or Thu night outside peak season dat will be reduced by 50%.*

General 🖵 P 🚐 🕆 🛢 🅿 ⊙ 🛢 🐕 ☼   Leisure ⚠ 🛶 ⚑

enjoyEngland ™

official tourist board guides

Hotels, including country house and town house hotels, metro and budget hotels in England 2008

£10.99

Guest accommodation, B&Bs, guest houses, farmhouses, inns, restaurants with rooms, campus and hostel accommodation in England 2008

£11.99

Self-catering holiday homes, including serviced apartments and approved caravan holiday homes, boat accommodation and holiday cottage agencies in England 2008

£11.99

Touring parks, camping holidays and holiday parks and villages in Britain 2008

£8.99

informative, easy to use and great value for money

Pet-friendly hotels, B&Bs and self-catering accommodation in England 2008

£9.99

Great ideas for places to visit, eat and stay in England

£10.99

Places to stay and visit in South West England

£9.99

Places to stay and visit in Northern England

£9.99

Accessible places to stay in Britain

£9.99

Now available in good bookshops.
For special offers on VisitBritain publications,
please visit **visitbritaindirect.com**

East of England

Bedfordshire, Cambridgeshire, Essex, Hertfordshire, Norfolk, Suffolk

Simple pleasures in a fascinating setting

There's more to the East of England than the Broads and teeming wildlife; explore this fascinating region and you'll discover fairytale castles, ancient cathedrals and exquisite gardens. (Oh, and dinosaurs and ghosts.)

East of England Tourism
visiteastofengland.com
(01284) 727470

Tring, Hertfordshire

Ely Cathedral, Cambridgeshire   Shuttleworth Collection, Bedfordshire

Southwold, Suffolk

The East of England is crammed full of secrets. Wander around the stupendous Ely Cathedral (star of the movie 'The Golden Age') that towers like a ship over the fens. Take a chariot-ride over to historic Colchester with its chilling links with Boudica. Journey to deepest Bedfordshire and feel like royalty at Wrest Park, a French- inspired Chateau with Versailles-like gardens. Explore the Swiss Garden at Old Warden, a charming Victorian folly garden complete with grotto, Monet bridges and peacocks. And discover the gigantic Dinosaur Adventure Park near Norwich for a monster day of family thrills and fact-finding. Finally, delight the ghostbuster in you and enter Castle Rising Castle, a 12th century Norman hall-keep near King's Lynn where the cries of Queen Isabella can still be heard on dark winter afternoons.

This region holds one of the nation's greatest relics – the astonishing treasure of the mystery Saxon King in his burial ship at Sutton Hoo. If contemporary treasures are more you, check out the landmark Firstsite visual arts centre in the heart of Colchester. And be sure to catch some of the colourful local events such as the World Snail Racing Championship in Congham where 300 snails battle for the silver tankard stuffed with lettuce. Time to up the tempo? Tune-in to the high-octane drag racing at Santa Pod, back a winner at Newmarket Races or head back to the coast for a lively fun-filled day at Great Yarmouth. And for a real echo of the past, gallop over to Royston Cave in Hertfordshire where you can see a bell-shaped chamber containing medieval carvings by the Knights Templar.

Whatever your interest, you'll find something to fascinate you in this unspoilt and very special corner of England.

Destinations

Cambridge

The name Cambridge instantly summons breathtaking images – the Backs carpeted with spring flowers, King's College Chapel, punting on the river Cam and, of course, the calm of the historic college buildings. Cambridge still has the atmosphere of a bustling market town, notwithstanding its international reputation. Explore its winding streets and splendid architecture, and choose from a range of attractions, museums, hotels, restaurants and pubs. Situated in the heart of East Anglia but less than an hour from London by high-speed rail link.

Colchester

If variety's the spice of life, Colchester's the place to savour it! Two thousand years of history and everything you need for a day trip, short break or longer stay. Art lovers will find cutting-edge contemporary galleries and there's a shopper's heaven of little specialist shops and big name stores. The range of cuisine makes Colchester a magnet for food lovers – don't miss the annual Colchester Oyster Feast. Find internationally important treasures located in award-winning museums and view lush landscapes in Victorian Castle Park. At night, discover clubs, theatres, music and open-air vibes.

Great Yarmouth

One of the UK's most popular seaside resorts, with an enviable mix of sandy beaches, attractions, entertainment, heritage and quality accommodation. And beyond the seaside fun is a charming town that is steeped in history. Visit the medieval town walls, stroll the historic South Quay and discover Nelson's 'other' column. When the sun goes down, Great Yarmouth becomes a wonderland of colour as the illuminations light your way to a night on the town. Full of holiday contrasts, the area also boasts 21 villages set in beautiful coastal and rural settings alongside the famous Norfolk Broads.

	50 miles
0	
0	75 kms

National Park & The Broads

Area of Outstanding Natural Beauty

Heritage Coast

National Trails
nationaltrail.co.uk

3 Sections of the National Cycle Network
nationalcyclenetwork.org.uk

Cromer
Hunstanton — Norfolk Coast
King's Lynn
PEDDARS WAY & NORFOLK COAST PATH
1
Great Yarmouth
Norwich
13
THE BROADS
Peterborough **63**
Welney
Lowestoft
Ely
Thetford
Suffolk Coast & Heaths
Southwold
Newmarket
Cambridge
Bury St Edmunds
Aldeburgh
Bedford
Lavenham
Ipswich
51
51
Saffron Walden — Dedham Vale
Royston
Luton — Stevenage
Colchester
Harwich
Dunstable
Coggeshall
Hertford
Clacton-on-Sea
St Albans — Chelmsford
6
Epping
Southend-on-Sea

River Cam, Cambridge

The Broads, near Great Yarmouth

Peterborough Cathedral

Colchester Castle Museum

Aldeburgh, near Ipswich

Luton Carnival

Ruins in Norwich Cathedral grounds

Ipswich

In England's oldest continuously settled Anglo-Saxon town, you'll find numerous architectural gems, including twelve medieval churches. Browse important collections of work by Constable and Gainsborough and enjoy the beautifully landscaped gardens and fine Tudor mansion at Christchurch Park. You'll be able to 'shop 'til you drop' in one of the region's best retail centres, and explore the historic waterfront where the Victorian wet dock is currently undergoing an exciting renaissance. Stay longer, and explore the beautiful, unspoilt Suffolk coastline.

Luton

Discover a friendly and cosmopolitan town. Luton is surprisingly 'green' with over 7% of its area made up of open space, with more than ten sites of importance for wildlife. Shoppers will be spoilt for choice with over 100 shops in the Arndale Centre and a large, thriving market. You'll find a lively and exciting night scene with bars and nightclubs playing music from the UK dance, house and garage scenes. Visit in the spring and catch Luton International Carnival.

Norwich

Norwich, county town of Norfolk, is an enchanting cathedral city and a thriving modern metropolis. See some of the finest medieval architecture in Britain in the cathedral and castle, and wander an intricate network of winding streets. The city's newest centrepiece, The Forum, represents contemporary architecture at its best. You'll find excellent shopping as well as a vibrant mix of theatres, cinemas, arts festivals, exhibitions, museums, and a vast array of restaurants.

Peterborough

With 3,000 years of heritage, Peterborough will exceed your expectations. Its magnificent Norman cathedral sits amid peaceful precincts just a few metres from the city's superb shopping and leisure facilities. You'll find a great range of outdoor activities in picturesque countryside – including 2,000 acres of riverside parkland. And there are plenty of attractions, events and festivals to thrill all ages and interests – just 45 minutes from central London by high-speed rail link.

Places to visit

Anglesey Abbey, Gardens and Lode Mill

near Cambridge
(01223) 810080
nationaltrust.org.uk
Abbey, Jacobean-style house and Fairfax collection

Audley End House and Gardens

Saffron Walden, Essex
(01799) 522399
english-heritage.org.uk
Sumptuous splendour of a grand stately home

Banham Zoo
Norfolk
(01953) 887771
banhamzoo.co.uk
Wildlife spectacular with tigers and leopards

Blickling Hall
near Norwich, Norfolk
(01263) 738030
nationaltrust.org.uk
Jacobean mansion with parkland and orangery

Bressingham Steam Experience and Gardens
near Diss, Norfolk
(01379) 686900
bressingham.co.uk
Fun-packed family day out

Colchester Castle
Essex
(01206) 282939
colchestermuseums.org.uk
Spectacular displays of Colchester's early history

Colchester Zoo

Essex
(01206) 331292
colchester-zoo.com
Over 250 species with superb cat and primate collections

Ely Cathedral
Cambridgeshire
(01353) 667735
cathedral.ely.anglican.org
One of England's finest cathedrals

Go Ape! High Wire Forest Adventure
Thetford Forest, Suffolk
0870 444 5562
goape.co.uk
Rope bridges, swings and zip slides

Hatfield House
Hertfordshire
(01707) 287010
hatfield-house.co.uk
Magnificent Jacobean house with exquisite gardens

Holkham Hall

near Wells-next-the-Sea, Norfolk
(01328) 710227
holkham.co.uk
Classic 18th-century Palladian-style mansion

Imperial War Museum Duxford
near Cambridge
(01223) 835000
duxford.iwm.org.uk
The sights, sound and power of aircraft

Knebworth House, Gardens and Park
near Stevenage, Hertfordshire
(01438) 812661
knebworthhouse.com
Re-fashioned Tudor manor house in 250-acre grounds

National Stud

Newmarket, Cambridgeshire
(01638) 663464
nationalstud.co.uk
Conducted tour of thoroughbreds

Norfolk Lavender Limited

near King's Lynn
(01485) 570384
norfolk-lavender.co.uk
Lavender farm and fragrant gardens

Norwich Cathedral
Norfolk
(01603) 218300
cathedral.org.uk
Imposing Norman cathedral with 14th-century roof bosses

The Royal Air Force Air Defence Radar Museum
Small Visitor Attraction of the Year – Gold Winner
Norwich, Norfolk
(01692) 631485
radarmuseum.co.uk
History of radar featuring Cold War Operations Room

RSPB Minsmere Nature Reserve
Saxmundham, Suffolk
(01728) 648281
rspb.org.uk
Bird-watching hides and trails plus year-round events

Sandringham House
Norfolk
(01553) 612908
sandringhamestate.co.uk
The country retreat of HM The Queen

Shuttleworth Collection

Biggleswade, Bedfordshire
(01767) 627927
shuttleworth.org
Unique collection of aircraft – see a Spitfire in flying condition

Diary dates 2008

Somerleyton Hall & Gardens
near Lowestoft, Suffolk
(01502) 734901
somerleyton.co.uk
Lavish early Victorian mansion

Sutton Hoo Burial Site
Woodbridge, Suffolk
(01394) 389700
nationaltrust.org.uk
Burial mounds overlooking River Deben

Thursford Collection
Norfolk
(01328) 878477
thursford.com
Organ collection with daily show

Verulamium Museum
St Albans, Hertfordshire
(01727) 751810
stalbansmuseums.org.uk
Re-creation of life in Roman Britain

Woburn Abbey
Bedfordshire
(01525) 290333
woburnabbey.co.uk
Palladian mansion set in 3,000-acre deer park

Woburn Safari Park
Bedfordshire
(01525) 290407
woburnsafari.co.uk
30 species of animals just a windscreen's width away

ZSL Whipsnade Zoo
Dunstable, Bedfordshire
(01582) 872171
zsl.org/zsl-whipsnade-zoo
More than 2,500 animals, many endangered in the wild

Whittlesea Straw Bear Festival
strawbear.org.uk
11 – 13 Jan

St George's Day Festival
Wrest Park, Bedfordshire
english-heritage.org.uk
19 – 20 Apr

Stilton Cheese Rolling Competition
Main Street, Stilton
stilton.org/about_rolling.html
5 May

Southend Air Show
The seafront
southendairshow.com
25 – 26 May

Luton International Carnival
Various locations, Luton
luton.gov.uk/carnival
26 May

Aldeburgh Festival
Snape, Suffolk
aldeburgh.co.uk
13 – 29 Jun

Royal Norfolk Show
Norwich
royalnorfolkshow.co.uk
25 – 26 Jun

Bedford River Festival
River Great Ouse
bedford.gov.uk
12 – 13 Jul

World Snail Racing Championships
The Cricket Field, Congham
snailracing.net
19 Jul

Annual British Crabbing Championship
The seafront, Walberswick
explorewalberswick.co.uk
10 Aug

Tourist Information Centres

When you arrive at your destination, visit an Official Partner Tourist Information Centre for quality assured help with accommodation and information about local attractions and events, or email your request before you go. To search for attractions and Tourist Information Centres on the move just text INFO to 62233, and a web link will be sent to your mobile phone.

Bishop's Stortford	The Old Monastery	(01279) 655831	tic@bishopsstortford.org
Bury St Edmunds	6 Angel Hill	(01284) 764667	tic@stedsbc.gov.uk
Flatford	Flatford Lane	(01206) 299460	flatfordvic@babergh.gov.uk
Harwich	Iconfield Park	(01255) 506139	harwichtic@btconnect.com
Hunstanton	The Green	(01485) 532610	hunstanton.tic@west-norfolk.gov.uk
Ipswich	St Stephens Lane	(01473) 258070	tourist@ipswich.gov.uk
King's Lynn	Purfleet Quay	(01553) 763044	kings-lynn.tic@west-norfolk.gov.uk
Lavenham*	Lady Street	(01787) 248207	lavenhamtic@babergh.gov.uk
Lowestoft	East Point Pavilion	(01502) 533600	touristinfo@waveney.gov.uk
Maldon	Coach Lane	(01621) 856503	tic@maldon.gov.uk
Saffron Waldon	1 Market Place	(01799) 510444	tourism@uttlesford.gov.uk
Southwold	69 High Street	(01502) 724729	southwold.tic@waveney.gov.uk
Stowmarket	The Museum of East Anglian Life	(01449) 676800	tic@midsuffolk.gov.uk
Sudbury	Market Hill	(01787) 881320	sudburytic@babergh.gov.uk

* seasonal opening

Knebworth House, Hertfordshire

Holkham Hall Estate, Norfolk

Find out more

East of England Tourism has a comprehensive website, updated daily. Log on to visiteastofengland.com

Online brochures and information sheets can be downloaded including Major Events; Lights, Camera, Action! (film and television locations); Stars and Stripes (connections with the USA) and a range of Discovery Tours around the region.

For more information, please call (01284) 727470 or email info@eet.org.uk

Travel info

By road:
The region is easily accessible: from London and the South via the A1(M), M11, M25, A10, M1 and A12; from the North via the A1(M), A17, A15, A5, M1 and A6; from the West via the A14, A47, A421, A428, A418, A41, A422 and A427.

By rail:
Regular fast and frequent trains run to all major cities and towns. London stations which serve the region are Liverpool Street, King's Cross, Fenchurch Street, Marylebone, St Pancras and Euston. Bedford, Luton and St Albans are on the Thameslink line which runs to King's Cross and on to London Gatwick Airport. There is also a direct link between London Stansted Airport and Liverpool Street. Through the Channel Tunnel, there are trains direct from Paris and Brussels to Waterloo Station, London. A short journey on the Underground will bring passengers to those stations operating services into the East of England. Further information on rail journeys in the East of England can be obtained on 0845 748 4950.

By air:
Fly into London Luton, London Stansted or Norwich International.

East of England

where to stay in
East of England

All place names in the blue bands are shown on the maps at the front of this guide.

A complete listing of all VisitBritain assessed parks in England appears at the back.

Accommodation symbols

Symbols give useful information about services and facilities. Inside the back-cover flap you can find a key to these symbols. Keep it open for easy reference.

BACTON-ON-SEA, Norfolk Map ref 3C1

★★★★★
HOLIDAY PARK
ROSE AWARD

🚐 (25) £116.00–£525.00

Cable Gap Holiday Park

Coast Road, Bacton, Norwich NR12 0EW **t** (01692) 650667 **f** (01692) 651388
e holiday@cablegap.co.uk **w** cablegap.co.uk

payment Credit/debit cards, cash/cheques

Cable Gap Holiday Park is a friendly family-run park. You will receive a warm welcome from both us and our staff. Our caravans are of a high standard with most double-glazed and centrally heated. We also have a brick built chalet suitable for the disabled. Open February to November.

⊕ Follow B1150 from Norwich or B1159 from Cromer.

♥ 10% discount on selected weeks for 2 persons or 2 persons and a baby under 2 years.

General P 🏸 📷 🗐 🐕

BUNGAY, Suffolk Map ref 3C1

★★★
TOURING &
CAMPING PARK

🚐 (45) £12.00–£16.00
🚕 (45) £12.00–£16.00
▲ (45) £12.00–£16.00
45 touring pitches

Outney Meadow Caravan Park

Outney Meadow, Bungay NR35 1HG **t** (01986) 892338 **f** (01986) 896627
e c.r.hancy@ukgateway.net **w** outneymeadow.co.uk

Within easy walking distance of the market town of Bungay. Situated between the River Waveney and the golf course. Ideal base for exploring the beautiful countryside. Fishing, bikes and canoes available. Open March to October.

payment Cash/cheques

General 🖾 🏕 P 🔌 🖰 🖺 🏸 ☉ 🗐 🐕 🛖 ☼ Leisure 🚣 ⼃ 🚴 🛶

CAISTER-ON-SEA, Norfolk Map ref 3C1

★★★★
HOLIDAY PARK

🚐 (30) £99.00–£495.00

Elm Beach Caravan Park

Manor Road, Caister-on-Sea, Great Yarmouth NR30 5HG **t** (01493) 721630 **f** (01493) 721640
e enquiries@elmbeachcaravanpark.com **w** elmbeachcaravanpark.com

Quiet caravan park situated on clean, sandy beach. Open from March through to the New Year. All caravans heated and fully equipped.

payment Credit/debit cards, cash/cheques

General P 🗐 🐕 ☼ Leisure ∪ ⼃ ⼁

CAMBRIDGE, Cambridgeshire Map ref 2D1

★★★★★
TOURING &
CAMPING PARK

🚐(60)   £12.10–£24.90
🚐(60)   £12.10–£24.90
⛺   on application
60 touring pitches

See Ad on inside front cover

Cherry Hinton Caravan Club Site

Lime Kiln Road, Cherry Hinton, Cambridge CB1 8NQ **t** (01223) 244088 **w** caravanclub.co.uk

open All year
payment Credit/debit cards, cash/cheques

Imaginatively landscaped site set in old quarry workings, bordered by a nature trail. Cambridge 0.5 miles (Park & Ride bus), Newmarket 14 miles. Open all year.

⊕ M11 jct 9 onto A11. After 7 miles slip road signposted Fulbourn and Tevisham. In Fulbourn continue to roundabout signposted Cambridge. At traffic lights turn left. Left again into Lime Kiln Road.

♥ Special member rates mean you can save your membership subscription in less than a week. Visit our website to find out more.

General 🖼 P 🔌 🚰 🍴 🚿 📷 ☉ 📵 📶 ⛺ ☼   Leisure ♩ ►

CAMBRIDGE, Cambridgeshire Map ref 2D1

★★★★★
TOURING &
CAMPING PARK

🚐(60)   £12.50–£15.00
🚐(60)   £12.50–£15.00
⛺(60)   £9.75–£15.00
120 touring pitches

Highfield Farm Touring Park

Long Road, Comberton, Cambridge CB23 7DG **t** (01223) 262308 **f** (01223) 262308
e enquiries@highfieldfarmtouringpark.co.uk **w** highfieldfarmtouringpark.co.uk

payment Cash/cheques, euros

A popular, family-run park with excellent facilities close to the university city of Cambridge, Imperial War Museum, Duxford. Ideally situated for touring East Anglia. Open April to October. Please view our website for further information.

⊕ From Cambridge, A428 to Bedford. After 3 miles, left at roundabout, follow sign to Comberton. From M11 jct 12, A603 to Sandy (0.5 miles). Then B1046 to Comberton.

♥ Low-season rate for Senior Citizens – 10% discount for stay of 3 nights or longer.

General 🖼 P 🔌 🚰 🍴 🚿 📷 ☉ 📵 📶 📶 ⛺ 🐾   Leisure ♨ ∪ ♩ ⚙

CROMER, Norfolk Map ref 3C1

★★★★
TOURING &
CAMPING PARK

🚐(101) £13.60–£25.60
🚐(101) £13.60–£25.60
101 touring pitches

See Ad on inside front cover

Seacroft Camping Park

Runton Road, Cromer NR27 9NH **t** (01263) 514938 **w** caravanclub.co.uk

payment Credit/debit cards, cash/cheques

An ideal site for a family holiday. Within walking distance of the beach. Heated swimming pool, communal barbecue, bar, restaurant, takeaway and a separate field for recreational use. Open May to January 2009.

⊕ Turn left off A149 (Cromer-Sheringham). Site entrance on left in 1 mile.

♥ Special member rates mean you can save your membership subscription in less than a week. Visit our website to find out more.

General 🖼 P 🔌 🚰 🍴 🚿 📷 📵 📶 ✕ ⛺   Leisure ≈ 📺 🍴 ♪ ⚡ ∪

Place index

If you know where you want to stay, the index at the back of the guide will give you the page number listing accommodation in your chosen town, city or village. Check out the other useful indexes too.

DUNWICH, Suffolk Map ref 3C2

★★★★
HOLIDAY PARK

🚐 (30) £14.00–£25.00
🚛 (20) £14.00–£25.00
⛺ (20) £14.00–£25.00

Cliff House Holiday Park

Minsmere Road, Dunwich, Saxmundham IP17 3DQ t (01728) 648282 f (01728) 648996
e info@cliffhouseholidays.co.uk w cliffhouseholidays.co.uk

Conservation area adjacent to Minsmere Nature Reserve. Secluded mature woodland site offering privacy with access to beach. Winner of Best Holiday Park in East Anglia. Gold David Bellamy Conservation Award.

open All year except Christmas and New Year
payment Credit/debit cards, cash/cheques

General 🚐 P ♨ 🚻 👤 🛒 ⊙ 🛎 🖥 🛒 ✕ 🐕 ☼ Leisure 📺 ⚑ 🎵 🔍 ⛰ 🎣 ⚓

EAST MERSEA, Essex Map ref 3B3

★★★★
HOLIDAY PARK

🚐 (30) £15.00–£25.00
🚛 (30) £15.00–£25.00
⛺ (30) £15.00–£25.00
90 touring pitches

Fen Farm Caravan and Camping Site

East Mersea, Colchester CO5 8UA t (01206) 383275 f (01206) 386316 e fenfarm@talk21.com

A quiet, rural, friendly, family site close to the sea and the country park.

payment Credit/debit cards, cash/cheques

General P ♨ 🚻 👤 🚐 🛒 ⊙ 🛎 🖥 🐕 🐾 ☼ Leisure ⛰

FAKENHAM, Norfolk Map ref 3B1

★★★
TOURING PARK

🚐 (120) £12.00–£25.00
🚛 (30) £12.00–£25.00
⛺ (30) £7.00–£25.00
120 touring pitches

Fakenham Racecourse

The Racecourse, Fakenham NR21 7NY t (01328) 862388 e caravan@fakenhamracecourse.co.uk
w fakenhamracecourse.co.uk

open All year
payment Credit/debit cards, cash/cheques

Fakenham Racecourse is the ideal base for caravanning and camping holidays in Norfolk. Just ten miles from a magnificent coastline and on the edge of the market town of Fakenham, the site is set in beautiful countryside and sheltered by conifers. The grounds and modern facilities are excellently maintained.

⊕ On all major approach routes to Fakenham follow brown signs stating 'Racecourse' and showing 'caravan and tent' symbols. Site entrance on Hempton Road.

♥ Open to all but with discounts for Caravan Club members. Special rates for rally groups. Check website for events.

General 🚐 P ♨ 🚻 👤 🚐 🛒 ⊙ 🛎 🖥 🛒 ✕ 🐕 🐾 ☼ Leisure ⚑ 🔍 🎣 ⚓

GREAT YARMOUTH, Norfolk Map ref 3C1

★★★★
HOLIDAY PARK

🚐 £8.00–£14.00
🚛 £8.00–£14.00
⛺ £7.00–£14.00
70 touring pitches

The Grange Touring Park

Yarmouth Road, Ormesby St Margaret, Great Yarmouth NR29 3QG t (01493) 730306
f (01493) 730188 e info@grangetouring.co.uk w grangetouring.co.uk

Level grassy park with lighting, made-up roadways and first-class facilities. Three miles north of Great Yarmouth, at the junction of A149 and B1159. Open from end of March to end of September.

payment Credit/debit cards, cash/cheques, euros

General P ♨ 🚻 👤 🛒 ⊙ 🛎 🖥 🐕 Leisure 🎣

GREAT YARMOUTH, Norfolk Map ref 3C1

★★★
TOURING PARK
(40) £11.00–£15.00
(6) £11.00–£15.00
(10) £100.00–£350.00
46 touring pitches

Grasmere Caravan Park

Bultitudes Loke, Yarmouth Road, Caister-on-Sea, Great Yarmouth NR30 5DH t (01493) 720382
f (01493) 377573 w grasmere-wentworth.co.uk

Small family park with no on-site entertainment. Approach Caister on A149, then follow brown tourist signs. Open April to October.

payment Credit/debit cards, cash/cheques

General

GREAT YARMOUTH, Norfolk Map ref 3C1

★★★★
TOURING PARK
(115) £12.10–£24.90
(115) £12.10–£24.90
115 touring pitches

See Ad on inside front cover

Great Yarmouth Caravan Club Site

Great Yarmouth Racecourse, Jellicoe Road, Great Yarmouth NR30 4AU t (01493) 855223
w caravanclub.co.uk

payment Credit/debit cards, cash/cheques

Spacious, level site in a very popular family resort offering wide, sandy beaches, countless seaside attractions and fishing, golf, sailboarding, ballroom dancing and bowls. Open March to November.

⊕ Travel north on A149, left at lights (within 1 mile past 40mph sign on southern outskirts of Caister) into Jellicoe Road. Within 0.25 miles, left into racecourse entrance.

♥ Special member rates mean you can save your membership subscription in less than a week. Visit our website to find out more.

THE CARAVAN CLUB

General   Leisure

HEMINGFORD ABBOTS, Cambridgeshire Map ref 3A2

★★★★
HOLIDAY, TOURING
& CAMPING PARK
(20) £12.50–£16.00
(20) £12.50–£16.00
(20) £12.50–£16.00
(9) £245.00–£370.00
20 touring pitches

Quiet Waters Caravan Park

Hemingford Abbots, Huntingdon PE28 9AJ t (01480) 463405 f (01480) 463405
e quietwaters.park@btopenworld.com w quietwaterscaravanpark.co.uk

A quiet riverside park situated in centre of picturesque village. Many local walks and cycle routes. Ideal for fishing from own banks. Family run. Open March to October.

payment Credit/debit cards, cash/cheques

General   Leisure

HUNSTANTON, Norfolk Map ref 3B1

★★★★★
HOLIDAY, TOURING
& CAMPING PARK
ROSE AWARD
(157) £12.00–£39.00
(50) £12.00–£39.00
(125) £11.00–£35.00
(156) £199.00–
£1,237.00
332 touring pitches

Searles Leisure Resort

South Beach Road, Hunstanton PE36 5BB t (01485) 534211 f (01485) 533815
e bookings@searles.co.uk w searles.co.uk

open All year except Christmas
payment Credit/debit cards, cash/cheques

Much more than quality family holidays. Family-run, and established for fifty years, Searles has something for everyone: excellent pitches and hook-ups, superb accommodation, bars, restaurants, entertainment, swimming pools, nine-hole golf-course, fishing lake and more – all 200yds from a sandy beach. The ideal base for exploring the Norfolk coast.

⊕ From King's Lynn take the A149 to Hunstanton. Upon entering Hunstanton follow B1161 to South Beach.

♥ Superb themed breaks every autumn. Beauty breaks, music weekends, Turkey and Tinsel breaks. Please check website for more details.

General   Leisure

HUNTINGDON, Cambridgeshire Map ref 3A2

★★★★
HOLIDAY &
TOURING PARK

🚐(76) £12.10–£24.90
🚍(76) £12.10–£24.90
76 touring pitches

See Ad on inside front cover

THE CARAVAN CLUB

Grafham Water Caravan Club Site

Church Road, Grafham, Huntingdon PE28 0BB t (01480) 810264 w caravanclub.co.uk

payment Credit/debit cards, cash/cheques

This is an attractive site situated half a mile west of picturesque Grafham village and a similar distance north of Grafham Water. Remarkably peaceful, surrounded by arable land and a narrow tree belt. Heated outdoor swimming pool and children's play area. Open March to November.

⊕ *Turn left off A1 at roundabout in Buckden onto B661; turn right and follow caravan signs.*

♥ *Special member rates mean you can save your membership subscription in less than a week. Visit our website to find out more.*

General P 🚐 🛁 🚻 📶 📶 ☺ 📵 🐕 ⑂ Leisure ⏃ 🎢 🎵

KESSINGLAND, Suffolk Map ref 3C2

★★
HOLIDAY PARK

🏠(8) £156.00–£355.00

Alandale Park

Bethel Drive, Kessingland, Lowestoft NR33 7SD t (01502) 740610 f (01502) 740610

Small holiday estate of mainly semi-detached two-bedroom holiday bungalows on western side of coastal slope on edge of village with direct access to beach. Open March to December.

payment Credit/debit cards, cash/cheques

General 🎮 📵 🐕 ☼

MERSEA ISLAND, Essex Map ref 3B3

★★★★
HOLIDAY, TOURING
& CAMPING PARK

🚐(60) £17.00–£25.00
🚍(60) £17.00–£25.00
▲(60) £17.00–£25.00
🏠(25) £220.00–£450.00
60 touring pitches

Waldegraves Holiday Park

Waldegraves Lane, Mersea Island, Colchester CO5 8SE t (01206) 382898 f (01206) 385359
e holidays@waldegraves.co.uk w waldegraves.co.uk

Ideal family park, grassland sheltered with trees and four fishing lakes, undercover golf driving range, pitch and putt, heated swimming pool, private beach, two play areas. Licensed bar and restaurant. Open 1 March to 30 November.

payment Credit/debit cards, cash/cheques

General 🖥 P 🚐 🛁 🚻 📶 📵 📖 ✕ 🐕 🛻 ☼ Leisure ⏃ 📺 🍷 🎵 🎯 🎢 🎵 🏌

MUNDESLEY, Norfolk Map ref 3C1

★★★
HOLIDAY &
TOURING PARK

🚐(40) £8.00–£20.00
🚍(40) £8.00–£20.00
🏠(2) £200.00–£395.00
40 touring pitches

Sandy Gulls Cliff Top Touring Park

Cromer Road, Mundesley, Norwich NR11 8DF t (01263) 720513

payment Cash/cheques

The area's only cliff-top touring park. Located just south of Cromer. All pitches have panoramic sea views, electric/TV hook-ups. Free access to superb shower facilities. Miles of clean, sandy beaches and rural footpaths. Managed by the owning family for forty years. We don't cater for children or teenagers. Silver David Bellamy Conservation Award.

⊕ *From Cromer drive south along coast road for 5 miles.*

General P 🚐 🛁 🚻 📶 ☺ 📵 🛒 🐕 🛻 Leisure ∪ 🎵 🏌

NORFOLK BROADS

See under Bungay, Caister-on-Sea, Great Yarmouth

PETERBOROUGH, Cambridgeshire Map ref 3A1

★★★★★
HOLIDAY PARK

(252) £12.10–£24.90
(252) £12.10–£24.90
252 touring pitches

See Ad on inside front cover

THE CARAVAN CLUB

Ferry Meadows Caravan Club Site

Ham Lane, Peterborough PE2 5UU t (01733) 233526 f (01733) 239880 w caravanclub.co.uk

open All year
payment Credit/debit cards, cash/cheques

Set in 500-acre Nene Country Park. Plenty of activities including canoeing, windsurfing and sailing. Also nature trails, two golf courses, pitch and putt and bird sanctuary.

⊕ *From any direction, on approaching Peterborough, follow the brown signs to Nene Park and Ferry Meadows.*

♥ *Special member rates mean you can save your membership subscription in less than a week. Visit our website to find out more.*

General 🖼 P 🔌 🕒 🍴 🚿 ﹝ ☺ 🛢 ⛺ ☼ Leisure ⚠ ⚓ ►

STANHOE, Norfolk Map ref 3B1

★★★★
TOURING PARK

£9.00–£11.00
£9.00–£11.00
£9.00–£11.00
30 touring pitches

The Rickels Caravan and Camping Park

Bircham Road, Stanhoe, King's Lynn PE31 8PU t (01485) 518671

From King's Lynn take A148 to Hillington, turn left onto B1153 to Great Bircham. Fork right onto B1155, to crossroads, straight over. Site 100yds on left. Open April to October. Adults only.

payment Cash/cheques

General ♿ P 🔌 🕒 🍴 🚿 ﹝ ☺ 🛢 ⛺ ﹡ ☼ Leisure ⚓ 🚲

WYTON, Cambridgeshire Map ref 3A2

★★★★
HOLIDAY PARK

(40) Min £14.50
(10) Min £14.50
(10) Min £11.00
40 touring pitches

Wyton Lakes Holiday Park

Banks End, Wyton, Huntingdon PE28 2AA t (01480) 412715 e loupeter@supanet.com
w wytonlakes.com

payment Cash/cheques

Adults-only park. Some pitches beside the on-site carp and coarse-fishing lakes. River frontage. Close to local amenities. Open April to October.

⊕ *Exit 23 off A14. Follow signs A141 March. Go past 4 roundabouts. At 4th roundabout take A1123 to St Ives. Park approx 1 mile on right.*

♥ *10% discount on all bookings 7 nights or over paid in full on arrival. 7 days' fishing for the price of 6.*

General P 🔌 🕒 🍴 ﹝ ☺ ⛺ ☼ Leisure ⚓

Key to symbols

The symbols at the end of each entry help you pick out the services and facilities which are most important to you. A key to the symbols can be found inside the back-cover flap. Keep this open for easy reference.

London

A city of secrets and surprises

So you think you know London? Take a closer look and you'll discover a treasure house of secret attractions just crying out to be explored. Just remember to leave yourself with enough time (a year should do).

Visit London
visitlondon.com
0870 156 6366

Wallce Collection, London

The Globe Theatre, Bankside   Hampton Court

South Bank

Marvel (and cringe) at how operations were performed in The Old Operating Theatre Museum in Southwark. This fascinating theatre along with its Herb Garret were built in the roof space of the English Baroque Church of St Thomas's. Get even more surreal and visit Dali Universe on the South Bank, where you can enter the psyche of the genius artist and see mind-bending furniture, film sets and original Dali sculptures. But if there's only one thing you see, make it the Tutankhamun and the Golden Age of the Pharaohs exhibition at The O2 (formerly the Dome). This is the first time in almost 30 years that artefacts of the boy-king's burial chamber have left their home in Egypt. See the fabulous golden canopic cofinette and get a glimpse of the golden age of the Pharaohs.

One of the joys of London is the shopping. From the 83 colourful street markets such as Brick Lane to the most exclusive designer stores on Bond Street, there's retail therapy enough to keep anyone sane. Check out the Mall Antiques Arcade in Islington. Set in a former tram station and packed with over 35 specialist dealers, it's a magnet for interior designers.

And did you know there's a viewing area inside Wellington Arch in Hyde Park Corner where you can see into the gardens of Buckingham Palace? Or that Britain's first botanical garden was at the enigmatic Chelsea Physic Garden? Or that at Firepower – the Royal Artillery Museum in Woolwich – you can trace the story of the Royal Arsenal from Henry VIII and the battle of Crecy to peacekeeping mission in Bosnia?

Another fascinating trip out is to HMS Belfast, the historic World War II battleship that's now a floating naval museum. Explore all nine decks from the Captain's Bridge to the boiler room.

Destinations

Greenwich

Stand with one foot in the East and one foot in the West astride the Greenwich Meridian, and set your watch by the red 'Time Ball' that drops each day at 1300hrs precisely and has done so for 170 years. There's a laid-back feel to Greenwich. Take time to browse the market stalls – crafts, antiques, records, bric-a-brac and, most famously, vintage clothing. Then pop into a riverside pub for lunch and some mellow jazz.

Kew

Stroll the finest botanic gardens in the country – 400 acres and 40,000 plant varieties. The Palm House hosts a tropical jungle of plants including bananas, pawpaws and mangoes. Marvel at the giant Amazonian water lily, aloe vera and several carnivorous plants in the Princess of Wales Conservatory where ten climatic zones are recreated. You'll find activities for children and a full calendar of special events.

Notting Hill

A colourful district filled with clubs, bars and dance venues, and now trendier than ever. Wander the celebrated Portobello Road market where over 1,500 traders compete for your custom at the Saturday antiques market. Find jewellery, silverware, paintings and more. Summertime is carnival time and the Caribbean influence has ensured the phenomenal growth of the world-famous, multi-cultural Notting Hill Carnival. Join the throng of millions – exotic costume recommended. On a quieter day, visit beautiful Holland Park, a haven of greenery with its own theatre.

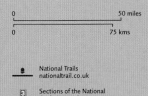

| 0 | | 50 miles |
| 0 | | 75 kms |

National Trails
nationaltrail.co.uk

3 Sections of the National Cycle Network
nationalcyclenetwork.org.uk

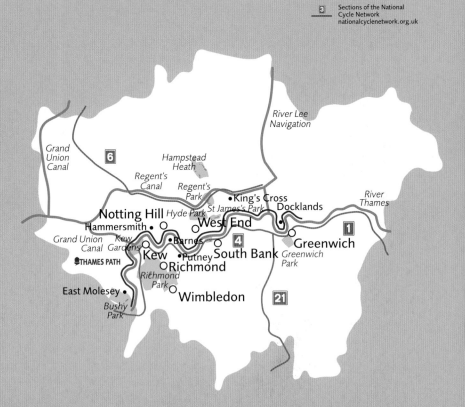

Notting Hill Carnival

Greenwich Park

West End

Tate Modern, South Bank

Wimbledon

Richmond Park

Palm House, Kew

Richmond

The River Thames runs through the heart of the beautiful borough of Richmond. Arrive by summer riverboat from Westminster Pier and explore the delightful village with its riverside pubs, specialist boutiques, galleries and museums. Glimpse herds of deer in the Royal parks and step into history in Henry VIII's magnificent Hampton Court Palace, the oldest Tudor palace in England. Round off your visit with a world-class rugby match at England's Twickenham Stadium.

South Bank

One of London's coolest quarters, the South Bank positively teems with must-see attractions and cultural highlights. Tate Modern has gained a reputation as one of the greatest modern art galleries in the world boasting works by Moore, Picasso, Dali, Warhol and Hepworth. Take in a play at the National Theatre or Shakespeare's magnificently restored Globe, and hit the heights on British Airways London Eye, the world's highest observation wheel.

West End

Shop in the best department stores and international designer boutiques in Oxford Street, Regent Street and Bond Street. Take lunch in a stylish eatery, and then see a major exhibition at the Royal Academy of Arts. At the heart of the West End are the landmarks of Trafalgar Square and Piccadilly Circus, and just a few minutes' stroll will take you into legendary Soho, the entertainment heart of the city, crammed with bars, pubs, clubs and restaurants.

Wimbledon

Wimbledon village is only ten miles from the centre of London but you could be in the heart of the countryside. Enjoy the open spaces of Wimbledon Common then wander along the charming high street with its unique medieval buildings, boutiques and pavement cafes. Visit the legendary All England Club where the Lawn Tennis Museum is a must-see for fans of the sport, not to mention the chance to tour the legendary Centre Court.

Places to visit

BBC Television Centre Tours

Shepherd's Bush, W12
0870 603 0304
bbc.co.uk/tours
Behind the scenes of world-famous television studios

Ben Uri Art Gallery, London Jewish Museum of Art

St John's Wood, NW8
(020) 7604 3991
benuri.org.uk
Europe's only dedicated Jewish museum of art

British Airways London Eye
South Bank, SE1
0870 990 8883
ba-londoneye.com
The world's largest observation wheel

British Museum
WC1
(020) 7323 8299
thebritishmuseum.ac.uk
One of the great museums of the world

Buckingham Palace
SW1
(020) 7766 7300
royalcollection.org.uk
HM The Queen's official London residence

Churchill Museum and Cabinet War Rooms
SW1
(020) 7930 6961
iwm.org.uk/cabinet
Churchill's wartime headquarters

Hampton Court Palace
East Molesey, KT8
0870 752 7777
hrp.org.uk
Outstanding Tudor palace with famous maze

HMS Belfast
Southwark, SE1
(020) 7940 6300
iwm.org.uk
World War II cruiser, now a naval time capsule

Imperial War Museum
Lambeth, SE1
(020) 7416 5320
iwm.org.uk
History of Britain at war since 1914

Kensington Palace State Apartments
W8
0870 751 5170
hrp.org.uk
Home to the Royal Ceremonial Dress Collection

Kew Gardens (Royal Botanic Gardens)
Richmond, TW9
(020) 8332 5655
kew.org
Stunning plant collections and magnificent glasshouses

London Aquarium
South Bank, SE1
(020) 7967 8000
londonaquarium.co.uk
Come face-to-face with two-metre long sharks

The London Dungeon
Southwark, SE1
(020) 7403 7221
thedungeons.com
So much fun it's frightening!

London Wetland Centre
Barnes, SW16
(020) 8409 4400
wwt.org.uk
Observe wildlife in recreated wetland habitats

Madame Tussauds and the London Planetarium
Marylebone, NW1
0870 999 0046
madame-tussauds.com
Meet the stars then enter the Chamber of Horrors

National Gallery
Trafalgar Square, WC2
(020) 7747 2885
nationalgallery.org.uk
One of the great collections of European art

National Maritime Museum
Outstanding Customer Service – Silver Winner
Greenwich, SE10
(020) 8858 4422
nmm.ac.uk

Over 2 million exhibits of seafaring history

Natural History Museum
Kensington, SW7
(020) 7942 5000
nhm.ac.uk
World-class collections bringing the natural world to life

Royal Observatory Greenwich
SE10
(020) 8858 4422
nmm.ac.uk
Explore the history of time and astronomy

Science Museum
Kensington, SW7
0870 870 4868
sciencemuseum.org.uk
State-of-the-art simulators, IMAX cinema and more

Diary dates 2008

Shakespeare's Globe Exhibition and Tour
Bankside, SE1
(020) 7902 1400
shakespeares-globe.org
A fascinating introduction to Shakespeare's London

Somerset House
Strand, WC2
(020) 7845 4600
somerset-house.org.uk
Magnificent art collections in grand 18th century house

Tate Britain
Millbank, SW1
(020) 7887 8888
tate.org.uk
The greatest single collection of British art

Tate Modern
Bankside, SE1
(020) 7887 8008
tate.org.uk
Britain's flagship museum of modern art

Tower Bridge Exhibition
SE1
(020) 7403 3761
towerbridge.org.uk
Learn all about the world's most famous bridge

Tower of London
EC3
0870 756 6060
hrp.org.uk
The Crown Jewels and 900 years of history

Victoria and Albert Museum
Kensington, SW7
(020) 7942 2000
vam.ac.uk
3,000 years of art and design

ZSL London Zoo
Regent's Park, NW1
(020) 7722 3333
londonzoo.co.uk
The hairiest and scariest animals on the planet

London Boat Show
ExCeL London, E16
londonboatshow.com
11 – 20 Jan

Oxford and Cambridge Boat Race
River Thames from Putney, SW15 to Mortlake, SW14
theboatrace.org
29 Mar

Chelsea Flower Show
rhs.org.uk
20 – 24 May*

Trooping the Colour
Horseguards Parade, SW1
royal.gov.uk
14 Jun

Wimbledon Lawn Tennis Championships
wimbledon.org
23 Jun – 6 Jul

The Proms
Royal Albert Hall, SW7
bbc.co.uk/proms
18 Jul – 13 Sep

Notting Hill Carnival
Streets around Ladbroke Grove, W10 and W11
visitlondon.com
24 – 25 Aug

The Mayor's Thames Festival
Westminster Bridge, SW1 to Tower Bridge, SE1,
thamesfestival.org
13 – 14 Sep

Lord Mayor's Show
From the Guildhall, EC2 to the Royal Courts of Justice, WC2 and back
lordmayorsshow.org
8 Nov

* provisional date at time of going to press

Tourist Information Centres

When you arrive at your destination, visit an Official Partner Tourist Information Centre for quality assured help with accommodation and information about local attractions and events, or email your request before you go. To search for attractions and Tourist Information Centres on the move just text INFO to 62233, and a web link will be sent to your mobile phone.

Britain & London Visitor Centre	1 Regent Street	0870 156636	blvcenquiries@visitlondon.com
Croydon	Katharine Street	(020) 8253 1009	tic@croydon.gov.uk
Greenwich	2 Cutty Sark Gardens	0870 608 2000	tic@greenwich.gov.uk
Lewisham	199-201 Lewisham High Street	(020) 8297 8317	tic@lewisham.gov.uk
Swanley	London Road	(01322) 614660	touristinfo@swanley.org.uk

The London Eye

Travel info

By road:
Major trunk roads into London include: A1, M1, A5, A10, A11, M11, A13, A2, M2, A23, A3, M3, A4, M4, A40, M40, A41, M25 (London orbital).
Transport for London is responsible for running London's bus services, the underground rail network and the DLR (Docklands Light Railway), and river and tram services.
(020) 7222 1234 (24-hour telephone service; calls answered in rotation).

By rail:
Main rail terminals: Victoria/Waterloo/ Charing Cross – serving the South/South East; King's Cross – serving the North East; Euston – serving the North West/Midlands; Liverpool Street – serving the East; Paddington – serving the Thames Valley/West.

By air:
Fly into London City, London Gatwick, London Heathrow, London Luton and London Stansted.

For more information, go to visitlondon.com/travel or tfl.gov.uk/journeyplanner

Find out more

By logging on to visitlondon.com
or calling 0870 1 LONDON for the following:

- **A London tourist information pack**

- **Tourist information on London**
  Speak to an expert for information and advice on
  museums, galleries, attractions, riverboat trips,
  sightseeing tours, theatre, shopping, eating out and
  much more! Or simply go to visitlondon.com.

- **Accommodation reservations**

Or visit one of London's tourist information centres
listed opposite.

Which part of London?

The majority of tourist accommodation is situated in the
central parts of London and is therefore very convenient
for most of the city's attractions and nightlife.

However, there are many establishments in Outer
London which provide other advantages, such as easier
parking. In the accommodation pages which follow, you
will find establishments listed under INNER LONDON
(covering the E1 to W14 London Postal Area) and
OUTER LONDON (covering the remainder of Greater
London). Colour maps 6 and 7 at the front of the guide
show place names and London postal area codes and will
help you to locate accommodation in your chosen area.

Horse Guards Parade

where to stay in
London

All place names in the blue bands are shown on the maps at the front of this guide.

A complete listing of all VisitBritain assessed parks in England appears at the back.

Accommodation symbols
Symbols give useful information about services and facilities. Inside the back-cover flap you can find a key to these symbols. Keep it open for easy reference.

INNER LONDON
LONDON SE2

★★★★★
TOURING &
CAMPING PARK

🚐 (220) £14.30–£27.70
🚍 (220) £14.30–£27.70
220 touring pitches

See Ad on inside front cover

CARAVAN CLUB

Abbey Wood Caravan Club Site

Federation Road, Abbey Wood, London SE2 0LS **t** (020) 8311 7708 **w** caravanclub.co.uk

open All year
payment Credit/debit cards, cash/cheques

Redeveloped to the highest standards, this site is th ideal base for exploring the capital. A green, gentl sloping site with mature trees screening its spaciou grounds.

⊕ On M2 turn off at A221. Then turn right into McLeod Roa right into Knee Hill and the site is the 2nd turning on th right.

♥ Special member rates mean you can save your membersh subscription in less than a week. Visit our website to fin out more.

General 🖳 P 🔌 🎮 🍴 🏕 🎫 ☉ 📠 🐾 ☼ Leisure 🏔 ⚑

LONDON SE19

★★★★★
TOURING &
CAMPING PARK

🚐 (126) £14.30–£27.70
🚍 (126) £14.30–£27.70
126 touring pitches

See Ad on inside front cover

CARAVAN CLUB

Crystal Palace Caravan Club Site

Crystal Palace Parade, London SE19 1UF **t** (020) 8778 7155 **f** (020) 8676 0980 **w** caravanclub.co.u

open All year
payment Credit/debit cards, cash/cheques

Popular with European families in the summer, a friendly site on the edge of a pleasant park, in clos proximity to all of London's attractions.

⊕ Turn off the A205, South Circular road at West Dulwich into Croxted Road. The site is adjacent to the BBC television mast.

♥ Special member rates mean you can save your membersh subscription in less than a week. Visit our website to fir out more.

General 🖳 P 🔌 🎮 🍴 🏕 🎫 ☉ 📠 🐾 ☼ Leisure 🏔 ⚑

Take a break

Look out for special promotions and themed breaks highlighted in colour.
(Offers subject to availability.)

Country ways

The Countryside Rights of Way Act gives people new rights to walk on areas of open countryside and registered common land.

To find out where you can go and what you can do, as well as information about taking your dog to the countryside, go online at countrysideaccess.gov.uk.

And when you're out and about...

Always follow the Country Code

- Be safe – plan ahead and follow any signs
- Leave gates and property as you find them
- Protect plants and animals, and take your litter home
- Keep dogs under close control
- Consider other people

South East England

Berkshire, Buckinghamshire, East Sussex,
Hampshire, Isle of Wight, Kent,
Oxfordshire, Surrey, West Sussex

Family fun in classic England

The South East is your quintessential slice of England. And whilst there's plenty for singles and couples to enjoy, this region is bursting with great family days out that the kids will treasure forever.

Tourism South East
visitsoutheastengland.com
(023) 8062 5400

Deal Beach, Kent Coast

Sheffield Park Garden, East Sussex   Winchester Cathedral, Hampshire

Uffington, Oxfordshire

With 400 miles of glorious coastline including the towering chalk cliff of Beachy Head and kid-friendly beaches galore, the South East has always been a family favourite. Add the gorgeous countryside of the South Downs, evocative castles like Leeds and a wealth of colourful venues such as Woburn Safari Park, and this region has it all. As you'd expect, sailing is big in these parts, and you can simply stroll around one of the many marinas or set sail for a course at Calshot Activities Centre near Southampton. And if you're really brave, try one of the extreme watersports like wakeboarding. Finally, head off to a rural inn where you can unwind, enjoy a pint of real ale and savour a superb bistro-like meal.

Experience life in the Dickens era at Dickens World Kent with its Victorian shopping mall, music hall and an exciting time travel ride. With a new Viking Land and two top-secret new rides, Legoland Windsor is even more of a draw for all the family (time your visit right and catch their flagship firework bonanza). And if you're in battle mood, charge over to the interactive visitor centre at Battle Abbey in East Sussex and experience the Battle of Hastings brought to terrifying life.

Check out the atmospheric Winchester Cathedral where the foundations were laid in 1079 in stone brought from the Isle of Wight. Drop anchor at the Portsmouth Historic Dockyard, too, and marvel at HMS Victory and the Mary Rose. And don't miss Oxford Castle, where boutique stalls, pulsating bars and a feast of visual arts are set against the prison backdrop.

South East England is a region rich in experiences. It has something to offer every age group and every traveller. Whether you are looking at visiting for a weekend or a month this region has everything you could want.

Destinations

Brighton

England's favourite seaside city, Brighton is historic, elegant and offbeat. Wander a beachfront packed with cafes and bars, then step into town for fine antiques and designer boutiques. Don't miss the Royal Pavilion, surely the most extravagant royal palace in Europe, and come in springtime for an arts festival second to none. Find the world's cuisine in over 400 restaurants, and then relax with dance, comedy or music in the thriving pub and club culture. Brighton has it all – and just 49 minutes from central London.

Dover

Discover the rich history of Dover – 'the lock and key of England' - and its celebrated White Cliffs. Tour Dover Castle and relive the epic sieges of 1216-17. Delve into the secrets contained in the Wartime Tunnels, nerve centre for the evacuation of Dunkirk and Command Centre from whose depths Churchill witnessed the Battle of Britain. Enjoy the pier and stroll the stylish marina before heading out of town to tour the scenic beaches of White Cliffs Country.

Canterbury

Marvel with fellow 'pilgrims' from the four corners of the world as Canterbury Cathedral dominates your approach to this World Heritage Site. Let Canterbury Tales 'Medieval Misadventures' take you on a journey back to Chaucer's England. Wander traffic-free daytime streets to enjoy historic buildings and modern attractions, and then head further afield to explore the valleys, woods and coastline of this beautiful region of Kent.

| 0 | | 50 miles |
| 0 | | 75 kms |

National Park

South Downs National Park (designated but not yet confirmed)

Area of Outstanding Natural Beauty

Heritage Coast

National Trails nationaltrail.co.uk

3 Sections of the National Cycle Network nationalcyclenetwork.org.uk

67 Regional Route

Ferry Routes

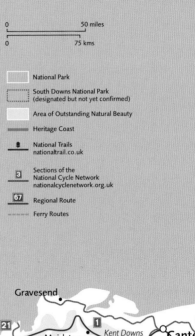

Windsor Castle

Canterbury Cathedral

Freshwater Bay, Isle of Wight

Dover Castle

New Forest

Oxford spires

Brighton seafront

Isle of Wight

Sixty miles of spectacular coastline, picturesque coves and safe bathing in bays of golden sand. Explore the maritime history of Cowes, the beautiful and historic town of Newport and take the family to the welcoming resorts of Shanklin and Ventnor. Follow the trail of dinosaurs, ancient tribes, Romans and monarchs in this diamond-shaped treasure trove.

New Forest

Roam a landscape little changed since William the Conqueror gave it his special protection over 900 years ago. You'll meet wild heath and dappled woodland, thatched hamlets, bustling market towns, and tiny streams meandering to the sparkling expanse of the Solent. Watch ponies eating by the roadside, pigs foraging for beechnuts, and donkeys ambling along the streets. As evening falls, hear the humming song of the nightjar, glimpse deer and watch bats flitting across the darkening sky.

Oxford

This ancient university city is both timeless and modern. Wander among its 'dreaming spires' and tranquil college quadrangles. Find national and international treasures, displayed in a family of museums whose scope and scholarship is second to none. Hire a punt and spend the afternoon drifting along the River Cherwell or seek out bustling shops and fashionable restaurants. Experience candlelit evensong in college chapels or Shakespeare in the park, and after dark enjoy the cosmopolitan buzz of countless cafés, pubs and theatres.

Windsor

Explore Windsor and the Royal Borough, to the west of London. Gaze at the priceless treasures in the Royal Collection at Windsor Castle, royal home and fortress for over 900 years. Henry VI founded Eton College in 1440. Lose yourself in the history of the cloisters and the chapel. Sail the churning rapids at Legoland's incredible Vikings' River Splash, and find peace and quiet in the rural landscape of Royal Berkshire, traversed by the timeless flow of the Thames.

Places to visit

Bedgebury National Pinetum & Forest
Goudhurst, Kent
(01580) 879820
forestry.gov.uk/bedgebury
World's finest conifer collection

Blenheim Palace
Woodstock, Oxfordshire
(01993) 811091
blenheimpalace.com
Baroque palace and beautiful parkland

Canterbury Cathedral
Kent
(01227) 762862
canterbury-cathedral.org
Seat of the Archbishop of Canterbury

Carisbrooke Castle
Newport, Isle Of Wight
(01983) 522107
english-heritage.org.uk
Splendid Norman castle

Dickens World
Chatham, Kent
(01634) 890421
dickensworld.co.uk
Fascinating journey through Dickens' lifetime

Dinosaur Isle
Sandown, Isle Of Wight
(01983) 404344
dinosaurisle.com
Britain's first purpose-built dinosaur attraction

Dover Castle and Secret Wartime Tunnels
Kent
(01304) 211067
english-heritage.org.uk
Historic nerve centre for Battle of Britain

Exbury Gardens and Steam Railway
Hampshire
(023) 8089 1203
exbury.co.uk.
Over 200 acres of woodland garden

Explosion! Museum of Naval Firepower
Gosport, Hampshire
(023) 9250 5600
explosion.org.uk
Naval firepower from gunpowder to the Exocet

Go Ape! High Wire Forest Adventure
Farnham, Surrey
0870 444 5562
goape.co.uk
Rope bridges, swings and zip slides

Groombridge Place Gardens and Enchanted Forest
Tunbridge Wells, Kent
(01892) 861444
groombridge.co.uk
Peaceful gardens and ancient woodland

Harbour Park (Family Amusement Park)
Littlehampton, West Sussex
(01903) 721200
harbourpark.com
Traditional ride favourites on the seafront

Hever Castle and Gardens
near Edenbridge, Kent
(01732) 865224
hevercastle.co.uk
Beautiful childhood home of Anne Boleyn

Highclere Castle and Gardens
Newbury, Hampshire
(01635) 253210
highclerecastle.co.uk
Imposing Victorian castle and parkland

The Historic Dockyard Chatham
Kent
(01634) 823800
thedockyard.co.uk
Maritime heritage site with stunning architecture

Howletts Wild Animal Park
Canterbury, Kent
0870 750 4647
totallywild.net
Wild animals in 90 acres of parkland

INTECH Science Centre
Winchester, Hampshire
(01962) 863791
intech-uk.com
Hands-on science and technology exhibits

LEGOLAND Windsor
Berkshire
0870 504 0404
legoland.co.uk
More Lego bricks than you ever dreamed possible

Loseley Park
Guildford, Surrey
(01483) 304440
loseley-park.com
Beautiful Elizabethan mansion and gardens

National Motor Museum Beaulieu
Brockenhurst, Hampshire
(01590) 612345
beaulieu.co.uk
Vintage cars and stately home in New Forest

Osborne House
East Cowes, Isle Of Wight
(01983) 200022
english-heritage.org.uk
Queen Victoria's seaside retreat

Paultons Park
Romsey, Hampshire
(023) 8081 4442
paultonspark.co.uk
Over 50 rides for all the family

Polesden Lacey
near Dorking, Surrey
(01372) 452048
nationaltrust.org.uk
*Opulent Edwardian interiors in
downland setting*

RHS Garden Wisley
Woking, Surrey
0845 260 9000
rhs.org.uk
*A working encyclopedia of British
gardening*

**Royal Botanic Gardens,
Wakehurst Place**
near Haywards Heath,
West Sussex
(01444) 894000
rbgkew.org.uk
*Beautiful gardens throughout the
seasons*

Spinnaker Tower
Portsmouth, Hampshire
(023) 9285 7520
spinnakertower.co.uk
*Breathtaking views from
170-metre landmark*

Thorpe Park
Chertsey, Surrey
0870 444 4466
thorpepark.com
*An adrenaline-charged day out for
all the family*

Windsor Castle
Berkshire
(020) 7766 7304
royalcollection.org.uk
*Official residence of HM
The Queen*

Diary dates 2008

New Year Steamday
Didcot Railway
didcotrailwaycentre.org.uk
1 Jan

Brighton Festival
Various locations, Brighton
brightonfestival.org
3 – 25 May*

Royal Windsor Horse Show
Windsor Castle
royal-windsor-horse-show.co.uk
8 – 11 May

Royal Ascot
ascot.co.uk
17 – 21 Jun

Henley Royal Regatta
River Thames
hrr.co.uk
2 – 6 Jul

Parham Garden Weekend
Pulborough, West Sussex
parhaminsussex.co.uk
5 – 6 Jul*

Farnborough International Air Show
farnborough.com
14 – 20 Jul

New Forest Show
Brockenhurst, Hampshire
newforestshow.co.uk
29 – 31 Jul

Cowes Week
The Solent, Isle of Wight
skandiacowesweek.co.uk
2 – 9 Aug

Ringwood Carnival
ringwoodcarnival.org
20 Sep

* provisional date at time of going to press

Tourist Information Centres

When you arrive at your destination, visit an Official Partner Tourist Information Centre for quality assured help with accommodation and information about local attractions and events, or email your request before you go. To search for attractions and Tourist Information Centres on the move just text INFO to 62233, and a web link will be sent to your mobile phone.

Bicester	Unit 86a, Bicester Village	(01869) 369055	bicester.vc@cherwell-dc.gov.uk
Brighton	Pavilion Buildings	0906 711 2255**	brighton-tourism@brighton-hove.gov.uk
Canterbury	12/13 Sun Street	(01227) 378100	canterburyinformation@canterbury.gov.uk
Chichester	29a South Street	(01243) 775888	chitic@chichester.gov.uk
Cowes	9 The Arcade	(01983) 813818	info@islandbreaks.co.uk
Dover	The Old Town Gaol	(01304) 205108	tic@doveruk.com
Hastings	Queens Square	0845 274 1001	hic@hastings.gov.uk
Lyndhurst & New Forest	Main Car Park	(023) 8028 2269	information@nfdc.gov.uk
Newport	High Street	(01983) 813818	info@islandbreaks.co.uk
Oxford	15/16 Broad Street	(01865) 726871	tic@oxford.gov.uk
Portsmouth	The Hard	(023) 9282 6722	vis@portsmouthcc.gov.uk
Rochester	95 High Street	(01634) 843666	visitor.centre@medway.gov.uk
Royal Tunbridge Wells	The Pantiles	(01892) 515675	touristinformationcentre@ tunbridgewells.gov.uk
Ryde	81-83 Union Street	(01983) 813818	info@islandbreaks.co.uk
Sandown	8 High Street	(01983) 813818	info@islandbreaks.co.uk
Shanklin	67 High Street	(01983) 813818	info@islandbreaks.co.uk
Southampton	9 Civic Centre Road	(023) 8083 3333	tourist.information@southampton.gov.uk
Winchester	High Street	(01962) 840500	tourism@winchester.gov.uk
Windsor	Windsor Royal Shopping	(01753) 743900	windsor.tic@rbwm.gov.uk
Yarmouth	The Quay	(01983) 813818	info@islandbreaks.co.uk

** *calls to this number are charged at premium rate*

The Lee, Buckinghamshire

Find out more

The following publications are available from Tourism South East by logging on to visitsoutheastengland.com or calling (023) 8062 5400:

Publications

- **Escape into the Countryside**
- **Great Days Out in Berkshire, Buckinghamshire and Oxfordshire**
- **Distinctive Country Inns**
- **We Know Just the Place**

E-Brochures

- **Family Fun**
- **Fine Tradition**
- **Just the Two of Us**
- **Great Days Out**
- **Go Golf**
- **Countryside**
- **Cities**

Travel info

By road:
From the North East – M1 & M25;
the North West – M6, M40 & M25;
the West and Wales – M4 & M25;
the East – M25;
the South West – M5, M4 & M25;
London – M25, M2, M20, M23, M3, M4 or M40.

By rail:
Regular services from London's Charing Cross, Victoria, Waterloo and Waterloo East stations to all parts of the South East. Further information on rail journeys in the South East can be obtained on 0845 748 4950.

By air:
Fly into London City, London Heathrow, London Gatwick, London Southend, Luton, Southampton, Shoreham (Brighton City) or Stanstead.

Chatham, Kent

where to stay in
South East England

All place names in the blue bands are shown on the maps at the front of this guide.

A complete listing of all VisitBritain assessed parks in England appears at the back.

Accommodation symbols
Symbols give useful information about services and facilities. Inside the back-cover flap you can find a key to these symbols. Keep it open for easy reference.

ANDOVER, Hampshire Map ref 2C2

★★★
TOURING & CAMPING PARK

🚐	£16.00–£20.00
🚎	£16.00–£20.00
Å	£14.00–£20.00

69 touring pitches

Wyke Down Touring Caravan & Camping Park

Picket Piece, Andover SP11 6LX t (01264) 352048 f (01264) 324661 e info2008@wykedown.co.uk
w wykedown.co.uk

Level, sheltered site with public house and restaurant. Also recreation room, play area and golf driving range. Follow caravan and camping park signs from A303.

open All year
payment Credit/debit cards, cash/cheques

General ▢ ♨ P 🔌 🔒 🌐 📡 ☉ ⊞ ✕ 🐾 ☼   Leisure ⌁ ▾ ⚲ ∪ ↝

ARRETON, Isle of Wight Map ref 2C3

★★
HOLIDAY PARK

🚐 (10)	£8.00–£9.00
🚎 (5)	£8.00–£9.00
Å (5)	

10 touring pitches

Perreton Farm

East Lane, Arreton, Newport PO30 3DL t (01983) 865218 e roger.perreton@virgin.net
w islandbreaks.co.uk

Farm with countryside views, quiet location. Ideal for walkers and cyclists with plenty of footpaths. Cycle track nearby with hire facilities on farm. Dogs welcome. Good pubs in village. Open April to October inclusive.

payment Cash/cheques

General ▢ ♨ P 🔌 🔒 📡 ☉ 🐾 🌿 ☼   Leisure ∪ ↝ ▸ ⚵ 🏛

ASHFORD, Kent Map ref 3B4

★★★★★
HOLIDAY, TOURING & CAMPING PARK

🚐	£12.00–£20.00
🚎	£12.00–£20.00
Å	£12.00–£20.00
🚏 (5)	£220.00–£450.00

70 touring pitches

Broadhembury Holiday Park

Steeds Lane, Kingsnorth, Ashford TN26 1NQ t (01233) 620859 f (01233) 620918
e holidaypark@broadhembury.co.uk w broadhembury.co.uk

For walking, cycling, visiting castles and gardens or just relaxing, Broadhembury, in quiet Kentish countryside, is a park for all seasons. Convenient for Channel crossings and Canterbury.

open All year
payment Credit/debit cards, cash/cheques, euros

General ▢ ♨ P 🔌 ⊙ 🔒 🌐 📡 ☉ ⊞🈐 ▦ 🐾 🌿 ☼   Leisure 📺 ⚲ ⋀ ∪ ↝ ▸

Key to symbols
Open the back flap for a key to symbols.

BANBURY, Oxfordshire Map ref 2C1

★★★★
HOLIDAY &
TOURING PARK

£15.00–£18.00
(30) £13.00–£15.00
98 touring pitches

Bo-Peep Caravan Park

Aynho Road, Adderbury, Banbury OX17 3NP **t** (01295) 810605 **f** (01295) 810605
e warden@bo-peep.co.uk **w** bo-peep.co.uk

Twelve-acre site with 98 all-electric pitches. Fine views, surrounded by farmland. Excellent campsite facilities. Central for Oxford, Blenheim, Stratford and Warwick. Access from M40 jct 10 and 11. Open April to October.

payment Cash/cheques

General ▤ P ⊕ ☺ ♿ ⊕ ⋔ ⊞ ⛺ ☂ Leisure ♪ ⚑

BATTLE, East Sussex Map ref 3B4

★★★★★
HOLIDAY PARK
ROSE AWARD

(54) £189.00–£920.00

Crowhurst Park

Telham Lane, Battle TN33 0SL **t** (01424) 773344 **f** (01424) 775727
e enquiries@crowhurstpark.co.uk **w** crowhurstpark.co.uk

payment Credit/debit cards, cash/cheques

Quality development of luxury Scandinavian-style pine lodges within the grounds of a 17thC country estate. Facilities include leisure club with indoor swimming pool, bar, restaurant and children's playground. Open 4 March to 6 January.

⊕ Two miles south of Battle on A2100.

♥ Christmas and New Year holidays available.

General ▣ P ⊞ ⛺ ✕ ☼ Leisure ☎ ⊺⊽ ♟ ♪ ♦ ⛰ ♫ ♪

BATTLE, East Sussex Map ref 3B4

★★★★★
TOURING PARK

(150) £12.10–£24.90
(150) £12.10–£24.90
150 touring pitches

See Ad on inside front cover

Normanhurst Court Caravan Club Site

Stevens Crouch, Battle TN33 9LR **t** (01424) 773808 **w** caravanclub.co.uk

payment Credit/debit cards, cash/cheques

An elegant site, set in the heart of 1066 Country. Visit historic Battle Abbey or picturesque Rye, littered with antique shops and tea rooms. Open March to November.

⊕ From Battle, turn left onto A271. Site is 3 miles on left.

♥ Special member rates mean you can save your membership subscription in less than a week. Visit our website to find out more.

THE
CARAVAN
CLUB

General ▤ P ⊕ ☺ ♿ ⊕ ⋔ ⊙ ⊞ ⛺ ☼ Leisure ⋔ ♪ ⚑

BEACONSFIELD, Buckinghamshire Map ref 2C2

★★★★
TOURING &
CAMPING PARK

(60) £15.00–£20.00
(60) £15.00–£20.00
(35) £10.00–£18.00
95 touring pitches

Highclere Farm Country Touring Park

Newbarn Lane, Seer Green, Beaconsfield HP9 2QZ **t** (01494) 874505 **f** (01494) 875238
e highclerepark@aol.com **w** highclerepark.co.uk

Quiet meadowland park, low-cost Tube prices to London (25 minutes). Eleven miles Legoland. Launderette, showers, superb toilet block, play area. Open March to January inclusive.

payment Credit/debit cards, cash/cheques

General ▤ P ⊕ ☺ ♿ ⊕ ⋔ ⊙ ⊞ ⛺ ☼ Leisure ⋔

BEMBRIDGE, Isle of Wight Map ref 2C3

★★★★
HOLIDAY PARK
🚐 (400) £10.00–£26.00
🚐 (400) £10.00–£26.00
⛺ (400) £10.00–£26.00
🚍 (230) £79.00–£789.00
400 touring pitches

Whitecliff Bay Holiday Park

Hillway Road, Bembridge PO35 5PL t (01983) 872671 f (01983) 872941
e holiday@whitecliff-bay.com w whitecliff-bay.com

payment Credit/debit cards, cash/cheques, euros

Situated in an Area of Outstanding Natural Beauty, the park offers great-value family holidays. There are facilities on site for all ages. Pets welcome in low season. Open March to October.

⊕ *From A3055 turn onto B3395 at Brading and follow signposts.*

❤ *Special offers are available from time to time – please visit our website for full details.*

General 🔌🚐P🔌🍴🐕🚽🏪🎡🌙😀⛱🎿✕☼ Leisure ⌇⌇♬🐾⚲ﾉ↱

BEXHILL-ON-SEA, East Sussex Map ref 3B4

★★★★
HOLIDAY, TOURING & CAMPING PARK
🚐 (55) £8.50–£9.50
🚐 (55) £8.20–£9.20
⛺ (55) £8.50–£9.50
🚍 (2) £130.00–£330.00
55 touring pitches

Cobbs Hill Farm Caravan & Camping Park

Watermill Lane, Sidley, Bexhill-on-Sea TN39 5JA t (01424) 213460 e cobbshillfarmuk@hotmail.com
w cobbshillfarm.co.uk

Quiet site in countryside with selection of farm animals. Touring and hire vans, level pitches, tent and rally fields. Near Hastings, Battle and Eastbourne.

payment Credit/debit cards, cash/cheques

General 🚐P🔌🍴🐕🏪🚽😀🏪🎡🐾🐾☼ Leisure ⌂

BEXHILL-ON-SEA, East Sussex Map ref 3B4

★★★★
TOURING & CAMPING PARK
🚐 £16.50–£22.50
🚐 £16.50–£22.50
⛺ £16.50–£22.50
50 touring pitches

Kloofs Caravan Park

Sandhurst Lane, Bexhill-on-Sea TN39 4RG t (01424) 842839 f (01424) 845669
e camping@kloofs.com w kloofs.com

open All year
payment Credit/debit cards, cash/cheques

Freedom all year round, whatever the weather! Fully serviced, hard, extra-large pitches. Modern facilities, private washing, central heating. In a quiet, rural setting.

General 🚐P🔌🍴🐕🏪🚽😀🏪🎡🐾🐾☼ Leisure ⌂∪ﾉ↱

The great outdoors

Discover Britain's green heart with this easy-to-use guide.
Featuring a selection of the most stunning gardens in the country, The Gardens Explorer is complete with a handy fold-out map and illustrated guide. You can purchase the Explorer series from good bookshops and online at visitbritaindirect.com.

BIRCHINGTON, Kent Map ref 3C3

★★★★★
HOLIDAY, TOURING
& CAMPING PARK

🚐 (100) £13.00–£22.00
🚌 (100) £13.00–£22.00
⛺ (100) £13.00–£22.00
300 touring pitches

Two Chimneys Holiday Park

Shottendane Road, Birchington CT7 0HD **t** (01843) 841068 **f** (01843) 848099
e info@twochimneys.co.uk **w** twochimneys.co.uk

payment Credit/debit cards, cash/cheques

A friendly, family-run country site near sandy beaches. Spacious, level pitches. Modern wc/shower and laundry facilities including disabled. Children's play and ball-games areas. Open Easter to 31 October.

⊕ A2 then A28 to Birchington. Turn right into Park Lane, bear left into Manston Road, left at crossroads (B2049), site on right.

General 📺 P 🔌 🌡 🍴 🚘 📻 ☉ 📼 🗄 🅰 ☼ Leisure 🎣 🍷 ⚓ 🎡 🔍 ∪ 🎿

BOGNOR REGIS, West Sussex Map ref 2C3

★★★★★
TOURING &
CAMPING PARK

🚐 (100) £12.10–£24.90
🚌 (100) £12.10–£24.90
⛺ on application
100 touring pitches

See Ad on inside front cover

THE
CARAVAN
CLUB

Rowan Park Caravan Club Site

Rowan Way, Bognor Regis PO22 9RP **t** (01243) 828515 **w** caravanclub.co.uk

payment Credit/debit cards, cash/cheques

A small, recently redeveloped site just two miles from Bognor. Award-winning beach, seaside attractions. Chichester, Arundel and Brighton within easy reach; also NT properties including Petworth. Open March to November.

⊕ From roundabout on A29, 1 mile north of Bognor, turn left into Rowan Way, site 100yds on right, opposite Halfords superstore.

♥ Special member rates mean you can save your membership subscription in less than a week. Visit our website to find out more.

General 📺 P 🔌 🌡 🍴 🚘 📻 📼 🗄 🐾 ☼ Leisure 🎡 🎿 🏇

BRIGHTON & HOVE, East Sussex Map ref 2D3

★★★★★
TOURING &
CAMPING PARK

🚐 (169) £14.30–£27.70
🚌 (169) £14.30–£27.70
⛺ on application
169 touring pitches

See Ad on inside front cover

THE
CARAVAN
CLUB

Sheepcote Valley Caravan Club Site

East Brighton Park, Brighton BN2 5TS **t** (01273) 626546 **w** caravanclub.co.uk

open All year
payment Credit/debit cards, cash/cheques

Located on the South Downs, just two miles from Brighton. Visit the Marina, with its shops, pubs, restaurants and cinema, and take a tour of the exotic Royal Pavilion.

⊕ M23/A23, join A27 (Lewes). B2123 (Falmer/Rottingdean). Right, onto B2123 (Woodingdean). In 2 miles, at traffic lights, right (Warren Road). In 1 mile, left (Wilson Avenue).

♥ Special member rates mean you can save your membership subscription in less than a week. Visit our website to find out more.

General 📺 P 🔌 🌡 🍴 🚘 📻 ☉ 📼 🗄 🐾 ☼ Leisure 🎡 🏇

Place index

If you know where you want to stay, the index at the back of the guide will give you the page number listing accommodation in your chosen town, city or village. Check out the other useful indexes too.

BURFORD, Oxfordshire Map ref 2B1

★★★★★
TOURING PARK

🚐(120) £12.10–£24.90
🚐(120) £12.10–£24.90
120 touring pitches

See Ad on inside front cover

THE
CARAVAN
CLUB

Burford Caravan Club Site

Bradwell Grove, Burford OX18 4JJ **t** (01993) 823080 **w** caravanclub.co.uk

payment Credit/debit cards, cash/cheques

Attractive, spacious site opposite Cotswold Wildlife Park. Burford has superb Tudor houses, a museum and historic inns. A great base from which to explore the Cotswolds. Open March to November.

⊕ *From roundabout at A40/A361 junction in Burford, take A361 signposted Lechlade. Site on right after 2.5 miles. Site signposted from roundabout.*

♥ *Special member rates mean you can save your membership subscription in less than a week. Visit our website to find out more.*

General 🖭 P 🔌 🛗 ♿ 🚿 ⊙ 📼 🐾 ☼ Leisure ⛰ ⚓ ►

CANTERBURY, Kent Map ref 3B3

★★★★
HOLIDAY, TOURING & CAMPING PARK

🚐(15) £14.00–£20.00
🚐(5) £14.00–£20.00
⛺(25) £12.00–£18.00
🏠(7) £175.00–£410.00
45 touring pitches

Yew Tree Park

Stone Street, Petham, Canterbury CT4 5PL **t** (01227) 700306 **f** (01227) 700306
e info@yewtreepark.com **w** yewtreepark.com

payment Credit/debit cards, cash/cheques

Picturesque country park close to Canterbury, centrally located for exploring Kent. Naturally landscaped touring and camping facilities. Self-catering apartments (not assessed) and holiday units. Outdoor pool.

⊕ *On B2068, 4 miles south of Canterbury, 9 miles north of M20, jct 11.*

General ♿ P 🔌 🛗 ♿ 🚿 ⊙ 📼 ☼ Leisure ⚓ ⛰

COTSWOLDS

See under Burford, Kingham, Standlake
See also Cotswolds in South West England section

DOVER, Kent Map ref 3C4

★★★★
HOLIDAY & TOURING PARK

🚐(10) £12.00–£22.00
🚐(10) £12.00–£22.00
⛺(10) £12.00–£22.00
🏠(5) £125.00–£550.00
35 touring pitches

Sutton Vale Country Club & Caravan Park

Vale Road, Sutton-by-Dover, Dover CT15 5DH **t** (01304) 374155 **f** (01304) 381132
e office@sutton-vale.co.uk **w** sutton-vale.co.uk

payment Credit/debit cards, cash, euros

Picturesque rural park in valley with country club. Heated swimming pool, restaurant and children's adventure playground. Closed February.

General ♿ 🖭 🚐 P 🔌 🛗 ♿ 🚿 ⊙ 📼 🛒 ✕ 🐕 🐾 ☼ Leisure ⚓ ⛰ 📺 ▮ 🎵 ⚛ ⛰ ∪ ⚓ ► 🐾

EASTBOURNE, East Sussex Map ref 3B4

★★★★
TOURING &
CAMPING PARK

🚐 (60) £11.50–£16.50
🚎 (60) £11.50–£16.50
⛺ (60) £11.50–£16.50
60 touring pitches

Fairfields Farm Caravan & Camping Park

Eastbourne Road, Westham, Pevensey BN24 5NG t (01323) 763165 f (01323) 469175
e enquiries@fairfieldsfarm.com w fairfieldsfarm.com

payment Credit/debit cards, cash/cheques

A quiet country touring site on a working farm. Clean facilities, lakeside walk with farm pets and free fishing for campers. Close to the beautiful seaside resort of Eastbourne, and a good base from which to explore the diverse scenery and attractions of south east England. Open April to October.

⊕ Signposted off A27 Pevensey roundabout. Straight through Pevensey and Westham villages towards castle. Then B2191 (left) to Eastbourne east, over level crossing on the left.

♥ Special low season midweek offer: 3 nights for the price of 2. Contact us for more details.

General 🏕 P 🚐 🕒 🚿 🌣 ⊙ 🔓 🐕 🌡 ☼ Leisure ⚓ 🚲

FOLKESTONE, Kent Map ref 3B4

★★★★★
TOURING &
CAMPING PARK

🚐 (140) £12.10–£24.90
🚎 (140) £12.10–£24.90
140 touring pitches

See Ad on inside front cover

CARAVAN
CLUB

Black Horse Farm Caravan Club Site

385 Canterbury Road, Densole, Folkestone CT18 7BG t (01303) 892665 w caravanclub.co.uk

open All year
payment Credit/debit cards, cash/cheques

Set in the heart of farming country in the Kentish village of Densole on the Downs. This is a quiet and relaxed country site, ideally suited for families wishing to visit the many interesting local attractions including the historic city of Canterbury. For nature lovers there are many walks.

⊕ From M20 jct 13 on A260 to Canterbury, 2 miles from junction with A20, site on left 200yds past Black Horse inn.

♥ Special member rates mean you can save your membership subscription in less than a week. Visit our website to find out more.

General 🖥 P 🚐 🕒 🚿 🚐 🌣 ⊙ 📦 🐕 ☼ Leisure ⚙ ♪ ⚓

FORDINGBRIDGE, Hampshire Map ref 2B3

GATWICK AIRPORT

See under Horsham, Redhill

HORAM, East Sussex Map ref 2D3

★★★★
TOURING &
CAMPING PARK

🚐 (40) £14.50
🚙 (10) £14.50
⛺ (40) £14.50
90 touring pitches

Horam Manor Touring Park

Horam, Heathfield TN21 0YD **t** (01435) 813662 **e** camp@horam-manor.co.uk **w** horam-manor.co.uk

An established park with modern facilities including free hot water and showers. A tranquil setting in an Area of Outstanding Natural Beauty. On the A267, ten miles north of Eastbourne. Open March to October.

payment Cash/cheques

General 🚘 P 🔌 🛗 🚻 ⌂ ☺ 🚮 🔟 🛒 ⛓ ☼   Leisure 🏔 🔍 ∪ ♪ ► 🚵

HORSHAM, West Sussex Map ref 2D2

★★★★
HOLIDAY PARK

🚐 (200) £17.00–£23.00
🚙 (100) £17.00–£23.00
⛺ (80) £15.00–£19.00
200 touring pitches

Honeybridge Park

Honeybridge Lane, Dial Post, Nr Horsham RH13 8NX **t** (01403) 710923 **f** (01403) 712815
e enquiries@honeybridgepark.co.uk **w** honeybridgepark.co.uk

open All year
payment Credit/debit cards, cash/cheques, euros

Delightfully situated within an Area of Outstanding Natural Beauty. A rural retreat with relaxed atmosphere providing exclusive holiday lodges for sale. Highest standards maintained with spacious touring pitches, heated amenity blocks, licensed shop, takeaway, play area. Seasonal pitches and storage facilities. Ideal touring base. Convenient to coast, London and theme parks.

⊕ On A24 travelling south, turn left 1 mile past Dial Post turning. At Old Barn Nurseries continue for 300yds and site is on the right.

♥ 10% discount on pitch fees for Senior Citizens, foreign camping carnet holders and 7 nights or more. Midweek special: £6 off (incl Tue).

General 🔲 P 🔌 🛗 🚻 🎠 🚮 ☺ 🔟 🛒 ⛓ ☼   Leisure ♦ 🏔 ♪ ► 🚵

HORSHAM, West Sussex Map ref 2D2

★★★★
TOURING PARK

🚐 (60) £14.50–£18.50
🚙 (60) £14.50–£18.50
⛺ (30) £14.50–£18.50

Sumners Ponds Fishery & Campsite

Slaughterford Farm, Chapel Road, Barns Green, Horsham RH13 0PR **t** (01403) 732539
e sumnersponds@dsl.pipex.com **w** sumnersponds.co.uk

open All year
payment Credit/debit cards, cash/cheques

A very beautiful site set on a working farm amongst three lakes, woodland and pastures. Excellent facilities and a village pub and shop five minutes' walk away. Excellent countryside for cyclists and walkers with South Downs Link nearby. Horsham town centre and supermarkets only ten minutes away.

⊕ From north and Horsham, follow A264. Turn left after humpback bridge signposted Barns Green. From south, head north to Barns Green from Coolham crossroads.

♥ Usually 2 or 3 events such as concerts or plays in summer. Check website or contact us directly.

General 🚘 P 🔌 🛗 🚲 🎠 ☺ 🔟 🛒 ✕ ⛓ 🐾 ☼   Leisure ♪ 🚵

HOVE

See under Brighton & Hove

Rest assured

All accommodation in this guide has been rated, or is awaiting assessment, by a professional assessor.

HURLEY, Berkshire Map ref 2C2

★★★★
HOLIDAY PARK
(138) £9.50–£15.50
(138) £9.50–£15.50
(62) £8.25–£14.25
(10) £200.00–£450.00
200 touring pitches

Hurley Riverside Park

Hurley, Maidenhead SL6 5NE t (01628) 824493 f (01628) 825533 e info@hurleyriversidepark.co.uk
w hurleyriversidepark.co.uk

payment Credit/debit cards, cash/cheques

Our family-run park is situated in the picturesque Thames Valley, surrounded by farmland. Access to the Thames Path. Ideal location for visiting Windsor Legoland, Oxford and London. Open March to October.

General P Leisure

ISLE OF WIGHT

See under Bembridge, Shanklin

KINGHAM, Oxfordshire Map ref 2B1

★★★★
HOLIDAY PARK
ROSE AWARD
(30) £420.00–
£1,125.00

Bluewood Park

Kingham, Chipping Norton OX7 6UJ t (01608) 659946 f (01608) 658317
e rachel@bluewoodpark.com w bluewoodpark.com

open All year
payment Credit/debit cards, cash/cheques

Escape to Bluewood Park, nestled in a bluebell wood in an Area of Outstanding Natural Beauty, the park is a superb base for exploring the Cotswolds. This exclusive development of luxury and contemporary accommodation, each with its own hot tub, is the perfect place to relax and unwind.

⊕ *Bluewood Park can be found near Kingham on the B4450 between Stow-on-the-Wold and Chipping Norton.*

General P Leisure

MARDEN, Kent Map ref 3B4

★★★★★
TOURING &
CAMPING PARK
(100) £13.00–£19.00
(33) £13.00–£19.00
(20) £13.00–£18.00
100 touring pitches

Tanner Farm Touring Caravan & Camping Park

Goudhurst Road, Tonbridge TN12 9ND t (01622) 832399 f (01622) 832472
e enquiries@tannerfarmpark.co.uk w tannerfarmpark.co.uk

open All year
payment Credit/debit cards, cash/cheques

Immaculate, secluded park surrounded by beautiful countryside on family farm. Ideal touring base for the area. Gold David Bellamy Conservation Award. Bed and breakfast also available. Green Tourism Business Scheme silver.

⊕ *From A21 or A229 onto B2079; midway between Marden and Goudhurst.*

♥ *Caravan Club AS.*

General P Leisure

MOLLINGTON, Oxfordshire Map ref 2C1

★★★★
TOURING &
CAMPING PARK

⊟ £11.50–£12.50
⊞ £11.50–£12.50
▲ (15) £6.00–£10.00
36 touring pitches

Anita's Touring Caravan Park

Church Farm, Mollington, Banbury OX17 1AZ t (01295) 750731 f (01295) 750731
e anitagail@btopenworld.com w caravancampingsites.co.uk

Family-run site on working farm. Quality toilet/
shower facility. Central to many places of interest,
the Cotswolds, National Trust properties,
Blenheim, Oxford, Stratford. Rallies welcome.
Three superb self-catering cottages for hire.

open All year
payment Cash/cheques

General 🎫 P 🔌 🍴 📺 📶 ☺ 🐕 🛉 ☼ Leisure ∪ ✂

NEW FOREST

See under Fordingbridge, Ower, Ringwood

OWER, Hampshire Map ref 2C3

★★★
TOURING PARK

⊟ £15.00
⊞ £15.00
▲ £12.00–£20.00
45 touring pitches

Green Pastures Caravan Park

Whitemoor Lane, Ower, Romsey SO51 6AJ t (023) 8081 4444 e enquiries@greenpasturesfarm.com
w greenpasturesfarm.com

Family-run farm and campsite on edge of New
Forest, convenient for ferries. Space to play within
view of units. Block with toilet/shower facilities
for disabled people. Day kennelling available.

payment Cash/cheques

General 🎫 P 🔌 🍴 📶 ☺ 📟 📼 🐕 🛉 Leisure ✂ ▶

PEVENSEY BAY, East Sussex Map ref 3B4

★★★
HOLIDAY, TOURING
& CAMPING PARK

⊟ (40) £14.50–£19.50
⊞ (4) £14.50–£19.50
▲ (50) £14.50–£19.50
⊡ (8) £180.00–£595.00
94 touring pitches

Bay View Park Ltd

Old Martello Road, Pevensey Bay BN24 6DX t (01323) 768688 f (01323) 769637
e holidays@bay-view.co.uk w bay-view.co.uk

Family site on a private road next to the beach.
Play area. New showers and laundry. Small, well-
stocked shop. Ideal touring base. Open March to
October.

payment Credit/debit cards, cash/cheques

General 📺 P 🔌 🍴 📺 📶 📟 📼 🐕 ☼ Leisure ⛺ ✂ ▶

READING, Berkshire Map ref 2C2

★★★★
TOURING &
CAMPING PARK

⊟ (58) £15.00–£22.00
⊞ (58) £15.00–£22.00
▲ (14) £13.00–£18.00
58 touring pitches

Wellington Country Park

Odiham Road, Riseley, Reading RG7 1SP t (0118) 932 6444 f (0118) 932 6445
e info@wellington-country-park.co.uk w wellington-country-park.co.uk

A wealth of enjoyment. Nature trails, children's
play areas, miniature railway, crazy golf. Special
events throughout the season. Open February to
October.

payment Credit/debit cards

General 📺 P 🔌 🍴 📶 ☺ 📟 ✕ 🐕 ☼ Leisure ⛺ ∪ ✂

Suit yourself

The symbols at the end of each entry mean you can enjoy virtually
made-to-measure accommodation with the services and facilities
most important to you. A key to the symbols can be found inside the
back-cover flap. Keep this open for easy reference.

REDHILL, Surrey Map ref 2D2

★★★★
TOURING PARK
(79) £12.10–£24.90
(79) £12.10–£24.90
79 touring pitches

See Ad on inside front cover

Alderstead Heath Caravan Club Site

Dean Lane, Redhill RH1 3AH **t** (01737) 644629 **w** caravanclub.co.uk

open All year
payment Credit/debit cards, cash/cheques

Quiet site with views over rolling, wooded North Downs. Denbies Wine Estate nearby. For day trips try Chessington and Thorpe Park and the lively city of Brighton. Non-members welcome.

M25 jct 8, A217 towards Reigate, fork left after 300yds towards Merstham. 2.5 miles, left at T-junction onto A23. 0.5 miles turn right into Shepherds Hill (B2031). 1 mile, lef into Dean Lane.

Special member rates mean you can save your membershi subscription in less than a week. Visit our website to fin out more.

THE CARAVAN CLUB

General Leisure

RINGWOOD, Hampshire Map ref 2B3

★★★★
TOURING & CAMPING PARK
(150) £16.50–£27.00
(150) £16.50–£27.00
(150) £16.50–£27.00
150 touring pitches

Shamba Holidays

230 Ringwood Road, St Leonards, Ringwood BH24 2SB **t** (01202) 873302 **f** (01202) 873392
e enquiries@shambaholidays.co.uk **w** shambaholidays.co.uk

Family-run touring and camping park close to the New Forest and Bournemouth with its fine beaches. Modern toilet/shower facilities, heated indoor/outdoor pool, licensed clubhouse, games room, takeaway, shop. Open March to October.

payment Credit/debit cards, cash/cheques

General Leisure

ROMSEY, Hampshire Map ref 2C3

★★★★
HOLIDAY, TOURING & CAMPING PARK
(70) £16.00–£26.00
(70) £16.00–£26.00
(40) £16.00–£26.00
(6) £220.00–£500.00
70 touring pitches

Hill Farm Caravan Park

Branches Lane, Sherfield English, Romsey SO51 6FH **t** (01794) 340402 **f** (01794) 342358
e gib@hillfarmpark.com **w** hillfarmpark.com

Set in 11 acres of beautiful countryside on the edge of the New Forest, our family-run site provides an ideal base from which to visit the area. Touring pitches from March to October, holiday homes from February to January.

payment Cash/cheques

General Leisure

ST HELENS, Isle of Wight Map ref 2C3

★★★
TOURING & CAMPING PARK
(70) £10.00
(70) £10.00
(70) £10.00
70 touring pitches

Carpenters Farm Campsite

Carpenters Road, St Helens, Ryde PO33 1YL **t** (01983) 874557 **e** info@carpentersfarm.co.uk
w carpentersfarm.co.uk

Farm campsite with beautiful views in picturesque rural setting, adjacent to RSPB Reserve and SSSI. Close to beaches and attractions. Relaxed atmosphere on site. Families, groups and pets very welcome.

open All year
payment Cash/cheques

General Leisure

It's all quality-assessed accommodation

Our commitment to quality involves wide-ranging accommodation assessment. Rating and awards were correct at the time of going to press but may change following a new assessment. Please check at time of booking.

ST HELENS, Isle of Wight Map ref 2C3

★★★★★
HOLIDAY PARK
ROSE AWARD

(51) £200.00–£820.00

Hillgrove Park

Field Lane, St Helens PO33 1UT **t** (01983) 872802 **f** (01983) 872100 **e** holidays@hillgrove.co.uk
w hillgrove.co.uk

open All year

payment Credit/debit cards, cash/cheques, euros

Quiet family park, close to local beach and harbour. Local shops, village inn and excellent restaurants within a few hundred yards. Many beautiful country walks, coastal path and cycle routes are all accessible. The outdoor heated pool, children's play areas, games room and sports field are all very popular in the summer months.

⊕ From Ryde take A3055 to Sandown and turn left onto B3330 at traffic lights. Field Lane is first on left on entering St Helens.

♥ Up to £100 discount for 2-week bookings. All prices include car ferry travel with Wight Link.

General 🏚🅖🐕☼ Leisure ⚓🎣⛰♨⚓♒

ST NICHOLAS AT WADE, Kent Map ref 3C3

★★
TOURING &
CAMPING PARK

(15) £12.00–£15.00
(5) £12.00–£14.00
Å (55) £9.00–£12.00
75 touring pitches

St Nicholas Camping Site

Court Road, St Nicholas at Wade, Birchington CT7 0NH **t** (01843) 847245

The site – flat, grassy and well-sheltered – is on the outskirts of the village, close to the village shop. The resort of Thanet is within easy reach. The site is signposted from the A299 and A28.

payment Cash/cheques

General P 🅖🅖🍴🄿☺🐕☼ Leisure ⛰

SELSEY, West Sussex Map ref 2C3

★★★★★
TOURING PARK

(250) £18.50–£32.00
(250) £18.50–£32.00
Å (50) £16.50–£30.00
250 touring pitches

Warner Farm Touring Park

Warners Lane, Selsey, Chichester PO20 9EL **t** (01243) 604499 & (01243) 606080 **f** (01243) 604095
e touring@bunnleisure.co.uk **w** bunnleisure.co.uk

payment Credit/debit cards, cash/cheques

Warner Farm is a top-quality camping and touring holiday park. With a choice of well-maintained standard, electric or super pitches and excellent wash facilities, you can have a relaxing and carefree holiday here. Bunn Leisure's fantastic entertainment and children's activities are also available to use. A friendly atmosphere and welcome awaits you! Open March to October.

General 🖥 P 🅖🅖🍴🗺🄿☺🏚🅖🍴✕🐕🛁☼ Leisure ⚓🎣🍹🎵🎣⛰🎱♨⚓🏇🚲

Country Code always follow the Country Code

- Be safe – plan ahead and follow any signs
- Leave gates and property as you find them
- Protect plants and animals, and take your litter home
- Keep dogs under close control
- Consider other people

SELSEY, West Sussex Map ref 2C3

★★★★
HOLIDAY PARK
ROSE AWARD

(250)   £135.00–
£1,425.00

West Sands Holiday Park

Mill Lane, Selsey, Chichester PO20 9BH t (01243) 606080 f (01243) 606068
e holidays@bunnleisure.co.uk w bunnleisure.co.uk

payment Credit/debit cards, cheques

Situated on the beachfront overlooking beautiful coastline, West Sands is our liveliest holiday park. With everything you could want for a fun-filled family holiday ... let your children play at the fun-fair and kids clubs; enjoy fantastic entertainment; relax at the superb Oasis pool complex...we can't wait to see you! Open March to October.

⊕ At Chichester take B2145 following signs to Selsey. When you reach Selsey continue through village, turn right into West Street and right into Mill Lane. Follow the road to the windmill and main reception.

♥ See website for details.

General Leisure

SHANKLIN, Isle of Wight Map ref 2C3

★★★★
TOURING &
CAMPING PARK

£13.00–£17.00
£13.00–£17.00
£13.00–£17.00
150 touring pitches

Landguard Camping Park

Landguard Manor Road, Shanklin PO37 7PH t (01983) 867028 f (01983) 865988
e landguard@weltinet.com w landguard-camping.co.uk

A family park for all touring units, within walking distance of Shanklin town and sandy beaches. Outdoor heated swimming pool. Take-away pizzeria. All 150 pitches have electrical hook-up. Open April to September.

payment Credit/debit cards, cash/cheques

General Leisure

STANDLAKE, Oxfordshire Map ref 2C1

WASHINGTON, West Sussex Map ref 2D3

★★★★
TOURING &
CAMPING PARK

(21)   Max £15.00
(5)   Max £15.00
(80)   Max £15.00
21 touring pitches

Washington Caravan & Camping Park

London Road, Washington, Pulborough RH20 4AJ t (01903) 892869 f (01903) 893252
e washcamp@amserve.com w washcamp.com

The park is set in beautifully landscaped grounds beneath the South Downs affording the right atmosphere for an enjoyable stay. Well situated for visiting places of interest.

open All year
payment Credit/debit cards, cash/cheques

General Leisure

A holiday on two wheels

For a fabulous freewheeling break, seek out accommodation participating in our Cyclists Welcome scheme. Look out for the symbol and plan your route online at nationalcyclenetwork.org.

WINCHESTER, Hampshire Map ref 2C3

★★★★
TOURING &
CAMPING PARK

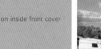

(139) £10.40–£22.40
(139) £10.40–£22.40
A   on application
139 touring pitches

See Ad on inside front cover

THE
CARAVAN
CLUB

Morn Hill Caravan Club Site

Morn Hill, Winchester SO21 2PH **t** (01962) 869877 **w** caravanclub.co.uk

payment Credit/debit cards, cash/cheques

Large, split-level site from which to explore Winchester. Oxford, Chichester, the New Forest, Salisbury and Stonehenge are all within an hour's drive. Open March to November.

⊕ *From M3 jct 10 A31 (signposted Alton). Left at roundabout (Percy Hobbs sign), signposted Easton. Immediate turn in front of pub, top of lane for Caravan Club.*

♥ *Midweek discount: pitch fee for standard pitches for stays on any Tue, Wed or Thu night outside peak season dates will be reduced by 50%.*

General 🖼 P 🍴 ☕ 🍽 🚐 📶 ☺ 🏧 ☀ Leisure /⋀ 🎣 🏌

Families Welcome

If you are looking for a great family break in quality-assessed accommodation, look out for the Families Welcome sign.

Participants in this scheme offer additional facilities and services catering for a range of ages and family units. For families with young children, they'll have facilities such as cots and highchairs, storage for push-chairs and somewhere to heat baby food or milk. Where meals are provided, children's choices will be clearly indicated, with healthy options available. They'll also have information on local walks, attractions, activities or events suitable for children, as well as local child-friendly pubs and restaurants.

Of course, not all accommodation is able to cater for all ages or combinations of family units, so do check when you book.

Wherever you're travelling in England, the Families Welcome scheme will help you find just the right place to stay to ensure everyone has a great time.

FAMILIES WELCOME · FAMILIES WELCOME · FAMILIES WELCOME

South West England

Bath, Bristol, Cornwall, Cotswolds and the Forest of Dean, Devon, Dorset, Gloucestershire, Isles of Scilly, Somerset, Wiltshire

Sun, surf, sensational wildlife – and so much more

The South West has always been a magnet for holidaymakers. And with a great climate, masses of activities, teeming wildlife and magical landscapes, is it any wonder?

South West Tourism
visitsouthwest.co.uk
(01392) 360050

Polzeath Beach, Cornwall

Forest of Dean, Gloucestershire   Tarr Steps, Exmoor National Park

Corfe, Dorset

The coastline is one of this region's real gems, from Dorset's spectacular Lulworth Cove and the fossil-rich Jurassic Coast to the elegant English Riviera and Devon's surf-piled north Atlantic coast. Look closely and you may spot whales, dolphins, basking sharks or even a dinosaur tooth or two. And with more Blue Flag beaches than anywhere else in England, you can enjoy high adrenaline watersports or simply build sandcastles to your heart's content. Inland you'll find the romantic wilderness of Dartmoor and Exmoor National Parks along with the scenic Forest of Dean, secret wooded valleys and the Tarka Trail. It's the perfect terrain for mountain biking and horse riding. And from family theme parks to special interest holidays in yoga or glass making, this region has it all.

One of the must-see attractions is 'Breaking the Chains', a major exhibition at Bristol's British Empire and Commonwealth Museum. Marking the bicentenary of the abolition of the slave trade, it's a moving account of one of the darkest episodes in human history. Another great new attraction is the Artificial Surf Reef at Boscombe seafront, set to deliver rollers on the calmest of days. And when you need a little peace and quiet, head off to Gloucester Cathedral. This architectural marvel features massive cylindrical pillars in the Norman nave, glorious fan-vaulted cloisters and the tomb of King Edward II.

Wherever you go you will see spectacular scenery, wonderful countryside and a beautiful coastline. Discover St Nectan's Glen near Tintagel, where a 60ft waterfall cascades into a stone basin before pouring out through an arch in the rock. Another mystical place is Silbury Hill near Marlborough, Wiltshire. Dating back to 2,780 BC and covering 5 acres, it's the largest man made mound in Europe and still shrouded in mystery.

Destinations

Bath

Beautiful Bath is not to be missed. Set in rolling countryside, less than two hours from London, this exquisite Georgian spa city was founded by the Romans and is now a World Heritage Site. Explore the compact city centre on foot and discover a series of architectural gems including the Roman baths and Pump Room, the 15th-century Abbey, and stunning Royal Crescent. Follow in the footsteps of Romans and Celts and bathe in the naturally warm waters of the Thermae Bath Spa.

Bournemouth

Award-winning Bournemouth is the perfect holiday and short-break destination, renowned for its seven miles of family-friendly, golden beaches, beautiful parks and gardens and cosmopolitan ambience. Enjoy the buzz of the town then head out and savour the beauty of the New Forest, the splendour of Dorset's spectacular World Heritage Jurassic Coastline, and the rolling countryside immortalised by Thomas Hardy.

Bristol

In bygone times, explorers and merchants set off on epic journeys from its harbour. Nowadays, Bristol's spirit of boldness and creativity expresses itself in art, architecture and an enviable quality of life. One of the UK's best short-break destinations – take in Georgian terraces, waterfront arts centres, green spaces, great shopping and acclaimed restaurants. The city's treasure chest of heritage glitters with the work of historic figures such as Isambard Kingdom Brunel, and all set against a truly classic view – the River Avon and its dramatic gorge reaching almost into the heart of the city.

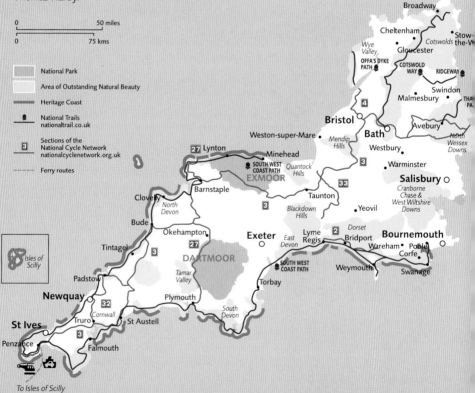

Pulteney Bridge, Bath

Russell-Cotes Museum, Bournemouth

SS Great Britain, Bristol

Tate St Ives

Newquay Zoo

Exeter Cathedral

Stonehenge

Exeter

Devon's regional capital for culture, leisure and shopping is a vibrant city, steeped in ancient history. Don't miss the superb Decorated Gothic cathedral. Stroll along the historic Quayside, once the setting for a thriving wool trade and now a bustling riverside resort. Choose from over 700 shops, join a free Red Coat-guided city tour and dine in any one of numerous acclaimed restaurants. You've also found the perfect base from which to explore the sweeping National Parks of Dartmoor and Exmoor.

Newquay

A beach paradise, stretching for seven miles, drawing all ages like a magnet and making this one-time fishing village Cornwall's premier resort. Soaring cliffs alternate with sheltered coves, and thundering surf with secluded rock pools, smugglers' caves and soft golden sands. Whatever the weather, make a splash at Waterworld, or visit Newquay Zoo, one of the best wildlife parks in the country. Newquay will offer you an unforgettable holiday memory.

St Ives

What was once a small, thriving fishing village is now an internationally renowned haven for artists, attracted by the unique light. Explore the narrow streets and passageways and come upon countless galleries, studios and craft shops. Don't miss the Tate Gallery and Barbara Hepworth Museum. Enjoy the natural beauty of the harbour and explore the Blue Flag beaches and coastal walks. Perfectly placed for all of West Cornwall's stunning scenery and famous attractions.

Salisbury

Nestling in the heart of southern England, Salisbury is every bit the classic English city. The majestic cathedral boasts the tallest spire in England and rises elegantly above sweeping lawns. Wander through this medieval city and you'll find first-class visitor attractions, theatre, shopping, food and drink. And, of course, no trip to Salisbury would be complete without the eight-mile pilgrimage to one of the greatest prehistoric sites in the world – Stonehenge.

Places to visit

Babbacombe Model Village
Torquay, Devon
(01803) 315315
babbacombemodelvillage.co.uk
England in miniature, in four acres of gardens

Bristol City Museum & Art Gallery
(0117) 922 3571
bristol.gov.uk
Art and archaeology in a magnificent baroque building

Bristol Zoo Gardens
(0117) 974 7399
bristolzoo.org.uk
Over 400 exotic and endangered species

Buckland Abbey
Yelverton, Devon
(01822) 853607
nationaltrust.org.uk
Home of seafarer Sir Francis Drake

Cheddar Caves & Gorge
Somerset
(01934) 742343
cheddarcaves.co.uk
Britain's finest caves and deepest gorge

Eden Project
St Austell, Cornwall
(01726) 811911
edenproject.com
A global garden for the 21st century

Exmoor Falconry & Animal Farm
Allerford, Somerset
(01643) 862816
exmoorfalconry.co.uk
Unique farm with falconry centre and activities

Flambards Experience
Helston, Cornwall
(01326) 573404
flambards.co.uk
Acclaimed exhibitions and family amusements

Kingston Lacy House and Gardens
Wimborne Minster, Dorset
(01202) 883402
nationaltrust.org.uk
Elegant country mansion with important collections

Living Coasts
Torquay, Devon
(01803) 202470
livingcoasts.org.uk
Fascinating coastal creatures in stunning location

Longleat
Warminster, Wiltshire
(01985) 844400
longleat.co.uk
Lions, tigers and a stately home

The Lost Gardens of Heligan
near St Austell, Cornwall
(01726) 845100
heligan.com
Beautifully restored gardens

Monkey World - Ape Rescue Centre
Wareham, Dorset
(01929) 462537
monkeyworld.org
Internationally acclaimed primate rescue centre

Morwellham Quay The Morwellham & Tamar Valley Trust
Tavistock, Devon
(01822) 832766
morwellham-quay.co.uk
Evocative museum and visitor centre

National Marine Aquarium
Plymouth, Devon
(01752) 600301
national-aquarium.co.uk
The ocean experience of a lifetime

National Maritime Museum Cornwall
Falmouth, Cornwall
(01326) 313388
nmmc.co.uk
Award-winning exhibitions and boat collections

Newquay Zoo
Cornwall
(01637) 873342
newquayzoo.org.uk
Exotic animals in sub-tropical lakeside gardens

Oceanarium
Bournemouth, Dorset
(01202) 311993
oceanarium.co.uk
Marine life from the furthest reaches of the globe

Paignton Zoo Environmental Park
Devon
(01803) 697500
paigntonzoo.org.uk
One of England's most beautiful zoos

Roman Baths
Bath, Somerset
(01225) 477785
romanbaths.co.uk
Magnificent Roman temple and hot spring baths

STEAM - Museum of the Great Western Railway
Swindon, Wiltshire
(01793) 466646
swindon.gov.uk/steam
Interactive story of pioneering railway network

Stonehenge and Avebury World Heritage Site
near Salisbury, Wiltshire
0870 333 1181
english-heritage.org.uk
World-famous prehistoric monument

Diary dates 2008

Stourhead House and Garden
Wiltshire
(01747) 841152
nationaltrust.org.uk
*Celebrated 18th century
landscaped gardens and mansion*

The Tank Museum
Wareham, Dorset
(01929) 405096
tankmuseum.co.uk
*The world's finest display of
armoured fighting vehicles*

Tate St Ives
St Ives, Cornwall
(01736) 796226
tate.org.uk/stives
A unique introduction to modern art

Thermae Bath Spa
Bath, Somerset
(01225) 335678
thermaebathspa.com
*Enjoy Britain's only natural thermal
waters*

**Wookey Hole Caves
and Papermill**
near Wells, Somerset
(01749) 672243
wookey.co.uk
*Spectacular caves and family
attractions*

**WWT Slimbridge
Wetlands Centre**
Gloucestershire
(01453) 891900
wwt.org.uk
*Wetland centre with amazing
array of wildlife*

South West England Food Festival
Various locations, Exeter
visitsouthwest.co.uk/foodfestival
4 – 6 Apr

Helston Flora Day
helstonfloraday.org.uk
8 May

Bath International Music Festival
Various locations, Bath
visitbath.co.uk
16 May – 1 Jun

Salisbury Festival
Various locations, Salisbury
salisburyfestival.co.uk
23 May – 8 Jun

Royal Bath and West Show
Bath & West Showground, Shepton Mallet
bathandwest.com
28 – 31 May

Golowan Festival Incorporating Mazey Day
Various locations, Penzance
golowan.org
22 – 29 Jun

Sidmouth Folk Week
Various locations, Sidmouth
sidmouthfolkweek.co.uk
1 – 8 Aug

Great Dorset Steam Fair
South Down Farm, Tarrant Hinton
gdsf.co.uk
27 – 31 Aug

Tar Barrels
Ottery St Mary
otterytourism.org.uk
5 Nov

Bridgwater Guy Fawkes Carnival Procession
bridgwaterguyfawkescarnival.co.uk
7 Nov

Tourist Information Centres

When you arrive at your destination, visit an Official Partner Tourist Information Centre for quality assured help with accommodation and information about local attractions and events, or email your request before you go. To search for attractions and Tourist Information Centres on the move just text INFO to 62233, and a web link will be sent to your mobile phone.

Avebury	Green Street	(01672) 539425	all.atic@kennet.gov.uk
Bath	Abbey Church Yard	0906 711 2000**	tourism@bathnes.gov.uk
Bodmin	Mount Folly Square	(01208) 76616	bodmintic@visit.org.uk
Bourton-on-the-Water	Victoria Street	(01451) 820211	bourtonvic@btconnect.com
Bridport	47 South Street	(01308) 424901	bridport.tic@westdorset-dc.gov.uk
Bristol Harbourside	Harbourside	0906 711 2191**	ticharbourside@destinationbristol.co.uk
Brixham	The Quay	(01803) 211211	holiday@torbay.gov.uk
Bude	The Crescent	(01288) 354240	budetic@visitbude.info
Burnham-on-Sea	South Esplanade	(01278) 787852	burnham.tic@sedgemoor.gov.uk
Camelford*	The Clease	(01840) 212954	manager@camelfordtic.eclipse.co.uk
Cartgate	A303/A3088 Cartgate Picnic Site	(01935) 829333	cartgate.tic@southsomerset.gov.uk
Cheddar	The Gorge	(01934) 744071	cheddar.tic@sedgemoor.gov.uk
Cheltenham	77 Promenade	(01242) 522878	info@cheltenham.gov.uk
Chippenham	Market Place	(01249) 665970	tourism@chippenham.gov.uk
Chipping Camden	High Street	(01386) 841206	information@visitchippingcamden.com
Christchurch	49 High Street	(01202) 471780	enquiries@christchurchtourism.info
Cirencester	Market Place	(01285) 654180	cirencestervic@cotswold.gov.uk
Coleford	High Street	(01594) 812388	tourism@fdean.gov.uk
Corsham	31 High Street	(01249) 714660	enquiries@corshamheritage.org.uk
Devizes	Market Place	(01380) 729408	all.dtic@kennet.gov.uk
Dorchester	11 Antelope Walk	(01305) 267992	dorchester.tic@westdorset-dc.gov.uk
Falmouth	11 Market Strand	(01326) 312300	info@falmouth.co.uk
Gloucester	28 Southgate Street	(01452) 396572	tourism@gloucester.gov.uk
Looe*	Fore Street	(01503) 262072	looetic@btconnect.com
Lyme Regis	Church Street	(01297) 442138	lymeregis.tic@westdorset-dc.gov.uk
Malmesbury	Market Lane	(01666) 823748	malmesburyip@northwilts.gov.uk
Moreton-in-Marsh	High Street	(01608) 650881	moreton@cotswolds.gov.uk
Padstow	North Quay	(01841) 533449	padstowtic@btconnect.com
Paignton	The Esplanade	(01803) 211211	holiday@torbay.gov.uk
Plymouth Mayflower	3-5 The Barbican	(01752) 306330	barbicantic@plymouth.gov.uk
Salisbury	Fish Row	(01722) 334956	visitorinfo@salisbury.gov.uk
Somerset	Sedgemoor Services	(01934) 750833	somersetvisitorcentre@ somerset.gov.uk
Sherborne	Digby Road	(01935) 815341	sherborne.tic@westdorset-dc.gov.uk
Stow-on-the-Wold	The Square	(01451) 831082	stowvic@cotswold.gov.uk
Stroud	George Street	(01453) 760960	tic@stroud.gov.uk

Swanage	Shore Road	(01929) 422885	mail@swanage.gov.uk
Swindon	37 Regent Street	(01793) 530328	infocentre@swindon.gov.uk
Taunton	Paul Street	(01823) 336344	tauntontic@tauntondeane.gov.uk
Tewkesbury	64 Barton Street	(01684) 295027	tewkesburytic@tewkesburybc.gov.uk
Torquay	Vaughan Parade	(01803) 211211	holiday@torbay.gov.uk
Truro	Boscawen Street	(01872) 274555	tic@truro.gov.uk
Wadebridge	Eddystone Road	(01208) 813725	wadebridgetic@btconnect.com
Wareham	South Street	(01929) 552740	tic@purbeck-dc.gov.uk
Warminster	off Station Rd	(01985) 218548	visitwarminster@westwiltshire.gov.uk
Wells	Market Place	(01749) 672552	touristinfo@wells.gov.uk
Weston-super-Mare	Beach Lawns	(01934) 888800	westontouristinfo@n-somerset.gov.uk
Weymouth	The Esplanade	(01305) 785747	tic@weymouth.gov.uk
Winchcombe	High Street	(01242) 602925	winchcombetic@tewkesbury.gov.uk
Yeovil	Hendford	(01935) 845946	yeoviltic@southsomerset.gov.uk

* seasonal opening ** calls to this number are charged at premium rate

Avebury, Wiltshire

Lydford, Devon

Find out more

Visit the following websites for further information on South West England (or call 01392 360050):

- visitsouthwest.co.uk
- swcp.org.uk
- accessiblesouthwest.co.uk

Also available from South West Tourism:

- The Trencherman's Guide to Top Restaurants in South West England
- Adventure South West
  Your ultimate activity and adventure guide.
- World Heritage Map
  Discover our World Heritage.

Travel info

By road:
The region is easily accessible from London, the South East, the North and the Midlands by the M6/M5 which extends just beyond Exeter, where it links in with the dual carriageways of the A38 to Plymouth, the A380 to Torbay and the A30 into Cornwall. The North Devon Link Road A361 joins junction 27 with the coast of North Devon and the A39, which then becomes the Atlantic Highway into Cornwall.

By rail:
The main towns and cities in the South West are served throughout the year by fast, direct and frequent rail services from all over the country. Trains operate from London (Paddington) to Chippenham, Swindon, Bath, Bristol, Weston-super-Mare, Taunton, Exeter, Plymouth and Penzance. A service runs from London (Waterloo) to Exeter, via Salisbury, Yeovil and Crewkerne.

By air:
Daily flights into Bristol, Bournemouth, Exeter, Gloucester, Isles of Scilly, Newquay and Plymouth operate from airports around the UK and Europe. For schedules, log on to visitsouthwest.co.uk/flights.

where to stay in
South West England

All place names in the blue bands are shown on the maps at the front of this guide.

A complete listing of all VisitBritain assessed parks in England appears at the back.

Accommodation symbols
Symbols give useful information about services and facilities. Inside the back-cover flap you can find a key to these symbols. Keep it open for easy reference.

ALDERHOLT, Dorset Map ref 2B3

★ ★ ★ ★
TOURING &
CAMPING PARK

(35) £12.00–£16.00
(35) £12.00–£16.00
Å (50) £10.00–£16.00
35 touring pitches

Hill Cottage Farm Camping & Caravan Park

Sandleheath Road, Alderholt, Fordingbridge SP6 3EG **t** (01425) 650513 **f** (01425) 652339
e hillcottagefarmcaravansite@supanet.com **w** hillcottagefarm.co.uk

payment Cash/cheques

Listed in Top 100 Parks Award (Practical Caravan). Set in 40 acres of Dorset countryside on the Hampshire/Dorset border. The New Forest is just two miles away. Luxury facilities. Small lakes for coarse fishing. Rally field available with use of function room/skittle alley. Open March to October.

⊕ *From Fordingbridge take the B3078 to Alderholt for two miles. On the sharp left-hand bend take a right, we are half a mile on the left.*

General 🔲 🏧 P 🔌 🛢 🍴 🚐 📶 ⊙ 🏪 📷 🐕 ✿ ☼ Leisure 🎣 ⚕ ∪ 🎣 🚲 ⛵

ASHBURTON, Devon Map ref 1C2

Parkers Farm Holiday Park

Higher Mead Farm, Ashburton, Devon, TQ13 7LJ
Tel: 01364 654869
E-mail: parkersfarm@btconnect.com · Web: www.parkersfarm.co.uk

Friendly family run site on edge of Dartmoor with spectacular views. Enjoy a relaxing holiday and visit the animals on a genuine farm.
Touring site with large, level terraced pitches.
Static caravans for hire. Indoor/outdoor play areas with trampolines.
Family bar and restaurant, shop etc. Dogs welcome. 12 miles to coast.
Short breaks available.

Place index

If you know where you want to stay, the index at the back of the guide will give you the page number listing accommodation in your chosen town, city or village. Check out the other useful indexes too.

AXMINSTER, Devon Map ref 1D2

★★★★
HOLIDAY, TOURING
& CAMPING PARK

🚐 (130)   £9.00–£17.00
🚍 (20)   £7.00–£17.00
⛺ (60)   £7.00–£17.00
210 touring pitches

Hunters Moon Country Estate

Hawkchurch, Axminster EX13 5UL   t (01297) 678402   f (01297) 678720
w ukparks.co.uk/huntersmoon

Set in glorious countryside with views over beautiful Axe Valley, near Lyme Regis. Seasonal pitches and short/long storage. Luxury holiday homes for sale. Prestige bar and restaurant. Primarily, though not exclusively, aimed at the adult market. Open March to November.

payment Credit/debit cards, cash/cheques

General P 🅿 🅖 🍴 🎱 ☉ 🔲 🕮 🗜 ✕ 🐾 🏕 ☼   Leisure 🍷 ♫ 🎢

BATH, Somerset Map ref 2B2

★★★★
TOURING &
CAMPING PARK

🚐 (90)   £17.95–£19.95
🚍 (90)   £17.95–£19.95
⛺ (105)   £13.50–£17.50
195 touring pitches

Newton Mill Camping

Twaebrook Ltd, Newton Mill Camping Park, Newton Road, Bath BA2 9JF   t (01225) 333909
e newtonmill@hotmail.com   w campinginbath.co.uk

open All year
payment Credit/debit cards, cash

Situated in an idyllic hidden valley close to the city centre with easy access by frequent, local buses or nearby level, traffic-free cycle path. Superb heated amenities (5-star Loo of the Year 2007) including showers, bathrooms and private facilities. Old Mill bar/restaurant open all year. David Bellamy Gold Award for Conservation. ADAC Campingplatz Auszeichnung 2007.

⊕ On A4 on outskirts of Bath towards Bristol, take exit signposted Newton St Loe at roundabout by the Globe pub. Site is 1 mile on left.

♥ 5% discount on stays of 7 days (selected periods). New Year package.

General 🖼 🚗 P 🅿 🅖 🍴 🚲 🎱 ☉ 🔲 🕮 🗜 ✕ 🐾 🏕 ☼   Leisure 📺 🍷 ♦ 🎢 U ⤵ ➤ ⚙

BERE REGIS, Dorset Map ref 2B3

★★★
TOURING &
CAMPING PARK

🚐 (71)   £11.00–£16.50
🚍 (71)   £11.00–£16.50
⛺ (71)   £11.00–£16.50
71 touring pitches

Rowlands Wait Touring Park

Rye Hill, Bere Regis, Wareham BH20 7LP   t (01929) 472727   f (01929) 472275
e enquiries@rowlandswait.co.uk   w rowlandswait.co.uk

payment Credit/debit cards, cash/cheques

Set in an Area of Outstanding Natural Beauty. Modern amenity block with family/disabled facilities. Centrally situated for many attractions and places of interest. Direct access to heathland, ideal for walkers, cyclists, couples, families and nature lovers. Open March to October, winter by arrangement.

⊕ At Bere Regis follow signs to Wool/Bovington. Rowlands Wait is 0.75 miles (1.2km) from the village, top of the hill on the right.

General 🚗 P 🅿 🅖 🍴 🚲 🎱 ☉ 🕮 🗜 🐾 ☼   Leisure ♦ 🎢 U ⤵ ➤ ⚙

It's all quality-assessed accommodation

Our commitment to quality involves wide-ranging accommodation assessment. Rating and awards were correct at the time of going to press but may change following a new assessment. Please check at time of booking.

BLACKWATER, Cornwall Map ref 1B3

★★★★
TOURING &
CAMPING PARK
ROSE AWARD

⊞ (30) £10.00–£15.00
⊟ (30) £10.00–£15.00
Å (30) £10.00–£15.00
⊟ (20) £140.00–£550.00
30 touring pitches

Trevarth Holiday Park

Blackwater, Truro TR4 8HR **t** (01872) 560266 **f** (01872) 560379 **e** trevarth@lineone.net
w trevarth.co.uk

payment Credit/debit cards, cash/cheques

Luxury caravan holiday homes, touring and camping.
A small, quiet park conveniently situated for north-
and south-coast resorts. Level touring and tent
pitches with electric hook-up. Open April to October.

⊕ Leave A30 at Chiverton roundabout (signed St Agnes). At
the next roundabout take the road to Blackwater. Park on
right after 200m.

General 🖃 🔌 🗘 🍴 ⊞ 🔘 ⊙ 🖽🗐 ☼ Leisure 🔦 🏕

BLANDFORD FORUM, Dorset Map ref 2B3

★★★★
TOURING &
CAMPING PARK

⊞ £12.00–£18.50
125 touring pitches

The Inside Park

Down House Estate, Blandford St Mary, Blandford Forum DT11 9AD **t** (01258) 453719
f (01258) 459921 **e** inspark@aol.com **w** members.aol.com/inspark/inspark

Secluded park and woodland with facilities built
into 18thC stable and coach house. Ideal location
for touring the county. One-and-a-half miles south
west of Blandford on road to Winterborne
Stickland. Open 1 April to 31 October.

payment Credit/debit cards, cash/cheques

General 🖃 P 🔌 🗘 🍴 🔘 ⊙ 🖽🗐 🖢 🐾 ☼ Leisure 🔦 🏕 ∪ ⚓

BRATTON CLOVELLY, Devon Map ref 1C2

★★★★
HOLIDAY, TOURING
& CAMPING PARK

⊞ (5) £11.50–£18.00
⊟ (20) £11.50–£18.00
Å (20) £11.50–£18.00
25 touring pitches

South Breazle Holidays

Okehampton EX20 4JS **t** (01837) 871752 **e** louise@southbreazleholidays.co.uk
w southbreazleholidays.co.uk

payment Credit/debit cards, cash/cheques

This peaceful family-owned site with 25 super-sized
pitches is set within a 100-acre organic farm, close to
Dartmoor and two miles from Roadford Lake. Well-
appointed shower block with power showers, on-site
shop. Wi-Fi. An ideal place to unwind, and explore
the local area. Open 1 March to 31 October.

⊕ Exit A30 at Stowford Cross. Follow signs for Roadford Lake.
After 1 mile turn right, then 2nd left (staggered
crossroads). 1st farm lane on right.

♥ Get 10% discount when you book 15 nights or more in low
or mid-season.

General 🖃 P 🔌 🍴 ⊞ 🔘 ⊙ 🗐 🖢 ☼ Leisure 🏕 ⚓

BRAUNTON, Devon Map ref 1C1

★★★★
TOURING &
CAMPING PARK

⊞ (100) £8.00–£24.00
⊟ (40) £8.00–£24.00
Å (40) £6.00–£24.00
180 touring pitches

Lobb Fields Caravan and Camping Park

Saunton Road, Braunton EX33 1EB **t** (01271) 812090 **f** (01271) 812090 **e** info@lobbfields.com
w lobbfields.com

Fourteen-acre grassy park with panoramic views
across the Taw Estuary. Situated one mile from
Braunton centre on B3231 and 1.5 miles from
Saunton beach and Biosphere reserve. Open
15 March to 26 October.

payment Credit/debit cards, cash/cheques

General 🖃 P 🔌 🗘 🍴 🔘 ⊙ 🖽🗐 🐾 🚗 ☼ Leisure 🏕 ∪ ⚓ ⚙

BREAN, Somerset Map ref 1D1

★★★
**TOURING &
CAMPING PARK**

🚐 (40)   £7.00–£13.00
🚍 (40)   £7.00–£13.00
⛺ (80)   £7.00–£13.00
200 touring pitches

Diamond Farm

Weston Road, Brean, Burnham-on-Sea TA8 2RL **t** (01278) 751263
e trevor@diamondfarm42.freeserve.co.uk **w** diamondfarm.co.uk

Quiet family site alongside River Axe and five minutes from beach. Fishing on site. Brean coast road and beach 800yds. Open March to October.

payment Cash/cheques

General 🏧 🖬 ♿ P 🔌 🛗 🚻 ☕ 🅰 ⊙ 📵 🛒 ✕ 🐕 🎯 ☼ Leisure 🎣 ∪ 🎿 ⚓

BREAN, Somerset Map ref 1D1

★★★★
**HOLIDAY, TOURING
& CAMPING PARK**

🚐 (350)   £6.25–£20.00
🚍 (350)   £6.25–£20.00
⛺ (150)   £6.25–£17.00
350 touring pitches

Northam Farm Touring Park

Brean Sands, Burnham-on-Sea TA8 2SE **t** (01278) 751244 **f** (01278) 751150
e enquiries@northamfarm.co.uk **w** northamfarm.co.uk

payment Credit/debit cards, cash

Attractive and well established family-run touring park situated 200m from five miles of sandy beach. 30-acre park offering children's outdoor play areas, fishing lake, cafe, mini-supermarket, launderette, dog walks, hardstanding and grass pitches. The Seagull Inn, our own family entertainment venue and restaurant, is within 600m. Open March to October.

⊕ M5 jct 22. Follow signs to Burnham-on-Sea, Brean. Continue through Brean and Northam Farm is on the right, 0.5 miles past Brean Leisure Park.

General P 🔌 🛗 🚻 ♿ 🅰 ⊙ 📵 🛒 ✕ 🐕 🎯 ☼ Leisure 🎣 ∪ 🎿 🚲

BREAN, Somerset Map ref 1D1

★★★★
**HOLIDAY, TOURING
& CAMPING PARK**

🚐   £7.00–£14.50
🚍   £7.00–£14.50
⛺   £7.00–£14.50
🏠 (11) £180.00–£480.00
575 touring pitches

Warren Farm Holiday Centre

Warren Road, Brean Sands, Burnham-on-Sea TA8 2RP **t** (01278) 751227 **f** (01278) 751033
e enquiries@warren-farm.co.uk **w** warren-farm.co.uk

Award-winning, family-run holiday centre close to beach. Friendly atmosphere, high standards of cleanliness, modern facilities and excellent value. Grass pitches, indoor/outdoor play facilities, pub, restaurant, nightly entertainment in high season. Open April to October.

payment Credit/debit cards, cash/cheques

General 🖬 P 🔌 🛗 🚻 ♿ 🅰 ⊙ 📵 🛒 ✕ 🐕 🎯 ☼ Leisure 📺 🍽 🎵 🍷 🎣 ∪ 🎿 🚲

BRIDGWATER, Somerset Map ref 1D1

★★★
TOURING &
CAMPING PARK

🚐 £9.00–£16.50
🚐 £9.00–£16.50
⛺ £4.00–£40.00
200 touring pitches

Fairways International Touring Caravan and Camping Park

Bath Road, Bawdrip, Bridgwater TA7 8PP t (01278) 685569 f (01278) 685569
e holiday@fairwaysinternational.co.uk w fairwaysinternational.co.uk

payment Credit/debit cards, cash/cheques, euros

International touring park in countryside, two miles off motorway in Glastonbury direction. On-site accessory centre for tents, caravans and motor homes. Storage, store and stay, storage on pitch, seasonals and rallies welcomed. Tents charged on size; caravans and motor homes charged on length. Fishing one mile, seaside six miles. Open 1 March to mid-November.

⊕ From M5 take signs towards Glastonbury/Street. At junction, again head towards Glastonbury/Street. Take left turning to Woolavington, approx 75yds on right. Park is behind garage.

❤ Senior Citizen weeks during Mar, Jun, Sep and Oct: all English and international camping cards accepted; caravan/ motorhome and hook-up for two people – £10 daily, £55.00 weekly.

General 🗺 🚫 P 🔌 🖰 🍴 🍲 📻 ☉ 📧 🖥 🔧 🐕 ☀ Leisure 📺 🔍 ⚓ 🎵

BRIDPORT, Dorset Map ref 2A3

★★★★
HOLIDAY, TOURING
& CAMPING PARK

🚐 (350) £11.00–£31.00
🚐 (50) £11.00–£31.00
⛺ (100) £11.00–£31.00
🏠 (60) £160.00–£740.00
500 touring pitches

Freshwater Beach Holiday Park

Burton Bradstock, Bridport DT6 4PT t (01308) 897317 f (01308) 897336
e office@freshwaterbeach.co.uk w freshwaterbeach.co.uk

payment Credit/debit cards, cash/cheques

Family park with a large touring and camping field. Own private beach on Dorset's spectacular World Heritage Coastline. Surrounded by countryside and within easy reach of Dorset's features and attractions. Free nightly family entertainment and children's activities. Horse and pony rides, donkey derby, beach fishing, cliff and seaside walks. Open mid-March to mid-November.

⊕ From Bridport take B3157, situated 2 miles on the right.

❤ Pitch prices include up to 6 people and club membership.

General 🗺 P 🔌 🖰 🍴 🍲 📻 ☉ 📧 🖥 🔧 ✕ 🐕 ☀ Leisure 🎣 📺 🍷 🎵 🔍 ⚓ ∪ 🎵

BRIDPORT, Dorset Map ref 2A3

★★★★★
HOLIDAY, TOURING
& CAMPING PARK
ROSE AWARD

🚐 £15.00–£27.00
🚐 £15.00–£27.00
⛺ (159) £13.00–£22.00
🏠 (12) £220.00–£560.00
108 touring pitches

Golden Cap Holiday Park

Seatown, Chideock, Bridport DT6 6JX t (01308) 422139 f (01308) 425672 e holidays@wdlh.co.uk
w wdlh.co.uk

One hundred metres from beach overlooked by Dorset's highest cliff top – Golden Cap – surrounded by countryside on this Heritage Coast. Open March to November.

payment Credit/debit cards, cash/cheques

General P 🔌 🖰 🍴 📻 ☉ 📧 🖥 🔧 🐕 ☀ Leisure ⚓ 🎵

Key to symbols
Open the back flap for a key to symbols.

BRIDPORT, Dorset Map ref 2A3

★★★★★
HOLIDAY, TOURING
& CAMPING PARK
ROSE AWARD

🚐	£15.00–£24.00
🚏	£15.00–£24.00
▲ (75)	£10.00–£18.00
🏠 (18)	£220.00–£560.00

120 touring pitches

Highlands End Holiday Park

Eype, Bridport DT6 6AR t (01308) 422139 f (01308) 425672 e holidays@wdlh.co.uk w wdlh.co.uk

Quiet, select, family park overlooking sea with exceptional views of Heritage Coast and Lyme Bay. Indoor swimming pool. Open March to November.

payment Credit/debit cards, cash/cheques

General ⬛ P 🚐 🖙 🚽 🚐 📻 ☺ 🚿 🛒 ✕ 🐴 ☼ Leisure 🎣 🍽 🔍 ⛰ 🎯 ✈ ⚓

BRISTOL, City of Bristol Map ref 2A2

★★★★
TOURING PARK

🚐 (55)	£14.30–£27.70
🚏 (55)	£14.30–£27.70

55 touring pitches

See Ad on inside front cover

THE
CARAVAN
CLUB

Baltic Wharf Caravan Club Site

Cumberland Road, Bristol BS1 6XG t (0117) 926 8030 w caravanclub.co.uk

open All year
payment Credit/debit cards, cash/cheques

A waterside site, right in the heart of Bristol's beautifully redeveloped dockland. Linked in the summer by a river ferry to the city centre. For families there is the zoo and Downs Park; a safe place for young children to play in and an ideal picnic spot.

⊕ M5 jct 18, A4, under bridge. Left lane, follow Historic Harbour/SS Great Britain, into Hotwells Road. Right lane at lights, left lane after pedestrian crossing. Over bridge, site on left.

♥ Special member rates mean you can save your membership subscription in less than a week. Visit our website to find out more.

General P 🚐 🖙 🚽 🚐 📻 🚿 📻 ☼ Leisure ▶

BRIXHAM, Devon Map ref 1D2

★★★★
TOURING &
CAMPING PARK

🚐 (60)	£9.60–£17.20
🚏 (10)	£9.60–£17.20
▲ (60)	£9.60–£17.20
🏠 (4)	£205.00–£515.00

120 touring pitches

Galmpton Touring Park

Greenway Road, Galmpton, Brixham TQ5 0EP t (01803) 842066
e galmptontouringpark@hotmail.com w galmptontouringpark.co.uk

payment Credit/debit cards, cash/cheques

Overlooking the River Dart with superb views from pitches. A quiet base for families and couples to explore Torbay and South Devon. Self-catering cottages available. Open Easter to September.

⊕ Take A380 Torbay ring road then A379 to Brixham. Take 2nd right to Galmpton Park through village to park. Site signposted.

♥ Off-peak reductions.

General ⬛ P 🚐 🖙 🚽 📻 🚿 📻 🛒 🐴 ☼ Leisure ⛰ ✈

Take a break

Look out for special promotions and themed breaks. This could be your chance to indulge an interest, find a new one, or just relax and enjoy exceptional value. Offers (highlighted in colour) are subject to availability.

BRIXHAM, Devon Map ref 1D2

★★★★★
TOURING &
CAMPING PARK

🚐 (239) £14.30–£32.00
🚎 (239) £14.30–£32.00
▲   on application
239 touring pitches

See Ad on inside front cover

THE
CARAVAN
CLUB

Hillhead Holiday Park Caravan Club Site

Hillhead, Brixham TQ5 0HH t (01803) 853204 w caravanclub.co.uk

payment Credit/debit cards, cash/cheques

In a great location, with many pitches affording stunning sea views. Swimming pool, evening entertainment, bar, restaurant and much more! Open March to January 2009.

⊕ Right off A380 (Newton Abbot). Three miles onto ring road (Brixham). Seven miles turn right, A3022. In 0.75 miles, right onto A379. Two miles keep left onto B3025. Site entrance on left.

♥ Special member rates mean you can save your membership subscription in less than a week. Visit our website to find out more.

General P 🚗 🅿 🍴 🚼 🗺 📻 ☉ 💷 🗑 🛒 ✕ 🐾 ☼   Leisure ⌇ 📺 🍷 🎵 🔍 🎣 ∪

BUDE, Cornwall Map ref 1C2

★★★★★
TOURING PARK

🚐 (145) £9.00–£24.00
🚎 (145) £9.00–£24.00
▲ (145) £9.00–£24.00
145 touring pitches

Budemeadows Park

Budemeadows, Bude EX23 0NA t (01288) 361646 f 0870 7064825 e infootb@budemeadows.com
w budemeadows.com

open All year
payment Credit/debit cards, cash/cheques

Superb centre for surfing, scenery and sightseeing. All usual facilities including heated pool, licensed bar, shop, launderette, playground. Well kept and maintained grounds.

⊕ Signposted on A39, 3 miles south of Bude, 200yds past crossroad to Widemouth Bay.

♥ Discounts for large families and longer stays. Please phone for details.

General 🗺 🚗 P 🚗 🅿 🍴 🚼 📻 ☉ 💷 🗑 🛒 🐾 ☼   Leisure ⌇ 📺 🍷 🔍 🎣 ∪ 🏊

BUDE, Cornwall Map ref 1C2

★★★★
HOLIDAY &
TOURING PARK

🚐 (20) £8.50–£19.50
🚎 (20) £8.50–£19.50
▲ (20) £8.50–£19.50
🏠 (150) £102.00–
          £579.00
60 touring pitches

Sandymouth Bay Holiday Park

Sandymouth Bay, Bude EX23 9HW t (01288) 352563 f (01288) 354822
e reception@sandymouthbay.co.uk w sandymouthbay.co.uk

payment Credit/debit cards, cash/cheques

Friendly family park set in 24 acres of meadowland in an area rich with beautiful beaches, bustling coastal resorts and picturesque fishing villages. Inland, the rolling countryside is a fascinating contrast to the rugged coast. Licensed club, indoor pool, sauna, crazy golf, toilets and launderette. Open March to October.

⊕ On M5 from north, exit jct 27. Travel on A361/A39 towards Bude. Just past the village of Kilkhampton, take right-hand turning signposted Sandymouth.

♥ Various promotions for certain times of the year – call us or see website.

General 🔥 🗺 🚗 P 🚗 🅿 🍴 📻 ☉ 💷 🗑 🛒 ✕ ☼   Leisure ⌇ 📺 🍷 🎵 🔍 🎣 ∪ 🏊 🚲

Using map references
Map references refer to the colour maps at the front of this guide.

BUDE, Cornwall Map ref 1C2

★★★★
HOLIDAY, TOURING
& CAMPING PARK

⛺ (65) £8.50–£15.50
🚐 (65) £8.50–£15.50
⛺ (65) £8.50–£15.50
🏠 (18) £155.00–£495.00
65 touring pitches

Upper Lynstone Caravan and Camping Site

Upton, Bude EX23 0LP **t** (01288) 352017 **f** (01288) 359034 **e** reception@upperlynstone.co.uk
w upperlynstone.co.uk

A quiet family-run park just 0.75 miles from the sandy beach and town centre. Enjoy the beauty of the coastal path from our site. Spacious camping and electric hook-up patches. Modern, well-equipped caravans for hire. Families and couples only. Open Easter to October.

⊕ *Half a mile south of Bude on coastal road to Widemouth Bay. Signposted.*

payment Credit/debit cards, cash/cheques

General P ⛽ 🅲 🕯 🏧 ☺ 🛢 🔌 🐕   Leisure ⛰ ∪ ♪

BUDE, Cornwall Map ref 1C2

★★★★★
HOLIDAY &
TOURING PARK

⛺ (50) £14.00–£24.00
🚐 (50) £14.00–£24.00
⛺ (40) £14.00–£24.00
🏠 (55) £190.00–£720.00
60 touring pitches

Wooda Farm Park

Poughill, Bude EX23 9HJ **t** (01288) 352069 **f** (01288) 355258 **e** enquiries@wooda.co.uk
w wooda.co.uk

Stunning views over Bude Bay and countryside; 1.5 miles from safe, sandy beaches. Family-owned and run with all facilities, fishing, sports barn, tennis court, woodland walks, golf. An ideal base. Open April to October.

payment Credit/debit cards, cash/cheques

General 📺 ⚡ P ⛽ 🅲 🕯 🚐 🏧 ☺ 🛢 🔌 🐕 🐾 ☀   Leisure 📺 ◉ ⛰ ⚲ ♪ ▶ ⛾

BURNHAM-ON-SEA, Somerset Map ref 1D1

Home Farm HOLIDAY PARK

Welcome to Somerset's ultimate holiday destination set in forty-four acres of beautiful parkland.

Home Farm has everything you could wish for to make your holiday a truly memorable experience, with fun for all the family including:

• Top-class entertainment in the Home Farm Country Club.
• A new colourful, safe playground for the children.
• Home Farm Country Club restaurant and bar and all day takeaway.

We have some great summer offers so why not give us a call today or check out our new website:

www.homefarmholidaypark.co.uk

The UK's favourite holiday park runner up in 2003 – voted by the readers of Caravan Magazine.

Booking hotline
01278 788888

Get away...

BURTON BRADSTOCK, Dorset Map ref 2A3

★★★
HOLIDAY, TOURING
& CAMPING PARK

⛺   £11.00–£19.00
🚐   £11.00–£19.00
⛺   £9.00–£16.00
40 touring pitches

Coastal Caravan Park

Annings Lane, Burton Bradstock, Bridport DT6 4QP **t** (01308) 897361 **f** (01308) 425672
e holidays@wdlh.co.uk **w** wdlh.co.uk

Small, non-commercial park in beautiful surroundings, situated 2.5 miles from A35 east of Bridport. Mainly privately-owned caravan holiday homes. Open April to September.

payment Credit/debit cards, cash/cheques

General P ⛽ 🕯 🏧 ☺ 🛢 🔌 🐕 ☀   Leisure ▶

If you have access needs...

Look for the National Accessible Scheme symbols if you have special hearing, visual or mobility needs.

CHARMOUTH, Dorset Map ref 1D2

★★★
HOLIDAY, TOURING & CAMPING PARK

(300) £10.00–£19.00
(300) £10.00–£19.00
(300) £10.00–£19.00
(6) £200.00–£650.00
300 touring pitches

Manor Farm Holiday Centre

The Street, Charmouth, Bridport DT6 6QL **t** (01297) 560226 **f** (01297) 560429
e enq@manorfarmholidaycentre.co.uk **w** manorfarmholidaycentre.co.uk

Large, open site in Area of Outstanding Natural Beauty close to the sea. From east end of Charmouth bypass, come into Charmouth and the site is 0.75 miles on the right.

open All year
payment Credit/debit cards, cash/cheques

General Leisure

CHARMOUTH, Dorset Map ref 1D2

★★★★
TOURING & CAMPING PARK

£12.60–£16.50
£12.60–£16.50
£12.60–£16.50
180 touring pitches

Monkton Wyld Farm Caravan & Camping Park

Monkton Wyld, Bridport DT6 6DB **t** (01297) 631131 **f** (01297) 33594 **e** simonkewley@mac.com
w monktonwyld.co.uk

Beautifully landscaped, level park. Only three miles from sandy beaches and surrounded by lovely countryside. Excellent access, yet away from noisy main roads. All the amenities of a quality park. Open mid-March to end October.

payment Credit/debit cards, cash/cheques, euros

General Leisure

CHARMOUTH, Dorset Map ref 1D2

SEADOWN HOLIDAY PARK

Bridge Road, Charmouth, Dorset DT6 6QS

Quiet family run park situated on Dorset's World Heritage Coast. The park has its own direct access to Charmouth's famous fossil beach.

T: (01297) 560154 F: (01297) 561130 www.seadownholidaypark.co.uk

CHARMOUTH, Dorset Map ref 1D2

★★★★★
HOLIDAY, TOURING & CAMPING PARK

(186) £12.50–£26.00
£12.50–£26.00
(20) £10.50–£22.00
(3) £220.00–£565.00
206 touring pitches

Wood Farm Caravan and Camping Park

Charmouth, Bridport DT6 6BT **t** (01297) 560697 **f** (01297) 561243 **e** holidays@woodfarm.co.uk
w woodfarm.co.uk

payment Credit/debit cards, cash/cheques

Breathtaking views and superb facilities are both on offer at Wood Farm. Our Heritage Coast and spectacular rural scenery are just waiting to amaze you. Open Easter to October.

From M5 jct 25 follow A358 to Chard then Axminster. Join A35 towards Bridport. After 4 miles, at roundabout take 1st exit to Wood Farm.

Low- and mid-season offers for 1- and 2-week stays.

General Leisure

To your credit

If you book by phone you may be asked for your credit card number. If so, it is advisable to check the proprietor's policy in case you have to cancel your reservation at a later date.

CHEDDAR, Somerset Map ref 1D1

★★★★
HOLIDAY, TOURING
& CAMPING PARK
ROSE AWARD

🚐 (100) £13.00–£25.00
🚎 (20) £11.00–£19.00
⛺ (80) £13.00–£24.00
🏠 (37) £180.00–£600.00
200 touring pitches

Broadway House Holiday Touring Caravan and Camping Park

Axbridge Road, Cheddar BS27 3DB t (01934) 742610 f (01934) 744950
e info@broadwayhouse.uk.com w broadwayhouse.uk.com

payment Credit/debit cards, cash/cheques, euros

Nestling at the foot of the Mendip Hills, this family run park is only one mile, and the closest of its kind to England's Grand Canyon: Cheddar Gorge. We have every facility your family could ever want: shop, bar, launderette, swimming pool, BMX track, skateboard park, nature trails, archery, caving and canoeing. Open March to November.

⊕ M5 jct 22. Eight miles. Midway between Cheddar and Axbridge on A371.

General 🖼 P ⊕ ⚲ 🚽 🚱 ⋒ ☉ 📶 ▣ ✕ 🐕 ⚡ ☼ Leisure ⬞ 📺 🍴 🔍 ⋔ ∪ ♪ ▶ 🚲

CHRISTCHURCH, Dorset Map ref 2B3

★★★
CAMPING PARK

🚐 (60) £13.00–£22.00
🚎 (60) £13.00–£22.00
⛺ (14) £13.00–£19.00
60 touring pitches

Harrow Wood Farm Caravan Park

Poplar Lane, Bransgore, Christchurch BH23 8JE t (01425) 672487 f (01425) 672487
e harrowwood@caravan-sites.co.uk w caravan-sites.co.uk

Quiet site bordered by woods and meadows. Take A35 from Lyndhurst, after approximately 11 miles turn right at Cat and Fiddle pub, site approximately 1.5 miles into Bransgore, first right after school. Open 1 March to 6 January.

payment Credit/debit cards, cash/cheques

General P ⊕ 🚽 🚱 ⚲ ⋒ ☉ 📶 ▣ ☼ Leisure ∪ ♪ 🚲

COMBE MARTIN, Devon Map ref 1C1

★★★★
TOURING &
CAMPING PARK

🚐 (610) £7.50–£21.25
🚎 (50) £8.50–£21.25
⛺ (50) £7.50–£24.25
710 touring pitches

Stowford Farm Meadows

Combe Martin, Ilfracombe EX34 0PW t (01271) 882476 f (01271) 883053
e enquiries@stowford.co.uk w stowford.co.uk

open All year
payment Credit/debit cards, cash/cheques

Recent winner of numerous awards and situated on the fringe of the Exmoor National Park, this park has a reputation for superb facilities and unrivalled value.

⊕ Situated on the A3123 Woolacombe to Combe Martin road, 4 miles west of Combe Martin.

♥ Low season: one week, only £39.90 (incl electric hook-up). Mid season: one week, only £59.90 (incl electric hook-up).

General 🖼 P ⊕ ⚲ 🚽 🚱 ⋒ 📶 ▣ 🚱 ✕ 🐕 ⚡ ☼ Leisure ⬞ 📺 🍴 🎵 🔍 ⋔ ∪ ♪ ▶ 🚲

WALKERS
WELCOME

WALKERS
WELCOME

Best foot forward

Walkers feel at home in accommodation participating in our Walkers Welcome scheme. Look out for the symbol. Consider walking all or part of a long-distance route – go online at nationaltrail.co.uk.

CONNOR DOWNS, Cornwall Map ref 1B3

★★★★
TOURING &
CAMPING PARK

🚐 (82) £10.00–£22.00
🚏 (82) £10.00–£22.00
⛺ (82) £10.00–£22.00
82 touring pitches

Higher Trevaskis Park

Gwinear Road, Connor Downs, Hayle TR27 5JQ t (01209) 831736

Big enough to cope, small enough to care! Friendly and secluded family-run countryside park. Well placed for local beaches. Terraced, level pitches in small enclosures to ensure privacy. Prices are for two adults and two children. Open 12 April to 5 October.

payment Cash/cheques

General 🖼 🏕 P 🔌 🕐 🚽 🎢 ☉ 🛢 🔖 ♨

CORFE CASTLE, Dorset Map ref 2B3

★★
HOLIDAY, TOURING
& CAMPING PARK

🚐 Min £11.00
🚏 Min £11.00
⛺ (60) Min £8.50
52 touring pitches

Norden Farm Campsite

Norden Farm, Wareham BH20 5DS t (01929) 480098 e nordenfarm@fsmail.net w nordenfarm.com

payment Credit/debit cards, cash/cheques

Level fields on working farm site in the beautiful Purbeck Valley. Excellent toilet/shower facilities. Good family location. Set away from main road but with easy access. Family-run business with adjoining farm shop and bed and breakfast with licensed restaurant open to non-residents. Open 1 March to 31 October.

⊕ A351 Wareham to Corfe Castle, follow signs for Norden Park'n'Ride and look for us on right-hand side as Castle comes into view.

♥ High season – 5% discount for 7 nights or more.

General P 🔌 🕐 🚽 🎢 ☉ 🛢 🔖 ✗ 🐴 ♨ Leisure ∪ 🎣 🏹 🚴

CORFE CASTLE, Dorset Map ref 2B3

★★
CAMPING PARK

🚏 (150) £10.00
⛺ (150) £10.00

Woodyhyde Farm Camping Park

Afflington, Corfe Castle, Wareham BH20 5HT t (01929) 480274 e camp@woodyhyde.fsnet.co.uk w woodyhyde.co.uk

Secluded family site. Easy access to beaches and local attractions. Ideal centre for walking holidays. Steam train station nearby. Open Easter to October.

payment Credit/debit cards, cash/cheques

General 🏕 P 🔌 🕐 🚽 🚇 🎢 ☉ 🔖 🐴 ♨ Leisure ∪ 🎣 🏹 🚴

COTSWOLDS

See under Moreton-in-Marsh, Tewkesbury
See also Cotswolds in South East England section

CRACKINGTON HAVEN, Cornwall Map ref 1C2

★★★
HOLIDAY, TOURING
& CAMPING PARK

🚐 (20) £10.00–£16.50
🚏 (12) £10.00–£16.50
⛺ (35) £10.00–£16.50
🚃 (8) £160.00–£560.00
43 touring pitches

Hentervene Caravan & Camping Park

Crackington Haven, Bude EX23 0LF t (01840) 230365 f (01840) 230065
e contact@hentervene.co.uk w hentervene.co.uk

Peaceful park in an Area of Outstanding Natural Beauty. Sandy beaches and coastal path nearby. Spacious, level pitches. Modern caravans to hire/buy. Excellent base for exploring North Cornwall and Devon.

open All year
payment Credit/debit cards, cash/cheques

General 🏕 P 🔌 🕐 🚽 🎢 ☉ 🛢 🔖 🐴 ♨ Leisure 📺 🎱 ⛰ ∪ 🎣

DARTMOOR

See under Ashburton, Tavistock

DAWLISH, Devon Map ref 1D2

★★★★
HOLIDAY, TOURING
& CAMPING PARK
ROSE AWARD

🚐 (450) £13.00–£23.00
🚏 (450) £13.00–£23.00
⛺ (450) £13.00–£23.00
🏚 (66) £170.00–£675.00
450 touring pitches

Cofton Country Holidays

Cofton, Starcross, Exeter EX6 8RP t (01626) 890111 f (01626) 891572 e info@coftonholidays.co.uk
w coftonholidays.co.uk

payment Credit/debit cards, cash/cheques

A glorious corner of Devon. Family-run holiday park
in 30 acres of delightful parkland. Some of the finest
pitches in South Devon. Heated outdoor swimming
pools. Fun-packed visitor attractions to suit all. David
Bellamy Gold Conservation Award. Two minutes
from Blue Flag beach. Open April to October.

⊕ *A379 Exeter to Dawlish road, 3 miles Exeter side of
Dawlish.*

♥ *£2 off standard pitch per night, low and mid season. Senior
Citizens save an extra £1 each per night (advance
bookings, minimum 3 nights' stay).*

General 🔌 📺 P 🎣 🚻 🍴 📻 ⊙ 📞 🗄 🥤 ✕ ☼ Leisure 🎣 🍴 🔍 ⛰ 🎵

DAWLISH, Devon Map ref 1D2

DORCHESTER, Dorset Map ref 2B3

★★
TOURING &
CAMPING PARK

🚐 (50)   £7.00–£12.00
🚏 (50)   £7.00–£12.00
⛺ (50)   £7.00–£12.00
50 touring pitches

Giants Head Caravan & Camping Park

Old Sherborne Road, Dorchester DT2 7TR t (01300) 341242 e holidays@giantshead.co.uk
w giantshead.co.uk

Two miles north-east of Cerne Abbas, three miles   payment Cash/cheques
south of Middlemarsh, eight miles from
Dorchester.

General 🔌 📺 🚲 P 🎣 🚻 🍴 📻 ⊙ 🗄 🥾 ✈ Leisure 🎵 🏴

Discover Britain's heritage

Discover the history and beauty of over 250 of Britain's best-known
historic houses, castles, gardens and small manor houses. You can
purchase Britain's Historic Houses and Gardens – Guide and Map
from good bookshops and online at visitbritaindirect.com.

DULVERTON, Somerset Map ref 1D1

★ ★ ★ ★
TOURING PARK

🚐 (64) £12.10–£24.90
🚐 (64) £12.10–£24.90
64 touring pitches

See Ad on inside front cover

Exmoor House Caravan Club Site

Dulverton TA22 9HL **t** (01398) 323268 **w** caravanclub.co.uk

payment Credit/debit cards, cash/cheques

Very quiet and secluded, in the heart of Lorna Doone country. Shops and pubs within walking distance, Exmoor is on the doorstep. Leave your car behind and explore this walker's paradise. Open March to January 2009.

⊕ *From M5 jct 27, B3222 to Dulverton, left over river bridge, 200yds on. Note: 2 narrow hump bridges on B3222, approach carefully.*

♥ *Special member rates mean you can save your membership subscription in less than a week. Visit our website to find out more.*

General P 🚐 🕁 ♨ 🚻 🅿 ⊙ 📵 🐕

DULVERTON, Somerset Map ref 1D1

★ ★ ★ ★ ★
TOURING PARK

🚐 (80) £14.30–£27.70
🚐 (80) £14.30–£27.70
80 touring pitches

See Ad on inside front cover

Lakeside Caravan Club Site

Higher Grants, Exebridge, Dulverton TA22 9BE **t** (01398) 324068 **w** caravanclub.co.uk

payment Credit/debit cards, cash/cheques

Recently redeveloped, Lakeside has splendid new facilities and all pitches (now level) boast superb views of surrounding hills and the Exe Valley. Within easy reach of the National Park and Lorna Doone country. Open March to November.

⊕ *From A396 site on left within 2.5 miles.*

♥ *Special member rates mean you can save your membership subscription in less than a week. Visit our website to find out more.*

General P 🚐 🕁 🅿 📵 🐕 Leisure 🌙

EXMOOR

See under Combe Martin, Dulverton, Porlock, Winsford

EXMOUTH, Devon Map ref 1D2

Using map references

The map references refer to the colour maps at the front of this guide. The first figure is the map number, the letter and figure that follow indicate the grid reference on the map.

FOWEY, Cornwall Map ref 1B3

★★★★
TOURING &
CAMPING PARK

🚐 (65) £12.00–£18.00
� (65) £12.00–£18.00
⛺ (65) £12.00–£18.00
65 touring pitches

Penmarlam Caravan & Camping Park

Bodinnick by Fowey, Fowey PL23 1LZ **t** (01726) 870088 **f** (01726) 870082
e info@penmarlampark.co.uk **w** penmarlampark.co.uk

payment Credit/debit cards, cash/cheques, euros

A quiet, grassy site on the Fowey Estuary, an Area of Outstanding Natural Beauty. Choose from our lawned, sheltered field or enjoy breathtaking views from the upper field. Shop and off-licence, immaculately clean heated amenity block, electric hook-ups and serviced pitches, Wi-Fi Internet access, boat launching and storage adjacent. Open Easter to October.

⊕ *A38 in Dowballs, take A390 (signposted St Austell). In East Taphouse, left onto B3359 (signposted Looe, Polperro). After 5 miles, right (signposted Bodinnick, Fowey via ferry). Site 5 miles.*

General ... Leisure ...

GLASTONBURY, Somerset Map ref 2A2

★★★★★
HOLIDAY PARK

🚐 (60) £12.50–£19.00
� (20) £12.50–£19.00
⛺ (20) £12.50–£19.00
100 touring pitches

The Old Oaks Touring Park

Wick, Glastonbury BA6 8JS **t** (01458) 831437 **e** info@theoldoaks.co.uk **w** theoldoaks.co.uk

An award-winning park, exclusively for adults, set in tranquil, unspoilt countryside with panoramic views, offering spacious, landscaped pitches and excellent amenities. Open 1 March to 20 November.

payment Credit/debit cards, cash/cheques

General ... Leisure ...

HAYLE, Cornwall Map ref 1B3

★★★★
HOLIDAY, TOURING
& CAMPING PARK

🚐 £8.00–£24.50
� £8.00–£24.50
⛺ £8.00–£24.50
🏠 £85.00–£725.00
84 touring pitches

Beachside Holiday Park

Lethlean Lane, Phillack, Hayle TR27 5AW **t** (01736) 753080 **f** (01736) 757252
e reception@beachside.demon.co.uk **w** beachside.co.uk

Beachside is a family holiday park amidst sand dunes beside the sea in the famous St Ives Bay. Our location is ideal for the beach and for touring the whole of West Cornwall. Open Easter to October.

payment Credit/debit cards, cash/cheques

General ... Leisure ...

HELSTON, Cornwall Map ref 1B3

★★★★
HOLIDAY, TOURING
& CAMPING PARK

🚐 (13) £8.50–£12.50
� (13) £8.50–£12.50
⛺ (13) £8.50–£12.50
🏠 (7) £135.00–£465.00
13 touring pitches

Poldown Camping & Caravan Park

Carleen, Breage, Helston TR13 9NN **t** (01326) 574560 **f** (01326) 574560 **e** info@poldown.co.uk
w poldown.co.uk

Small and pretty countryside site. Peace and quiet guaranteed. Within easy reach of West Cornwall's beaches, walks and attractions. Very good touring facilities. Modern holiday caravans.

payment Cash/cheques, euros

General ... Leisure ...

It's all in the detail

Please remember that all information in this guide has been supplied by the proprietors well in advance of publication. Since changes do sometimes occur it's a good idea to check details at the time of booking.

ILFRACOMBE, Devon Map ref 1C1

★ ★ ★ ★ ★
HOLIDAY PARK
🚐 (27) £175.00–£700.00

Beachside Holiday Park

33 Beach Road, Hele, Ilfracombe EX34 9QZ t (01271) 863006 f (01271) 867296
e enquiries@beachsidepark.co.uk w beachsidepark.co.uk

open All year
payment Credit/debit cards, cash/cheques

At Beachside, sea views and the beach are right outside your door; you don't have to get in the car and drive. Peaceful, relaxing, tranquil, unspoilt, quiet, great for all ages and families alike – these are words often used to describe a holiday at Beachside. Open all year round.

⊕ Just off the A399 between Ilfracombe and Combe Martin.

♥ Short breaks out of high season. For specials see our website.

General ⌂ P ℝ 🗐 🐕 ☼ Leisure ∪ ⤨ ►

ILFRACOMBE, Devon Map ref 1C1

★ ★ ★ ★
HOLIDAY, TOURING
& CAMPING PARK
ROSE AWARD

🚐 (8) £11.00–£22.00
▲ (50) £11.00–£27.00
🚐 (20) £180.00–£710.00

Hele Valley Holiday Park

Hele Bay, Ilfracombe EX34 9RD t (01271) 862460 f (01271) 867926 e holidays@helevalley.co.uk
w helevalley.co.uk

open All year
payment Credit/debit cards, cash/cheques

A family-run haven set in a charming peaceful valley within walking distance of Hele Bay beach and Ilfracombe town. An ideal location for touring the beautiful rugged North Devon coastline. Luxury accommodation with private spas. Hele Valley has everything you need for a perfectly peaceful holiday.

⊕ From Ilfracombe High Street travel east towards Combe Martin. Swimming baths on your left then follow brown tourist signs for Hele Valley.

General ⌂ 🖥 P 🔌 ◔ 🚻 🚐 ℝ ☺ 🗐 🔠 🐕 ⛺ ☼ Leisure ⟁ ∪ ⤨ ► 🚲

KENTISBEARE, Devon Map ref 1D2

★ ★ ★ ★
HOLIDAY &
TOURING PARK
ROSE AWARD

🚐 £12.50–£17.00
🚐 £12.50–£17.00
▲ £10.00–£14.00
🚐 (26) £185.00–£450.00
80 touring pitches

Forest Glade Holiday Park

Kentisbeare, Cullompton EX15 2DT t (01404) 841381 f (01404) 841593
e nwellard@forest-glade.co.uk w forest-glade.co.uk

payment Credit/debit cards, cash/cheques

Free indoor heated pool on small, family-managed park surrounded by forest with deer. Large, flat, sheltered pitches. Luxury, all-serviced holiday homes for hire. Open mid-March to end of October.

⊕ From Honiton, take Dunkerswell road, follow Forest Glade signs. From M5, A373, 2.5 miles at Keepers Cottage inn then 2.5 miles on Sheldon road.

♥ Club members £1 per night discount on pitch fees. Short breaks available in holiday homes during most of season. Pet-free and non-smoking holiday homes available.

General ⌂ 🖥 🖥 P 🔌 ◔ 🚻 🚐 ℝ ☺ 🗐 🔠 🐕 ☼ Leisure ⛲ 🎣 ⟁ 🎱 ∪ ⤨

Check it out
Please check prices, quality ratings and other details when you book.

LACOCK, Wiltshire Map ref 2B2

★★★★★
TOURING &
CAMPING PARK

🚐 (39) £12.50–£14.50
🚎 (39) £12.50–£14.50
⛺ (4)   £12.50–£14.50
43 touring pitches

Piccadilly Caravan Park Ltd

Folly Lane (West), Lacock, Chippenham SN15 2LP t (01249) 730260 e piccadillylacock@aol.com

This well-maintained and peaceful site stands in open countryside 0.5 miles from the historic National Trust village of Lacock. Open April to October.

payment Cash/cheques

General P 🔌 🗗 🍴 🌂 ☺ 📮 🔆 ⛺ ✿ Leisure ⛰ 🚣

LANDRAKE, Cornwall Map ref 1C2

Rating Applied For
TOURING &
CAMPING PARK

🚐 (60) £10.80–£18.60
🚎 (60) £10.80–£18.60
⛺ (11) £3.50–£18.60
60 touring pitches

Dolbeare Caravan & Camping Park

St Ive Road, Landrake, Saltash PL12 5AF t (01752) 851332 f (01752) 547871
e reception@dolbeare.co.uk w dolbeare.co.uk

open All year
payment Credit/debit cards, cash/cheques

Friendly, well-maintained park which offers you that personal touch. Set amidst rolling countryside from which to explore varied coastal resorts. Enjoy both Cornwall and Devon from Dolbeare. Internet and Wi-Fi available.

General 🖥 P 🔌 🗗 🍴 🌐 🌂 ☺ 📮 🔆 ✿ Leisure ⛰ 🚣 🏇

LAND'S END, Cornwall Map ref 1A3

★★★
TOURING &
CAMPING PARK

🚐   £8.00–£14.50
🚎   £8.00–£14.50
⛺   £8.00–£14.50
105 touring pitches

Cardinney Caravan & Camping Park

Penberth Valley, St Buryan, Penzance TR19 6HJ t (01736) 810880 f (01736) 810998
e cardinney@btinternet.com w cardinney-camping-park.co.uk

Quiet, family-run site set in rural area. Peaceful, central for the Land's End peninsula.

payment Credit/debit cards, cash/cheques

General P 🔌 🗗 🍴 🌂 ☺ 🔆 ✕ ✿ Leisure 📺 🍴 ⚓ ∪

LANIVET, Cornwall Map ref 1B2

★★★
HOLIDAY PARK

🏠 (5) £150.00–£330.00

Kernow Caravan Park

Clann Lane, Lanivet, Bodmin PL30 5HD t (01208) 831343

payment Cash/cheques

Kernow Caravan Park is quiet and peaceful, in a tranquil setting. Personally supervised by a Cornish family. An ideal touring location to visit Eden Project, Heligan Lost Gardens, Lanhydrock, Camel Trail, Saints Way or Wenford Steam Railway. Site is a few minutes' walk from Lanivet village shop, pub, fish and chip restaurant. Open March to October.

⊕ *Leave A30 Innis Downs roundabout. Follow sign to Lanivet 0.75 miles. Left in village centre, opposite shop. Along Clann Lane 300m left into concrete drive.*

♥ *Weekend and mini-breaks subject to availability.*

General P 📮 ☀

Confirm your booking

It's always advisable to confirm your booking in writing.

LOOE, Cornwall Map ref 1C2

★ ★ ★ ★
HOLIDAY, TOURING
& CAMPING PARK

⌂ (100)	£9.20–£14.00
⊞ (40)	£9.20–£14.00
Å (100)	£9.20–£14.00
⌷ (100)	£120.00–£450.00

240 touring pitches

Tencreek Caravan Park

Polperro Road, Looe PL13 2JR t (01503) 262447 f (01503) 262760 e reception@tencreek.co.uk
w dolphinholidays.co.uk

open All year
payment Credit/debit cards, cash/cheques

Lying close to the South Cornwall coast, in a rural but not isolated position, Tencreek Holiday Park is ideal for exploring Cornwall and South Devon. Tencreek is the closest park to Looe and lies in Daphne du Maurier Country; beyond are Bodmin Moor, Dartmoor, traditional Cornish towns and picturesque beaches and ports.

⊕ *A38 from Tamar bridge. Left at roundabout. follow Looe signs. Right onto A387, becomes B3253. Through Looe towards Polperro. Tencreek 1.25 miles from Looe bridge.*

♥ *Various promotions for certain times of the year – call us or see website.*

General 🏕🍴P🍽🚻🚿♨☉🏪🛒✕🐕🎣☀ Leisure 🏊🎱🍷🎵🎯🏛⛵♣🚲

LYME REGIS, Dorset Map ref 1D2

10 acre level site • On the Devon & Dorset border • Pitches for tents, motor vans & caravans • Electric hook ups • Spacious modern shower block • Large children's play area • Crazy golf • Dog walking area • Rallies welcome • Off peak special offers • Colour brochure

ROUSDON • LYME REGIS • DORSET DT7 3XW
TEL: (01297) 442227 FAX (01297) 446086
email: enqshrubberypark@tiscali.co.uk
www.ukparks.co.uk/shrubbery

MEVAGISSEY, Cornwall Map ref 1B3

★ ★ ★ ★ ★
HOLIDAY, TOURING
& CAMPING PARK
ROSE AWARD

⌂ (189)	£7.00–£30.00
⊞ (189)	£7.00–£30.00
Å (189)	£7.00–£30.00
⌷ (38)	£149.00–£999.00

189 touring pitches

Sea View International

Boswinger, Gorran, St Austell PL26 6LL t (01726) 843425 f (01726) 843358
e holidays@seaviewinternational.com w seaviewinternational.com

payment Credit/debit cards, cash/cheques

Close to Eden Project and New Maritime Museum. AA's best campsite many times. 3.5 miles south west of Mevagissey, parkland setting with panoramic views. Luxury caravans and chalets, mains services, colour television etc. Statics: mid-March to end of October. Touring: May to end of September.

⊕ *From St Austell roundabout take B3273 to Mevagissey. Prior to village turn right and follow signs to Gorran and Gorran Haven and brown tourism signs to park.*

♥ *Please visit the website for special offers.*

General 🏕🖼🍴P🍽🚻🚿🍳♨☉🏪🛒🐕🎣☀ Leisure 🏊♣🏛♠⛵♣🚲

Suit yourself

The symbols at the end of each entry mean you can enjoy virtually made-to-measure accommodation with the services and facilities most important to you. A key to the symbols can be found inside the back-cover flap. Keep this open for easy reference.

MODBURY, Devon Map ref 1C3

★★★★
TOURING PARK
(112) £12.10–£24.90
(112) £12.10–£24.90
112 touring pitches

See Ad on inside front cover

Broad Park Caravan Club Site

Higher East Leigh, Modbury, Ivybridge PL21 0SH t (01548) 830714 w caravanclub.co.uk

payment Credit/debit cards, cash/cheques

Situated between moor and sea, this makes a splendid base from which to explore South Devon. Head for Dartmoor, or seek out the small villages of the South Hams. Open March to November.

⊕ From B3207, site on left.

♥ Midweek discount: pitch fee for standard pitches for stays on any Tue, Wed or Thu night outside peak season dates will be reduced by 50%.

General P 🔌 🖰 🚰 🍴 🛒 🐕 🏕.

MOORSHOP, Devon Map ref 1C2

★★★★
TOURING &
CAMPING PARK
(80)   £6.00–£12.00
(10)   £6.00–£12.00
(40)   £5.00–£12.00
(4) £150.00–£480.00
100 touring pitches

Higher Longford Caravan & Camping Park

Moorshop, Tavistock PL19 9LQ t (01822) 613360 f (01822) 618722 e stay@higherlongford.co.uk w higherlongford.co.uk

Beautiful, quiet family-run park with scenic views of Dartmoor. Spacious pitches, electric hook-ups, grass, hardstanding and multiserviced pitches available all year. Modern, clean and warm facilities. Dogs welcome. Ideal for Devon, Cornwall and Dartmoor.

open All year
payment Credit/debit cards, cash/cheques

General 🔧 P 🔌 🖰 🍴 🛒 🐕 🏕. ☼ Leisure 📺 🎯 U J ♪ ♿

MORETON-IN-MARSH, Gloucestershire Map ref 2B1

★★★★★
TOURING PARK
(182) £14.30–£27.70
(182) £14.30–£27.70
182 touring pitches

See Ad on inside front cover

Moreton-in-Marsh Caravan Club Site

Bourton Road, Moreton-in-Marsh GL56 0BT t (01608) 650519 w caravanclub.co.uk

open All year
payment Credit/debit cards, cash/cheques

An attractive, well-wooded site within easy walking distance of the market town of Moreton-in-Marsh. On-site facilities include crazy golf, volleyball and boules. Large dog-walking area.

⊕ From Moreton-in-Marsh on A44 the site entrance is on the right 250yds past the end of the speed limit sign.

♥ Special member rates mean you can save your membership subscription in less than a week. Visit our website to find out more.

General P 🔌 🖰 🍴 🚰 🍴 ⊙ 🛒 🐕 🏕. ☼ Leisure 🏕 J

MORTEHOE, Devon Map ref 1C1

★★★★
HOLIDAY, TOURING
& CAMPING PARK
(25)   £13.00–£19.00
        £12.00–£19.00
(150)   £12.00–£16.00
(24) £225.00–£540.00

North Morte Farm Caravan and Camping Park

North Morte Road, Mortehoe, Woolacombe EX34 7EG t (01271) 870381 f (01271) 870115 e info@northmortefarm.co.uk w northmortefarm.co.uk

Set in beautiful countryside overlooking Rockham Bay, close to village of Mortehoe, and Woolacombe. Open April to September.

payment Credit/debit cards, cash/cheques

General P 🍴 ⊙ 🛒 🐕 🏕. ☼ Leisure 🏕 U J

CHOOSE YOUR BEST HOLIDAY EVER FROM ONE OF NEWQUAY'S FINEST PARKS.

...independent, top quality rated parks, especially for families and couples.

CARAVAN AND CAMPING PARK

Trevella Park
Crantock • Newquay • Cornwall TR8 5EW

- Set in beautiful parkland surroundings.
- Modern facilities including heated swimming & paddling pools.
- Luxury Rose Award caravans.
- Nature reserve & two fishing lakes.
- Seventh year David Bellamy Gold Award.
- Online booking available.

Email: **holidays@trevella.co.uk**
01637 830308
www.trevella.co.uk

Chalet Bungalows • Caravans • Camping • Tourers • Families and Couples only

Mawgan Porth's 5 Star Park

Sun Haven Valley
HOLIDAY PARK

- "Families & Couples only" -NO club, NO bar,
- 5 star park - tents, touring & static caravans
- Surrounded by Cornish countryside
- 10min. walk from glorious golden beach,
- Children's play area, TV room, Games Room,
- Sheltered level camping area with electric
- Large central grass area for family games
- Laundry & optional private bathrooms
- Luxury shower block, (no charge).
- Campers microwave & ice pack freezer,
- Washing up area (Free Hot Water)
- Fishing lake 'on-site'; adjacent to golf club
- V. Small shop on site & Calor Gas stockist

Mawgan Porth, Nr Newquay, Cornwall TR8 4BQ
Telephone (01637) 860373
Email: sunhaven@sunhavenvalley.com
www.sunhavenvalley.com

Newquay's Family Fun Holiday Park

Cornwall's Holiday Park of the Year!
Fun for families and couples, with excellent, top quality touring, camping and luxury holiday homes - relaxing, safe and added value holidays.

free days ....
the superb Oasis indoor and outdoor fun pools, and acres beautiful landscaped park for relaxing, playing or just chilling out with Newquay's golden beaches only minutes away.

and laid back evenings
however way you like to chill out, from high energy cabaret lounge to a quiet drink and supper overlooking the pools, have FREE entertainment and FREE children's club included!

Hendra
HOLIDAY PARK

Click and explore
www.hendra-holidays.com
for your best holiday ever!

For a brochure call FREE on **0500 242 523**
or click enquiries@hendra-holidays.com

Hendra Holidays, NEWQUAY, Cornwall TR8 4NY. Telephone: 01637 875778

NEWPERRAN
Holiday Park

Peaceful family holiday park, renowned for its spacious, flat perimeter pitching, with breathtaking open countryside and sea views.

❖ New luxury toilet blocks
❖ free showers
❖ family rooms
❖ disabled facilities
❖ launderette
❖ premium all-service pitches
❖ shop/offlicence ❖ cafe/takeaway
❖ entertainments ❖ TV/games room ❖ Cottage Inn
❖ crazy golf ❖ aviary ❖ adventure playground
❖ toddlers play area ❖ outdoor heated swimming pool
with sunbathing terraces

Luxury Holiday Units for Hire/sale

A warm welcome awaits you

Rejerrah, Newquay, Cornwall TR8 5QJ
Tel: 0845 1668407 (local rate) ❖ Fax: 01872 571254

www.newperran.co.uk
Call Keith or Christine Brewer for a Free Colour Brochure

NEWQUAY, Cornwall Map ref 1B2

★★★★
HOLIDAY PARK
ROSE AWARD

🚐	£9.00–£14.90
🚍	£9.00–£14.90
⛺	£9.00–£14.90
🏠 (5)	£235.00–£620.00

395 touring pitches

Newperran Holiday Park

Rejerrah, Newquay TR8 5QJ t (01872) 572407 f (01872) 571254 e holidays@newperran.co.uk
w newperran.co.uk

Peaceful family holiday park renowned for its spacious perimeter pitching, with breathtaking open countryside and sea views. Caravans, motor homes, tents and holiday caravans for hire. Open Easter to 31 October.

payment Credit/debit cards, cash/cheques

General ▣▣P▣◐☎▣◓☉▣▣▣✕🐾▪☼ Leisure ⚡📺♿♪♣⚲∪♪▶

NEWQUAY, Cornwall Map ref 1B2

★★★★
HOLIDAY, TOURING
& CAMPING PARK
ROSE AWARD

🚐	£10.00–£36.00
🚍	£10.00–£36.00
⛺	£8.00–£36.00
🏠 (18)	£210.00–£705.00

200 touring pitches

Porth Beach Tourist Park

Porth, Newquay TR7 3NH t (01637) 876531 f (01637) 871227 e info@porthbeach.co.uk
w porthbeach.co.uk

payment Credit/debit cards, cash/cheques

Situated in a valley with small trout stream, and only 100m from Porth Beach – the perfect family beach. Premium pitches have all facilities including satellite hook-up, as do the 18 static caravans. Bookings only accepted from families or couples (maximum three couples). Open March to November.

⊕ A30 then A392 Newquay Road. At Quintrell Downs roundabout follow signs for Porth. Turn right at Porth Four Turnings, Park is 0.5 miles on.

General ▣P▣◐☎▣◓☉▣▣☼ Leisure ⚲∪♪▶🦶

NEWQUAY, Cornwall Map ref 1B2

★★★★
HOLIDAY, TOURING
& CAMPING PARK

🚐	£13.00–£17.00
🏠 (19)	£200.00–£675.00

98 touring pitches

Riverside Holiday Park

Gwills Lane, Newquay TR8 4PE t (01637) 873617 f (01637) 877051
e info@riversideholidaypark.co.uk w riversideholidaypark.co.uk

Peaceful riverside family park. Two miles to Newquay. Sheltered, level touring pitches, luxury lodges and caravans. Covered, heated pool and bar. Open March to October.

payment Credit/debit cards, cash/cheques

General ▣P▣◐☎▣▣▣▣✕🐾 Leisure ⚡📺♿♣♪

NEWQUAY, Cornwall Map ref 1B2

★★★★
TOURING &
CAMPING PARK

🚐 (140)	£8.50–£14.50
🚍 (140)	£8.50–£14.50
⛺ (140)	£8.50–£14.50

140 touring pitches

Treloy Touring Park

Newquay TR8 4JN t (01637) 872063 & (01637) 876279 e treloy.tp@btconnect.com w treloy.co.uk

payment Credit/debit cards, cash/cheques

A family-run park catering exclusively for touring caravans, tents and motor homes. We aim to offer fun and enjoyable holidays for families and couples in a pleasant, relaxed setting with clean, modern facilities. Nearby is Treloy Golf Club and driving range. Coarse fishing available at Porth Reservoir, one mile away. Open April to September.

⊕ Leave A30 at Highgate Hill, take 3rd exit (Newquay). At Halloon roundabout take A39 Wadebridge (3rd exit). Then Trekenning roundabout 1st left, Treloy 4 miles.

♥ Free-night offers early and late season. Conditions apply.

General ▣P▣◐☎▣◓☉▣▣▣✕🐾▪☼ Leisure ⚡📺♿♪♣⚲∪♪▶

NEWTON ABBOT, Devon Map ref 1D2

★★★★★
TOURING &
CAMPING PARK

🚐 (135) £12.50–£19.80
🚐   £12.50–£19.80
⛺   £13.50–£20.80

Dornafield

Two Mile Oak, Newton Abbot TQ12 6DD **t** (01803) 812732 **f** (01803) 812032
e enquiries@dornafield.com **w** dornafield.com

payment Credit/debit cards, cash/cheques

Beautiful 14thC farmhouse located in 30 acres of glorious South Devon countryside. So quiet and peaceful, yet so convenient for Torbay and Dartmoor. Superb facilities to suit the discerning caravanner, including many hardstanding, all-service pitches. Shop, games room, adventure play area, tennis and golf. Our brochure is only a phone call away.

⊕ Take A381 Newton Abbot to Totnes road. In 2.5 miles at Two Mile Oak Inn turn right. In 0.5 miles 1st turn to left. Site 200yds on right.

♥ Early- and late-season bookings. Book for 7 days and only pay for 5. Details on request.

General 🖵 P 🔌 🛈 🚻 🚐 🍴 ☉ 📱 ▣ 🛒 🐕 🎪 ☼   Leisure 📺 ☎ ⚲ ⚲ 🏃

PADSTOW, Cornwall Map ref 1B2

★★★★
TOURING &
CAMPING PARK

🚐   £14.00
🚐   £14.00
⛺   £14.00

30 touring pitches

The Laurels

Padstow Road, Whitecross, Wadebridge PL27 7JQ **t** (01209) 313474 **e** jamierielly@btconnect.com
w thelaurelsholidaypark.co.uk

payment Cash/cheques

Manicured touring park with top-quality shower and toilet block kept to an extremely high standard. The grounds of the park are simply beautiful. The guest book on our website tells all – visitors are so pleased to have chosen our park. New separate ball games area, pets welcome. Padstow five miles. Open April to October.

⊕ Just 0.5 miles from the Royal Cornwall Showground on A39. At the junction of A39 and A389 towards Padstow.

General P 🔌 🚻 🍴 ☉ ▣ 🐕 🎪 ☼ Leisure ∪ ♪ 🏃 ⚲

PADSTOW, Cornwall Map ref 1B2

★★★★★
HOLIDAY, TOURING
& CAMPING PARK
ROSE AWARD

🚐 (118) £12.00–£43.00
🚐 (118) £12.00–£43.00
⛺ (124) £12.00–£43.00
🏕 (51) £190.00–£920.00
26 touring pitches

Mother Iveys Bay Caravan Park

Trevose Head, Padstow PL28 8SL **t** (01841) 520990 **f** (01841) 520550 **e** info@motheriveysbay.com
w motheriveysbay.com

Cornwall Tourism Awards 2002 – Holiday/
Caravan Park of the Year 'Highly Commended'.
Situated on the coast with spectacular sea views
and our own private sandy beach, perfect for
traditional family holidays. Open 15 March to
2 November.

payment Cash/cheques

General P 🔌 🛈 🚻 🍴 📱 ▣ 🛒 🐕 Leisure ♪ 🏃

PADSTOW, Cornwall Map ref 1B2

★★★
TOURING &
CAMPING PARK

🚐 (180) £10.00–£17.50
🚐 (180) £10.00–£17.50
⛺ (180) £10.00–£17.50
80 touring pitches

Padstow Touring Park

Padstow PL28 8LE **t** (01841) 532061 **e** mail@padstowtouringpark.co.uk **w** padstowtouringpark.co.uk

Located one mile from Padstow with footpath
access; panoramic views; quiet family park; open
all year; sandy beaches two miles; some en suite
pitches; easy access from main road.

open All year
payment Credit/debit cards, cash/cheques

General 🖵 🚮 P 🔌 🛈 🚻 🚐 🍴 ☉ 📱 ▣ 🛒 🐕 🎪 ☼ Leisure 🎪 ∪ ♪ ⚲

PAIGNTON, Devon Map ref 1D2

★★★★★
HOLIDAY, TOURING
& CAMPING PARK
ROSE AWARD

🚐	£14.25–£36.00
🚐	£14.25–£36.00
⛺	£11.00–£30.00
🏠 (189)	£145.00–£950.00

175 touring pitches

Beverley Park

Goodrington Road, Paignton TQ4 7JE t (01803) 843887 f (01803) 845427
e info@beverley-holidays.co.uk w beverley-holidays.co.uk

open All year except Christmas and New Year
payment Credit/debit cards

Superb luxury holiday park overlooking Torbay with fabulous sea views. South West Tourism 'Caravan Park of the Year' 2004/2005. David Bellamy Gold Conservation Award. Indoor/outdoor pools, tennis, gym, crazy golf, playground, restaurant, bar, shop, plus golf, watersports, and unlimited coastal walks nearby. Less than one mile to the beach.

⊕ Follow the A380/A3022 from the English Riviera roundabout towards Brixham for 5.6 miles. Turn left into Goodrington Road at the traffic lights at the garage.

♥ Special discounts for over-50s and under-5s in holiday caravans. 7 nights touring for 6. Specific dates apply.

General 🔌🖥P🔌🚻🍴📶🛒✕ Leisure ⛱🏊🍴🎵🎯🎣

PAIGNTON, Devon Map ref 1D2

★★★★
HOLIDAY, TOURING
& CAMPING PARK

🚐 (80)	£8.00–£14.00
🚐 (80)	£8.00–£14.00
⛺ (80)	£8.00–£14.00
🏠 (18)	£140.00–£450.00

80 touring pitches

Higher Well Farm Holiday Park

Waddeton Road, Stoke Gabriel, Totnes TQ9 6RN t (01803) 782289 e higherwell@talk21.com
w higherwellfarmholidaypark.co.uk

Secluded farm park with static caravans and separate area welcoming touring caravans, tents and motor homes. Within one mile of Stoke Gabriel and the River Dart. Four miles to Paignton.

payment Credit/debit cards, cash/cheques

General 🚲P🔌🚻🍴📶☺📶🛒🐾🚜☀ Leisure 🎯

PAIGNTON, Devon Map ref 1D2

★★★★
HOLIDAY, TOURING
& CAMPING PARK

🚐	£12.00–£26.00
🚐	£12.00–£26.00
⛺	£11.00–£25.00
🏠 (60)	£135.00–£600.00

260 touring pitches

Whitehill Country Park

Stoke Road, Paignton TQ4 7PF t (01803) 782338 f (01803) 782722 e info@whitehill-park.co.uk
w whitehill-park.co.uk

payment Credit/debit cards

Beautifully situated in rolling Devon countryside yet within easy reach of the sea, the bright lights of Torbay, and Dartmoor. Outdoor swimming pool, play area, craft room, table tennis, amusements, cycle and walking trails, bar and restaurant. Open Easter to September.

⊕ From the A358 Totnes Road, turn left at the Parker's Arm. We are one mile along towards Stoke Gabriel.

♥ £20 off per week in a caravan for 2 people. 7 nights touring for 6 – specific dates apply.

General P🔌🚻🍴📶📶🛒✕☀ Leisure 🎯🍴🎣🏔

Town, country or coast

The entertainment, shopping and innovative attractions of the big cities, the magnificent vistas of the countryside or the relaxing and refreshing coast – this guide will help you find what you're looking for.

PENZANCE, Cornwall Map ref 1A3

★★★
HOLIDAY, TOURING
& CAMPING PARK

🚐	£10.50–£15.00
🚐	£10.50–£16.00
▲	£8.50–£13.00
🏕 (5)	£150.00–£400.00

102 touring pitches

Tower Park Caravans & Camping

St Buryan, Penzance TR19 6BZ t (01736) 810286 f (01736) 810286
e enquiries@towerparkcamping.co.uk w towerparkcamping.co.uk

open All year
payment Credit/debit cards, cash/cheques

Friendly, family-run site in peaceful rural setting adjoining St Buryan village. Large, sheltered, level pitches for tents and tourers and static holiday caravans for hire. Ideally situated for beaches and Minack Theatre and popular with families, walkers, divers, climbers, surfers, birdwatchers and cyclists. Open March to January.

⊕ From the A30 Lands End road, fork left onto the B3283 signposted St Buryan. On entering the village, turn right. Site is 300yds from village.

♥ Camping – 7 nights for the price of 6 (low/mid-season). Short breaks for static holiday homes (except Jul & Aug).

General 📺 P 🚐 🗘 🚻 🏪 ⊙ 🗑 🐾 🐕 ⛲ ☼   Leisure 📺 🎯 ⛰ ∪ 🎣 ♿

PLYMOUTH, Devon Map ref 1C2

★★★★
HOLIDAY &
TOURING PARK

🚐 (60)	£8.60–£18.00
🚐 (60)	£8.60–£18.00

60 touring pitches

See Ad on inside front cover

Plymouth Sound Caravan Club Site

Bovisand Lane, Down Thomas, Plymouth PL9 0AE t (01752) 862325 w caravanclub.co.uk

payment Credit/debit cards, cash/cheques

Within easy reach of the historic port. Superb views over the Sound. Close to the South West Coast Path and lovely beaches. Open March to October.

⊕ Turn right at village signposted Down Thomas into Bovisand Lane. Site on right.

♥ Special member rates mean you can save your membership subscription in less than a week. Visit our website to find out more.

General P 🚐 🗘 📺 🐕 🎯   Leisure ▶

POLRUAN-BY-FOWEY, Cornwall Map ref 1B3

★★★★
HOLIDAY, TOURING
& CAMPING PARK

🚐 (7)	£10.00–£15.50
🚐 (7)	£10.00–£15.50
▲ (40)	£7.50–£15.50
🏕 (10)	£165.00–£470.00

47 touring pitches

Polruan Holidays (Camping & Caravanning)

Townsend, Polruan PL23 1QH t (01726) 870263 f (01726) 870263 e polholiday@aol.com

Small, peaceful, coastal holiday park surrounded by sea, river and National Trust farmland. Walking, sailing, fishing, boating and beaches nearby.

payment Cash/cheques

General 🚐 P 🚐 🗘 🚻 📺 🏪 ⊙ 🗑 🗑 🐾 🐕 ☼   Leisure ⛰ ∪ 🎣

PORLOCK, Somerset Map ref 1D1

★★★★
HOLIDAY, TOURING
& CAMPING PARK

🚐 (54) £10.00–£15.00
🚚 (54) £10.00–£15.00
▲ (66) £8.00–£13.00
🏚 (19) £140.00–£375.00
120 touring pitches

Burrowhayes Farm Caravan and Camping Site and Riding Stables

West Luccombe, Porlock, Minehead TA24 8HT **t** (01643) 862463 **e** info@burrowhayes.co.uk
w burrowhayes.co.uk

payment Credit/debit cards, cash/cheques

Real family site situated in glorious National Trust scenery in Exmoor National Park. Ideal for walking and riding, with stables on site. New heated toilet and shower block with disabled and baby-changing facilities. Open mid-March to end October.

⊕ From Minehead, A39 towards Porlock; 1st left after Allerford to Horner and West Luccombe; Burrowhayes is 0.25 miles along on right before hump-backed bridge.

General 🔲 P 🔌 🖰 👕 🚾 ⋔ ☉ 📶 🔲 🛄 ⋔ ☼ Leisure ∪ ♪

PORTHTOWAN, Cornwall Map ref 1B3

★★★★
TOURING &
CAMPING PARK

🚐 (22) £8.50–£14.50
🚚 (6) £8.50–£14.50
▲ (22) £8.50–£14.50
80 touring pitches

Porthtowan Tourist Park

Mile Hill, Porthtowan, Truro TR4 8TY **t** (01209) 890256 **e** admin@porthtowantouristpark.co.uk
w porthtowantouristpark.co.uk

payment Cash/cheques

This quiet, family-run park offers plenty of space and level pitches. Superb new toilet/laundry facilities with family rooms. Close to a sandy surfing beach, coastal path and Portreath to Devoran cycle trail, it's an excellent base from which to discover the delights of Cornwall. David Bellamy Silver Award. Open Apr to September.

⊕ From A30, take 3rd exit off the roundabout signed Redruth/Porthtowan. Follow this road for 2 miles. Turn right at T-junction. Site on left after 0.5 miles.

♥ Off-peak special offers – see our website for details.

General P 🔌 🖰 👕 ⋔ ☉ 📶 🔲 🛄 ⋔ ⋌ ☼ Leisure ♣ ∆ ∪ ♪ ⚙

PORTREATH, Cornwall Map ref 1B3

★★★
TOURING &
CAMPING PARK

🚐 £8.00–£14.00
🚚 £8.00–£14.00
▲ £8.00–£14.00
60 touring pitches

Cambrose Touring Park

Portreath Road, Cambrose, Redruth TR16 4HT **t** (01209) 890747 **f** (01209) 891665
e cambrosetouringpark@supanet.com **w** cambrosetouringpark.co.uk

Six acres of well-sheltered land in a valley. Excellent suntrap. Most roads are tarmac finished. Facilities for the disabled. Open April to October inclusive.

payment Cash/cheques

General P 🔌 🖰 👕 ⋔ ☉ 📶 🔲 🛄 ⋔ ☼ Leisure ⤜ ♣ ∆ ∪ ♪ ⚙ 🏞

Don't forget www.

Web addresses throughout this guide are shown without the prefix www. Please include www. in the address line of your browser.
If a web address does not follow this style it is shown in full.

PORTREATH, Cornwall Map ref 1B3

Tehidy Holiday Park

★★★★
HOLIDAY, TOURING
& CAMPING PARK

🚐 (18) £10.00–£14.00
🚙 (3) £10.00–£14.00
⛺ (18) £10.00–£14.00
🏠 (20) £140.00–£575.00

Harris Mill, Illogan, Redruth TR16 4JQ **t** (01209) 216489 **e** holiday@tehidy.co.uk **w** tehidy.co.uk

payment Credit/debit cards, cash/cheques

Tehidy Holiday Park has been developed to a high standard and includes a range of clean and modern facilities to ensure you have a comfortable and enjoyable stay. Children's play area. Shop/off licence, payphone, games room. Toilet block with laundrette. Open from March to November.

⊕ *Off A30 at Redruth, right to Porthtowan. After 275m left onto B3300 (Portreath). Straight over at crossroads. Past Cornish Arms. Site 500m on left.*

General 🔌 P 🔲 🗘 🔱 🌡 ⊙ 🏕 🔲 🦮 Leisure 📺 🔍 ⚲ ∪ 🎣 🚴

REDRUTH, Cornwall Map ref 1B3

Lanyon Caravan & Camping Park

★★★★
HOLIDAY, TOURING
& CAMPING PARK

🚐 (25) £16.00
🚙 (25) £16.00
⛺ (50) £16.00
🏠 (16) £210.00–£540.00
25 touring pitches

Loscombe Lane, Four Lanes, Redruth TR16 6LP **t** (01209) 313474 **e** jamierielly@btconnect.com **w** lanyonholidaypark.co.uk

open All year
payment Credit/debit cards, cash/cheques

Lovely, well-kept, friendly park set in the heart of the beautiful Cornish countryside with distant sea views. Ideal touring base. Three modern toilet/shower blocks. Free hot water. Pets welcome.

General 🔌 🔲 P 🔲 🌡 🆆🅿 🏕 ⊙ 🔲 🦮 ✕ 🏇 🎠 ☼ Leisure 🎣 🍴 🎵 🔍 ⚲ ∪ 🎣 ➤ 🚴

ROSUDGEON, Cornwall Map ref 1B3

Kenneggy Cove Holiday Park

★★★★
HOLIDAY, TOURING
& CAMPING PARK
ROSE AWARD

🚐 £10.00–£18.50
🚙 £10.00–£18.50
⛺ £10.00–£18.50
🏠 (9) £185.00–£495.00
50 touring pitches

Higher Kenneggy, Rosudgeon, Penzance TR20 9AU **t** (01736) 763453 **e** enquiries@kenneggycove.co.uk **w** kenneggycove.co.uk

payment Cash/cheques, euros

Flat, lawned pitches in a beautiful garden setting with panoramic sea views. Twelve minutes' walk to South West Coast Path and secluded, sandy beach. Home-made breakfasts available. Please note: this is a quiet site, operating a policy of no noise between 2200 and 0800. German and French spoken. Open May to October.

⊕ *Take the lane to Higher Kenneggy, south off the A394 at the Helston end of Rosudgeon. The park is 0.5 miles down the lane on the left.*

♥ *No single-sex groups or large parties.*

General P 🔲 🗘 🌡 🏕 ⊙ 🔲 🦮 🎠 ☼ Leisure ⚲ ∪ 🎣 ➤ 🚴

Mention our name
Please mention this guide when making your booking.

RUAN MINOR, Cornwall Map ref 1B3

★★★★
HOLIDAY, TOURING
& CAMPING PARK

🚐 (15) £11.00–£17.00
🚐 (15) £11.00–£17.00
⛺ (20) £10.00–£14.00
🏠 (14) £99.00–£417.00
35 touring pitches

Silver Sands Holiday Park

Gwendreath, Nr Kennack Sands, Ruan Minor, Helston TR12 7LZ **t** (01326) 290631 **f** (01326) 290631
e enquiries@silversandsholidaypark.co.uk **w** silversandsholidaypark.co.uk

payment Credit/debit cards, cash/cheques

A quiet family-run park set in nine acres of landscaped grounds, offering peace and tranquillity. The large, well-spaced touring emplacements are individually marked and bounded by trees and shrubs. A short, enchanting woodland walk through the Lizard nature reserve brings you to award-winning sandy beaches. David Bellamy Gold award. Open Easter to September.

⊕ A3083 from Helston past RNAS Culdrose, left onto B3293 (St Keverne). Right turn after passing Goonhilly satellite station. Left after 1.5 miles to Gwendreath.

General ⚡ P 🚐 🌀 🍴 ♿ 🚾 📶 ⊙ 🎣 🐕 🔥 ☼   Leisure ⛵ ⋃ 🎵

ST AGNES, Cornwall Map ref 1B3

★★★★
TOURING PARK

🚐 (70) £14.00–£19.00
🚐 (70) £14.00–£19.00
⛺ (70) £14.00–£19.00
70 touring pitches

Beacon Cottage Farm Touring Park

Beacon Drive, St Agnes TR5 0NU **t** (01872) 552347 **e** beaconcottagefarm@lineone.net
w beaconcottagefarmholidays.co.uk

Peaceful, secluded park on a working farm in an Area of Outstanding Natural Beauty. Pitches in six small, landscaped paddocks. Beautiful sea views, lovely walks, ten minutes' walk to sandy beach. Open April to October.

payment Credit/debit cards, cash/cheques

General ⚡ 📺 ⚡ P 🚐 🌀 🍴 ♿ 🚾 📶 ⊙ 🎣 🐕 🔥 ☼   Leisure ⛵ ⋃ 🎵 🚴 🎣

ST AUSTELL, Cornwall Map ref 1B3

visit**Britain**.com

Get in the know – log on for a wealth of information and inspiration. All the latest news on places to visit, events and quality-assessed accommodation is literally at your fingertips. Explore all that Britain has to offer.

ST AUSTELL, Cornwall Map ref 1B3

★ ★ ★ ★ ★
HOLIDAY, TOURING
& CAMPING PARK
ROSE AWARD

£12.00–£26.00
£12.00–£26.00
£12.00–£26.00
(40) £250.00–£650.00
45 touring pitches

River Valley Holiday Park

Pentewan Road, London Apprentice, St Austell PL26 7AP   t (01726) 73533   f (01726) 73533
w cornwall-holidays.co.uk

payment Credit/debit cards, cash/cheques

Stay at River Valley and you will enjoy our high standards. Quality caravans to hire, or bring your own and stay in our level, sheltered meadow. Surrounded by woodlands and bordered by a river with lots of walks. Indoor swimming pool, cycle trail to the beach, immaculate toilet block. Open April to October.

⊕ Take B3273 from St Austell to Mevagissey. When entering London Apprentice, park is on left-hand side.

♥ Short-break offers in static vans. 7 nights for the price of 5 in the touring meadow.

General 🖵 P 🚗 🔌 🍴 💻 📶 ⊙ 🏪 🛒 🐕 ✕ ☼   Leisure ⌇ 🔍 ⚲ 🚲

ST IVES, Cornwall Map ref 1B3

★ ★ ★ ★
TOURING &
CAMPING PARK

(168) £11.50–£21.00
(168) £11.50–£21.00
(235) £11.50–£21.00
234 touring pitches

Little Trevarrack Holiday Park

Laity Lane, Carbis Bay, St Ives TR26 3HW   t (01736) 797580   e info@littletrevarrack.co.uk
w littletrevarrack.co.uk

payment Credit/debit cards, cash/cheques

Little Trevarrack Holiday Park is ideally located for exploring the beautiful West Cornwall peninsula. Our range of superb facilities includes a heated outdoor swimming pool with sun terrace (Whitsun to mid-September). Approximately one mile from the stunning Carbis Bay beach and the coastal footpath into St Ives. Open April to September.

⊕ From A30 take A3074 to St Ives. Signposted left opposite turning for Carbis Bay beach. Straight across at next crossroads. Approx 200m on right.

♥ Please telephone reception for details.

General 🖵 P 🚗 📷 🍴 📶 ⊙ 🏪 🐕 ✕ ☼   Leisure ⌇ 🔍 ⚲ ♪ ✈

ST IVES, Cornwall Map ref 1B3

★ ★ ★ ★ ★
TOURING &
CAMPING PARK

£11.00–£27.00
£11.00–£27.00
£11.00–£25.00
260 touring pitches

Polmanter Tourist Park

St Ives TR26 3LX   t (01736) 795640   f (01736) 793607   e reception@polmanter.com
w polmanter.com

Family park in lovely countryside with sea views, within walking distance of St Ives and beaches. Heated toilets/showers. Hard-standings. Open April to October.

payment Credit/debit cards, cash/cheques

General 🖵 P 🚗 📷 🍴 📶 ⊙ 🏪 🛒 ✕ 🐕 ✕ ☼   Leisure ⌇ ⚑ 🔍 ⚲ ♪ ✈

Take a break

Look out for special promotions and themed breaks. It's a golden opportunity to indulge an interest, find a new one, or just relax and enjoy exceptional value. Offers and promotions are highlighted in colour (and are subject to availability).

ST JUST-IN-PENWITH, Cornwall Map ref 1A3

★★★★
HOLIDAY, TOURING
& CAMPING PARK

🚐 (10)   £10.00–£12.50
🚗 (7)   £10.00–£12.50
⛺ (14)   £8.00–£10.00
🏠 (15) £190.00–£450.00
17 touring pitches

Roselands Caravan Park

Dowran, St Just, Penzance TR19 7RS t (01736) 788571 e info@roselands.co.uk w roselands.co.uk

payment Credit/debit cards, cash/cheques

Roselands is a quiet, secluded, family-run park ideal for coastal and moorland walks. Close to beaches and attractions including golf course. Luxury six-berth caravans. Level touring pitches. Bar, evening meals, in our new conservatory. Open 1 January to 31 October.

⊕ From the A30 Penzance bypass, turn right for St Just on the A3071. Half a mile before reaching St Just, turn left at the caravan sign.

♥ Over 55s, 10% off one week's holiday before 14 Jul or after 8 Sep, excl Easter.

General P 🚐 🅿 🛁 🚰 🔥 ⊙ 📷 🔋 ✕ 🐕 🏧 ☀ Leisure 🎣 🍴 ⛰ ♪ ► 🚲

ST JUST IN ROSELAND, Cornwall Map ref 1B3

★★★★★
TOURING &
CAMPING PARK

🚐 (84)   £14.00–£20.00
🚗 (50)   £14.00–£20.00
⛺ (35)   £14.00–£20.00
84 touring pitches

Trethem Mill Touring Park

Trethem, St Just in Roseland TR2 5JF t (01872) 580504 f (01872) 580968 e reception@trethem.com w trethem.com

payment Credit/debit cards

We offer peace and tranquillity with an exceptional standard of facilities. Cornwall Tourism Awards: 'Consistent winners offering consistent quality.' Open April to mid-October. Say hello to a new experience.

⊕ A3078 towards Tregony/St Mawes, over Tregony bridge. After 5 miles follow brown caravan and camping signs from Trewithian. Site 2 miles beyond on right-hand side.

General 🔗 P 🚐 🅿 🚰 🛜 🔥 ⊙ 📷 🔋 🐕 🏧 ☀ Leisure ⛰ ♪ 🚲

ST MERRYN, Cornwall Map ref 1B2

★★★★
HOLIDAY, TOURING
& CAMPING PARK

🚐   £8.00–£12.00
🚗   £8.00–£12.00
⛺   £8.00–£12.00
🏠 (3)   £175.00–£450.00
70 touring pitches

Trevean Farm

St Merryn, Padstow PL28 8PR t (01841) 520772 f (01841) 520772 e trevean.info@virgin.net

Small, pleasant farm site one mile from the sea. Ideally situated for beaches, walking and many visitor attractions. Open Easter to end of October.

payment Cash/cheques, euros

General 📺 🔗 P 🚐 🅿 🚰 🔥 ⊙ 📷 🔋 🐕 ☀ Leisure ⛰ ♪

SALCOMBE REGIS, Devon Map ref 1D2

★★★★
TOURING &
CAMPING PARK

🚐 (100) £10.80–£16.48
🚗 (100) £10.80–£16.48
⛺ (100) £10.80–£16.48
100 touring pitches

Kings Down Tail Caravan & Camping Park

Salcombe Regis, Sidmouth EX10 0PD t (01297) 680313 f (01297) 680313
e info@kingsdowntail.co.uk w kingsdowntail.co.uk

Level, grassy, sheltered park. Central area for East Devon coast and countryside access. Three miles east of Sidmouth. Adjacent A352, opposite Branscombe water tower, not in any village. Open 15 March to 15 November.

payment Credit/debit cards, cash/cheques

General 📺 P 🚐 🅿 🚰 🔥 ⊙ 🔋 🐕 ☀ Leisure 🍴 ⛰

SALISBURY PLAIN

See under Warminster

SIDBURY, Devon Map ref 1D2

★ ★ ★ ★ ★
TOURING PARK
🚐 (113) £12.10–£24.90
🚎 (113) £12.10–£24.90
113 touring pitches

See Ad on inside front cover

THE
CARAVAN
CLUB

Putts Corner Caravan Club Site

Sidbury, Sidmouth EX10 0QQ **t** (01404) 42875 **w** caravanclub.co.uk

payment Credit/debit cards, cash/cheques

A quiet site in pretty surroundings, with a private path to the local pub. Bluebells create a sea of blue in spring, followed by foxgloves. Open March to November.

⊕ From M5 jct 25, A375 signposted Sidmouth. Turn right at Hare and Hounds onto B3174. In about 0.25 miles turn right into site entrance.

♥ Special member rates mean you can save your membership subscription in less than a week. Visit our website to find out more.

General 🖵 P 🔌 🕭 🚿 🚽 📻 ☺ 📶 🔚 🐕 ☼ Leisure ⚠ ▶

SIDMOUTH, Devon Map ref 1D2

★ ★ ★ ★ ★
HOLIDAY, TOURING
& CAMPING PARK
ROSE AWARD

🚐 (40) £10.00–£18.20
🚎 (40) £10.00–£18.20
▲ (60) £10.00–£18.20
🏠 (10) £175.00–£510.00
100 touring pitches

Salcombe Regis Camping and Caravan Park

Salcombe Regis, Sidmouth EX10 0JH **t** (01395) 514303 **f** (01395) 514314
e contact@salcombe-regis.co.uk **w** salcombe-regis.co.uk

Situated 1.5 miles east of Sidmouth in Area of Outstanding Natural Beauty. A good base for visiting East Devon. Short walk to coastal path. Great walking country.

payment Credit/debit cards, cash/cheques

General P 🔌 🕭 🚿 🚽 📻 ☺ 📶 🔚 🚿 🐕 🐾 ☼ Leisure ⚠ ▶

SWANAGE, Dorset Map ref 2B3

★ ★ ★ ★ ★
TOURING PARK
🚐 (53) £13.60–£25.60
🚎 (53) £13.60–£25.60
53 touring pitches

See Ad on inside front cover

THE
CARAVAN
CLUB

Haycraft Caravan Club Site

Haycrafts Lane, Swanage BH19 3EB **t** (01929) 480572 **w** caravanclub.co.uk

payment Credit/debit cards, cash/cheques

Peaceful site located five miles from Swanage, with its safe, sandy beach. Spectacular cliff-top walks, Corfe Castle, Lulworth Cove and Durdle Door within easy reach. There are numerous public footpaths and coastal walks nearby. Open March to November.

⊕ Midway between Corfe Castle and Swanage. Take A351 from Wareham to Swanage, at Harmans Cross turn right into Haycrafts Lane, site 0.5 miles on the left.

♥ Special member rates mean you can save your membership subscription in less than a week. Visit our website to find out more.

General P 🔌 🕭 🚿 🚽 📻 ☺ 📶 🔚 🐕 ☼ Leisure ♫ ▶

Friendly help and advice

Tourist Information Centres offer friendly help with accommodation and holiday ideas as well as suggestions of places to visit and things to do. You'll find contact details at the beginning of each regional section.

TAUNTON, Somerset Map ref 1D1

★★★
HOLIDAY, TOURING
& CAMPING PARK

🚐 (20) £10.00–£12.50
🚏 (10) £10.00–£12.50
▲ (10) £10.00–£12.50
🏠 (2) £120.00–£175.00
30 touring pitches

Ashe Farm Caravan and Campsite

Thornfalcon, Taunton TA3 5NW t (01823) 442567 f (01823) 443372
e camping@ashe-farm.fsnet.co.uk

Quiet farm site, lovely views, easy access. Central
for touring. Easy reach coast and hills. Family run
and informal. Open April to October.

payment Cash/cheques

General 🚬 P 🔌 🕐 🍴 ℞ ☉ 🗑 🐾 ⚡ Leisure ✦ ⚲ ⚑

TAUNTON, Somerset Map ref 1D1

★★★★
TOURING &
CAMPING PARK

🚐 (30) £12.00–£15.00
🚏 (30) £12.00–£15.00
▲ (10) £10.00–£13.00
40 touring pitches

Holly Bush Park

Culmhead, Taunton TA3 7EA t (01823) 421515 e info@hollybushpark.com w hollybushpark.com

A small, clean, quiet and friendly park. Ideal for
walking, relaxing or touring. Excellent local inn
150 yds. Opposite woodlands and in an Area of
Outstanding Natural Beauty.

open All year
payment Credit/debit cards, cash/cheques

General P 🔌 🕐 🍴 ℞ ☉ 🗑 🐾 ⚡ Leisure ◡ ⚑

TAVISTOCK, Devon Map ref 1C2

★★★★
HOLIDAY, TOURING
& CAMPING PARK
ROSE AWARD

🚐 (40) £9.50–£14.50
🚏 (40) £9.50–£14.50
▲ (40) £9.50–£14.50
🏠 (12) £195.00–£445.00
120 touring pitches

Harford Bridge Holiday Park

Peter Tavy, Tavistock PL19 9LS t (01822) 810349 f (01822) 810028 e enquiry@harfordbridge.co.uk
w harfordbridge.co.uk

open All year
payment Credit/debit cards, cash/cheques

Beautiful, level, sheltered park set in Dartmoor with
delightful views of Cox Tor. The River Tavy forms a
boundary, offering riverside and other spacious,
level camping pitches. Luxury, self-catering caravan
holiday homes. Ideal for exploring Devon and
Cornwall, walking the moor or just relaxing on this
beautiful park.

⊕ M5 onto A30 to Sourton Cross; take left turn onto A386
Tavistock Road; 2 miles north of Tavistock, take the Peter
Tavy turning; entrance 200yds on left.

♥ Holiday let: £15 off 2-week booking. £10 Senior Citizen
discount.

General 🏕 🚬 P 🔌 🕐 🍴 🚐 ℞ ☉ 🗑 🐾 ⚡ ☀ Leisure 📺 ✦ 🎢 ⚲ ◡ ♪ ⚑ 🚵 🛶

TAVISTOCK, Devon Map ref 1C2

★★★★
HOLIDAY, TOURING
& CAMPING PARK
ROSE AWARD

🚐 (40) £10.00–£12.00
🚏 (40) £10.00–£12.00
▲ (40) £10.00–£12.00
🏠 (7) £165.00–£400.00
40 touring pitches

Langstone Manor Caravan and Camping Park

Moortown, Tavistock PL19 9JZ t (01822) 613371 f (01822) 613371 e jane@langstone-manor.co.uk
w langstone-manor.co.uk

payment Credit/debit cards, cash/cheques

Fantastic location with direct access onto moor.
Peace and quiet, with secluded pitches. Bar and
restaurant. Excellent base for South Devon and
Cornwall. Discover Dartmoor's secret!

⊕ Take the B3357 Princetown road from Tavistock. After
approx 1.5 miles, signs to Langstone Manor. Turn right, go
over cattle grid, up hill, left following signs.

♥ £25 discount for 2-week booking in holiday homes. 20%
discount for 2 people sharing on weekly bookings in
holiday accommodation (off-peak).

General 🏕 🚬 P 🔌 🕐 🍴 ℞ ☉ 🗑 ✕ 🐾 ⚡ ☀ Leisure 📺 🍷 ✦ 🎢 ◡ ⚑ 🚵

TEDBURN ST MARY, Devon Map ref 1D2

★★★
HOLIDAY, TOURING
& CAMPING PARK

🚐 (38)   £12.00–£20.00
🚐 (2)   £12.00–£20.00
⛺ (10)   £10.00–£20.00
🏠 (6)   £200.00–£450.00
50 touring pitches

Springfield Holiday Park

Tedburn St Mary, Exeter EX6 6EW **t** (01647) 24242 **e** enquiries@springfieldholidaypark.co.uk
w springfieldholidaypark.co.uk

Peaceful, beautiful location in central Devon. Ideal
family park, close to Dartmoor National Park,
coastal resorts and Exeter. Open 15 March to
15 October.

open All year except Christmas and New Year
payment Credit/debit cards, cash/cheques,
euros

General 🛗 P 🔌 ☕ 🍴 🕻 ⊙ 🗓 ☼   Leisure 🕽 🎣 ⚲ ♬ ⚑

TEIGNGRACE, Devon Map ref 1D2

★★★★
TOURING &
CAMPING PARK

🚐 (25)   £8.00–£13.00
🚐 (25)   £8.00–£13.00
⛺   £8.00–£13.00
25 touring pitches

Twelve Oaks Farm Caravan Park

Teigngrace, Newton Abbot TQ12 6QT **t** (01626) 352769 **f** (01626) 352769
e info@twelveoaksfarm.co.uk **w** twelveoaksfarm.co.uk

A working farm specialising in Charolais beef
cattle. Friendly, personal service. Luxury showers
and toilets, heated swimming pool. Coarse
fishing.

open All year
payment Credit/debit cards, cash/cheques

General 🖭 P 🔌 ☕ 🍴 🚐 🕻 ⊙ 📧 🗓 🐴 ☼   Leisure 🕽 ∪ ♬

TEWKESBURY, Gloucestershire Map ref 2B1

★★★★
TOURING &
CAMPING PARK

🚐 (154)   £12.10–£24.90
🚐 (154)   £12.10–£24.90
⛺   on application
154 touring pitches

See Ad on inside front cover

Tewkesbury Abbey Caravan Club Site

Gander Lane, Tewkesbury GL20 5PG **t** (01684) 294035 **w** caravanclub.co.uk

payment Credit/debit cards, cash/cheques

Impressive location next to Tewkesbury Abbey. Only
a short walk into the old town of Tewkesbury where
there is much to explore. Open March to November.

⊕ From M5 leave by exit 9 onto A438. In about 3 miles in
town centre, at cross-junction turn right. After 200yds turn
left into Gander Lane. From M50 leave by exit 1 on A38.
For details on other routes visit caravanclub.co.uk.

♥ Special member rates mean you can save your membership
subscription in less than a week. Visit our website to find
out more.

General 🖭 P 🔌 ☕ 🍴 🚐 🕻 ⊙ 📧 🗓 🐴 ☼   Leisure ♬ ⚑

TINTAGEL, Cornwall Map ref 1B2

★★★★★
TOURING &
CAMPING PARK

🚐 (142)   £13.60–£25.60
🚐 (142)   £13.60–£25.60
⛺   on application
142 touring pitches

See Ad on inside front cover

Trewethett Farm Caravan Club Site

Trethevy, Tintagel PL34 0BQ **t** (01840) 770222 **w** caravanclub.co.uk

payment Credit/debit cards, cash/cheques

Cliff-top site with breathtaking views. Walk to
Boscastle, with its pretty harbour and quayside, or
Tintagel to see its dramatic castle. Non-members
welcome. Open March to November.

⊕ From A30 onto A395 signposted Camelford. Right onto
A39 signposted Bude. Left just before transmitter. Right
onto B3266 signposted Boscastle. Left onto B3263. Site
entrance is on the right in about 2 miles.

♥ Special member rates mean you can save your membership
subscription in less than a week. Visit our website to find
out more.

General P 🔌 ☕ 🚐 🕻 ⊙ 📧 🗓 🐴 ☼   Leisure ♬ ⚑

What's in an award?
Further information about awards can be found at the front of this guide.

TOTNES, Devon Map ref 1D2

★★★★
TOURING &
CAMPING PARK

£8.00–£15.00
£8.00–£15.00
£8.00–£15.00
35 touring pitches

Broadleigh Farm Park

Coombe House Lane, Aish, Stoke Gabriel, Totnes TQ9 6PU **t** (01803) 782309 **f** (01803) 782422
e enquiries@broadleighfarm.co.uk **w** gotorbay.com/accommodation

Situated in beautiful South Hams village of Stoke
Gabriel close to the River Dart and Torbay's
wonderful, safe beaches. Many local walks. Bus
stop at end of lane. Dartmoor within easy reach
by car. Open March to end of October.

payment Cash/cheques

General P 🚐 🔧 🏪 ⛽ 🌙 🔘 🐕 ☀ Leisure ◢ ▶ 🏊

TRURO, Cornwall Map ref 1B3

★★★★
TOURING PARK

(40) £10.00–£13.00
(5) £10.00–£13.00
(15) £10.00–£13.00
60 touring pitches

Summer Valley Touring Park

Shortlanesend, Truro TR4 9DW **t** (01872) 277878 **e** res@summervalley.co.uk **w** summervalley.co.uk

Situated in a sheltered valley surrounded by
woods and farmland, we have been awarded for
our peaceful, rural environment. We have the
ideal site for visiting the gardens in spring. Open
April to October.

payment Credit/debit cards, cash/cheques

General 🏕 P 🚐 🔧 🏪 ⛽ 🌙 🔘 🐕 ☀ Leisure 🎱 ◢

WAREHAM, Dorset Map ref 2B3

WARMINSTER, Wiltshire Map ref 2B2

★★★★★
TOURING PARK

(165) £14.30–£27.70
(165) £14.30–£27.70
165 touring pitches

See Ad on inside front cover

THE
CARAVAN
CLUB

Longleat Caravan Club Site

Longleat, Warminster BA12 7NL **t** (01985) 844663 **w** caravanclub.co.uk

payment Credit/debit cards, cash/cheques

Close to Longleat House, this is the only site where
you can hear lions roar at night! Cafés, pubs and
restaurants within walking distance. Non-members
welcome. Open March to November.

⊕ *Take A362, signed for Frome, 0.5 miles at roundabout turn
left (2nd exit) onto Longleat Estate. Through toll booths,
follow caravan and camping pennant signs for 1 mile.*

♥ *Special member rates mean you can save your membership
subscription in less than a week. Visit our website to find
out more.*

General 🚐 P 🚐 🔧 🏪 ⛽ 🌙 🔘 🐕 ☀ Leisure 🎱 ◢

Travel update
Get the latest travel information – just dial RAC on 1740 from your mobile phone.

WARMWELL, Dorset Map ref 2B3

★★★★
HOLIDAY, TOURING
& CAMPING PARK

🚐 (37) £12.95–£15.95
🚛 (9) £12.95–£15.95
⛺ (5) £10.40–£13.40
40 touring pitches

Warmwell Caravan Park

Warmwell, Dorchester DT2 8JD **t** (01305) 852313 **f** (01305) 851824
e stay@warmwellcaravanpark.co.uk **w** warmwellcaravanpark.co.uk

The park is set in an Area of Outstanding Natural Beauty in the heart of Thomas Hardy country in Dorset. Open 1 March to 2 January.

payment Credit/debit cards, cash/cheques

General 🖵 🚮 P 🔌 🖰 🕯 � 🗱 🗐 🐾 🛏 ☼ Leisure 🍷 🎵

WATERROW, Somerset Map ref 1D1

★★★★★
TOURING &
CAMPING PARK
ROSE AWARD

🚐 (38) £13.00–£20.00
🚛 (38) £13.00–£20.00
⛺ (7) £13.00–£20.00
🏠 (1) £270.00–£415.00
45 touring pitches

Waterrow Touring Park

Waterrow, Taunton TA4 2AZ **t** (01984) 623464 **f** (01984) 624280 **w** waterrowpark.co.uk

A gently sloping, grassy site with landscaped hardstandings in the peaceful Tone Valley. An ideal base from which to explore this beautiful unspoilt area. One holiday caravan for hire. Adults only.

open All year
payment Credit/debit cards, cash/cheques

General P 🔌 🖰 🕯 🖳 ês ⊙ 🗐 🗐 🛏 🐾 ☼ Leisure 🎵 🏞

WESTON-SUPER-MARE, Somerset Map ref 1D1

★★★★
HOLIDAY, TOURING
& CAMPING PARK

🚐 (120) £12.00–£22.00
🚛 (120) £12.00–£22.00
⛺ (120) £12.00–£22.00
120 touring pitches

Country View Holiday Park

29 Sand Road, Sand Bay, Weston-super-Mare BS22 9UJ **t** (01934) 627595 **w** cvhp.co.uk

Country View is a beautifully kept site surrounded by the countryside and just 200yds from the Sand Bay beach. Heated pool, bar, shop and children's play area. Fantastic new toilet and shower facilities.

open All year
payment Cash/cheques

General 🚮 P 🔌 🖰 🕯 🖳 ês ⊙ 🗐 🗐 🛏 ☼ Leisure ✧ 🍷 🔍 ⚠ 🏳

WESTON-SUPER-MARE, Somerset Map ref 1D1

★★★
TOURING &
CAMPING PARK

🚐 (57) £10.00–£17.00
🚛 (5) £10.00–£17.00
⛺ (25) £8.00–£15.00
87 touring pitches

Dulhorn Farm Camping Site

Weston Road, Lympsham, Weston-super-Mare BS24 0JQ **t** (01934) 750298 **f** (01934) 750913

A family site on a working farm set in the countryside, approximately four miles from the beach, midway between Weston and Burnham. Ideal for touring. Easily accessible from M5. Open March to October.

payment Cash/cheques

General 🗔 🖵 🚮 P 🔌 🖰 🕯 🖳 ês ⊙ 🗐 🛏 🐾 ☼ Leisure ⚠ ∪ 🎵

Country Code always follow the Country Code

- Be safe – plan ahead and follow any signs
- Leave gates and property as you find them
- Protect plants and animals, and take your litter home
- Keep dogs under close control
- Consider other people

WEYMOUTH, Dorset Map ref 2B3

★★★★
TOURING PARK
(120) £11.20–£22.40
(120) £11.20–£22.40
120 touring pitches

See Ad on inside front cover

THE CARAVAN CLUB

Crossways Caravan Club Site

Crossways, Dorchester DT2 8BE **t** (01305) 852032 **w** caravanclub.co.uk

payment Credit/debit cards, cash/cheques

Set in 35 acres of woodland. Dorchester is nearby, also Weymouth's award-winning, sandy beach. Visit Lawrence of Arabia's house at Cloud's Hill. If you want to leave the car behind for the day, the railway station is just five minutes' walk from the site. Open March to October.

⊕ *North from A35 or south from A352, join B3390. Site on right within 1 mile. Entrance to site by forecourt of filling station.*

❤ *Midweek discount: pitch fee for standard pitches for stays on any Tue, Wed or Thu night outside peak season dates will be reduced by 50%.*

General · Leisure

WIMBORNE MINSTER, Dorset Map ref 2B3

★★★★★
TOURING & CAMPING PARK
(60) £12.00–£22.00
(60) £12.00–£22.00
(25) £12.00–£22.00
85 touring pitches

Wilksworth Farm Caravan Park

Cranborne Road, Furzehill, Wimborne BH21 4HW **t** (01202) 885467
e rayandwendy@wilksworthfarmcaravanpark.co.uk **w** wilksworthfarmcaravanpark.co.uk

payment Credit/debit cards, cash/cheques

A popular and attractive park set in the grounds of a Grade II* Listed farmhouse, tranquilly placed in the heart of rural Dorset. Facilities include an outdoor heated swimming pool, large play area, completely refurbished toilet block, café, takeaway, shop and games room. Close to Kingston Lacy, Poole and Bournemouth. Open 1 April to 30 October.

⊕ *1 mile north of Wimborne on B3078 (Cranborne Road).*

❤ *7-night booking outside peak times – 1 night free.*

General · Leisure

WINSFORD, Somerset Map ref 1D1

★★★★
TOURING & CAMPING PARK
(22) £10.00–£12.00
(22) £10.00–£12.00
(22) £10.00–£12.00
44 touring pitches

Halse Farm Caravan & Tent Park

Winsford, Minehead TA24 7JL **t** (01643) 851259 **f** (01643) 851592 **e** brit@halsefarm.co.uk
w halsefarm.co.uk

payment Credit/debit cards, cash/cheques

Exmoor National Park, small, peaceful, working farm with spectacular views. Paradise for walkers and country lovers. David Bellamy Gold Conservation Award. Open 23 March to 31 October.

⊕ *Signposted from A396. In Winsford turn left and bear left past Royal Oak Inn. One mile up hill. Entrance immediately after cattle grid on left.*

❤ *10% discount for 1 week or more, paid 10 days in advance*

General · Leisure

Star ratings

Detailed information about star ratings can be found at the back of this guide.

WOOL, Dorset Map ref 2B3

★★★★
TOURING &
CAMPING PARK

🚐 (95) £8.50–£14.50
🚐 (95) £8.50–£14.50
⛺ (95) £8.50–£14.50
95 touring pitches

Whitemead Caravan Park

East Burton Road, Wool, Wareham BH20 6HG **t** (01929) 462241 **f** (01929) 462241
e whitemeadcp@aol.com **w** whitemeadcaravanpark.co.uk

Within easy reach of beaches and beautiful countryside, this friendly site is maintained to a high standard of cleanliness. Turn west off the A352 near Wool level crossing. Open 18 March to 31 October.

payment Cash/cheques

General 🖵 P 🕭 🖰 🗑 🌥 ☺ 🗐🗄 🐾 ❄️ Leisure ⚓ /🏔

YEOVIL, Somerset Map ref 2A3

★★★★
HOLIDAY, TOURING
& CAMPING PARK

🚐 (30) £16.00
🚐 (30) £16.00
⛺ (30) £16.00
🏠 (3) £350.00–£800.00
60 touring pitches

Long Hazel Park

High Street, Sparkford, Yeovil BA22 7JH **t** (01963) 440002 **f** (01963) 440002
e longhazelpark@hotmail.com **w** sparkford.f9.co.uk/lhi.htm

Adult-only park set in 3.5 acres of level, landscaped grounds. Recreation area, picnic tables and full disabled facilities. Two fully heated lodges. Close to restaurant, bar, shop, post office, garage and bus stop.

open All year
payment Credit/debit cards, cash/cheques, euros

General 🖵 🚮 P 🕭 🖰 🗑 🖵 🌥 ☺ 🗐🗄 🐾 ❄️ Leisure ∪ 🎣 🚲

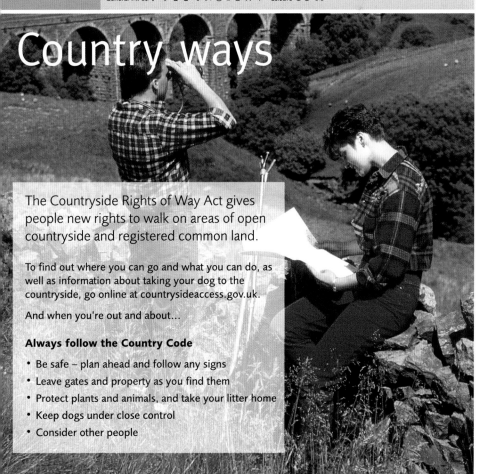

Country ways

The Countryside Rights of Way Act gives people new rights to walk on areas of open countryside and registered common land.

To find out where you can go and what you can do, as well as information about taking your dog to the countryside, go online at countrysideaccess.gov.uk.

And when you're out and about...

Always follow the Country Code

- Be safe – plan ahead and follow any signs
- Leave gates and property as you find them
- Protect plants and animals, and take your litter home
- Keep dogs under close control
- Consider other people

Loch Lomond and the Trossachs
National Park, Perthshire

Scotland

Outstanding natural beauty and rich in culture

If you're looking for a place to revive and clear your mind then head for Scotland. Dramatic landscapes and mist-shrouded lochs, spectacular wildlife, world-class shopping and an unrivalled arts festival – you just can't beat it.

VisitScotland
visitscotland.com
(0131) 472 2222

Kellie Castle Garden, Fife

Edinburgh Military Tattoo

Kirkhope Tower, Scottish Borders

For the perfect escape from modern life, start with the magical corner of Dumfries and Galloway. Walk along deserted beaches where Robert Burns journeyed on horseback to catch whisky smugglers. Both landscapes and wildlife are at their most spectacular in Scotland's two National Parks – Loch Lomond & The Trossachs, and the Cairngorms. Journey through heather-clad peaks on The Trossachs Trail. Travel to the islands to truly experience another world. Dreamy beaches are found in the Outer Hebrides and puffins by the million await bird-watchers in Shetland. Prefer to get out rather than chill out? Golfing, fishing, cycling, hillwalking, snowboarding, whitewater canoeing... the list is endless.

Scotland's great cities beckon. In Edinburgh, follow the cobbled 'Royal Mile' from the ancient castle to Holyrood Palace. Visit in August for entertainment galore at the celebrated arts and fringe festivals and enjoy the pomp and splendour of the Edinburgh Military Tattoo. Glasgow has become one of Europe's great cultural capitals with more than 30 art galleries and museums. Shop 'til you drop with outlets to rival London's best then dine in style in an art nouveau brasserie. Aberdeen is a great place from which to explore the treasures on its doorstep including the eight distilleries on the world's only Malt Whisky Trail.

Castles are plentiful – put Culzean, Braemar or Balmoral on your day-trip list. For fascinating history and an opportunity to sight the Loch Ness monster head for Urquhart Castle. Experience the breathtaking vista at Eilean Donan where the dramatic castle ruins and surrounding mountains are mirrored in the waters of the loch. Stay in the Highlands and get close to nature. You may get lucky and spot dolphins, whales, eagles, deer, otters and much more besides.

Destinations

Aberdeen

Prosperous and cosmopolitan, the 'Granite City' can hold its own as a cultural and academic centre. You'll find spectacular architecture, captivating museums, a wealth of art and culture and a lively social scene. The famous 'Granite Mile', Union Street, is the gateway to over 800 shops, restaurants and bars. Wander the cobbled lanes of Old Aberdeen and soak up the life and colour of the historic harbour. Find flower-filled parks and even a two-mile sweep of golden, sandy beach.

Dundee

The 'City of Discovery' is Scotland's sunniest city. You'll find superb shopping and a lively pub and club scene. Step into a bygone age on Captain Scott's famous polar exploration ship Discovery or check out the hip and exciting Dundee Contemporary Arts, a stunning complex on Nethergate. Enjoy panoramic views from Dundee Law – the plug of an extinct volcano – and nearby Broughty Ferry has one of the cleanest beaches in the UK.

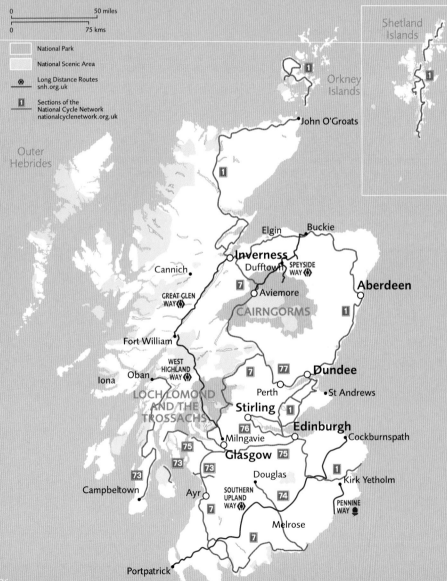

0	50 miles
0	75 kms

National Park

National Scenic Area

Long Distance Routes
snh.org.uk

1 Sections of the
National Cycle Network
nationalcyclenetwork.org.uk

Shetland
Islands

Orkney
Islands

John O'Groats

Outer
Hebrides

Elgin   Buckie

Inverness   SPEYSIDE
WAY

Cannich

Dufftown

GREAT GLEN
WAY

7   Aviemore

Aberdeen

CAIRNGORMS

Fort William

WEST
HIGHLAND
WAY

Iona   Oban

7   77   Dundee

Perth   St Andrews

LOCH LOMOND
AND THE
TROSSACHS

Stirling   1

76   Edinburgh

Milngavie

75   Glasgow   75   Cockburnspath

73

Campbeltown

73   73

Ayr

Douglas

SOUTHERN
UPLAND
WAY

74   Kirk Yetholm

7

PENNINE
WAY

Melrose

7

Portpatrick

Mitchell Library, Glasgow

Maritime centre, Dundee

Edinburgh Castle

Duthie Park Winter Garden, Aberdeen

Stirling Castle

Inverness

Edinburgh

One of the most visited cities in Europe, the capital of Scotland is historic, cosmopolitan and cultured. Its magnificent castle dominates the city-centre skyline. The Old and New Towns are a World Heritage Site: explore the winding alleys of the medieval Old Town and the neoclassical buildings and broad, straight streets of the New Town. Edinburgh is not called the Festival City lightly, as its incredible calendar of annual events clearly shows.

Glasgow

Glasgow, Scotland's capital of style, is positively oozing with things to see and do. From superb shopping and a vibrant nightlife, to some of the best free museums and galleries in the country. At The Lighthouse, a Charles Rennie Mackintosh conversion, you'll find dynamic art and architecture exhibitions and a stunning, uninterrupted view over the city. Or take a stroll through the city's West End, a bohemian district of cafés, bars, clubs and boutiques.

Inverness

Visit Inverness for the perfect cocktail of city life and adventure sports enjoyed in the great outdoors. Crowned by a Gothic red sandstone castle, the compact city centre is lavishly decorated with flowers. You'll find great shopping, food and drink and plenty of places to relax. See the tropical gardens at the Floral Hall, head out to Culloden, site of the famous battle, or go monster-spotting on nearby Loch Ness.

Stirling

Stirling may be Scotland's youngest city, but, as the centre of Braveheart country, you can touch and feel the sense of history that marks it out as unique. Take in the magnificent view from the ramparts of the cliff-top castle, or meander along the compact heritage mile of the Old Town, boasting the finest concentration of historic buildings in Scotland. Modern Stirling has a bustling centre with a cosmopolitan edge, quality local attractions and a café culture.

Places to visit

Aberdeen Art Gallery
(01224) 523700
aagm.co.uk
Marble-lined galleries and impressive collections

Bannockburn Heritage Centre
Stirling
0844 493 2139
nts.org.uk
Historic battlefield with famous Bruce statue

Benmore Botanic Garden
Dunoon, Argyll and Bute
(01369) 706261
rbge.org.uk
Spectacular gardens with avenue of giant redwoods

Blair Castle
near Pitlochry, Perth and Kinross
(01796) 481207
blair-castle.co.uk
Scotland's most visited historic house

Braemar Castle
Aberdeenshire
(01339) 741219
braemarscotland.co.uk
Seventeenth century castle with star-shaped curtain wall

Burns National Heritage Centre
Ayr
(01292) 443700
burnsheritagepark.com
Experience the power, pride and passion of Robert Burns

Cairngorm Reindeer Centre
Aviemore, Highlands
(01479) 861228
reindeer-company.demon.co.uk
Wander freely amongst the herd

Caledonian Railway
Brechin, Angus
(01356) 622992
caledonianrailway.co.uk
Travel back in time to the Bridge of Dun

Carlyle's Birthplace
Lockerbie, Dumfries and Galloway
0844 493 2247
nts.org.uk
Home and relics of the famous historian and social reformer

Clydebuilt (Scottish Maritime Museum Braehead)
Glasgow
(0141) 886 1013
scottishmaritimemuseum.org
Interactive history of Glasgow's emblematic river

Deep Sea World
North Queensferry, Fife
(01383) 411880
deepseaworld.com
Take a dive in shark-infested waters

Edinburgh Castle
(0131) 225 9846
historic-scotland.gov.uk
Magnificent fortress dominating the capital's skyline

Edinburgh Zoo
(0131) 334 9171
edinburghzoo.org.uk
From the tiny blue poison arrow frog to the massive rhino

Glamis Castle
near Forfar, Angus
(01307) 840393
glamis-castle.co.uk
Childhood home of HM Queen Elizabeth The Queen Mother

The Glenlivet Distillery Visitor Centre
Ballindalloch, Moray
(01340) 821720
glenlivetestate.co.uk/glenlivet_distillery.html
Interactive tour of a distillery producing a fine single malt

Hunterian Art Gallery
Glasgow
(0141) 330 5431
hunterian.gla.ac.uk
Housing the University of Glasgow's outstanding art collections

Hunterian Museum
Glasgow
(0141) 330 4221
hunterian.gla.ac.uk
The oldest museum in Scotland, housed in Gothic splendour

Laphroaig Distillery
Isle of Islay, Argyll and Bute
(01496) 302418
laphroaig.com
Visit the distillers of a fine single malt

Mercat Walking Tours of Edinburgh
(0131) 225 5445
mercattours.com
Take a trip into the dark, magical history of Edinburgh

National Gallery of Scotland
Edinburgh
(0131) 624 6200
nationalgalleries.org
Scotland's greatest collection of painting and sculpture

National Wallace Monument
Causewayhead, Stirling
(01786) 472140
nationalwallacemonument.com
Spectacular tower commemorating Scotland's 'Braveheart'

Diary dates 2008

Palace of Holyroodhouse
Edinburgh
(0131) 556 5100
royal.gov.uk
HM The Queen's official residence in Scotland, founded in 1128

The Royal Yacht Britannia
Leith Docks, Edinburgh
(0131) 555 5566
royalyachtbritannia.co.uk
Tour the most famous yacht in the world

Scottish Maritime Museum
Irvine, North Ayrshire
(01294) 278283
scottishmaritimemuseum.org
Scotland's influence on the world's maritime history

Scottish National Portrait Gallery
Edinburgh
(0131) 624 6200
natgalscot.ac.uk
Portraits of those who shaped Scottish history

The Tall Ship at Glasgow Harbour
(0141) 222 2513
thetallship.com
Discover life aboard a tall ship

World Famous Old Blacksmith's Shop Centre
Gretna, Dumfries and Galloway
(01461) 338441
gretnagreen.com
Follow a thousand eloping couples to the original Blacksmith's Shop

Celtic Connections
Glasgow
celticconnections.com
16 Jan – 3 Feb

Shetland Folk Festival
shetlandfolkfestival.com
1 – 4 May

Isle of Bute Jazz Festival
butejazz.com
1 – 5 May

UCI Mountain Bike World Cup
Fort William
fortwilliamworldcup.co.uk
7 – 8 Jun

Taste of Grampian
Inverurie, Aberdeenshire
tasteofgrampian.co.uk
14 Jun

Edinburgh Military Tattoo
edintattoo.co.uk
1 – 23 Aug

Blair Castle International Horse Trials and Country Fair
Blair Atholl
blairhorsetrials.co.uk
21 – 24 Aug

The Braemar Gathering
braemargathering.org
6 Sep

Glasgay
Glasgow
glasgay.co.uk
Oct – Nov*

Edinburgh's Hogmany
edinburghshogmanay.org
29 Dec – 1 Jan

* provisional date at time of going to press

Tourist Information Centres

When you arrive at your destination, visit a Tourist Information Centre for help with accommodation and information about local attractions and events. Alternatively call **0845 22 55 121** to receive information and book accommodation before you go.

Aberdeen	23 Union Street		Dunvegan	2 Lochside
Aberfeldy	The Square		Durness*	Sangomore
Aberfoyle	Trossachs Discovery Centre		Edinburgh	Princess Mall, 3 Princes Street
Abington	Junction 13, M74 Services		Edinburgh Airport	Main Concourse
			Elgin	17 High Street
Alford*	Old Station Yard		Eyemouth*	Auld Kirk, Manse Road
Alva	Mill Trail Visitor Centre		Falkirk	2-4 Glebe Street
Anstruther*	Scottish Fisheries Museum		Forres*	116 High Street
Arbroath	Gravesend		Fort William	Cameron Square
Ardgartan*	By Arrochar		Fraserburgh*	3 Saltoun Square
Aviemore	Grampian Road		Gatehouse of Fleet*	Car Park
Ayr	22 Sandgate		Glasgow	11 George Square
Ballater	Station Square		Glasgow Airport	International Arrivals Hall
Balloch*	The Old Station Building		Grantown on Spey*	54 High Street
Banchory*	Bridge Street		Gretna	Gretna Gateway Outlet Village
Banff*	Collie Lodge			
Biggar*	155 High Street		Hawick*	Drumlanrig's Tower
Blairgowrie	26 Wellmeadow		Helensburgh*	The Clock Tower
Bo'ness*	Union Street		Huntly*	9a The Square
Bowmore	The Square		Inveraray	Front Street
Braemar	Mar Road		Inverness	Castle Wynd
Brechin*	Pictavia Centre		Inverurie*	18 High Street
Brodick	The Pier		Jedburgh	Murrays Green
Callander*	Rob Roy Centre		Kelso	The Square
Campbeltown	The Pier		Killin*	Breadalbane Folklore Centre
Castlebay*	Main Street			
Castle Douglas*	Market Hill Car Park		Kinross*	Junction 6, M90
Craignure	The Pier		Kirkcaldy	339 High Street
Crail*	Crail Museum, 62 Marketgate		Kirkcudbright	Harbour Square
			Kirkwall	6 Broad Street
Crathie*	The Car Park		Lanark	Horsemarket, Ladyacre Road
Crieff	High Street			
Daviot Wood*	Picnic Area, A9		Largs*	Main Street
Drumnadrochit	The Car Park		Lerwick	The Market Cross
Dufftown*	The Square		Linlithgow*	Burgh Halls, The Cross
Dumbarton	Milton, A82 Northbound		Loch Lomond Gateway Centre	Loch Lomond Shores
Dumfries	64 Whitesands		Lochboisdale*	Pier Road
Dunbar*	141 High Street		Lochgilphead*	Lochnell Street
Dundee	21 Castle Street		Lochinver*	Kirk Lane
Dunfermline	1 High Street		Lochmaddy*	Pier Road
Dunkeld	The Cross		Melrose	Abbey Street
Dunoon	7 Alexandra Parade		Moffat*	Churchgate

Newtongrange*	Scottish Mining Museum		Stornoway	26 Cromwell Street
Newton Stewart*	Dashwood Square		Stranraer	Burns House, 28 Harbour Street
North Berwick	Quality Street		Stromness	Ferry Terminal Building
North Kessock*	Car Park, Picnic Site		Strontian*	Acharacle
Oban	Argyll Square		Sumburgh	Sumburgh Airport
Paisley	9A Gilmour Street		Tarbert (Harris)*	Pier Road
Peebles	High Street		Tarbert (Loch Fyne)*	Harbour Street
Perth	West Mill Street		Tarbet (Loch Lomond)*	Main Street
Pitlochry	22 Atholl Road		Thurso*	Riverside Road
Portree	Bayfield Road		Tobermory*	The Pier
Rothesay	Winter Gardens		Tomintoul*	The Square
St Andrews	70 Market Street		Tyndrum	Main Street
Selkirk*	Halliwells House		Ullapool	Argyle Street
Stirling	41 Dumbarton Road			
Stirling (Pirnhall)	Junction 9, M9 Services		*seasonal opening	
Stonehaven*	66 Allardice Street			

South Ayrshire coast by Girvan

Travel info

By road:
The A1 and M6 bring you quickly over the border and immerse you in beautiful scenery. Scotland's network of excellent roads span out from Edinburgh – Glasgow takes approximately one hour and 15 minutes by car; Aberdeen two hours 30 minutes and Inverness three hours.

By rail:
The cross-border service from England and Wales to Scotland is fast and efficient, and Scotrail trains offer overnight Caledonian sleepers to make the journey even easier. Telephone 0845 755 0033 for further details.

By air:
Fly into Aberdeen, Dundee, Edinburgh, Glasgow or Inverness.

Find out more

The following publications and more are available online from VisitScotland.com or by calling the information and booking service on 0845 22 55 121:

Where to Stay Hotels & Guest Houses £8.99

Over 2,100 places to stay in Scotland – from luxury town houses and country hotels to budget-priced guesthouses. Details of prices and facilities, with location maps.

Where to Stay Bed & Breakfast £6.99

Over 1,900 Bed and Breakfast establishments throughout Scotland offering inexpensive accommodation – the perfect way to enjoy a budget trip and meet Scottish folk in their own homes. Details of prices and facilities, with location maps.

Where to Stay Caravan & Camping £4.99

Over 350 parks detailed with prices, available facilities and lots of other useful information. Parks inspected by the British Holiday Parks Grading Scheme. Also includes caravan homes for hire, with location maps.

Where to Stay Self Catering £5.99

Over 3,500 cottages, apartments and chalets to let – many in scenic areas. Details of prices and facilities, with location maps.

Touring Guide to Scotland £7.99

A fully revised edition of this popular guide which now lists over 1,700 things to do and places to visit in Scotland. Easy to use index and locator maps. Details of opening hours, admission charges, general description and information on disabled access.

Touring Map of Scotland £4.99

An up-to-date touring map of Scotland. Full colour with comprehensive motorway and road information, the map details over 20 categories of tourist information and names over 1,500 things to do and places to visit in Scotland.

Loch Awe and Kilchurn Castle, Argyll

where to stay in
Scotland

All place names in the blue bands are shown on the maps at the front of this guide.

Accommodation symbols
Symbols give useful information about services and facilities. Inside the back-cover flap you can find a key to these symbols. Keep it open for easy reference.

AYR, South Ayrshire Map ref 6B2

★★★★★
TOURING PARK
(90) £12.10–£24.90
(90) £12.10–£24.90
90 touring pitches

See Ad on inside front cover

Craigie Gardens Caravan Club Site

Craigie Road, Ayr KA8 0SS **t** (01292) 264909

open All year
payment Credit/debit cards, cash/cheques

Set in a beautiful park, a short walk from Ayr. This area, known as 'The Golf Coast', has 40 golf courses! Learn about 'Rabbie Burns', the greatest Scottish poet, with the Burns Heritage Trail nearby. Open all year.

A77 Ayr bypass to Whitletts roundabout, then A719 via racecourse. Left at lights into Craigie Road. 0.5 miles, then after right-hand bend left into Craigie Gardens. Site 400yds on right.

Special member rates mean you can save your membership subscription in less than a week. Visit our website to find out more.

THE CARAVAN CLUB

General Leisure

AYR, South Ayrshire Map ref 6B2

★★★★
HOLIDAY PARK
(20) £11.50–£16.50
(8) £10.00–£15.00
(8) £10.00–£16.50
(10) £160.00–£550.00
36 touring pitches

Heads of Ayr Caravan Park

Dunure Road, Ayr KA7 4LD **t** (01292) 442269 **f** (01292) 500298 **e** stay@headsofayr.com
w headsofayr.com

Situated five miles south of Ayr on the A719. Facilities include bar, shop, laundry, play area and beach. Seasonal entertainment. Caravans to hire. Tourers and tents welcome. Open March to October.

payment Cash/cheques

General Leisure

Place index

If you know where you want to stay, the index at the back of the guide will give you the page number listing accommodation in your chosen town, city or village. Check out the other useful indexes too.

BALLOCH, West Dunbartonshire Map ref 6B2

★★★★★
HOLIDAY PARK
THISTLE AWARD

🚐 £15.00–£20.00
🚃 £15.00–£20.00
🏠 (6) £195.00–£550.00
120 touring pitches

Lomond Woods Holiday Park

Tullichewan, Old Luss Road, Balloch, Loch Lomond G83 8QP t (01389) 759475 f (01389) 755563
e lomondwoods@holiday-parks.co.uk w holiday-parks.co.uk

Beside Loch Lomond and at the gateway to the National Park, this superbly appointed, family-run park offers pine lodges and caravans for holiday hire and sunny, secluded pitches for touring caravans and motor homes.

open All year
payment Credit/debit cards, cash/cheques

General 🔌📺P🔥🚿🚰📻☉📟🔋🐾🏕☀ Leisure 📺🔍⛰∪♪▶🚲

BALMACARA, Highland Map ref 7B3

★★★★
TOURING PARK

🚐 (40) Min £11.00
🚃 (40) Min £11.00
⛺ (5) Min £11.00
45 touring pitches

Reraig Caravan Site

Balmacara, Kyle of Lochalsh IV40 8DH t (01599) 566215 e warden@reraig.com w reraig.com

Small family-run site, four miles from bridge to Isle of Skye. Booking not necessary. No awnings during July and August. Tents: only small tents permitted. No youth groups. Open May to September.

payment Credit/debit cards, cash/cheques

General 🔥P🔥🚰📻☉🏕

BOAT OF GARTEN, Highland Map ref 7C3

★★★★
HOLIDAY PARK

🏠 (3) £250.00–£375.00

Loch Garten Lodges & Caravan Park

Loch Garten Road, Boat of Garten PH24 3BY t (01479) 831769 f (01479) 831708
e m.ireland@totalise.co.uk w lochgarten.co.uk

Close by the ospreys on the outskirts of Boat of Garten beside the Speyside Way. A quiet location with squirrels, deer and rampant bird life. This is luxury in a wilderness setting. Self catering at its most comfortable.

open All year
payment Cash/cheques

General 🔌P📟🐾☀ Leisure ∪♪▶🚲

BRAEMAR, Aberdeenshire Map ref 7C3

★★★★
TOURING PARK

🚐 (97) £12.10–£24.90
🚃 (97) £12.10–£24.90
97 touring pitches

See Ad on inside front cover

The Invercauld Caravan Club Site

Glenshee Road, Braemar, Ballater AB35 5YQ t (01342) 326944 w caravanclub.co.uk

payment Credit/debit cards, cash/cheques

Set on the edge of Braemar village, gateway to the Cairngorms. Ideal centre for mountain lovers. See red deer, caper caillie and golden eagles. Open December 2007 to October 2008.

⊕ On A93 on southern outskirts of village.

♥ Special member rates mean you can save your membership subscription in less than a week. Visit our website to find out more.

General 🔌P🔥🚿🚰📻☉📟🔋🐾☀ Leisure ⛰♪▶

It's all quality-assessed accommodation

Our commitment to quality involves wide-ranging accommodation assessment. Rating and awards were correct at the time of going to press but may change following a new assessment. Please check at time of booking.

CALLANDER, Stirling Map ref 6B1

★★★★★
HOLIDAY PARK

🚐 (128)　Min £18.00
🚐 (128)　Min £18.00
128 touring pitches

Gart Caravan Park

Stirling Road, Callander FK17 8LE　t (01877) 330002　f (01877) 330002
e enquiries@theholidaypark.co.uk　w theholidaypark.co.uk

payment Credit/debit cards, cash/cheques

A peaceful and spacious park maintained to a very high standard with modern, heated shower block facilities. The ideal centre for cycling, walking and fishing.

⊕ Leave jct 10 of the M9, west to Callander.

♥ Reduced rates for the over 50s. Winner – Calor Gas Best Park in Britain 2003.

General 🖼 P 🔌 🗗 🕿 🖼 🟤 ☉ 🗐🗐 🐴 ☼　Leisure ⚠ ∪ ♪ ▶ ⅋

CULLODEN, Highland Map ref 7C3

★★★★★
TOURING PARK

🚐 (97)　£12.10–£24.90
🚐 (97)　£12.10–£24.90
97 touring pitches

See Ad on inside front cover

Culloden Moor Caravan Club Site

Newlands, Inverness IV2 5EF　t (01463) 790625　w caravanclub.co.uk

payment Credit/debit cards

A gently sloping site with glorious views over the Nairn Valley. Inverness, with impressive castle, great shops and fascinating museums, is six miles away. Open March to January 2009.

⊕ From A9 south of Inverness, take B9006 signposted Croy, site on left 1 mile past Culloden field memorial.

♥ Special member rates mean you can save your membership subscription in less than a week. Visit our website to find out more.

General 🖼 P 🔌 🗗 🕿 🖼 🟤 ☉ 🗐🗐 🐴 ☼　Leisure ⚠ ♪

DIRLETON, East Lothian Map ref 6D2

★★★★★
TOURING PARK

🚐 (116)　£13.60–£25.60
🚐 (116)　£13.60–£25.60
116 touring pitches

See Ad on inside front cover

Yellowcraig Caravan Club Site

Dirleton, North Berwick EH39 5DS　t (01620) 850217　w caravanclub.co.uk

payment Credit/debit cards, cash/cheques

This is a great choice for family holidays with acres of golden sands and rock pools close by. Pitching areas separated by sandy dunes, shrubs and roses. Open March to November.

⊕ From North Berwick take A198, signposted Edinburgh. Turn right off bypass for Dirleton, then right again at International Camping sign.

♥ Special member rates mean you can save your membership subscription in less than a week. Visit our website to find out more.

General 🖼 P 🔌 🗗 🕿 🖼 🟤 ☉ 🗐🗐 🐴 ☼　Leisure ⚠ ▶

DUNBAR, East Lothian Map ref 6D2

★★★★
HOLIDAY PARK
THISTLE AWARD

🚐 (53) £12.00–£21.00
🚎 (53) £12.00–£21.00
▲ (53) £12.00–£21.00
🏠 (5) £245.00–£560.00
53 touring pitches

Belhaven Bay Caravan and Camping Park

Belhaven Bay, Dunbar EH42 1TU **t** (01368) 865956 **f** (01368) 865022
e belhaven@meadowhead.co.uk **w** meadowhead.co.uk

payment Credit/debit cards, cash/cheques, euros

Bordered by one of Britain's cleanest beaches and a tranquil pond. Set on the edge of the John Muir Country Park but only 30 minutes to Edinburgh's city centre! Perfect for a quiet and relaxing break. Open 1 March to 7 January.

⊕ From A1 north Thistly Cross roundabout take A199 then A1087 at Beltonford roundabout (signposted Dunbar). Continue through West Barns. Belhaven Bay on left.

♥ See website for special offers.

General 🖵 P 🔌 🛗 🍴 🚐 📶 ☉ 🛒 🗑 🐕 ☼ Leisure 🏕 🏊

DUNKELD, Perth and Kinross Map ref 6C1

★★★★
TOURING PARK

🚐 £13.00–£14.00
🚎 £13.00–£14.00
▲ (15) £11.00–£14.00
50 touring pitches

Inver Mill Farm Caravan Park

Inver, Dunkeld PH8 0JR **t** (01350) 727477 **f** (01350) 727477 **e** invermill@talk21.com
w visitdunkeld.com/perthshire-caravan-park.htm

We are situated in a very tranquil, scenic and beautiful part of Perthshire, an ideal location to explore a large part of Scotland. Open March to October.

payment Cash/cheques

General P 🔌 🛗 🍴 📶 ☉ 🛒 🗑 🐕 ☼ Leisure 🏊 ►

EDINBURGH, Edinburgh Map ref 6C2

DRUMMOHR CARAVAN PARK

Levenhall, Musselburgh, Edinburgh EH21 8JS T: (0131) 665 6867 F: (0131) 653 6859

Premier park close to Princes Street, Edinburgh, and the coast of East Lothian. Excellent bus service to city with many retail outlets in the area.

E: bookings@drummohr.org www.drummohr.org

EDINBURGH, Edinburgh Map ref 6C2

★★★★★
TOURING PARK

🚐 (80) £15.00–£18.00
🚎 (40) £15.00–£18.00
▲ (28) £15.00–£18.00
🏠 (12) £300.00–£800.00
108 touring pitches

See Ad above

Drummohr Caravan Park

Levenhall, Musselburgh, Edinburgh EH21 8JS **t** (0131) 665 6867 **f** (0131) 653 6859

payment Credit/debit cards, cash/cheques

Premier park close to Princes Street, Edinburgh and the coast of East Lothian. Excellent bus service to city with many retail outlets in the area.

⊕ From south (A1), take A199 Musselburgh, then B1361. Follow park signs. From west (A1), come off at Wallyford slip road and follow Park and Mining Museum signs.

General 🔌 P 🔌 🛗 🍴 🚐 📶 ☉ 🛒 🗑 🐄 🐕 🐾 ☼ Leisure 🏕

Key to symbols
Open the back flap for a key to symbols.

★★★★★
TOURING PARK
🚐 (197) £13.60–£25.60
🚐 (197) £13.60–£25.60
197 touring pitches

See Ad on inside front cover

Edinburgh Caravan Club Site

35-37 Marine Drive, Edinburgh EH4 5EN **t** (0131) 312 6874

open All year
payment Credit/debit cards, cash/cheques

Situated to the north of the city on the Firth of Forth, the site provides easy access to Edinburgh. It's a historic setting – yet Edinburgh is a friendly, modern, cosmopolitan city with something for everyone.

⊕ *From A901 turn left at traffic lights; at roundabout turn right into Marine Drive. Site on left.*

♥ *Special member rates mean you can save your membership subscription in less than a week. Visit our website to find out more.*

General P 🍴 ➕ 🛁 🛖 📷 🐴 🚽 Leisure ▶

★★★★
TOURING PARK
🚐 (50) £12.00–£15.00
🚐 (50) £12.00–£15.00
⛺ (10) £10.00–£13.00
60 touring pitches

Linwater Caravan Park

West Clifton, East Calder EH53 0HT **t** (0131) 333 3326 **f** (0131) 333 1952 **e** linwater@supanet.com **w** linwater.co.uk

A peaceful park seven miles west of Edinburgh. Excellent facilities. Ideal for visiting Edinburgh, Royal Highland Showground, Falkirk Wheel, or as a stop-over on your way north or south. Open 14 March to 2 November.

payment Credit/debit cards, cash/cheques, euros

General 📷 🚲 P 🍴 ➕ 🛁 🛖 ☺ 📷 🐴 🚽 ☼ Leisure ∪ ♪

★★★
HOLIDAY PARK
🚐 (11) £10.00–£11.50
🚐 (11) £10.00–£11.50
⛺ (11) £7.00–£10.00
🏠 (3) £250.00
11 touring pitches

Brownmuir Caravan Park

Fordoun, Laurencekirk AB30 1SJ **t** (01561) 320786 **f** (01561) 320786
e brownmuircaravanpark@talk21.com **w** brownmuircaravanpark.co.uk

A quiet park set in the Howe-of-the-Mearns not far from Royal Dee Side, ideal for cycling and fishing. Top golf courses are nearby. Children's play area on site. Open April to October.

payment Cash/cheques

General 📷 🚲 P 🍴 ➕ 🛁 🛖 ☺ 📷 🐴 🚽 ☼ Leisure ⚲ ⚲ ∪ ♪ ▶

★★★★★
TOURING PARK
🚐 (99) £13.60–£25.60
🚐 (99) £13.60–£25.60
99 touring pitches

See Ad on inside front cover

Bunree Caravan Club Site

Onich, Fort William PH33 6SE **t** (01855) 821283 **w** caravanclub.co.uk

payment Credit/debit cards, cash/cheques

Your van can be parked almost at the water's edge of Loch Linnhe for wonderful views of the mountains across the water. This site is breathtaking. Try a visit to Ben Nevis or Glencoe. Open March to November.

⊕ *Turn left off A82 1 mile past Onich and follow Club Site signs.*

General P 🍴 ➕ 🛁 📷 🛖 ☺ 📷 🐴 ☼ Leisure ⚲ ⚲ ♪

Scotland

FORT WILLIAM, Highland Map ref 6B1

★★★★★
HOLIDAY PARK

⊕ £13.00–£19.00
🚐 £13.00–£19.00
▲ (300) £10.20–£15.50
🏠 (22) £235.00–£525.00
250 touring pitches

Glen Nevis Caravan & Camping Park

Glen Nevis, Fort William PH33 6SX t (01397) 702191 f (01397) 703904
e cottages@glen-nevis.co.uk w glen-nevis.co.uk

Our award-winning touring caravan and camping park has a magnificent location in one of Scotland's most famous highland glens at the foot of mighty Ben Nevis. Closed during the winter.

payment Credit/debit cards, cash/cheques

General ⬛ Leisure

FORT WILLIAM, Highland Map ref 6B1

★★★★★
HOLIDAY PARK

⊕ (65) £16.00–£18.50
🚐 (65) £16.00–£18.50
▲ (15) £13.00–£16.00
🏠 (60) £265.00–£520.00
80 touring pitches

Linnhe Lochside Holidays

Corpach, Fort William PH33 7NL t (01397) 772376 f (01397) 772007
e relax@linnhe-lochside-holidays.co.uk w linnhe-lochside-holidays.co.uk

payment Credit/debit cards, cash/cheques

Almost a botanical garden. Winner of 'Best Park in Scotland 1999' award. Free fishing. Colour brochure sent with pleasure. Also self-catering. Open 15 December to 31 October.

⊕ On A830 1.5 miles (3km) west of Corpach village, 5 miles from Fort William.

♥ Discounts for senior citizen groups and for 2nd week. Rallies – no charge for awnings.

General ⬛ Leisure

GLENCOE, Highland Map ref 6B1

★★★★★
HOLIDAY PARK
THISTLE AWARD

⊕ Min £17.00
🚐 Min £17.00
▲ Min £15.00
🏠 £270.00–£450.00
60 touring pitches

Invercoe Caravan & Camping Park

Invercoe, Glencoe PH49 4HP t (01855) 811210 f (01855) 811210 e holidays@invercoe.co.uk
w invercoe.co.uk

open All year
payment Credit/debit cards, cash/cheques

Situated on the shores of Loch Leven and surrounded by spectacular scenery, Invercoe is a small, award-winning, family-run park and is an excellent base for exploring the West Highlands. Booking advisable during high season (minimum three nights).

⊕ Site is 0.25 miles from Glencoe crossroads (A82) on the Kinlochleven road (B863).

General ⬛ Leisure

Our quality rating schemes

For a detailed explanation of the quality and facilities represented by the stars, please refer to the information pages at the back of this guide.

GRANTOWN-ON-SPEY, Highland Map ref 7C3

★★★★★
HOLIDAY PARK
(136) £15.00–£23.00
(136) £15.00–£23.00
Δ (40) £10.00–£17.00
136 touring pitches

Grantown on Spey Caravan Park

Seafield Avenue, Grantown on Spey PH26 3JQ t (01479) 872474 f (01479) 873696
e warden@caravanscotland.com w caravanscotland.com

open All year
payment Credit/debit cards, cash/cheques

A scenic park in a mature setting near the river and town, surrounded by hills, mountains, moors and woodland. The park is very well landscaped, and is in a good location for golf, fishing, mountaineering, walking, sailing and canoeing.

⊕ Take A9 to A95 north of Aviemore. Follow A95 into Grantown. Turn north on Seafield Avenue by Bank of Scotland.

General 🗺 🚗 P 🔌 🏕 🛒 🚐 📶 ☉ 🏪 🐕 🐎 ☼ Leisure 🎣 ⛰ ♪ ⛳ 🚴 ⛵

INVERNESS, Highland Map ref 7C3

★★★★
HOLIDAY PARK
 £11.00–£15.00
 £11.00–£15.00
Δ (30) £8.00–£10.00
(11) £160.00–£300.00
45 touring pitches

Auchnahillin Caravan and Camping Park

Daviot East, Inverness IV2 5XQ t (01463) 772286 e info@auchnahillin.co.uk w auchnahillin.co.uk

Warm welcome awaits at friendly, informal, family-run park. Ten acres, peaceful, scenic, rural location but convenient for many attractions, ideal base for touring. Refurbished amenities, small shop, play area, laundrette. Open March to October.

payment Credit/debit cards, cash/cheques

General 🔌 🗺 🚗 P 🔌 🏕 🛒 🚐 📶 ☉ 🏪 🐕 🐎 ☼ Leisure ⛰ ♪

JOHN O'GROATS, Highland Map ref 7D1

★★★
TOURING PARK
(90) Min £10.00
(90) Min £10.00
Δ (90) Min £10.00
90 touring pitches

John O' Groats Caravan Park

John O' Groats, Wick KW1 4YR t (01955) 611329 & (01955) 611744
e info@johnogroatscampsite.co.uk w johnogroatscampsite.co.uk

On seashore overlooking Orkney Islands (day trips available). Hotel restaurant 400m, harbour 150m, sea birds 3km. Cliff scenery. Open April to September.

payment Cash/cheques

General P 🔌 🏕 🛒 🚐 📶 ☉ 🏪 🐕 Leisure ∪ ♪

KILLIN, Stirling Map ref 6B1

★★★★★
TOURING PARK
(100) £13.60–£25.60
(100) £13.60–£25.60
100 touring pitches

See Ad on inside front cover

Maragowan Caravan Club Site

Aberfeldy Road, Killin FK21 8TN t (01567) 820245 w caravanclub.co.uk

payment Credit/debit cards, cash/cheques

An ideal family holiday base, set on one bank of the River Lochay and within walking distance of the shops and restaurants of the little holiday town of Killin. Open March to November.

⊕ Site on right of A827 (Killin-Kenmore) 0.5 miles past end of village.

♥ Special member rates mean you can save your membership subscription in less than a week. Visit our website to find out more.

THE CARAVAN CLUB

General P 🔌 🏕 🛒 🚐 📶 ☉ 🏪 🐕 Leisure ♪

KIRKCOWAN, Dumfries & Galloway Map ref 6B3

Rating Applied For

(21)	£13.00–£16.00
(21)	£13.00–£16.00
(9)	£8.00–£16.00
(8)	£170.00–£418.00

31 touring pitches

Three Lochs Estate

Kirkcowan, Newton Stewart DG8 0EP **t** (01671) 830304 **f** (01671) 830335
e parkmanager01@btconnect.com **w** 3lochs.co.uk

Three Lochs Holiday Park, one of the most reputed UK caravan parks, offers a lifestyle as varied and interesting as the seasons themselves.

open All year except Christmas and New Year
payment Credit/debit cards, cash/cheques

General ☐ ☐ P ☐ ☐ ☐ ☐ ☐ ☐ ☐ ☐ ☐ ☐ ☀ Leisure ☐ ☐ ☐ ☐ ☐ ☐

LAURENCEKIRK, Aberdeenshire Map ref 6D1

★★★★
HOLIDAY PARK

(25)	£11.00–£12.00
(25)	£11.00–£12.00
(25)	£8.00–£9.00
(1)	£220.00–£250.00

25 touring pitches

Dovecot Caravan Park

Northwaterbridge, Laurencekirk AB30 1QL **t** (01674) 840630 **f** (01674) 840630
e info@dovecotcaravanpark.com **w** dovecotcaravanpark.com

Dovecot is a peaceful, rural site located halfway between Dundee and Aberdeen. Ideal location for touring. Sandy beaches eight miles and Angus Glens on our doorstep. Open April to mid-October.

payment Cash/cheques

General P ☐ ☐ ☐ ☐ ☐ ☐ ☐ ☐ ☐ ☐ ☐ Leisure ☐ ☐ ☐

LINLITHGOW, West Lothian Map ref 6C2

★★★★
TOURING PARK

(36)	£12.00–£16.00
(36)	£12.00–£16.00
(20)	£10.00–£19.00

56 touring pitches

Beecraigs Caravan and Camping Site

Beecraigs Country Park, The Park Centre, Linlithgow EH49 6PL **t** (01506) 844516 **f** (01506) 846256
e mail@beecraigs.com **w** beecraigs.com

open All year
payment Credit/debit cards, cash/cheques

Open all year. Situated near historic Linlithgow town. On-site facilities include electric hook-ups, barbecues, play area, modern toilet facilities with privacy cubicles, baby-change and laundry. Pets welcome. Leaflets available. Great for exploring central Scotland and the Lothians.

⊕ *From Linlithgow, follow Beecraigs Country Park and International Caravan Park signposts. Park is 2 miles south of Linlithgow. From M8, follow B792. From M9, follow A803.*

♥ *1 October 2007 – 9 March 2008: 10% discount for Senior Citizens (proof required) and 10% discount for 7-night stay if paid in advance (excl Senior Citizens).*

General P ☐ ☐ ☐ ☐ ☐ ☐ ☐ ☐ × ☐ ☀ Leisure ☐ ☐ ☐ ☐ ☐

LOCKERBIE, Dumfries & Galloway Map ref 6C3

★★★★★
HOLIDAY PARK

(100)	£7.50–£14.00
(100)	£7.50–£14.00
(30)	£6.50–£14.00

130 touring pitches

Hoddom Castle Caravan Park

Hoddom, Lockerbie DG11 1AS **t** (01576) 300251 **e** hoddomcastle@aol.com **w** hoddomcastle.co.uk

Part of 10,000-acre estate. Beautiful, peaceful, award-winning park. Own 9-hole golf course. Salmon, seatrout and coarse fishing. Nature trails and walks in surrounding countryside. Open April to October.

payment Credit/debit cards, cash/cheques

General ☐ ☐ P ☐ ☐ ☐ ☐ ☐ ☐ ☐ ☐ ☐ × ☐ ☐ ☀ Leisure ☐ ☐ ☐ ☐ ☐ ☐ ☐ ☐ ☐

Using map references
Map references refer to the colour maps at the front of this guide.

MELROSE, Scottish Borders Map ref 6C2

★★★★★
TOURING PARK

🚐 (60) £13.60–£25.60
🚙 (60) £13.60–£25.60
🛖 on application
60 touring pitches

See Ad on inside front cover

CARAVAN CLUB

Gibson Park Caravan Club Site

High Street, Melrose TD6 9RY t (01896) 822969 w caravanclub.co.uk

open All year
payment Credit/debit cards, cash/cheques

Peaceful, award-winning site on edge of town. Adjacent tennis courts and playing fields. Melrose Abbey, where Robert the Bruce's head is buried, is within walking distance. Non-members welcome.

⊕ Site adjacent to main road (A6091) close to centre of town. Approx 6 miles (10km) from A68 Edinburgh/Newcastle road.

♥ Special member rates mean that you can save your membership subscription in less than a week. Visit our website to find out more.

General 🖼 P 🔌 🚻 🍴 🚐 📶 ☉ 🔘 🐾 ☼ Leisure ⚲ 🎣 ⚑

NORTH BERWICK, East Lothian Map ref 6D2

★★★★★
HOLIDAY PARK

THISTLE AWARD

🚐 (147) £13.00–£22.00
🚙 (147) £13.00–£22.00
🛖 (40) £13.00–£22.00
🏠 (10) £275.00–£625.00
147 touring pitches

Tantallon Caravan Park

Dunbar Road, North Berwick EH39 5NJ t (01620) 893348 f (01620) 895623
e tantallon@meadowhead.co.uk w meadowhead.co.uk

payment Credit/debit cards, cash/cheques, euros

Relaxing park that's ideal for exploring the classy golfing capital of North Berwick and East Lothian beyond. Overlooks Glen Golf Course with views of the Forth, Bass Rock, Isle of May and Fife. Local bus and trains connect us to Edinburgh. Open 1 March to 7 January.

⊕ From North Berwick, A198 towards Dunbar. From the south, turn off at A1 north of Dunbar and follow signs for North Berwick and Tantallon Park.

♥ See website for special offers.

General 🖼 P 🔌 🚻 🍴 🚐 📶 ☉ 📧🔘 🛒 🐾 ☼ Leisure 📺 ⚫ 🎿 ⚑

PARTON, Dumfries & Galloway Map ref 6C3

★★★★
HOLIDAY PARK

🚐 (52) £16.00–£18.00
🚙 (4) £16.00–£18.00
🛖 (50) £12.00–£16.00
🏠 (10) £260.00–£480.00
56 touring pitches

Loch Ken Holiday Park

Parton, Castle Douglas DG7 3NE t (01644) 470282 e penny@lochkenholidaypark.co.uk
w lochkenholidaypark.co.uk

payment Credit/debit cards, cash/cheques

A popular park situated on the shores of Loch Ken. There is a natural emphasis on water activities; excellent fishing, sailing, water-skiing. Family-owned and run. It is in a beautiful spot, opposite the RSPB reserve. An uncommercialised, natural, peaceful place for a relaxing family holiday. David Bellamy Gold Conservation Award. Open March to November.

⊕ Take the A713 from A75 at Castle Douglas. 7m to Loch Ken Holiday Park.

♥ Short breaks for static holiday homes Mar-Jul, Sep-Nov.

General 🛁 P 🔌 🚻 🍴 📶 📧🔘 🛒 🐾 🍴 ☼ Leisure ∪ 🎣 ⚑ 🚵

Friendly help and advice

Tourist Information Centres offer friendly help with accommodation and holiday ideas as well as suggestions of places to visit and things to do. You'll find contact details at the beginning of each regional section.

PITLOCHRY, Perth and Kinross Map ref 6C1

★★★★
HOLIDAY PARK
THISTLE AWARD

🚐	£14.00–£16.50
🚙	£14.00–£16.50
⛺	£14.00–£16.50
🏠 (36)	£240.00–£430.00

154 touring pitches

Milton of Fonab Caravan Site

Bridge Road, Pitlochry PH16 5NA t (01796) 472882 f (01796) 474363 e info@fonab.co.uk
w fonab.co.uk

Quiet, family-run site on the banks of the River Tummel, 0.5 miles south of Pitlochry and a five minute walk from Pitlochry Festival Theatre. Mountain-bike hire, free trout fishing. Open March to October.

payment Cash/cheques

General 🖰 P 🚐 🖰 🛡 ⋔ ⊙ 🖳📷 🐾 🐕 🐄 ☼ Leisure ♪ ► ⚲

PORT LOGAN, Dumfries & Galloway Map ref 6B3

★★★★
TOURING PARK

🚐 (158)	£10.40–£22.40
🚙 (158)	£10.40–£22.40

158 touring pitches

See Ad on inside front cover

New England Bay Caravan Club Site

Port Logan, Stranraer DG9 9NX t (01776) 860275 w caravanclub.co.uk

payment Credit/debit cards, cash/cheques

On the edge of Luce Bay, an ideal site for children with direct access to a safe, clean, sandy beach. Sailing, sea-angling, golf, green bowling, pony-trekking. Open March to November.

⊕ From Newton Stewart take A75, then A715, then A716. Site on left 2.7 miles past Ardwell Filling Station.

♥ Special member rates mean you can save your membership subscription in less than a week. Visit our website to find out more.

General 🖵 P 🚐 🛡 🖵 ⋔ ⊙ 🖳📷 🐾 ☼ Leisure ⚓ ⛰ ∪

SHIEL BRIDGE, Highland Map ref 7B3

★★★★★
TOURING PARK

🚐 (106)	£12.10–£24.90
🚙 (106)	£12.10–£24.90
⛺	on application

106 touring pitches

See Ad on inside front cover

Morvich Caravan Club Site

Inverinate, Kyle IV40 8HQ t (01599) 511354 w caravanclub.co.uk

payment Credit/debit cards, cash/cheques

Morvich has all the amenities for an ideal family holiday base. All around there are hills and mountains and the most dazzling scenery. Great for walkers – so take your boots and binoculars. Open March to November.

⊕ Turn right off A87 1.25 miles past Shiel Bridge. In 1 mile turn right into road to site entrance. Site on left in 150yds.

♥ Special member rates mean you can save your membership subscription in less than a week. Visit our website to find out more.

General P 🚐 🖰 🛡 🖵 ⋔ ⊙ 🖳📷 🐾 ☼ Leisure ⚓ ♪

STEPPS, North Lanarkshire Map ref 6B2

★★★
HOLIDAY PARK

🚐 (14)	£13.50–£15.00
🚙 (13)	£13.50–£15.00
⛺ (30)	£14.25–£16.25
🏠 (17)	£150.00–£400.00

27 touring pitches

Craigendmuir Caravan and Camping Park

Craigendmuir Park, Stepps G33 6AF t (0141) 779 4159 f (0141) 779 4057
e info@craigendmuir.co.uk w craigendmuir.co.uk

Craigendmuir Park offers substantial touring caravan and camping areas, together with fully equipped chalets and static caravans.

open All year
payment Credit/debit cards, cash/cheques

General ⛽ P 🚐 🖰 🛡 ⋔ ⊙ 🖳📷 ⋔ ☼ Leisure ∪ ♪ ►

STIRLING, Stirling Map ref 6C2

★★★★★
TOURING PARK

🚐(60)   £12.00–£16.00
🚎(60)   £12.00–£16.00
🅰(60)   £10.00–£16.00
60 touring pitches

Witches Craig Caravan Park

Blairlogie, Stirling FK9 5PX   t (01786) 474947   f (01786) 447286   e info@witchescraig.co.uk
w witchescraig.co.uk

Winner of numerous awards, Witches Craig is attractive and exceptionally well maintained. Peacefully situated below the picturesque Ochil Hills, an ideal place to unwind. Great base for travelling. Superb modern facilities. Open 1 April to 31 October.

payment Credit/debit cards, cash/cheques

General 🖵 ♿ P 🕭 🗗 🍴 🖨 📷 ☉ 🍴🖼 🐕 ☼   Leisure ⛰ ∪ ⌘

THURSO, Highland Map ref 7C1

★★★★★
TOURING PARK

🚐(57)   £12.90–£24.90
🚎(57)   £12.90–£24.90
57 touring pitches

See Ad on inside front cover

Dunnet Bay Caravan Club Site

Dunnet, Thurso KW14 8XD   t (01847) 821319   w caravanclub.co.uk

payment Credit/debit cards, cash/cheques

A good place for those who like to be solitary. Views to Dunnet Head, northernmost point of mainland Britain. Good for bird-watching and fishing. Open April to October.

⊕ *From east (John O'Groats) on A836. Site on right past Dunnet village.*

♥ *Special member rates mean you can save your membership subscription in less than a week. Visit our website to find out more.*

General P 🕭 🗗 🖼 📷 📷 🐕   Leisure ⌘

Wales

Fascinating land of the ancient Celts

For a small country Wales is big on things to see and do. We're not just talking about mountains, valleys and beaches – culture, exercise, adventure and peace and quiet, they're all here too.

Visit Wales
visitwales.com
0870 121 1251

Portmeirion, Gwynedd

Caernarfon Castle

Llyn Gwynant, Gwynedd

You can feel the draw of Wales with three National Parks, each with differing landscapes, a turbulent history which comes alive in its castles and hundreds of miles of seashore which have been declared Areas of Outstanding Natural Beauty and Heritage Coast. Ascend to the summit of Mount Snowdon by foot or train. Try parascending or white-water rafting. Prefer to travel in style? Climb aboard a vintage steam locomotive and journey through the beautiful Brecon Beacons. Don your swimmers and take a dip from one of the many award-winning beaches or spot Bottlenose dolphins along the coast of Cardigan Bay. After all that adventure tuck into local delicacies such as cockles, laverbread and traditional welshcakes.

Set your course for the Maritime Quarter in Swansea to visit Wales' newest museum, the National Waterfront Museum which showcases new technologies in science, manufacturing and medicine. Stroll through romantic Italian-style Portmeirion Village and Gardens or make a bee-line for The National Botanic Garden of Wales in Carmarthenshire. Join the cafe culture and Dr Who in Cardiff and admire the stunning waterfront along Cardiff Bay. Don't forget to check out the sporting fixtures and concerts at Cardiff's Millennium Stadium.

Castles, of course, are what Wales does very well, from Harlech, Beaumaris, Caernarfon and Conwy, to romantic hilltop fortresses such as Carreg Cennen near Llandeilo. It's easy to conjure up images of princes, wizards and dragons as you climb the ramparts or explore the underground passages. Descend below the surface again at the Llechwedd Slate Caverns and the Big Pit at Blaenavon to image the life of a coal miner. Want to entertain the kids? Set them on the Childen's Puzzle Trail at dramatic Lake Vyrnwy, west of Welshpool, where they can seek out beautifully crafted wooden animals hidden in the trees.

Destinations

Bangor

This university and cathedral city is located in a breathtaking landscape, with Snowdonia National Park to the south and the Isle of Anglesey to the north. The city centre combines historic atmosphere with the best of modern amenities. Visit the cathedral, founded on one of the earliest Christian settlements in Britain, or the restored Victorian pier, extending out into the Menai Straits and surrounded by traditional pubs and restaurants, or head further afield to explore local villages.

Cardiff

The capital city of Wales has plenty to keep you entertained. Wine and dine al fresco at a wide range of restaurants in the city centre's new Brewery Quarter, or stroll through the regenerated Cardiff Bay and catch a performance at the spectacular Wales Millennium Centre or a top-class sporting event at the Millennium Stadium. Feeling brave? Get up close to a cyberman and a dalek at the interactive Dr Who exhibition in the Red Dragon Centre.

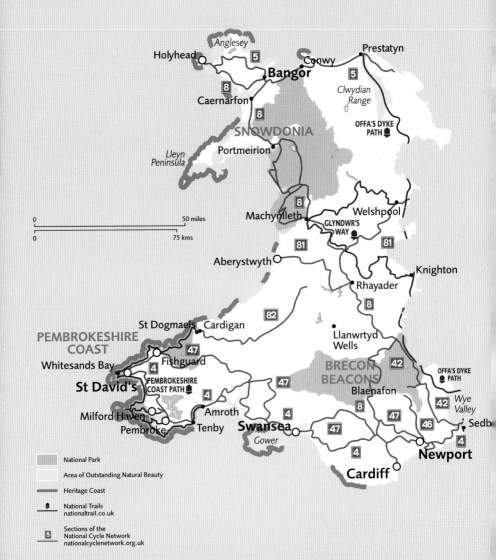

Millennium Centre, Cardiff

St David's Cathedral

Penrhyn Castle, Bangor

Celtic Manor Resort, Newport

Three Cliffs Bay, Gower

Newport

Newport is a city of contrasts – where medieval cathedral and castle rub shoulders with exuberant Victorian architecture, and Roman walls and amphitheatre contrast with high-tech developments. Visit one of the last working transporter bridges in the world, tour the fascinating Roman site at Caerleon, or take in a show at the impressive new Riverfront Arts Centre. For golf lovers, there's the world-class Celtic Manor Resort, venue for the 2010 Ryder Cup.

St David's

Britain's smallest city, located in the Pembrokeshire Coast National Park, has been a favourite destination for pilgrims, travellers and artists through the ages. Visit the starkly beautiful cathedral, reputedly founded on the site of St David's 6th-century monastery and enjoy fresh local food in the newly opened refectory. Walk coastal paths amid some of the finest natural scenery in Europe, relax on unspoilt beaches or take a boat trip to spot dolphins and whales.

Swansea

Wales' 'City by the Sea' is the only place in the UK where you can shop, eat out and enjoy a vibrant arts, entertainment and club scene yet be so close to an Area of Outstanding Natural Beauty. Visit the stunning new National Waterfront Museum or sample local delicacies such as cockles and laverbread at the largest indoor market in Wales. If you're looking for sun, sand and watersports, the beaches stretch from Swansea Bay to the rugged beauty of the Gower peninsula.

Places to visit

Bala Lake Railway
Llanuwchllyn, Gwynedd
(01678) 540666
bala-lake-railway.co.uk
Nine-mile lakeside steam journey in Snowdonia National Park

Beaumaris Castle
Isle of Anglesey
(01248) 810361
cadw.wales.gov.uk
Awesome, unfinished masterpiece begun in 1295

Big Pit National Mining Museum of Wales
Blaenavon, Torfaen
(029) 2039 7951
nmgw.ac.uk/bigpit
Travel 300ft underground with an ex-miner as your guide

Bodelwyddan Castle
near Rhyl, Denbighshire
(01745) 584060
bodelwyddan-castle.co.uk
Outstation of the National Portrait Gallery in magnificent parkland

Brecon Beacons Mountain Centre
Libanus, Powys
(01874) 623366
brecon-beacons.com/mountain-centre.htm
Stunning views of four mountain ranges

Brecon Mountain Railway
Pontsticill, Powys
(01685) 722988
breconmountainrailway.co.uk
Seven-mile steam journey with mountain, lake and forest views

Caernarfon Castle
Gwynedd
(01286) 677617
cadw.wales.gov.uk
Mighty medieval fortress, now a World Heritage Site

Cardiff Bay Visitor Centre
(029) 2046 3833
cardiffharbour.com
Enter the 'Tube' for a preview of Cardiff's superb maritime future

Cardiff Castle
(029) 2087 8100
cardiffcastle.com
Fairy-tale castle spanning 2,000 years of history

Denbigh Castle
(01745) 813385
cadw.wales.gov.uk
Intriguing thirteenth-century castle crowning the town

Ffestiniog Railway
Porthmadog, Gwynedd
(01766) 516000
festrail.co.uk
One of North Wales' leading attractions, established in 1832

Gower Heritage Centre
Parkmill, Abertawe
(01792) 371206

gowerheritagecentre.co.uk
Family day out on the beautiful Gower peninsula

Harlech Castle
Gwynedd
(01766) 780552
cadw.wales.gov.uk
Magnificent thirteenth-century castle and World Heritage Site

Inigo Jones Slate Works
Caernarfon, Gwynedd
(01286) 830242
inigojones.co.uk
Engrave your own piece of slate

King Arthur's Labyrinth
Corris, Gwynedd
(01654) 761584
kingarthurslabyrinth.com
Take an underground boat trip through spectacular caverns

Llechwedd Slate Caverns
Blaenau Ffestiniog, Gwynedd
(01766) 830306
llechwedd-slate-caverns.co.uk
Descend to underground lakes on the steepest passenger railway in Britain

Millennium Stadium Tours
Cardiff
(029) 2082 2228
millenniumstadium.com
Follow the footsteps of sporting greats

National Botanic Garden of Wales
Llanarthney, Carmarthenshire
(01558) 668768
gardenofwales.org.uk
Important botanic collection featuring Foster's Great Glasshouse

National Coracle Centre
Cenarth, Carmarthenshire
(01239) 710980
coracle-centre.co.uk
Unique collection of coracles beside the beautiful Cenarth falls

National Cycle Collection
Llandrindod Wells, Powys
(01597) 825531
cyclemuseum.org.uk
From the penny-farthing to today's carbon-fibre machines

Diary dates 2008

National Museum
and Gallery of Wales

Cardiff
(029) 2039 7951
nmgw.ac.uk
*Dazzling displays of art, science
and natural history*

National Waterfront
Museum
Swansea, Abertawe
(01792) 638950
museumwales.ac.uk
*Inspirational museum of Wales'
industrial and maritime history*

National Wetlands
Centre, Wales
Llwynhendy,
Carmarthenshire
(01554) 741087
wwt.org.uk/centre/120/visit/llane
lli/.html
*Beautiful wetland reserve, home
to countless wild species*

Nelson Museum
Monmouth
(01600) 710630
monmouthshire.gov.uk
*Superb collection of materials
relating to the famous admiral*

St Davids Cathedral
Pembrokeshire
(01437) 720691
stdavidscathedral.org.uk
*One of the great historic shrines of
Christendom with roots in the
sixth century*

St Fagan's National
History Museum
Cardiff
(029) 2057 3500
museumwales.ac.uk
*One of Europe's biggest open-air
museums*

Snowdon
Mountain Railway
Llanberis, Gwynedd
0870 458 0033
snowdonrailway.co.uk
*Take a spectacular ride to the
summit of Snowdon*

White Christmas
Wales Millennium Centre, Cardiff
wmc.org.uk
To 12 Jan

Wales v Scotland Six Nations
Wales Millennium Centre, Cardiff
millenniumstadium.com
9 Feb

World Wetlands Day
Newport Wetlands Reserve
rspb.org.uk
28 Feb

St David's Day Food & Craft Fair
Saundersfoot Harbour, Pembrokeshire
visit-saundersfoot.com
1 – 2 Mar

Conwy Seed Fair
conwybeekeepers.org.uk
26 Mar

Celtic Festival of Wales
Trecco Bay, Porthcawl
cwlwmceltaidd.com
6 – 9 Mar

Llangollen International Musical Eisteddfod
international-eisteddfod.co.uk
8 – 13 Jul

Royal Welsh Show
Bluith Wells, Powys
rwas.co.uk
21 – 24 Jul

Anglesey Beer Festival
angleseybeerfestival.com
13 – 14 Sep*

Abergavenny Food Festival
abergavennyfoodfestival.com
20 – 21 Sep

* provisional date at time of going to press

Tourist Information Centres

When you arrive at your destination, visit a Tourist Information Centre for help with accommodation and information about local attractions and events, or email your request before you go.

Aberaeron	The Quay	(01545) 570602	aberaerontic@ceredigion.gov.uk
Aberdulais Falls	The National Trust	(01639) 636674	aberdulais@nationaltrust.org.uk
Aberdyfi *	The Wharf Gardens	(01654) 767321	tic.aberdyfi@eryri-npa.gov.uk
Abergavenny	Monmouth Road	(01873) 853254	abergavennytic@breconbeacons.org
Aberystwyth	Terrace Road	(01970) 612125	aberystwythtic@ceredigion.gov.uk
Bala *	Pensarn Road	(01678) 521021	bala.tic@gwynedd.gov.uk
Bangor *	Deiniol Road	(01248) 352786	bangor.tic@gwynedd.gov.uk
Barmouth	Station Road	(01341) 280787	barmouth.tic@gwynedd.gov.uk
Barry Island *	The Promenade	(01446) 747171	barrytic@valeofglamorgan.gov.uk
Beddgelert *	Canolfan Hebog	(01766) 890615	tic.beddgelert@eryri-npa.gov.uk
Betws y Coed	Royal Oak Stables	(01690) 710426	tic.byc@eryri-npa.gov.uk
Blaenau Ffestiniog *	Unit 3, High Street	(01766) 830360	tic.blaenau@eryri-npa.gov.uk
Blaenavon *	North Street	(01495) 792615	blaenavon.ironworks@btopenworld.com
Borth *	Cambrian Terrace	(01970) 871174	borthtic@ceredigion.gov.uk
Brecon	Cattle Market Car park	(01874) 622485	brectic@powys.gov.uk
Bridgend	Bridgend Designer Outlet	(01656) 654906	bridgendtic@bridgend.gov.uk
Builth Wells	The Groe Car Park	(01982) 553307	builtic@powys.gov.uk
Caerleon	5 High Street	(01633) 422656	caerleon.tic@newport.gov.uk
Caernarfon	Castle Street	(01286) 672232	caernarfon.tic@gwynedd.gov.uk
Caerphilly	The Twyn	(029) 2088 0011	tourism@caerphilly.gov.uk
Cardiff	The Old Library	0870 121 1258	visitor@cardiff.gov.uk
Cardigan	Bath House Road	(01239) 613230	cardigantic@ceredigion.gov.uk
Carmarthen	113 Lammas Street	(01267) 231557	carmarthentic@carmarthenshire.gov.uk
Chepstow	Bridge Street	(01291) 623772	chepstow.tic@monmouthshire.gov.uk
Conwy	Castle Buildings	(01492) 592248	conwytic@conwy.gov.uk
Dolgellau	Eldon Square	(01341) 422888	tic.dolgellau@eryri-npa.gov.uk
Fishguard Harbour	The Parrog	(01348) 872037	fishguardharbour.tic@ pembrokeshire.gov.uk
Fishguard Town	Market Square	(01437) 776636	fishguard.tic@pembrokeshire.gov.uk
Harlech *	High Street	(01766) 780658	tic.harlech@eryri-npa.gov.uk
Haverfordwest	Old Bridge	(01437) 763110	haverfordwest.tic@ pembrokeshire.gov.uk
Holyhead	Stena Line, Terminal 1	(01407) 762622	holyhead@nwtic.com
Knighton	West Street	(01547) 529424	oda@offasdyke.demon.co.uk
Lake Vyrnwy	Unit 2, Vyrnwy Craft Workshops	(01691) 870346	laktic@powys.gov.uk
Llanberis *	41b High Street	(01286) 870765	llanberis.tic@gwynedd.gov.uk
Llandovery	Kings Road	(01550) 720693	llandovery.ic@breconbeacons.org
Llandrindod Wells	Temple Street	(01597) 822600	llandtic@powys.gov.uk
Llandudno	Mostyn Street	(01492) 876413	llandudnotic@conwy.gov.uk
Llanelli	North Dock	(01554) 777744	DiscoveryCentre@ carmarthenshire.gov.uk

Llanfairpwllgwyngyll	Station Site	(01248) 713177	llanfairpwll@nwtic.com
Llangollen	Castle Street	(01978) 860828	llangollen@nwtic.com
Machynlleth	Penrallt Street	(01654) 702401	mactic@powys.gov.uk
Merthyr Tydfil	14a Glebeland Street	(01685) 379884	tic@merthyr.gov.uk
Milford Haven *	94 Charles Street	(01646) 690866	milford.tic@pembrokeshire.gov.uk
Mold	Earl Road	(01352) 759331	mold@nwtic.com
Monmouth	Agincourt Square	(01600) 713899	monmouth.tic@monmouthshire.gov.uk
Mumbles	Mumbles Road	(01792) 361302	info@mumblestic.co.uk
New Quay *	Church Street	(01545) 560865	newquaytic@ceredigion.gov.uk
Newport	John Frost Square	(01633) 842962	newport.tic@newport.gov.uk
Newport (pembs) *	Long Street	(01239) 820912	newporttic@pembrokeshirecoast.org.uk
Newtown	Back Lane	(01686) 625580	newtic@powys.gov.uk
Oswestry Mile End	Mile End Services	(01691) 662488	tic@oswestry-bc.gov.uk
Oswestry Town	2 Church Terrace	(01691) 662753	ot@oswestry-welshborders.org.uk
Pembroke *	Commons Road	(01646) 622388	pembroke.tic@pembrokeshire.gov.uk
Porthcawl *	John Street	(01656) 786639	porthcawltic@bridgend.gov.uk
Porthmadog	High Street	(01766) 512981	porthmadog.tic@gwynedd.gov.uk
Presteigne *	Broad Street	(01544) 260650	presteignetic@powys.gov.uk
Pwllheli	Station Square	(01758) 613000	pwllheli.tic@gwynedd.gov.uk
Rhayader	North Street	(01597) 810591	rhayader.tic@powys.gov.uk
Rhyl	West Parade	(01745) 355068	rhyl.tic@denbighshire.gov.uk
Saundersfoot *	Harbour Car Park	(01834) 813672	saundersfoot.tic@pembrokeshire.gov.uk
St Davids	1 High Street	(01437) 720392	enquiries@ stdavids.pembrokeshirecoast.org.uk
Swansea	Plymouth Street	(01792) 468321	tourism@swansea.gov.uk
Tenby	Unit 2, The Gateway Complex	(01834) 842402	tenby.tic@pembrokeshire.gov.uk
Tywyn *	High Street	(01654) 710070	tywyn.tic@gwynedd.gov.uk
Welshpool	Church Street	(01938) 552043	weltic@powys.gov.uk
Wrexham	Lambpit Street	(01978) 292015	tic@wrexham.gov.uk

* seasonal opening

Find out more

For any further information contact:

Visit Wales
Welsh Assembly Government, Brunel House,
2 Fitzalan Road, Cardiff CF24 0UY
t 0870 830 0306
   0870 121 1255 (minicom)
w visitwales.com

Travel info

By road:
Travelling to South and West Wales is easy on the M4 and
the dual carriageway network. The new Second Severn
Crossing gives two ways to enter Wales, but those
wishing to visit Chepstow and the Wye Valley should use
the original Severn Bridge and the M48 (originally part of
the M4). In North Wales the A55 'Expressway' has made
travelling speedier, whilst Mid Wales is accessible via the
M54 which links with the M6, M5 and M1.

By rail:
Fast and frequent Great Western Intercity trains travel
between London Paddington and Cardiff, departing
hourly and half-hourly at peak times, and taking only two
hours. Newport, Bridgend, Port Talbot, Neath and
Swansea are also accessible through this service, which
encompasses most of West Wales.
London Euston links to the North Wales coast via Virgin
Trains, who also run a service between the North East of
England and South Wales. In addition, Wales and West
Passenger Trains run Alphaline services from London
Waterloo, Manchester and the North East, Brighton and
the South, and Nottingham and the Heart of England. For
further rail enquiries, please telephone 0845 748 4950.

By air:
Fly into Cardiff International Airport.

Barafundle Bay, Pembrokeshire

where to stay in
Wales

All place names in the blue bands are shown on the maps at the front of this guide.

Accommodation symbols
Symbols give useful information about services and facilities. Inside the back-cover flap you can find a key to these symbols. Keep it open for easy reference.

ABERAERON, Ceredigion Map ref 8A2

★★★★
HOLIDAY, TOURING
& CAMPING PARK

🚐 £14.00–£23.00
🚐 £14.00–£23.00
▲ £14.00–£23.00
100 touring pitches

Aeron Coast Caravan Park

North Road, Aberaeron SA46 0JF t (01545) 570349 e enquiries@aeroncoast.co.uk
w aeroncoast.co.uk

Flat coastal park only 500yds from the picturesque harbour and shops of Aberaeron. Quiet out of season but good facilities for families and free evening entertainment in school holidays.

payment Credit/debit cards, cash/cheques

General ♿ P 🚐 🕒 🍴 🆓 📶 ⊙ 📳 🔋 🐕 ☼ Leisure ⚓ 📺 🍽 ◆ ⑂ ⚲ ∪ ⛵ ▶

ABERGAVENNY, Monmouthshire Map ref 8B3

★★★★
TOURING PARK

🚐 (53) £12.10–£24.90
🚐 (53) £12.10–£24.90
53 touring pitches

See Ad on inside front cover

Pandy Caravan Club Site

Pandy, Abergavenny NP7 8DR t (01873) 890370 w caravanclub.co.uk

payment Credit/debit cards, cash/cheques

Level and green site scattered with mature trees. Abergavenny has a fine castle. Walkers will be delighted to try out the Offa's Dyke Path. Open March to November.

⊕ *Turn left off A465, in 6.5 miles by The Old Pandy Inn into minor road. Site on left.*

THE
CARAVAN
CLUB

General P 🚐 🕒 🍴 🆓 📶 ⊙ 📳 🐕 🐾 Leisure ⛵

Place index

If you know where you want to stay, the index at the back of the guide will give you the page number listing accommodation in your chosen town, city or village. Check out the other useful indexes too.

AMROTH, Pembrokeshire Map ref 8A3

★★★★★
HOLIDAY, TOURING
& CAMPING PARK

🚐	£14.00–£21.00
🚃	£14.00–£21.00
⛺ (60)	£14.00–£21.00
🏠 (13)	£240.00–£600.00

56 touring pitches

Little Kings Park

Amroth Road, Ludchurch, Narberth SA67 8PG **t** (01834) 831330 **f** (01834) 831161
e littlekingspark@btconnect.com **w** littlekings.co.uk

payment Credit/debit cards, cash/cheques

Quiet park with view across open land to sea. Beac
1.5 miles. Covered, heated pool, bar/restaurant, tw
toilet blocks, laundry, shop, mains hook-up, games
room, children's play area, dog walk. Open from
1 March to first week in January.

⊕ *On A477 heading south west. 2m from Llanteg turn left
(Amroth, Wiseman's Bridge). 1m later, at crossroads, tur
right. Site on left in 0.75m.*

General P 🚫 🚻 🛉 📶 🚿 ⊙ 📵 🛒 ✕ 🐾 🎣 ☼ Leisure 🎣 🍴 🔍 ⚗ ⛱ 🏃

AMROTH, Pembrokeshire Map ref 8A3

★★★★★
HOLIDAY PARK

🏠 (12) £120.00–£630.00

Pendeilo Dragon Award Caravans

Pendeilo Leisure Park, Amroth, Narberth SA67 8PR **t** (01834) 831259 **f** (01834) 831702
e pendeiloholidays@aol.com **w** pendeilo.co.uk

payment Credit/debit cards, cash/cheques

This is an award-winning park set amid the beautif
countryside of the Pembrokeshire Coast National
Park and yet only five minutes' drive from the wic
expanse of Amroth's clean, golden sands. Choose
from two- and three-bedroom static caravans or co
cottage for two. Central heating and double glazir
available on top-of-range homes. Open March to
October.

⊕ *From Camarthen take A40 to St Clears (9 miles). Take A4
(signed Pembroke Dock). At Llanteg (8 miles) turn sout
following signs to Colby Woodlands. We are approx
0.5 miles from A477 on right.*

♥ *Fortnightly bookings: 5% discount, couples only. 10%
discount Mar, Apr, May, late Sep, Oct (but not school
holidays).*

General P 📵 🐾 🛉 ☼ Leisure 🎣

BARMOUTH, Gwynedd Map ref 8A2

★★★★
HOLIDAY PARK

🏠 (70) £274.00–£550.00

Parc Caerelwan

Talybont, Barmouth LL43 2AX **t** (01341) 247236 **f** (01341) 247711
e enquiries@parccaerelwan.co.uk **w** parccaerelwan.co.uk

Top-quality caravan-bungalows and caravans
available at quiet, family-run park. Near safe,
sandy beach with mountain views. Low season
short breaks available. Pets welcome.

open All year
payment Credit/debit cards, cash/cheques

General 🔌 P 🚻 🚿 📵 🛒 🐾 ☼ Leisure 🎣 🔍 ⚗ ⛱ ⚓

It's all quality-assessed accommodation

Our commitment to quality involves wide-ranging accommodation assessment. Rating
and awards were correct at the time of going to press but may change following a
new assessment. Please check at time of booking.

BENLLECH, Isle of Anglesey Map ref 8A1

★★★★★
TOURING PARK
🚐 (92) £12.90–£24.90
🚐 (92) £12.90–£24.90
92 touring pitches

See Ad on inside front cover

THE
CARAVAN
CLUB

Penrhos Caravan Club Site

Brynteg, Benllech LL78 7JH **t** (01248) 852617 **w** caravanclub.co.uk

payment Credit/debit cards, cash/cheques

An ideal site for a family holiday, five minutes' drive from a safe, sandy beach. Open March to October.

⊕ *From A5025, turn left onto B5110 (Llangefni). Continue straight on at crossroads. Site on right.*

♥ *Special member rates mean you can save your membership subscription in less than a week. Visit our website to find out more.*

General P 🔌 🕗 🍽 🇷 🏧 ▣ 🐕 🐾 Leisure ⚠ ▶

CAERNARFON, Gwynedd Map ref 8A1

CAERNARFON, Gwynedd Map ref 8A1

★★★
TOURING &
CAMPING PARK
🚐 (30) £11.50–£16.50
🚐 (5) £11.50–£16.50
⛺ (25) £8.50–£16.50
60 touring pitches

Cwm Cadnant Valley

Llanberis Road, Caernarfon LL55 2DF **t** (01286) 673196 **f** (01286) 675941
e visitwales@cadnantvalley.co.uk **w** cwmcadnant.co.uk

A ten-minute stroll to Caernarfon town and Castle. Hot showers available and toilet block. A quiet family site with children's play area and friendly atmosphere. Open March to November.

payment Credit/debit cards, cash/cheques

General P 🔌 🕗 🍽 🇷 ☉ ▣ 🐕 🌣 Leisure ⚠

CARDIGAN, Ceredigion Map ref 8A2

★★★★★
HOLIDAY PARK
🚐 (10) £14.00–£24.00
🚐 (10) £14.00–£24.00
⛺ (10) £14.00–£24.00
🏠 (3) £205.00–£565.00
30 touring pitches

Cenarth Falls Holiday Park

Cenarth, Newcastle Emlyn SA38 9JS **t** (01239) 710345 **f** (01239) 710344
e enquiries@cenarth-holipark.co.uk **w** cenarth-holipark.co.uk

Family-run, award-winning park. Excellent facilities. Indoor/outdoor swimming pools, spa, sauna/steam, gym, restaurant, bar. Fishing, golf, lovely beaches nearby. Pricing per pitch valid for up to four people. Open 1 March to 18 December.

payment Credit/debit cards, cash/cheques

General P 🔌 🕗 🍽 🇷 ☉ ▣ ✕ 🐕 🌣 Leisure 🏊 🎾 📺 🍽 ♥ ⚠ ∪ ♪ ▶ 🚲

Mention our name
Please mention this guide when making your booking.

COLWYN BAY, Conwy Map ref 8B1

★★★★★
TOURING PARK
🚐 (120) £16.00–£20.00
� (10) £16.00–£20.00
130 touring pitches

Bron-Y-Wendon Touring Caravan Park

Wern Road, Llanddulas, Colwyn Bay LL22 8HG t (01492) 512903 f (01492) 512903
e stay@northwales-holidays.co.uk w northwales-holidays.co.uk

Award-winning park, all pitches overlooking the sea. Ideally situated for touring Snowdonia, Llandudno, Chester. Leave the A55 at Llanddulas, junction 23 (A547), and follow Tourist Information signs to the park.

open All year
payment Credit/debit cards, cash/cheques

General 🖵 🚿 P 🔌 🕛 🍴 🚐 🌂 ⊙ 📷 🐕 ☼ Leisure 📺 🍺 ∪ ⌗

CWMCARN, Newport Map ref 8B3

★★★
TOURING &
CAMPING PARK
🚐 (23) £8.50–£10.00
� (23) £8.50–£10.00
🛆 (27) £6.00–£9.50
27 touring pitches

Cwmcarn Forest Drive and Campsite

Nantcarn Road, Cwmcarn, Cross Keys, Newport NP11 7FA t (01495) 272001 f (01495) 271403
e cwmcarn-vc@caerphilly.gov.uk w caerphilly.gov.uk/visiting

Set amongst rolling hills and green forests, this quiet campsite is close to Cardiff, Newport and Brecon Beacons. Ideal base for touring. Mountain-bike trails, walking routes, visitor centre, cafe and gift shop on-site.

open All year except Christmas and New Year
payment Credit/debit cards, cash/cheques

General P 🔌 🍴 🌂 ⊙ 📷 ✕ 🐕 ☼ Leisure ⌗

FISHGUARD, Pembrokeshire Map ref 8A2

★★★★
HOLIDAY, TOURING
& CAMPING PARK
🚐 £13.00–£15.00
� £13.00–£15.00
🛆 (30) £12.00–£14.00
🏠 (14) £220.00–£480.00
20 touring pitches

Fishguard Bay Caravan & Camping Park

Garn Gelli, Fishguard SA65 9ET t (01348) 811415 f (01348) 811425 e enquiries@fishguardbay.com
w fishguardbay.com

Enjoy your stay on this beautiful stretch of Pembrokeshire National Park coastline. Ideal centre for walking and touring. Quiet, family-run park. Open March to November.

payment Credit/debit cards, cash/cheques

General P 🔌 🕛 🍴 🌂 📷 🛒 🐕 ☼ Leisure 📺 🍺 ⚠ ∪

FISHGUARD, Pembrokeshire Map ref 8A2

★★★★
TOURING PARK
🚐 (19) £13.00–£14.00
� (20) £13.00–£14.00
🛆 (8) £10.00–£13.00
28 touring pitches

Gwaun Vale Touring Park

Llanychaer, Fishguard SA65 9TA t (01348) 874698 e info@gwaunvale.co.uk w gwaunvale.co.uk

Situated in the beautiful Gwaun Valley, overlooking Pembrokeshire National Park. Ideal for walking, sightseeing or just relaxing. Close to Irish ferry.

payment Cash/cheques

General P 🔌 🕛 🍴 🌂 ⊙ 📷 🛒 🐕 🎣 ☼ Leisure ⌗

Key to symbols

The symbols at the end of each entry help you pick out the services and facilities which are most important to you. A key to the symbols can be found inside the back-cover flap. Keep this open for easy reference.

FRESHWATER EAST, Pembrokeshire Map ref 8A3

★★★★★
TOURING PARK

(130) £12.90–£24.90
(130) £12.90–£24.90
▲ on application
130 touring pitches

See Ad on inside front cover

THE CARAVAN CLUB

Freshwater East Caravan Club Site

Trewent Hill, Freshwater East, Pembroke SA71 5LJ t (01646) 672341 w caravanclub.co.uk

payment Credit/debit cards, cash/cheques

Only a few minutes from a beautiful stretch of beach, this hill-bottom site is flanked by trees on one side with a selection of grass or hardstanding pitches. This location offers fantastic walks with magnificent cliff-top views. Open March to October.

♥ Midweek discount: pitch fee for standard pitches for stays on any Tue, Wed or Thur night outside peak season dates will be reduced by 50%.

General P 🐾 🕩 🚿 💧 🛒 📶 🌳 ☺ 🚮 🗑 🐕 Leisure 🏊

LLANBRYNMAIR, Powys Map ref 8B2

★★★★
TOURING PARK

(38) £8.60–£18.00
(38) £8.60–£18.00
38 touring pitches

See Ad on inside front cover

THE CARAVAN CLUB

Gwern-y-Bwlch Caravan Club Site

Llanbrynmair SY19 7EB t (01342) 326944 w caravanclub.co.uk

payment Credit/debit cards, cash/cheques

A gem of a site in a lovely setting, lost in Mid Wales between Snowdonia and Montgomeryshire. A great site for country pursuits like birdwatching or fishing. Own sanitation required. Open April to October.

⊕ From A470 in 4 miles turn left at Club Site sign.

♥ Midweek discount: pitch fee for standard pitches for stays on any Tue, Wed or Thu night outside peak season dates will be reduced by 50%.

General P 🐾 🕩 🚿 📶 🗑 🐕 🚮.

LLANELLI, Carmarthenshire Map ref 8A3

★★★★★
TOURING PARK

(130) £13.60–£25.60
(130) £13.60–£25.60
130 touring pitches

See Ad on inside front cover

THE CARAVAN CLUB

Pembrey Country Park Caravan Club Site

Pembrey, Llanelli SA16 0EJ t (01554) 834369 w caravanclub.co.uk

payment Credit/debit cards, cash/cheques

Situated on the edge of a 520-acre country park with a vast range of outdoor sporting activities, and including use of a seven-mile stretch of safe, sandy beach, only a mile away. Open March to January 2009.

⊕ From A484 follow signs for country park.

♥ Special member rates mean you can save your membership subscription in less than a week. Visit our website to find out more.

General P 🐾 🕩 🚿 💧 📶 🌳 ☺ 🚮 🗑 🐕 ☀ Leisure 🏊

Take a break

Look out for special promotions and themed breaks. This could be your chance to indulge an interest, find a new one, or just relax and enjoy exceptional value. Offers (highlighted in colour) are subject to availability.

LLANGADOG, Carmarthenshire Map ref 8B3

★★★★
TOURING &
CAMPING PARK

🚐 (60) £9.00–£11.00
🚎 (60) £9.00–£11.00
⛺ (28) £8.50–£11.00
88 touring pitches

Abermarlais Caravan Park

Llangadog SA19 9NG **t** (01550) 777868 & (01550) 777797 **w** ukparks.co.uk/abermarlais

payment Credit/debit cards, cash/cheques

A tranquil site in a beautiful woodland valley at the western end of the Brecon National Park, ideal for nature lovers and bird-watchers. The site's facilities are of the highest standard with excellent shower and toilet block. Camp shop and reception with comprehensive selection of groceries, gas, etc. Open March to November.

⊕ Situated on A40, 6 miles west of Llandovery or 6 miles east of Llandeilo. Signposted.

General 🏠 🖫 P 🖾 🖰 🔐 🥅 ⊙ 🕮 🐾 🐕 🚻 ☼ Leisure 🏔 ∪ 🎣

LLIGWY BAY, Isle of Anglesey Map ref 8A1

★★★★★
HOLIDAY PARK

🏠 (4) £140.00–£575.00

Minffordd Caravan Park

Lligwy, Dulas LL70 9HJ **t** (01248) 410678 **f** (01248) 410378 **e** enq@minffordd-holidays.com **w** minffordd-holidays.com

Beautiful small garden park near Lligwy beach. Parking alongside each caravan, two of which are designed for physically disabled guests. Many local walks and cycle routes. Ideal countryside for bird-watchers. Open 1 April to 31 October.

payment Cash/cheques

General P 🖾 🥅 🕮 🐕 🚻 ☼ Leisure 🏔 🎣 ► 🚲 🏠

NEWPORT, Newport Map ref 8B3

★★★★★
TOURING &
CAMPING PARK

🚐 (80) £12.10–£24.90
🚎 (80) £12.10–£24.90
80 touring pitches

See Ad on inside front cover

Tredegar House Country Park Caravan Club Site

Coedkernew, Newport NP10 8TW **t** (01633) 815600 **w** caravanclub.co.uk

open All year
payment Credit/debit cards, cash/cheques

High-standard site within the park, bordering one of the ornamental lakes. Just off the M4, seven miles from Cardiff. Non-members welcome.

⊕ M4 jct 28 via slip road. At roundabout turn onto A48 (signposted Tredegar House). Roundabout 0.25 miles, turn left. Next roundabout, turn left into Tredegar House.

♥ Special member rates mean you can save your membership subscription in less than a week. Visit our website to find out more.

THE
CARAVAN
CLUB

General P 🖾 🥅 🖾 🔐 ⊙ 🖻 🐕 ☼ Leisure 🏔 🎣 ►

PRESTATYN, Denbighshire Map ref 8B1

★★★★★
HOLIDAY PARK

🏠 (4) £120.00–£500.00

Silver Birch Caravan Park

Chester Road, Prestatyn CH8 9JN **t** (01745) 853749 **f** (01745) 854147 **e** parks@bancroftleisure.co.uk **w** bancroftleisure.co.uk

Select landscaped park between Talacre and Gronant beaches. Family-run. Luxury holiday homes for sale or hire. Peaceful yet near all attractions for a fun-filled holiday. 104 static caravans, three available for hire. Open March to November.

payment Credit/debit cards, cash/cheques

General P 🕮 🖻 🐕 ☼ Leisure 🏀 🏔 ∪ 🎣 ►

★★★★★
HOLIDAY PARK
(2) £120.00–£500.00

Tan y Don Caravan Park

263 Victoria Road, Prestatyn LL19 7UT **t** (01745) 853749 **f** (01745) 854147
e parks@bancroftleisure.co.uk

Select landscaped park situated on the main A548 coast road. Close to Ffrith Beach Festival Gardens, beach and indoor bowls centre. Luxury caravans for sale or hire. Fully landscaped, peaceful and relaxing. Open March to November.

payment Credit/debit cards, cash/cheques

General Leisure

★★★
**TOURING &
CAMPING PARK**
£14.50–£22.00
£14.50–£22.00
£8.00–£25.00
100 touring pitches

Pitton Cross Caravan Park

Pitton Cross, Rhossili, Swansea SA3 1PH **t** (01792) 390593 **f** (01792) 391010
e admin@pittoncross.co.uk **w** pittoncross.co.uk

Set amid scenic coastline, rugged cliffs, sandy beaches and secluded coves, 100 pitches spread through six small fields, some sheltered, others offering coastal views. Gower Kite Centre on site. Surf equipment available for hire.

open All year
payment Credit/debit cards, cash/cheques, euros

General Leisure

★★★★
**HOLIDAY, TOURING
& CAMPING PARK**
(26) £11.00–£15.50
(15) £9.50–£15.50
(69) £9.50–£13.00
(9) £200.00–£400.00
110 touring pitches

Caerfai Bay Caravan and Tent Park

St Davids, Haverfordwest SA62 6QT **t** (01437) 720274 **f** (01437) 720577 **e** info@caerfaibay.co.uk
w caerfaibay.co.uk

A quiet, family-run park. Turn off A487 (Haverfordwest to St Davids) in St Davids at Visitor Centre. The park is at road end, one mile, on the right. Signposted. Open April to mid-November. No dogs in tent fields during school summer holidays.

payment Credit/debit cards, cash/cheques

General Leisure

★★★★
TOURING PARK
(130) £12.10–£24.90
(130) £12.10–£24.90
130 touring pitches

See Ad on inside front cover

Gowerton Caravan Club Site

Pont-Y-Cob Road, Gowerton, Swansea SA4 3QP **t** (01792) 873050 **w** caravanclub.co.uk

payment Credit/debit cards, cash/cheques

A level, well-designed site within an easy drive of the whole range of superb beaches on the Gower peninsula, such as Oxwich and Caswell Bays. Open March to November.

⊕ From B2496 turn right at traffic lights. In 0.5 miles turn right at traffic lights into Pont-y-Cob Road. Site on right.

♥ Special member rates mean you can save your membership subscription in less than a week. Visit our website to find out more.

General

British Graded Holiday Parks Scheme

On the following pages you will find an exclusive listing of every park in England assessed under the British Graded Holiday Parks Scheme.

The information includes brief contact details together with its star rating and classification. The listing also shows if an establishment has a National Accessible rating or participates in the Welcome schemes: Cyclists Welcome, Walkers Welcome, Welcome Pets! and Families Welcome (see the front of the guide for further information).

Parks are listed by region and then alphabetically by place name. They may be located in, or a short distance from, the places in the blue bands.

More detailed information on all the places shown in black can be found in the regional sections (where parks have paid to have their details included). To find these entries please refer to the park index at the back of this guide.

The list which follows was compiled slightly later than the regional sections. For this reason you may find that, in a few instances, a star rating may differ between the two sections. This list contains the most up-to-date information and was correct at the time of going to press. Please note that it does not include parks in Scotland and Wales.

ENGLAND'S NORTHWEST

AINSDALE
Merseyside

Willowbank Holiday Home and Touring Park ★★★★★
Holiday & Touring Park
Coastal Road, Ainsdale,
Southport PR8 3ST
t (01704) 571566
e info@willowbankcp.co.uk
w willowbankcp.co.uk

ALLONBY
Cumbria

Manor House Caravan Park ★★★
Holiday, Touring & Camping Park
Edderside Road, Allonby,
Maryport CA15 6RA
t (01900) 881236
e holidays@manorhousepark.
co.uk
w manorhousepark.co.uk

Spring Lea Caravan Park ★★★★
Holiday, Touring & Camping Park
Main Road, Allonby, Maryport
CA15 6QF
t (01900) 881331

AMBLESIDE
Cumbria

Skelwith Fold Caravan Park ★★★★★
Holiday & Touring Park
Skelwith Fold, Ambleside
LA22 0HX
t (015394) 32277
e info@skelwith.com
w skelwith.com

APPLEBY-IN-WESTMORLAND
Cumbria

Wild Rose Park ★★★★★
Holiday, Touring & Camping Park
Ormside, Appleby-in-
Westmorland CA16 6EJ
t (017683) 51077

ARMATHWAITE
Cumbria

Inglethwaite Hall Caravan Club Site ★★★★
Touring Park
Armathwaite, Carlisle CA4 9SY
t (01228) 560202
e enquiries@caravanclub.co.
uk

BASSENTHWAITE
Cumbria

Bassenthwaite Lakeside Lodges ★★★★★
Holiday Park
Scarness, Keswick CA12 4QZ
t (01768) 776641
e enquiries@bll.ac
w bll.ac

BLACKPOOL
Lancashire

Marton Mere Holiday Village ★★★★
Holiday & Touring Park
Mythop Road, Blackpool
FY4 4XN
t (01253) 767544
w martonmere-park.co.uk

Newton Hall Holiday Park ★★★★
Holiday Park
Staining Road, Blackpool
FY3 0AX
t (01253) 882512
e reception@newtonhall.net
w partingtons.com

Sunset Park ★★★★★
Holiday Park
Sower Carr Lane, Hambleton,
Poulton-le-Fylde FY6 9EQ
t (01253) 700222
e sales@sunsetpark.co.uk
w sunsetpark.co.uk

Windy Harbour Holiday Centre ★★★
Holiday, Touring & Camping Park
Windy Harbour Road,
Singleton FY6 8NB
t (01253) 883064
e info@windyharbour.net
w windyharbour.net

BOOT
Cumbria

Eskdale Camping and Caravanning Club Site
Rating Applied For
Holiday, Touring & Camping Park
Holmrook CA19 1TH
t 0845 130 7631

BOTHEL
Cumbria

Skiddaw View Holiday Park ★★★★
Holiday Park
Bassenthwaite, Keswick
CA7 2JG
t (01697) 320919
e office@skiddawview.com
w skiddawview.co.uk/ctb

BOUTH
Cumbria

Black Beck Caravan Park ★★★★★ ROSE AWARD
Holiday & Touring Park
Bouth, Ulverston LA12 8JN
t (01229) 861274
e reception@blackbeck.com

BRAYSTONES
Cumbria

Tarnside Caravan Park
Rating Applied For
Holiday & Touring Park
Braystones, Beckermet,
Egremont CA21 2YL
t (01946) 822777
e tom@seacote.com
w tarnsidepark.co.uk

BURY
Greater Manchester

Burrs Country Park Caravan Club Site ★★★★★
Touring Park
Woodhill Road, Bury BL8 1BN
t (0161) 761 0489
w caravanclub.co.uk

CABUS
Lancashire

Claylands Caravan Park ★★★★
Holiday, Touring & Camping Park
Weavers Lane, Cabus, Preston
PR3 1AJ
t (01524) 791242
e alan@claylandscaravanpark.
co.uk
w claylandscaravanpark.co.uk

CAPERNWRAY
Lancashire

Old Hall Caravan Park ★★★★★
Holiday & Touring Park
Capernwray, Carnforth
LA6 1AD
t (01524) 733276
w oldhall.uk.com/

CARLISLE
Cumbria

Dandy Dinmont Caravan and Camping Site ★★★★
Touring & Camping Park
Blackford, Carlisle CA6 4EA
t (01228) 674611
e dandydinmont@
btopenworld.com
w caravan-camping-carlisle.
itgo.com

CARNFORTH
Lancashire

Netherbeck Holiday Home Park ★★★★★
Holiday Park
North Road, Carnforth
LA5 9NG
t (01524) 735101
e info@netherbeck.co.uk
w netherbeck.co.uk

Redwell Fisheries ★★★
Touring & Camping Park
Kirkby Lonsdale Road, Mere
House, Carnforth LA6 1BQ
t (01524) 221979
e kenanddiane@
redwellfisheries.co.uk
w redwellfisheries.co.uk

CHESTER
Cheshire

Chester Fairoaks Caravan Club Site ★★★★★
Touring & Camping Park
Rake Lane, Little Stanney,
Chester CH2 4HS
t (0151) 355 1600
w caravanclub.co.uk

Manor Wood Country Caravan Park ★★★★★
Holiday, Touring & Camping Park
Manor Wood, Coddington,
Chester CH3 9EN
t (01829) 782990 &
07762 817827
e info@manorwoodcaravans.
co.uk
w cheshire-caravan-sites.co.uk

CHRISTLETON
Cheshire

Parkfields Farm Camping Site ★★
Touring Park
Plough Lane, Christleton
CH3 7BA
t 07914 734260
e a.kelly@chester.gov.uk
w visitchester.com/site/where-
to-stay/parkfields-farm-
camping-site-p44281

CLITHEROE
Lancashire

The Camping & Caravanning Club Site ★★★★
Touring & Camping Park
Edisford Road, Clitheroe
BB7 3LA
t (01200) 425294
w campingandcaravanning
club.co.uk

COCKERHAM
Lancashire

Moss Wood Caravan Park ★★★★★
Holiday & Touring Park
Crimbles Lane, Cockerham
LA2 0ES
t (01524) 791041
w mosswood.co.uk

COCKERMOUTH
Cumbria

Violet Bank Holiday Home Park ★★★★
Holiday Park
Simonscales Lane,
Cockermouth CA13 9TG
t (01900) 822169
w violetbank.co.uk

CONISTON
Cumbria

Crake Valley Holiday Park ★★★★★ ROSE AWARD
Holiday Park
Lake Bank, Water Yeat,
Ulverston LA12 8DL
t (01229) 885203
e crakevalley@coniston1.fslife.
co.uk
w crakevalley.co.uk

Park Coppice Caravan Club Site ★★★★
Touring & Camping Park
Park Gate, Coniston LA21 8LA
t (015394) 41555
w caravanclub.co.uk

Delamere Forest Camping and Caravanning Club Site ★★★★
Touring & Camping Park
Station Road, Northwich
CW8 2HZ
t 0845 130 7631

Cala Gran ★★★★
Holiday Park
Fleetwood Road, Fleetwood
FY7 8JY
t (01253) 872555
e enquiries@british-holidays.co.uk
w calagran-park.co.uk

Lakeland Leisure Park ★★★★
Holiday, Touring & Camping Park
Moor Lane, Flookburgh,
Grange-over-Sands LA11 7LT
t (015395) 58556
w lakeland-park.co.uk

Ridgeway Country Holiday Park ★★★★
Holiday Park
The Ridgeway, Frodsham
WA6 6XQ
t (01928) 734981
e sue@ridgewaypark.com
w ridgewaypark.com

The Beeches Caravan Park ★★★★
Holiday Park
Gilcrux, Wigton, Cockermouth
CA7 2QX
t (01697) 321555
e holiday@thebeechescaravanpark.com
w thebeechescaravanpark.com

Greaves Farm Caravan Park ★★★★ ROSE AWARD
Holiday & Touring Park
Field Broughton, Grange-over-Sands LA11 6HR
t (015395) 36329 & (015395) 36587

Meathop Fell Caravan Club Site ★★★★★
Touring Park
Meathop, Grange-over-Sands
LA11 6RB
t (015395) 32912
w caravanclub.co.uk

Old Park Wood Caravan Park ★★★★★
Holiday Park
Holker, Grange-over-Sands
LA11 7PP
t (015395) 58266
e pobatopw@aol.com
w holker-estate-parks.co.uk

The Croft Caravan and Camp Site ★★★★
Holiday, Touring & Camping Park
North Lonsdale Road,
Hawkshead, Ambleside
LA22 0NX
t (015394) 36374
e enquiries@hawkshead-croft.com
w hawkshead-croft.com

Ocean Edge Leisure Park ★★★
Holiday, Touring & Camping Park
Moneyclose Lane, Morecambe
LA3 2XA
t 0870 7744024
e enquiries@southlakelandparks.co.uk
w southlakelandparks.co.uk

Gelder Wood Country Park ★★★★★
Touring & Camping Park
Oak Leigh Cottage, Ashworth Road, Rochdale OL11 5UP
t (01706) 364858
e gelderwood@aol.com

Seven Acres Caravan Park ★★★
Holiday, Touring & Camping Park
Holmrook, Ravenglass, St Bees
CA19 1YD
t (01946) 822777
e reception@seacote.com
w sevenacres.info

Camping & Caravanning Club – Kendal ★★★★
Touring Park
Millcrest, Shap Road, Kendal
LA9 6NY
t 0845 130 7633
w campingandcaravanning club.co.uk

Low Park Wood Caravan Club Site ★★★★
Touring Park
Sedgwick, Kendal LA8 0JZ
t (015395) 60186
w caravanclub.co.uk

Waters Edge Caravan Park ★★★★
Holiday, Touring & Camping Park
Crooklands, Milnthorpe
LA7 7NN
t (015395) 67708
w watersedgecaravanpark.co.uk

Camping & Caravanning Club – Derwentwater ★★★
Touring & Camping Park
Crow Park Road, Keswick
CA12 5EN
t 0845 130 7633
w campingandcaravanning club.co.uk

Camping & Caravanning Club – Keswick ★★★
Holiday & Touring Park
Crow Park Road, Keswick
CA12 5EP
t 0845 130 7633
w campingandcaravanning club.co.uk

Castlerigg Farm Camping and Caravan Site ★★★★
Touring & Camping Park
Castlerigg, Keswick CA12 4TE
t (017687) 72479
e info@castleriggfarm.com
w castleriggfarm.com

Castlerigg Hall Caravan & Camping Park ★★★★
Holiday, Touring & Camping Park
Castlerigg Hall, Keswick
CA12 4TE
t (017687) 74499
e info@castlerigg.co.uk
w castlerigg.co.uk

Low Briery Holiday Village ★★★★ ROSE AWARD
Holiday Park
Penrith Road, Keswick
CA12 4RN
t (01768) 772044
e lowbriery@wyrenet.co.uk
w keswick.uk.com

Scotgate Holiday Park ★★★★
Holiday, Touring & Camping Park
Braithwaite, Keswick CA12 5TF
t (01768) 778343
e info@scotgateholidaypark.co.uk
w scotgateholidaypark.co.uk

Woodclose Caravan Park ★★★★★
Holiday, Touring & Camping Park
Kirkby Lonsdale LA6 2SE
t (01524) 271597
e info@woodclosepark.com
w woodclosepark.com

Pennine View Caravan Park ★★★★★
Touring & Camping Park
Station Road, Kirkby Stephen
CA17 4SZ
t (017683) 71717

Mowbreck Holiday and Residential Park ★★★★★
Holiday Park
Mowbreck Lane, Wesham
PR4 3HA
t (01772) 682494
e info@mowbreckpark.co.uk
w mowbreckpark.co.uk

Dockray Meadow Caravan Club Site ★★★★
Touring Park
Lamplugh CA14 4SH
t (01946) 861357
w caravanclub.co.uk

Inglenook Caravan Park ★★★★
Holiday, Touring & Camping Park
Lamplugh, Workington
CA14 4SH
t (01946) 861240

New Parkside Farm Caravan Park ★★★
Touring & Camping Park
Denny Beck, Caton Road,
Lancaster LA2 9HH
t (01524) 770723

Wyreside Lakes Fishery ★★★★
Touring & Camping Park
Sunnyside Farmhouse, Gleave Hill Road, Lancaster LA2 9DC
t (01524) 792093
e wyreside2003@yahoo.co.uk
w wyresidelakes.co.uk

Beacon Fell View ★★★
Holiday, Touring & Camping Park
110 Higher Road, Longridge,
Preston PR3 2TF
t (01772) 783233
e info@hagansleisure.co.uk
w hagansleisure.co.uk

LOUGHRIGG
Cumbria

Neaum Crag ★★★★★
Holiday Park
Loughrigg, Ambleside
LA22 9HG
(015394) 33221
e neaumcrag@ktdbroadband.
com
w neaumcrag.co.uk

LYTHAM ST ANNES
Lancashire

Eastham Hall Caravan Park
★★★★
Holiday & Touring Park
Saltcotes Road, Lytham St
Annes FY8 4LS
(01253) 737907
e ehcplytham@aol.com
w ukparks.co.uk/easthamhall

MILNTHORPE
Cumbria

Fell End Caravan Park
★★★★★
Holiday, Touring & Camping
Park
Slack Head Road, Hale,
Milnthorpe LA7 7BS
(015395) 62122
e enquiries@southlakeland-
caravans.co.uk
w southlakeland-caravans.co.
uk

MORECAMBE
Lancashire

Regent Leisure Park ★★★★
Holiday Park
Westgate, Morecambe
LA3 3DF
0870 774 4024
e enquiries@
southlakelandparks.co.uk
w southlakelandparks.co.uk

Venture Caravan Park
★★★
Holiday, Touring & Camping
Park
Langridge Way, Westgate,
Morecambe LA4 4TQ
(01524) 412986
e mark@venturecaravanpark.
co.uk
w venturecaravanpark.co.uk

Westgate Caravan Park
★★★
Holiday & Touring Park
Westgate, Morecambe
LA3 3DE
(01524) 411448
w westgatecaravanpark.co.uk/

NETHER KELLET
Lancashire

The Hawthorns Caravan
Park ★★★★★
Holiday Park
Nether Kellet, Carnforth
LA6 1EA
(01524) 732079
w hawthornscaravanpark.co.
uk/

NEW HUTTON
Cumbria

Ashes Exclusively Adult
Caravan Park ★★★★★
Touring Park
New Hutton, Kendal LA8 0AS
t (01539) 731833
e info@ashescaravanpark.co.
uk
w ashescaravanpark.co.uk

NEWBY BRIDGE
Cumbria

Newby Bridge Country
Caravan Park ★★★★★
Holiday Park
Canny Hill, Newby Bridge
LA12 8NF
t (015395) 31030
e info@cumbriancaravans.co.
uk
w cumbriancaravans.co.uk

NEWLANDS
Cumbria

Low Manesty Caravan Club
Site ★★★★
Touring Park
Manesty, Keswick CA12 5UG
t (01768) 777275
e enquiries@caravanclub.co.
uk

ORTON
Cumbria

Westmorland Touring &
Caravan Park ★★★★
Holiday & Touring Park
Orton, Penrith CA10 3SB
t (01539) 711322
e caravans@westmorland.com
w westmorland.com

PENRITH
Cumbria

Flusco Wood Caravan Park
★★★★★
Holiday & Touring Park
Flusco, Penrith CA11 0JB
t (01768) 480020

Lowther Holiday Park
★★★★★
Holiday, Touring & Camping
Park
Eamont Bridge, Penrith
CA10 2JB
t (01768) 863631
e info@lowther-holidaypark.
co.uk
w lowther-holidaypark.co.uk

Troutbeck Head Caravan
Club Site ★★★★★
Touring Park
Troutbeck, Penrith CA11 0SS
t (01768) 483521
w caravanclub.co.uk

PLANTATION BRIDGE
Cumbria

Camping & Caravanning
Club – Windermere
★★★★★
Holiday, Touring & Camping
Park
Ashes Lane, Staveley,
Windermere LA8 9JS
t 0845 130 7633
w campingandcaravanning
club.co.uk

POOLEY BRIDGE
Cumbria

Waterside House Campsite
★★★★
Camping Park
Waterside House, Howtown,
Penrith CA10 2NA
t (017684) 86332
e enquire@watersidefarm-
campsite.co.uk
w watersidefarm-campsite.co.
uk

POULTON-LE-FYLDE
Lancashire

Poulton Plaiz Holiday Park
★★★★
Holiday, Touring & Camping
Park
Garstang Road West, Poulton-
le-Fylde FY6 8AR
t (01253) 888930
e info@poultonplaiz.co.uk

RAVENGLASS
Cumbria

Camping & Caravanning
Site-Ravenglass ★★★★
Holiday, Touring & Camping
Park
Ravenglass CA18 1SR
t (01229) 717250
w campingandcaravanning
club.co.uk

RIMINGTON
Lancashire

Rimington Caravan Park
★★★★★
Holiday & Touring Park
Hardacre Lane, Gisburn, Nr
Clitheroe BB7 4EE
t (01200) 445355
e rimingtoncaravanpark@
btinternet.com
w rimingtoncaravanpark.co.uk

ROCHDALE
Greater Manchester

Hollingworth Lake Caravan
Park ★★★
Holiday, Touring & Camping
Park
Roundhouse Farm,
Hollingworth Lake,
Littleborough OL15 0AT
t (01706) 378661

ST BEES
Cumbria

Seacote Park ★★★★
Holiday, Touring & Camping
Park
The Beach, St Bees CA27 0ET
t (01946) 822777
e reception@seacote.com
w seacote.com

SCARISBRICK
Lancashire

Hurlston Hall Caravan Park
★★★★
Holiday & Touring Park
Hurlston Lane, Scarisbrick
L40 8HB
t (01704) 841064

SILLOTH
Cumbria

Seacote Caravan Park
★★★★
Holiday & Touring Park
Skinburness Road, Silloth
CA7 4QJ
t (01697) 331121
e seacote@bfcltd.co.uk

Solway Holiday Village ★★
Holiday, Touring & Camping
Park
Skinburness Drive, Silloth
CA7 4QQ
t (01697) 331236
e solway@hagansleisure.co.uk
w hagansleisure.co.uk

Stanwix Park Holiday Centre
★★★★★
Holiday, Touring & Camping
Park
Greenrow, Silloth CA7 4HH
t (01697) 332666
e enquiries@stanwix.com
w stanwix.com

Tanglewood Caravan Park
★★★
Holiday, Touring & Camping
Park
Causewayhead, Silloth
CA7 4PE
t (01697) 331253
e tanglewoodcaravanpar@
hotmail.com
w tanglewoodcaravanpark.co.
uk

SILVERDALE
Lancashire

Far Arnside Caravan Park
★★★★★
Holiday Park
Holgates Caravan Parks Ltd,
Middlebarrow Plain, Carnforth
LA5 0SH
t (01524) 701508
e caravan@holgates.co.uk
w holgates.co.uk

Holgates Caravan Park
★★★★★
Holiday, Touring & Camping
Park
Cove Road, Silverdale,
Carnforth LA5 0SH
t (01524) 701508
e caravan@holgates.co.uk
w holgates.co.uk

THURSTASTON
Merseyside

Wirral Country Park Caravan Club Site ★★★★
Touring & Camping Park
Station Road, Thurstaston,
Wirral CH61 0HN
t (0151) 648 5228
w caravanclub.co.uk

TROUTBECK
Cumbria

Camping & Caravanning Site – Troutbeck
Rating Applied For
Holiday, Touring & Camping Park
Hutton Moor End, Troutbeck,
Penrith CA11 0SX
t (01768) 779615
e troutbeck@campingandcaravanningclub.co.uk
w campingandcaravanningclub.co.uk

ULLSWATER
Cumbria

Quiet Site Caravan Park ★★★★★
Holiday, Touring & Camping Park
Ullswater, Penrith CA11 0LS
t (01768) 486337
e info@thequietsite.fsnet.co.uk
w thequietsite.co.uk

Waterfoot Caravan Park ★★★★★
Holiday & Touring Park
Pooley Bridge, Penrith
CA11 0JF
t (017684) 86302
e enquiries@waterfootpark.co.uk
w waterfootpark.co.uk

ULVERSTON
Cumbria

Bardsea Leisure Park ★★★★
Holiday & Touring Park
Priory Road, Ulverston
LA12 9QE
t (01229) 584712

WASDALE
Cumbria

Church Stile Holiday Park ★★★★
Holiday, Touring & Camping Park
Church Stile Farm, Wasdale
CA20 1ET
t (01946) 726252
e church-knight@btconnect.com
w churchstile.com

WEST BRADFORD
Lancashire

Three Rivers Woodland Park ★★★
Holiday, Touring & Camping Park
Eaves Hall Lane, West
Bradford, Clitheroe BB7 3JG
t (01200) 423523
w threeriverspark.co.uk

WHINFELL
Cumbria

Center Parcs Whinfell Forest ★★★★★
Forest Holiday Village
Whinfell Forest, Penrith
CA10 2DW
t 0870 067 3030
w centerparcs.co.uk

WHITEGATE
Cheshire

Lamb Cottage Caravan Park ★★★★★
Holiday & Touring Park
Dalefords Lane, Whitegate,
Northwich CW8 2BN
t (01606) 882302
w lambcottage.co.uk

WINDERMERE
Cumbria

Braithwaite Fold Caravan Club Site ★★★★
Touring Park
Glebe Road, Bowness-on-
Windermere, Windermere
LA23 3GZ
t (015394) 42177
w caravanclub.co.uk

Fallbarrow Park ★★★★★
Holiday & Touring Park
Rayrigg Road, Bowness-on-
Windermere, Windermere
LA23 3DL
t 0870 774 4024
w southlakelandparks.co.uk

Hill of Oaks and Blakeholme Caravans ★★★★★
Holiday & Touring Park
Newby Bridge, Nr Ulverston
LA12 8NR
t (015395) 31578
e enquiries@hillofoaks.co.uk
w hillofoaks.co.uk

Limefitt Park ★★★★★ ROSE AWARD
Holiday, Touring & Camping Park
Patterdale Road, Windermere
LA23 1PA
t 0870 774 4024
e enquiries@southlakelandparks.co.uk
w southlakelandparks.co.uk

Park Cliffe Caravan and Camping Estate ★★★★★
Holiday, Touring & Camping Park
Birks Road, Windermere
LA23 3PG
t (015395) 31344
e info@parkcliffe.co.uk
w parkcliffe.co.uk

White Cross Bay Holiday Park and Marina ★★★★
Holiday & Touring Park
Ambleside Road, Troutbeck
Bridge, Windermere LA23 1LF
t 0870 774 4024
e enquiries@southlakelandparks.co.uk
w southlakelandparks.co.uk

WINSFORD
Cheshire

Elm Cottage Caravan Park ★★★
Touring & Camping Park
Chester Lane, Little Budworth
Winsford CW7 2QJ
t (01829) 760544
e chris@elmcottagecp.co.uk
w elmcottagecp.co.uk

Lakeside Caravan Park ★★★★
Holiday Park
Stocks Hill, Winsford CW7 4E
t (01606) 861043
e enquiries@thornleyleisure.co.uk

WREA GREEN
Lancashire

Ribby Hall Village ★★★★
Ribby Road, Wrea Green,
Preston PR4 2PR
t (01772) 671111
e enquiries@ribbyhall.co.uk
w ribbyhall.co.uk

NORTH EAST ENGLAND

ALNWICK
Northumberland

Alnwick Rugby Football Club ★
Touring & Camping Park
Greensfield, Alnwick
NE66 1BG
t (01665) 602342
w alnwickrugby.com

ASHINGTON
Northumberland

Wansbeck Riverside Park Caravan and Camp Site ★★
Touring & Camping Park
Ashington NE63 8TX
t (01670) 812323
e traceyproudlock@fsmail.net
w wansbeck.gov.uk

BAMBURGH
Northumberland

Bradford Kaims Caravan Park ★★★
Holiday, Touring & Camping Park
Bradford House, Bamburgh
NE70 7JT
t (01668) 213432
e lwrob@tiscali.co.uk
w bradford-leisure.co.uk

Glororum Caravan Park ★★★
Holiday & Touring Park
Glororum, Bamburgh
NE69 7AW
t (01668) 214457
e info@glororum-caravanpark.co.uk
w glororum-caravanpark.co.uk

Meadowhead's Waren Caravan and Camping Park ★★★★ ROSE AWARD
Holiday, Touring & Camping Park
Waren Mill, Belford NE70 7EE
t (01668) 214366
e waren@meadowhead.co.uk
w meadowhead.co.uk

BARDON MILL
Northumberland

Winshields Camp Site ★★★
Camping Park
Bardon Mill, Hexham
NE47 7AN
t (01434) 344243
w winshields.co.uk

BEADNELL
Northumberland

The Camping and Caravanning Site Beadnell Bay ★★
Touring & Camping Park
The Camping and Caravanning
Club Site, Chathill NE67 5BX
t (01665) 720586
w campingandcaravanningclub.co.uk

BEAL
Northumberland

Haggerston Castle ★★★★
Holiday & Touring Park
Haggerston Castle Holiday
Park, Haggerston, Berwick-
upon-Tweed TD15 2PA
t (01289) 381333
e enquiries@british-holidays.co.uk
w haggerstoncastle-park.co.uk

Bobby Shafto Caravan Park ★★★★
Holiday, Touring & Camping Park
Money Hills DH9 0RY
t (0191) 370 1776
e jeffharlepeel@hotmail.co.uk
w ukparks.co.uk/bobbyshafto

BELFORD
Northumberland

South Meadows Caravan Park ★★★★★
Holiday, Touring & Camping Park
South Meadows, Belford
NE70 7DP
t (01668) 213326
e g.mcl@btinternet.com
w southmeadows.co.uk

BELLINGHAM
Northumberland

Brown Rigg Camping & Caravanning Club Site
Rating Applied For
Touring & Camping Park
Tweed House, The Croft,
Bellingham NE48 2JY
t (01434) 220175
e caroleandbarry@gmail.com
w campingandcaravanning
club.co.uk

Demesne Farm Campsite & Bunkhouse ★★★
Touring & Camping Park
Demesne Farm, Bellingham
NE48 2BS
t (01434) 220258
e stay@
demesnefarmcampsite.co.uk
w demesnefarmcampsite.co.uk

BERWICK-UPON-TWEED
Northumberland

Beachcomber Campsite ★★
Touring & Camping Park
Goswick, Berwick-upon-Tweed
TD15 2RW
t (01289) 381217
e johngregson@micro-plus-web.net
w lindisfarne.org.uk/
beachcomber

Berwick Holiday Park ★★★★★
Holiday Park
Magdalene Fields, Berwick-upon-Tweed NE61 1NE
t (01289) 307113
e berwick@bourne-leisure.co.uk
w british-holidays.co.uk

Seaview Caravan Club Site ★★★★
Touring & Camping Park
Billendean Road, Berwick-upon-Tweed TD15 1QU
t (01289) 305198
w caravanclub.co.uk

BLACKHALL COLLIERY
County Durham

Crimdon Dene Holiday Park ★★★
Holiday & Touring Park
Coast Road, Blackhall Colliery
TS27 4BN
t (01429) 267801
w park-resorts.com

CASTLESIDE
County Durham

Manor Park Caravan Park ★★
Holiday, Touring & Camping Park
Broadmeadows, Rippon Burn,
Consett DH8 9HD
t (01207) 501000

CORBRIDGE
Northumberland

Well House Farm – Corbridge ★★★
Touring & Camping Park
Newton, Stocksfield NE43 7UY
t (01661) 842193
e info@wellhousefarm.co.uk
w wellhousefarm.co.uk

COTHERSTONE
County Durham

Doe Park Caravan Site ★★★★
Touring Park
Cotherstone DL12 9UQ
t (01833) 650302

CRASTER
Northumberland

Proctors Stead Caravan Site ★★★
Holiday, Touring & Camping Park
Dunstan Village, Dunstan
NE66 3TF
t (01665) 576613

CRESSWELL
Northumberland

Cresswell Towers Holiday Park ★★★
Holiday Park
Cresswell, Morpeth NE61 5JT
t 0871 664 9734
e holidaysales.
cresswelltowers@
gbholidayparks.co.uk
w gbholidayparks.co.uk

Golden Sands Holiday Park ★★★★★
Holiday Park
Beach Road, Cresswell
NE61 5LF
t (01670) 860256
e enquiries@
northumbrianleisure.co.uk
w northumbrianleisure.co.uk

DARLINGTON
Tees Valley

Newbus Grange Country Park ★★★★
Touring & Camping Park
Hurworth Road, Neasham
DL2 1PE
t (01325) 720973

DUNSTAN
Northumberland

Camping and Caravan Club Site Dunstan Hill ★★★★
Touring & Camping Park
Dunstan, Alnwick NE66 3TQ
t (01665) 576310
w campingandcaravanning
club.co.uk

DURHAM
County Durham

Finchale Abbey Caravan Park ★★★★
Touring Park
Finchale Abbey Farm, Finchale
Abbey, Durham DH1 5SH
t (0191) 386 6528 &
07989 854704
e godricawatson@hotmail.com
w finchaleabbey.co.uk

Grange Caravan Club Site ★★★★★
Touring & Camping Park
Meadow Lane, Durham
DH1 1TL
t (0191) 384 4778
w caravanclub.co.uk

Strawberry Hill Farm Camping & Caravanning Park ★★★★ ROSE AWARD
Holiday, Touring & Camping Park
Running Waters, Old Cassop,
Durham DH6 4QA
t (0191) 372 3457
e info@strawberryhf.co.uk
w strawberry-hill-farm.co.uk

EAST ORD
Northumberland

Ord House Country Park ★★★★★
Holiday, Touring & Camping Park
East Ord, Berwick-upon-Tweed
TD15 2NS
t (01289) 305288
e enquiries@ordhouse.co.uk
w ordhouse.co.uk

EBCHESTER
County Durham

Byreside Caravan Site ★★★★
Touring & Camping Park
Hamsterley Colliery NE17 7RT
t (01207) 560280

GREENHEAD
Northumberland

Roam-n-Rest Caravan Park ★★★
Touring & Camping Park
Raylton House, Greenhead
CA8 7HA
t (01697) 747213

HALTWHISTLE
Northumberland

Camping & Caravanning Club Site Haltwhistle ★★★★
Touring & Camping Park
Park Burnfoot Farm,
Haltwhistle NE49 0JP
t (01434) 320106
w campingandcaravanning
club.co.uk

HAYDON BRIDGE
Northumberland

Poplars Riverside Caravan Park ★★★★
Holiday, Touring & Camping Park
East Lands Ends, Haydon
Bridge, Hexham NE47 6BY
t (01434) 684427

HEXHAM
Northumberland

Fallowfield Dene Caravan and Camping Park ★★★★
Touring & Camping Park
Acomb, Hexham NE46 4RP
t (01434) 603553
e den@fallowfielddene.co.uk
w fallowfielddene.co.uk

Hexham Racecourse Caravan Site ★★★
Touring & Camping Park
Yarridge Road, High Yarridge,
Hexham NE46 2JP
t (01434) 606847
e hexrace@aol.com
w hexham-racecourse.co.uk

KIELDER
Northumberland

Kielder Water Caravan Club Site
Touring & Camping Park
Leaplish Waterside Park,
Falstone, Hexham NE48 1AX
t (01434) 250278
w caravanclub.co.uk

LARTINGTON
County Durham

Camping and Caravanning Club Site Barnard Castle ★★★★★
Touring & Camping Park
Dockenflats Lane, Barnard
Castle DL12 9DG
t (01833) 630228
w campingandcaravanning
club.co.uk

LONGHORSLEY
Northumberland

Forget-Me-Not Holiday Park ★★★★
Holiday, Touring & Camping Park
Croftside, Morpeth NE65 8QY
t (01670) 788364
e info@forget-me-notholidaypark.co.uk
w forget-me-notholidaypark.co.uk

MELKRIDGE
Northumberland

Hadrian's Wall Caravan and Camping Site ★★★
Touring & Camping Park
Melkridge Tilery, Haltwhistle NE49 9PG
t (01434) 320495
e info@romanwallcamping.co.uk
w romanwallcamping.co.uk

NEWBIGGIN-BY-THE-SEA
Northumberland

Church Point Holiday Park ★★★★
Holiday Park
Newbiggin-by-the-Sea NE64 6DP
t (01670) 817443
w park-resorts.com

NORTH SEATON
Northumberland

Sandy Bay Holiday Park ★★★
Holiday & Touring Park
North Seaton NE63 9YD
t 0871 664 9764
e holidaysales.sandybay@park-resorts.com
w park-resorts.com

OVINGHAM
Northumberland

The High Hermitage Caravan Park ★★★
Holiday, Touring & Camping Park
The Hermitage, Main Road, Ovingham NE42 6HH
t (01661) 832250
e highhermitage@onetel.com

POWBURN
Northumberland

River Breamish Caravan Club Site ★★★★★
Touring & Camping Park
Powburn, Alnwick NE66 4HY
t (01665) 578320
w caravanclub.co.uk

RAMSHAW
County Durham

Craggwood Caravan Park ★★★
Holiday, Touring & Camping Park
Gordon Lane, Ramshaw, Bishop Auckland DL14 0NS
t (01388) 835866
e billy6482@btopenworld.com
w craggwoodcaravanpark.co.uk

ROTHBURY
Northumberland

Coquetdale Caravan Park ★★★
Holiday & Touring Park
Whitton, Morpeth NE65 7RU
t (01669) 620549
e enquiry@coquetdalecaravanpark.co.uk
w coquetdalecaravanpark.co.uk

Nunnykirk Caravan Club Site ★★★★

Touring Park
Nunnykirk Caravan Park, Nunnykirk, Morpeth NE61 4PZ
t (01669) 620762
w caravanclub.co.uk

SEAHOUSES
Northumberland

Seafield Caravan Park ★★★★★ ROSE AWARD
Holiday & Touring Park
Seafield Road, Seahouses NE68 7SP
t (01665) 720628
e info@seafieldpark.co.uk
w seafieldpark.co.uk

STOCKTON-ON-TEES
Tees Valley

White Water Caravan Club Park ★★★★★
Touring Park
Tees Barrage, Stockton-on-Tees TS18 2QW
t (01642) 634880
w caravanclub.co.uk

STONEHAUGH
Northumberland

Stonehaugh Campsite ★★
Touring & Camping Park
The Old Farmhouse, Stonehaugh Shields NE48 3BU
t (01434) 230798
e carole@stonehaugh.fsbusiness.co.uk
w stonehaugh.fsbusiness.co.uk

WHITLEY BAY
Tyne and Wear

Whitley Bay Holiday Park ★★★★
Holiday Park
The Links, Whitley Bay NE16 4BR
t 0871 664 9800
e holidaysales.whitleybay@park-resorts.com
w park-resorts.com

WINSTON
County Durham

Winston Caravan Park ★★★
Holiday & Touring Park
Front Street, Winston DL2 3RH
t (01325) 730228
e m.willetts@ic24.net
w touristnetuk.com/ne/winston

YORKSHIRE

ACASTER MALBIS
North Yorkshire

Moor End Farm ★★★★
Holiday, Touring & Camping Park
Moor End, Acaster Malbis, York YO23 2UQ
t (01904) 706727
e moorendfarm@acaster99.fsnet.co.uk
w ukparks.co.uk/moorend

ALLERSTON
North Yorkshire

Vale of Pickering Caravan Park ★★★★★
Touring & Camping Park
Allerston, Pickering YO18 7PQ
t (01723) 859280
e tony@valeofpickering.co.uk
w valeofpickering.co.uk

BARDSEY
West Yorkshire

Haighfield Caravan Park ★★★★★
Holiday Park
5 Blackmoor Lane, Leeds LS17 9DY
t (01937) 574658

BARMSTON
East Riding of Yorkshire

Barmston Beach Holiday Park ★★★★
Holiday Park
Sands Lane, Hornsea YO25 8PJ
t (01442) 830185
e angie.pyle@park-resorts.com
w park-resorts.com

BEDALE
North Yorkshire

Pembroke Caravan Park ★★★★
Touring & Camping Park
19 Low Street, Leeming Bar, Northallerton DL7 9BW
t (01677) 422652

BEVERLEY
East Riding of Yorkshire

Barmston Farm Caravan Park ★★★★★
Holiday Park
Barmston Farm, Barmston Lane, Woodmansey, Beverley HU17 0TP
t (01482) 863566 & 07970 042587
e enquiry@barmstonfarm.co.uk
w barmstonfarm.co.uk

BOLTON ABBEY
North Yorkshire

Howgill Lodge ★★★★★
Holiday, Touring & Camping Park
Barden, Skipton BD23 6DJ
t (01756) 720655
e info@howgill-lodge.co.uk
w howgill-lodge.co.uk

Strid Wood Caravan Club Site ★★★★★
Touring Park
Skipton BD23 6AN
t (01756) 710433
w caravanclub.co.uk

BRANDESBURTON
East Riding of Yorkshire

Dacre Lakeside Park ★★★★
Holiday & Touring Park
Leven Road, Brandesburton, Driffield YO25 8RT
t 0800 180 4556
e chalets@dacrepark.co.uk
w dacrepark.co.uk

Fosse Hill Caravan Park ★★★
Touring & Camping Park
Catwick Lane, Brandesburton, Hornsea YO25 8SB
t (01964) 542608
e tony@fossehill.co.uk
w fossehill.co.uk

BRIDLINGTON
East Riding of Yorkshire

North Bay Leisure Limited ★★★★ ROSE AWARD
Holiday Park
Lime Kiln Lane, Bridlington YO16 6TG
t (01262) 673733
e enquiries@northbayleisure.co.uk
w northbayleisure.co.uk

The Poplars Touring Park
★★★★
Touring & Camping Park
45 Jewison Lane, Sewerby,
Bridlington YO15 1DX
t (01262) 677251
w the-poplars.co.uk

South Cliff Caravan Park
★★★★
Holiday, Touring & Camping Park
Wilstrorpe, Bridlington
YO15 3QN
t (01262) 671051
e southcliff@eastriding.gov.uk
w southcliff.co.uk

BURTON-IN-LONSDALE
North Yorkshire

Gallaber Farm Caravan Park
★★★★
Holiday, Touring & Camping Park
Gallaber Farm, Burton in
Lonsdale, Carnforth LA6 3LU
t (01524) 261361
e gallaber@btopenworld.com
w gallaber.btinternet.co.uk

CAYTON BAY
North Yorkshire

Cayton Bay Holiday Park
★★★★
Holiday Park
Mill Lane, Cayton Bay,
Scarborough YO11 3NJ
t (01442) 830185
e angie.pyle@park-resorts.com
w park-resorts.com

Cliff Farm Caravan Park
★★★★★
Holiday Park
Mill Lane, Cayton Bay,
Scarborough YO11 3NN
t (01723) 582239

CLAXTON
North Yorkshire

Foxhill Park ★★★
Holiday, Touring & Camping Park
Claxton To Harton Lodge Road,
Claxton, Malton YO60 7RX
t (01904) 468355
e enquiries@foxhillpark.com

CONSTABLE BURTON
North Yorkshire

Constable Burton Hall Caravan Park ★★★★
Touring Park
Constable Burton, Leyburn
DL8 5LJ
t (01677) 450428

DUNNINGTON
North Yorkshire

Ashfield Caravan Park
★★★★
Touring & Camping Park
Hagg Lane, York YO19 5PE
t (01904) 489147
w ashfieldtouringcaravanpark.co.uk

ESCRICK
North Yorkshire

The Hollicarrs ★★★★★
Holiday Park
Riccall Road, York YO19 6EA
t 0800 980 8070
e sales@thehollicarrs.com
w thehollicarrs.com

FARNHAM
North Yorkshire

Kingfisher Caravan and Camping Park ★★★★
Holiday, Touring & Camping Park
Low Moor Lane, Scotton,
Knaresborough HG5 9JB
t (01423) 869411

FILEY
North Yorkshire

Filey Brigg Caravan & Country Park ★★★★
Touring & Camping Park
Church Cliff Drive, North Cliff,
Arndale, Filey YO14 9ET
t (01723) 513852
e fileybrigg@scarborough.gov.uk
w scarborough.gov.uk

Orchard Farm Holiday Village ★★★★★
Holiday Park
Stonegate, Hunmanby, Filey
YO14 0PU
t (01723) 891582

Primrose Valley Holiday Park ★★★★★
Holiday & Touring Park
Primrose Valley, Filey
YO14 9RF
t (01723) 513771
w primrosevalley-park.co.uk/

FLAMBOROUGH
East Riding of Yorkshire

Thornwick & Sea Farm Holiday Centre ★★★★
Holiday, Touring & Camping Park
North Marine Road,
Flamborough, Bridlington
YO15 1AU
t (01262) 850369
e enquiries@thornwickbay.co.uk
w thornwickbay.co.uk

FOLLIFOOT
North Yorkshire

Great Yorkshire Showground Caravan Club
★★★★
Touring Park
Wetherby Road, Harrogate
HG3 1TZ
t (01423) 560470
e natalie.tiller@caravanclub.co.uk
w caravanclub.co.uk

GILLING WEST
North Yorkshire

Hargill House Caravan Club Site ★★★★
Touring Park
Gilling West, Richmond
DL10 5LJ
t (01342) 336732
e natalie.tiller@caravanclub.co.uk
w caravanclub.co.uk

GRISTHORPE BAY
North Yorkshire

Blue Dolphin Holiday Park
★★★★
Holiday, Touring & Camping Park
Gristhorpe Bay, Filey
YO14 9PU
t (01723) 515155
w bluedolphin-park.co.uk

HARDEN
West Yorkshire

Harden & Bingley Holiday Park ★★★★
Holiday & Touring Park
Goit Stock Private Estate, Goit
Stock Lane, Bradford
BD16 1DF
t (01535) 273810
e pauldavisdunham@tiscali.co.uk
w ukparks.co.uk/harden

HARMBY
North Yorkshire

Lower Wensleydale Caravan Club Site ★★★
Touring & Camping Park
Harmby, Leyburn DL8 5NU
t (01969) 623366

HARROGATE
North Yorkshire

High Moor Farm Park
★★★★★
Holiday & Touring Park
Skipton Road, Felliscliffe,
Harrogate HG3 2LT
t (01423) 563637
e highmoorfarmpark@btconnect.com

Reynard Crag Park ★★★★
Holiday Park
Reynard Crag Lane, Burstwith,
Harrogate HG3 2JQ
t (01423) 772828
e reynardcrag@btconnect.com
w reynardcragpark.co.uk

Ripley Caravan Park
★★★★★
Holiday, Touring & Camping Park
Knaresborough Road, Ripley
HG3 3AU
t (01423) 770050
w ripleycaravanpark@talk21.com

Rudding Holiday Park
★★★★★ ROSE AWARD
Holiday, Touring & Camping Park
Follifoot, Harrogate HG3 1JH
t (01423) 870439
e holiday-park@ruddingpark.com
w ruddingpark.com

Warren Forest Caravan Park
★★★★★
Holiday Park
Warsill, Harrogate HG3 3LH
t (01765) 620683
e enquiries@warrenforestpark.co.uk
w warrenforestpark.co.uk

HATFIELD
South Yorkshire

Hatfield Water Park ★★★
Touring & Camping Park
Old Thorn Road, Doncaster
DN7 6EQ
t (01302) 841572

HAWES
North Yorkshire

Bainbridge Ings Caravan and Camping Site ★★
Holiday, Touring & Camping Park
Hawes DL8 3NU
t (01969) 667354
e janet@bainbridge-ings.co.uk
w bainbridge-ings.co.uk

Honeycott Caravan Park
★★★★
Holiday, Touring & Camping Park
Ingleton Road, Hawes DL8 3LH
t (01969) 667310
e info@honeycott.co.uk
w honeycott.co.uk

HAWORTH
West Yorkshire

Upwood Holiday Park
★★★★
Holiday, Touring & Camping Park
Blackmoor Road, Oxenhope,
Haworth, Keighley BD22 9SS
t (01535) 644242
e info@upwoodpark.co.uk
w upwoodpark.co.uk

HEBDEN BRIDGE
West Yorkshire

Lower Clough Foot Caravan Club Site ★★★★★
Touring Park
Cragg Vale, Hebden Bridge
HX7 5RU
t (01422) 882531
w caravanclub.co.uk

HELMSLEY
North Yorkshire

Foxholme Touring Caravan Park ★★★★★
Touring & Camping Park
Harome, Helmsley YO62 5JG
t (01439) 771241

Golden Square Caravan and Camping Park ★★★★★
Touring & Camping Park
Oswaldkirk, Helmsley, York
YO62 5YQ
t (01439) 788269
e barbara@
goldensquarecaravanpark.
freeserve.co.uk
w goldensquarecaravanpark.
com

HIGH BENTHAM
North Yorkshire

Riverside Caravan Park ★★★★★
Holiday, Touring & Camping Park
Wenning Avenue, Lancaster
LA2 7LW
t (01524) 261272
e info@riversidecaravanpark.
co.uk
w riversidecaravanpark.co.uk

HINDERWELL
North Yorkshire

Serenity Touring Caravan & Camping Park ★★★★
Touring & Camping Park
Saltburn-by-the-Sea TS13 5JH
t (01947) 841122

HOLMFIRTH
West Yorkshire

Holme Valley Camping and Caravan Park ★★★★
Touring & Camping Park
Thongsbridge, Holmfirth
HD9 7TD
t (01484) 665819
e enquiries@
homevalleycamping.com
w holmevalleycamping.com

HUTTON-LE-HOLE
North Yorkshire

Hutton le Hole Caravan Park ★★★★
Touring & Camping Park
Westfield Lodge, Hutton-le-Hole, York YO62 6UG
t (01751) 417261
e rwstrickland@
farmersweekly.net
w westfieldlodge.co.uk

INGLETON
North Yorkshire

Parkfoot Holiday Homes ★★★★★
Holiday Park
Bentham Road, Carnforth
LA6 3HR
t (01524) 261833
e parkfoot.ingleton@virgin.net
w parkfoot.co.uk

KEARBY WITH NETHERBY
North Yorkshire

Maustin Park Ltd ★★★★★
Holiday, Touring & Camping Park
Wharfe Lane, Kearby,
Wetherby LS22 4DA
t (0113) 288 6234
e info@maustin.co.uk
w maustin.co.uk

KILNSEA
East Riding of Yorkshire

Sandy Beaches Caravan Site ★★
Holiday Park
Kilnsea Road, Kilnsea, Hull
HU12 0UB
t (01964) 650372
e sandybeacheskiln@aol.com
w sandybeaches.co.uk

KNARESBOROUGH
North Yorkshire

Knaresborough Caravan Club Site ★★★★★
Touring Park
New Road, Scotton,
Knaresborough HG5 9HH
t (01342) 336732
w caravanclub.co.uk

LANGTHORPE
North Yorkshire

Old Hall Holiday Park ★★★★
Holiday & Touring Park
Skelton Road, Langthorpe,
Boroughbridge, Harrogate
YO51 9BZ
t (01423) 323190
e phil.brierley@which.net
w yhcparks.info

LEEDS
West Yorkshire

St Helena's Caravan Site ★★★★
Holiday, Touring & Camping Park
Otley Old Road, Leeds
LS18 5HZ
t (0113) 284 1142

LITTLE WEIGHTON
East Riding of Yorkshire

Croft Park ★★★★★
Touring & Camping Park
55 Rowley Road, Little
Weighton, Hull HU20 3XJ
t (01482) 840600
e steve@croftpark.fsnet.co.uk
w croftpark.net

LOFTHOUSE
North Yorkshire

Studfold Farm Caravan and Camping Park ★★★★
Touring & Camping Park
Studfold Farm, Lofthouse,
Pateley Bridge HG3 5SG
t (01423) 755210
e ianwalker@studfold.fsnet.
co.uk
w studfoldfarm.co.uk

LONG PRESTON
North Yorkshire

Gallaber Park ★★★★
Holiday & Touring Park
Skipton BD23 4QF
t (01729) 851397
e info@gallaberpark.com
w gallaberpark.com

MALTON
North Yorkshire

Wolds Way Caravan and Camping ★★★★
Touring & Camping Park
West Farm, West Knapton,
Malton YO17 8JE
t (01944) 728463
e knapton.wold.farms@
farming.co.uk
w ryedalesbest.co.uk

MARKINGTON
North Yorkshire

J S Brayshaw Caravans Limited ★★★★
Holiday, Touring & Camping Park
High Street, Markington,
Pateley Bridge HG3 3NR
t (01765) 677327
e yorkshirehussar@yahoo.co.
uk

MASHAM
North Yorkshire

Black Swan Holiday Park ★★★★
Holiday, Touring & Camping Park
Rear Black Swan Hotel,
Masham, Ripon HG4 4NF
t (01765) 689477
e info@blackswanholiday.co.
uk
w blackswanholiday.co.uk

NAWTON
North Yorkshire

Wrens of Ryedale Caravan and Camp Site ★★★★
Touring & Camping Park
Gale Lane, Nawton, York
YO62 7SD
t (01439) 771260
e dave@wrensofryedale.fsnet.
co.uk
w wrensofryedale.co.uk

NEWTON-LE-WILLOWS
North Yorkshire

Lindale Holiday Park – Caravan Park ★★★★
Holiday Park
Lindale Holiday Park, Newton-le-Willows, Bedale DL8 1TA
t (01677) 450842
e info@lindalepark.co.uk
w lindalepark.co.uk

NORTHALLERTON
North Yorkshire

Cote Ghyll Caravan & Camping Park ★★★★
Holiday, Touring & Camping Park
Osmotherley, Northallerton
DL6 3AH
t (01609) 883425
e hills@coteghyll.com
w coteghyll.com

NOSTELL
West Yorkshire

Nostell Priory Holiday Home Park ★★★★★
Holiday, Touring & Camping Park
Nostell Priory Estate, Wakefield
WF4 1QE
t (01924) 863938
e info@
nostellprioryholidaypark.co.uk
w nostellprioryholidaypark.co.
uk

PATRINGTON
East Riding of Yorkshire

Patrington Haven Leisure Park Ltd ★★★★★
Holiday Park
Patrington Haven, Hull
HU12 0PT
t (01964) 630071
e guy@phlp.co.uk
w phlp.co.uk

PICKERING
North Yorkshire

Wayside Caravan Park ★★★★
Holiday, Touring & Camping Park
Pickering YO18 8PG
t (01751) 472608
e waysideparks@freenet.co.uk
w waysideparks.co.uk

POCKLINGTON
East Riding of Yorkshire

South Lea Caravan Park ★★★★
Touring & Camping Park
The Balk, York YO42 2NX
t (01759) 303467
e southlea@fsmail.net
w south-lea.co.uk

REIGHTON GAP
North Yorkshire

Reighton Sands Holiday Park ★★★
Holiday, Touring & Camping Park
Reighton Gap, Filey YO14 9SJ
t (01723) 890476
w reightonsands-park.co.uk/

RIPON
North Yorkshire

River Laver Holiday Park ★★★★★
Holiday & Touring Park
Studley Road, Ripon HG4 2QR
t (01765) 690508
e riverlaver@lineone.net
w riverlaver.co.uk

Sleningford Watermill Caravan & Camping Park ★★★★★
Touring & Camping Park
North Stainley, Ripon
HG4 3HQ
t (01765) 635201
e sleningford@hotmail.co.uk
w ukparks.co.uk/sleningford

**Woodhouse Farm Caravan &
Camping Park** ★★★★
*Holiday, Touring & Camping
Park*
Winksley, Ripon HG4 3PG
t (01765) 658309
e woodhouse.farm@talk21.
com
w woodhousewinksley.com

**Camping & Caravanning
Club Boroughbridge**
★★★★★
Touring & Camping Park
Bar Lane, Roecliffe, Harrogate
YO51 9LS
t (01423) 322683
w campingandcaravanning
club.co.uk

**Sand-le-Mere Caravan &
Leisure Park** ★★★★
Holiday & Touring Park
Seaside Lane, Richmond
HU12 0JQ
t (01964) 670403
e info@sand-le-mere.co.uk
w sand-le-mere.co.uk

**Thorpe Hall Caravan and
Camping Site** ★★★★
Touring & Camping Park
Thorpe Hall, Rudston, Driffield
YO25 4JE
t (01262) 420393
e caravansite@thorpehall.co.
uk
w thorpehall.co.uk

Whitby Holiday Park
★★★★
Holiday & Touring Park
Saltwick Bay, Whitby YO22 4JX
t (01947) 602664
e info@whitbyholidaypark.co.
uk

Browns Caravan Park
★★★★★
Holiday & Touring Park
Mill Lane, Cayton Bay,
Scarborough YO11 3NN
t (01723) 582303
e info@brownscaravan.co.uk
w brownscaravan.co.uk

**Camping & Caravanning
Club Scarborough** ★★★★★
Touring Park
Field Lane, Burniston Road,
Scarborough YO13 0DA
t (01423) 322683
w campingandcaravanning
club.co.uk

Cayton Village Caravan Park
★★★★★
Touring & Camping Park
Mill Lane, Cayton Bay,
Scarborough YO11 3NN
t (01723) 583171
e info@caytontouring.co.uk
w caytontouring.co.uk

Crows Nest Caravan Park
★★★★ **ROSE AWARD**
Holiday Park
Gristhorpe, Filey YO14 9PS
t (01723) 582206
e enquiries@
crowsnestcaravanpark.com
w crowsnestcaravanpark.com

**Flower of May Holiday Parks
Ltd** ★★★★★
ROSE AWARD
*Holiday, Touring & Camping
Park*
Lebberston, Scarborough
YO11 3NU
t (01723) 584311
e info@flowerofmay.com
w flowerofmay.com

Jasmine Park ★★★★★
*Holiday, Touring & Camping
Park*
Cross Lane, Snainton,
Scarborough YO13 9BE
t (01723) 859240
e info@jasminepark.co.uk
w jasminepark.co.uk

Lebberston Touring Park
★★★★★
Touring Park
Lebberston, Scarborough
YO11 3PE
t (01723) 585723
e info@lebberstontouring.co.
uk
w lebberstontouring.co.uk

Scalby Close Park ★★★★
*Holiday, Touring & Camping
Park*
Burniston Road, Scarborough
YO13 0DA
t (01723) 365908
e info@scalbyclose.co.uk
w scalbyclosepark.co.uk

Langcliffe Park ★★★★
*Holiday, Touring & Camping
Park*
Settle BD24 9LX
t (01729) 822387
e info@langcliffe.com
w langcliffe.com

**Camping & Caravanning
Club Sheriff** ★★★★
Touring & Camping Park
Bracken Hill, Sheriff Hutton,
Malton YO60 6QG
t (01347) 878660
e info@
campingandcaravanningclub.
co.uk
w campingandcaravanning
club.co.uk

Far Grange Park Ltd
★★★★★
Holiday Park
Hornsea Road, Driffield
YO25 8SY
t (01262) 468010
e andy.such@bourne-leisure.
co.uk
w fargrangepark.co.uk

**Skipsea Sands Holiday
Village** ★★★★
*Holiday, Touring & Camping
Park*
Mill Lane, Skipsea, Hornsea
YO25 8TZ
t (01262) 468210
e info@skipseasands.co.uk

Skirlington Leisure Park
★★★★★
*Holiday, Touring & Camping
Park*
Hornsea Road, Skipsea,
Driffield YO25 8SY
t (01262) 468213
e enquiries@skirlington.com
w skirlington.com

**Burton Constable Holiday
Park & Arboretum** ★★★★★
*Holiday, Touring & Camping
Park*
The Old Lodges, Sproatley,
Hull HU11 4LN
t (01964) 562508
e info@burtonconstable.co.uk
w burtonconstable.co.uk

**Camping & Caravanning
Club Site Slingsby** ★★★★★
Touring & Camping Park
Railway Street, York YO62 4AA
t 0870 243 3331
w campingandcaravanning
club.co.uk

**Robin Hood Caravan &
Camping Park** ★★★★★
ROSE AWARD
*Holiday, Touring & Camping
Park*
Green Dyke Lane, Slingsby,
York YO62 4AP
t (01653) 628391
e info@
robinhoodcaravanpark.co.uk
w robinhoodcaravanpark.co.uk

Low Moor Caravan Club Site
★★★★
Touring Park
Sneaton, Whitby YO22 5JE
t (01947) 810505
e natalie.tiller@caravanclub.
co.uk

**Knight Stainforth Hall
Caravan and Campi** ★★★★
*Holiday, Touring & Camping
Park*
Little Stainforth, Settle
BD24 0DP
t (01729) 822200
e info@knightstainforth.co.uk
w knightstainforth.co.uk

Moorside Caravan Park
★★★★
Touring Park
Lords Moor Lane, Strensall,
York YO32 5XJ
t (01904) 491208
w moorsidecaravanpark.co.uk

**Thirsk Racecourse Caravan
Club Site** ★★
Touring & Camping Park
Thirsk Racecourse, Station
Road, Thirsk YO7 1QL
t (01845) 525266
e enquiries@caravanclub.co.
uk

York House Caravan Park
★★★★
*Holiday, Touring & Camping
Park*
Balk, Thirsk YO7 2AQ
t (01423) 323190
e phil.brierley@which.net
w yhcparks.info

Elder House Touring Park
★★★★
Touring Park
Elder House Farm, Crow Tree
Bank, Doncaster DN8 5TD
t (01405) 813173

Overbrook Caravan Park
★★★★
Touring Park
Maltongate, Pickering
YO18 7SE
t (01751) 474417
e overbrook@breathe.com
w overbrookcaravanpark.co.uk

Long Ashes Park ★★★★
Holiday Park
Threshfield, Skipton BD23 5PN
t (01756) 752261
e info@longashespark.co.uk
w longashespark.co.uk

Wood Nook Caravan Park
★★★★
*Holiday, Touring & Camping
Park*
Skirethorns, Threshfield,
Skipton BD23 5NU
t (01756) 752412
e enquiries@woodnook.net
w woodnook.net

Flask Holiday Home Park
★★★★ ROSE AWARD
Holiday Park
Robin Hood's Bay, Fylingdales,
Whitby YO22 4QH
t (01947) 880592
e flaskinn@aol.com
w flaskinn.com

**Ladycross Plantation
Caravan Park** ★★★★★
Touring & Camping Park
Whitby YO21 1UA
t (01947) 895502
e enquiries@
ladycrossplantation.co.uk
w ladycrossplantation.co.uk

**Middlewood Farm Holiday
Park** ★★★★★
ROSE AWARD
*Holiday, Touring & Camping
Park*
Middlewood Lane,
Fylingthorpe, Robin Hood's
Bay, Whitby YO22 4UF
t (01947) 880414
e info@middlewoodfarm.com
w middlewoodfarm.com

**Northcliffe & Seaview
Holiday Parks** ★★★★★
*Holiday, Touring & Camping
Park*
Bottoms Lane, High Hawsker,
Whitby YO22 4LL
t (01947) 880477
e enquiries@northcliffe-
seaview.com
w northcliffe-seaview.com

**Partridge Nest Farm Holiday
Caravans** ★★★
Holiday Park
Eskdaleside, Sleights, Whitby
YO22 5ES
t (01947) 810450
e barbara@partridgenestfarm.
com
w partridgenestfarm.com

**Sandfield House Farm
Caravan Park** ★★★★★
Touring Park
Sandsend Road, Whitby
YO21 3SR
t (01947) 602660
e info@sandfieldhousefarm.
co.uk
w sandfieldhousefarm.co.uk

**The White House Caravan
Park** ★★★★★
Holiday Park
Wilsthorpe, Bridlington
YO15 3QN
t (01262) 673894

**Park Resorts Withernsea
Sands** ★★★★
Holiday Park
North Road, Withernsea
HU19 2BS
t (01442) 830185
e angie.pyle@park-resorts.
com
w park-resorts.com

Willows Holiday Park
★★★★
*Holiday, Touring & Camping
Park*
Hollym Road, Withernsea
HU19 2PN
t (01964) 612233
e info@highfield-caravans.co.
uk
w highfield-caravans.co.uk

Wombleton Caravan Park
★★★★★
Touring & Camping Park
Moorfield Lane, York
YO62 7RY
t (01751) 431684
e info@
wombletoncaravanpark.co.uk
w wombletoncaravanpark.co.
uk

Alders Caravan Park
★★★★★
Touring & Camping Park
Home Farm, Monk Green,
Alne, York YO61 1RY
t (01347) 838722
e enquiries@homefarmalne.
co.uk
w alderscaravanpark.co.uk

Allerton Park Caravan Park
★★★★ ROSE AWARD
*Holiday, Touring & Camping
Park*
Allerton Park, Knaresborough
HG5 0SE
t (01423) 330569
e enquiries@
yorkshireholidayparks.co.uk
w yorkshireholidayparks.co.uk

**Beechwood Grange Caravan
Club Site** ★★★★★
Touring Park
Malton Road, York YO32 9TH
t (01904) 424637
w caravanclub.co.uk

Goosewood Holiday Park
★★★★★
*Holiday, Touring & Camping
Park*
Goose Lane, York YO61 1ET
t (01347) 810829
e enquiries@goosewood.co.
uk
w goosewood.co.uk

**Mount Pleasant Holiday
Park and Park Home Estate**
★★★★
Holiday Park
Mount Pleasant Holiday Park
and Park Hom, York YO23 2UA
t (01904) 707078
e mountpleasant@holgates.
com
w holgates.com

**Rowntree Park Caravan Club
Site** ★★★★★
Touring & Camping Park
Terry Avenue, York YO3 1JQ
t (01904) 658997
w caravanclub.co.uk

Weir Caravan Park ★★★★
ROSE AWARD
*Holiday, Touring & Camping
Park*
Buttercrambe Road, Stamford
Bridge, York YO41 1AN
t (01759) 371377
e enquiries@
yorkshireholidayparks.co.uk
w yorkshireholidayparks.co.uk

**YCP York Caravan Park and
Storage** ★★★★
Touring Park
Stockton Lane, York YO32 9UB
t (01904) 424222
e andrew-wilson125@hotmail.
com
w yorkcaravanpark.com

York Touring Caravan Site
★★★★
Touring & Camping Park
Towthorpe Lane, Towthorpe,
York YO32 9ST
t (01904) 499275
e info@yorkcaravansite.co.uk
w yorkcaravansite.co.uk

Kingfisher Holiday Park
★★★★★
Holiday Park
Fradley Junction, Alrewas,
Burton-on-Trent DE13 7DN
t (01283) 790407
e mail@kingfisherholidaypark.
com
w kingfisherholidaypark.com

**Island Meadow Caravan
Park** ★★★
*Holiday, Touring & Camping
Park*
The Mill House, Aston Cantlow
B95 6JP
t (01789) 488273
e holiday@
islandmeadowcaravanpark.co.
uk
w islandmeadowcaravanpark.
co.uk

Chapel Lane Caravan Park
★★★★★
Touring Park
Chapel Lane, Wythall,
Birmingham B47 6JX
t (01564) 826483
w caravanclub.co.uk

**Blackshaw Moor Caravan
Club Site** ★★★★★
Touring Park
Blackshaw Moor, Leek
ST13 8TW
t (01538) 300203
w caravanclub.co.uk

**Kingsbury Camping &
Caravan Club** ★★★★★
Touring & Camping Park
Bodymoor Heath Lane,
Bodymoor Heath, Sutton
Coldfield B76 0DY
t (01827) 874101

Look out for parks participating in the National Accessible Scheme

BREWOOD
Staffordshire

Homestead Caravan Park
★★★★
Holiday Park
Shutt Green, Brewood,
Wolverhampton ST19 9LX
t (01902) 851302
e david@caravanpark.
fsbusiness.co.uk
w caravanparkstaffordshire.co.
uk

BRIDGNORTH
Shropshire

Park Grange Holidays
★★★★
Holiday Park
Morville, Bridgnorth
WV16 4RN
t (01746) 714285
e info@parkgrangeholidays.
co.uk
w parkgrangeholidays.co.uk

Stanmore Hall Touring Park
★★★★★
Holiday & Touring Park
Stourbridge Road, Bridgnorth
WV15 6DT
t (01746) 761761
e stanmore@morris-leisure.co.
uk
w morris-leisure.co.uk

CHEDDLETON
Staffordshire

Glencote Caravan Park
★★★★★
*Holiday, Touring & Camping
Park*
Station Road, Cheddleton,
Leek ST13 7EE
t (01538) 360745
e canistay@glencote.co.uk
w glencote.co.uk

ELLESMERE
Shropshire

Fernwood Caravan Park
★★★★★
Holiday & Touring Park
Lyneal, Ellesmere SY12 0QF
t (01948) 710221
e enquiries@fernwoodpark.
co.uk
w fernwoodpark.co.uk

EVESHAM
Worcestershire

The Ranch Caravan Park
★★★★★
Holiday & Touring Park
Station Road, Honeybourne,
Evesham WR11 7PR
t (01386) 830744
e enquiries@ranch.co.uk
w ranch.co.uk

HANLEY SWAN
Worcestershire

**Blackmore Camping and
Caravanning Club Site**
★★★★★
Touring & Camping Park
Camp Site No 2, Hanley Swan
WR8 0EE
t (01684) 310280
w campingandcaravanning
club.co.uk

HAUGHTON
Shropshire

**Ebury Hill Camping &
Caravanning Club Site**
★★★★
Touring & Camping Park
Ebury Hill, Haughton, Telford
TF6 6BU
t (01743) 709334
w stmem.com/eburyhill/

HEREFORD
Herefordshire

**Lucksall Caravan and
Camping Park** ★★★★★
Holiday & Touring Park
Mordiford, Hereford HR1 4LP
t (01432) 870213
e karen@lucksallpark.co.uk
w lucksallpark.co.uk

HOPTON HEATH
Shropshire

**Ashlea Pools Country Park-
Log Cabins** ★★★★
Holiday Park
Hopton Heath, Craven Arms
SY7 0QD
t (01547) 530430
e ashleapools@surfbay.dircon.
co.uk
w ashleapools.co.uk

KINNERLEY
Shropshire

**Oswestry Camping &
Caravanning Club Site**
Rating Applied For
*Holiday, Touring & Camping
Park*
Oswestry SY10 8DY
t 0845 130 7631

LEEK
Staffordshire

**Leek Camping and
Caravanning Club Site**
★★★★
Touring & Camping Park
Blackshaw Grange, Leek
ST13 8TL
t 0845 130 7633
w campingandcaravanning
club.co.uk

LEOMINSTER
Herefordshire

Fairview Caravan Park ★★★
Holiday Park
c/o The Willows, Hatfield,
Leominster HR6 0SF
t (01568) 760428
e fairviewcaravanpark@
supanet.com

LITTLE TARRINGTON
Herefordshire

The Millpond ★★★★★
Touring & Camping Park
Little Tarrington, Hereford
HR1 4JA
t (01432) 890243
e enquiries@millpond.co.uk
w millpond.co.uk
🅰

LUDLOW
Shropshire

**Orleton Rise Holiday Home
Park** ★★★★★
Holiday & Touring Park
Green Lane, Orleton, Ludlow
SY8 4JE
t (01584) 831617
e enquiries@orletonrisepark.
co.uk

MERIDEN
West Midlands

Somers Wood Caravan Park
★★★★★
Touring Park
Somers Road, Meriden
CV7 7PL
t (01676) 522978
e somerswoodcpk@aol.com
w somerswood.co.uk

PEMBRIDGE
Herefordshire

Townsend Touring Park
★★★★★
Touring & Camping Park
East Street, Pembridge,
Leominster HR6 9HB
t (01544) 388527
e info@townsend-farm.co.uk
w townsend-farm.co.uk

PETERCHURCH
Herefordshire

Poston Mill Park C & C
★★★★★
Holiday & Touring Park
Peterchurch, Golden Valley
HR2 0SF
t (01981) 550225
e enquiries@poston-mill.co.uk
w bestparks.co.uk

PRESTHOPE
Shropshire

Presthope Caravan Club Site
★★★
Touring Park
Stretton Road, Much Wenlock
TF13 6DQ
t (01746) 785234
w caravanclub.co.uk
🅰

ROMSLEY
Worcestershire

**Clent Hills Camping &
Caravanning Club Site**
★★★★
Touring Park
Fieldhouse Lane, Romsley, Nr
Bromsgrove B62 0NH
t (01562) 710015
w campingandcaravanning
club.co.uk

ROSS-ON-WYE
Herefordshire

Broadmeadow Caravan Park
★★★★★
Touring & Camping Park
Broadmeadows, Ross-on-Wye
HR9 7BW
t (01989) 768076
e broadm4811@aol.com

RUGELEY
Staffordshire

**Camping & Caravanning
Club** ★★★★
Touring & Camping Park
Old Youth Hostel, Wandon,
Rugeley WS15 1QW
t (01889) 582166
w campingandcaravanning
club.co.uk

Silver Trees Caravan Park
★★★★
Holiday Park
Stafford Brook Road, Penkridge
Bank, Rugeley WS15 2TX
t (01889) 582185
e enquiries@
silvertreescaravanpark.co.uk
w silvertreescaravanpark.co.uk

SHOBDON
Herefordshire

Pearl Lake Leisure Park
★★★★★
Holiday Park
Shobdon, Leominster
HR6 9NQ
t (01568) 708326
e info@pearllake.co.uk
w bestparks.co.uk

SHREWSBURY
Shropshire

**Beaconsfield Farm Caravan
Park** ★★★★★
Holiday & Touring Park
Upper Battlefield, Shrewsbury
SY4 4AA
t (01939) 210370
e mail@beaconsfield-farm.co.
uk
w beaconsfield-farm.co.uk

Oxon Hall Touring Park
★★★★★
Holiday & Touring Park
Welshpool Road, Oxon,
Shrewsbury SY3 5FB
t (01743) 340868
e oxon@morris-leisure.co.uk
w morrisleisure.com

STOKE-ON-TRENT
Staffordshire

**Star Caravan & Camping
Park – Pitches** ★★★★★
*Holiday, Touring & Camping
Park*
Star Road, Cotton ST10 3BZ
t (01538) 702219
w starcaravanpark.co.uk
🔲

STOURPORT-ON-SEVERN
Worcestershire

Lickhill Manor Caravan Park
★★★★★
Holiday Park
Stourport-on-Severn DY13 8RL
t (01299) 871041
e excellent@lickhillmanor.co.
uk
w lickhillmanor.co.uk

STRATFORD-UPON-AVON
Warwickshire

Dodwell Park ★★★
Touring & Camping Park
Evesham Rd, Stratford-upon-Avon CV37 9SR
t (01789) 204957
e enquiries@dodwellpark.co.uk
w dodwellpark.co.uk

SYMONDS YAT WEST
Herefordshire

Sterrett's Caravan Park ★★★★
Holiday & Touring Park
Symonds Yat West, Ross-on-Wye HR9 6BY
t (01594) 832888

UTTOXETER
Staffordshire

Uttoxeter Racecourse Caravan Club Site ★★
Touring Park
Uttoxeter Racecourse, Wood Lane, Uttoxeter ST14 8BD
t (01889) 564172
w caravanclub.co.uk

WARWICK
Warwickshire

Warwick Racecourse ★★★
Touring Park
Hampton Street, Warwick CV34 6HN
t (01926) 495448
e enquiries@caravanclub.co.uk
w caravanclub.co.uk

WOLVERLEY
Worcestershire

Wolverley Camping & Caravanning Club Site ★★★
Touring & Camping Park
Brown Westhead Park, Wolverley, Nr Kidderminster DY10 3PX
t (01562) 850909
w campingandcaravanningclub.co.uk

WYRE PIDDLE
Worcestershire

Rivermead Holiday Home Park ★★★★★
Holiday Park
Church Street, Wyre Piddle, Pershore WR10 2JF
t (01386) 561250
e enquiries@rivermeadcaravanpark.co.uk
w rivermeadcaravanpark.co.uk

EAST MIDLANDS

ALSOP-EN-LE-DALE
Derbyshire

Rivendale Caravan and Leisure Park ★★★★
Holiday, Touring & Camping Park
Buxton Road, Alsop en le Dale, Ashbourne DE6 1QU
t (01335) 310311
e greg@rivendalecaravanpark.co.uk
w rivendalecaravanpark.co.uk

ANDERBY CREEK
Lincolnshire

Anderby Springs Caravan Estate ★★★
Holiday Park
Sea Road, Anderby Creek, Skegness PE24 5XW
t (01754) 872265

ASHBOURNE
Derbyshire

Blackwall Plantation Caravan Club Site ★★★★
Touring Park
Kirk Ireton, Ashbourne DE6 3JL
t (01335) 370903

Callow Top Holiday Park ★★★★
Holiday, Touring & Camping Park
Buxton Road, Sandybrook, Ashbourne DE6 2AQ
t (01335) 344020
e enquiries@callowtop.co.uk
w callowtop.co.uk

BAKEWELL
Derbyshire

Chatsworth Park Caravan Club Site ★★★★★
Touring Park
Chatsworth, Bakewell DE45 1PN
t (01246) 582226
w caravanclub.co.uk

BARTON-UPON-HUMBER
Lincolnshire

Silver Birches Tourist Park ★★★
Touring & Camping Park
Waterside Road, Barton-upon-Humber DN18 5BA
t (01652) 632509

BELPER
Derbyshire

Broadholme Lane Caravan Park ★★★
Touring Park
Broadholme Lane, Belper DE56 2JF
t (01773) 823517
w broadholme-caravanpark.co.uk

BOSTON
Lincolnshire

Orchard Caravan Park ★★★
Holiday, Touring & Camping Park
Frampton Lane, Hubberts Bridge, Boston PE20 3QU
t (01205) 290328
w orchardpark.co.uk

BURGH-LE-MARSH
Lincolnshire

Sycamore Farm Park ★★★
Holiday, Touring & Camping Park
Chalk Lane, Skegness PE24 5HN
t (01754) 810833
e lloyd@sycamorefarm.net
w sycamorefarm.net

Sycamore Lakes Touring Site ★★★★
Touring & Camping Park
Skegness Road, Burgh le Marsh PE24 5LN
t (01754) 811411
w sycamorelakes.co.uk

BUXTON
Derbyshire

Cottage Farm Caravan Park ★★★
Touring & Camping Park
Beech Croft, Blackwell, Buxton SK17 9TQ
t (01298) 85330
e mail@cottagefarmsite.co.uk
w cottagefarmsite.co.uk

Grin Low Caravan Club Site ★★★★★
Touring & Camping Park
Grin Low Road, Ladmanlow, Buxton SK17 6UJ
t (01298) 77735
w caravanclub.co.uk

Lime Tree Park ★★★★ ROSE AWARD
Holiday, Touring & Camping Park
Dukes Drive, Buxton SK17 9RP
t (01298) 22988
e info@limetreeparkbuxton.co.uk
w limetreeparkbuxton.co.uk

Longnor Wood Caravan and Camping Park ★★★★
Holiday, Touring & Camping Park
Fawfieldhead, Longnor, Buxton SK17 0NG
t (01298) 83648
e info@longnorwood.co.uk
w longnorwood.co.uk

Newhaven Caravan and Camping Park ★★★
Holiday, Touring & Camping Park
Newhaven, Nr Buxton SK17 0DT
t (01298) 84300
e bobmacara@ntlworld.com
w newhavencaravanpark.co.uk

CASTLETON
Derbyshire

Losehill Caravan Club Site ★★★★★
Touring & Camping Park
Castleton, Hope Valley S33 8WB
t (01433) 620636
w caravanclub.co.uk

CHAPEL ST LEONARDS
Lincolnshire

Tomlinsons Leisure Park ★★★★
Holiday Park
South Road, Chapel St Leonards, Skegness PE24 5TL
t (01754) 872241
w tomlinsons-leisure.co.uk

CROFT
Lincolnshire

Pine Trees Leisure Park ★★★
Touring Park
Croft Bank, Croft, Skegness PE24 4RE
t (01754) 762949
e holidays@pine148.fsnet.co.uk
w pinetreesholidays.co.uk

DERBY
Derbyshire

Elvaston Castle Caravan Club Site ★★★
Touring Park
Borrowash Road, Elvaston, Derby DE72 3EP
t (01332) 571342

EAST FIRSBY
Lincolnshire

Manor Farm Caravan and Camping Site ★★★
Touring & Camping Park
Manor Farm, East Firsby, Market Rasen LN8 2DB
t (01673) 878258
e info@lincolnshire-lanes.com
w lincolnshire-lanes.com

FINESHADE
Northamptonshire

Top Lodge Caravan Club Site ★★★★
Touring Park
Fineshade, Duddington, Corby
NN17 3BB
t (01780) 444617
w caravanclub.co.uk

FLAGG
Derbyshire

Pomeroy Caravan and Camping Park ★★
Touring & Camping Park
Street House Farm, Pomeroy,
Buxton SK17 9QG
t (01298) 83259

FLEET HARGATE
Lincolnshire

Delph Bank Touring Caravan & Camping Park – Just for Adults. ★★★★
Touring & Camping Park
Old Main Road, Fleet Hargate,
Spalding PE12 8LL
t (01406) 422910
e enquiries@delphbank.co.uk
w delphbank.co.uk

FOLKINGHAM
Lincolnshire

Low Farm Touring Park ★★★
Touring Park
Spring Lane, Folkingham
NG34 0SJ
t (01529) 497322

HADFIELD
Derbyshire

Camping and Caravanning Club Site Crowden ★★★
Touring & Camping Park
Crowden, Glossop SK13 1HZ
t (01457) 866057

HAYFIELD
Derbyshire

Camping and Caravanning Club Site Hayfield ★★★
Camping Park
Kinder Road, Hayfield, High
Peak SK22 2LE
t (01663) 745394

HORNCASTLE
Lincolnshire

Ashby Park ★★★★
Holiday, Touring & Camping Park
Horncastle, West Ashby
LN9 5PP
t (01507) 527966
e ashshbyparklakes@aol.com
w ukparks.co.uk/ashby

Elmhirst Lakes Caravan Park ★★★★
Holiday Park
Elmhirst Road, Horncastle
LN9 5LU
t (01507) 527533
w elmhirstlakes.co.uk

HUMBERSTON
North East Lincolnshire

Thorpe Park Holiday Centre ★★★★
Holiday Park
Grimsby DN35 0PW
t (01442) 868325
e theresa.ludlow@bourne-leisure.co.uk
w british-holidays.co.uk

INGOLDMELLS
Lincolnshire

Coastfield Caravan Park ★★★
Holiday Park
Vickers Point, Roman Bank,
Ingoldmells, Skegness
PE25 1JU
t (01754) 872592

Country Meadows Touring Park ★★★★
Holiday & Touring Park
Anchor Lane, Ingoldmells,
Skegness PE25 1LZ
t (01754) 874455
e bookings@countrymeadows.co.uk
w countrymeadows.co.uk

Golden Beach Holiday Park ★★★★
Holiday Park
Roman Bank, Ingoldmells,
Skegness PE25 1LT
t (01754) 873000

Ingoldale Park ★★★
Holiday Park
Beach Estate, Roman Bank,
Skegness PE25 1LL
t (01754) 872335

Kingfisher Park ★★★
Holiday Park
Sea Lane, Ingoldmells
PE25 1PG
t (01754) 872465
e kingfisherpark@e-lindsey.gov.uk

KIRKBY-ON-BAIN
Lincolnshire

Camping and Caravanning Club Site Woodhall Spa ★★★★★
Touring & Camping Park
Wellsyke Lane, Kirkby-on-Bain,
Woodhall Spa LN10 6YU
t (01526) 352911
w campingandcaravanningclub.co.uk

LINCOLN
Lincolnshire

Hartsholme Country Park ★★★
Touring Park
Skellingthorpe Road, Lincoln
LN6 0EY
t (01522) 873578
e hartsholmecp@lincoln.gov.uk
w lincoln.gov.uk

MABLETHORPE
Lincolnshire

Camping and Caravanning Club Site Mablethorpe ★★★★
Touring & Camping Park
Highfield, 120 Church Lane,
Mablethorpe LN12 2NU
t (01507) 472374
e campingandcaravanningclub.co.uk
w club.co.uk

Golden Sands Holiday Park ★★★
Holiday & Touring Park
Quebec Road, Mablethorpe
LN12 1QJ
t (01507) 477871
w goldensands-park.co.uk

Grange Leisure Park ★★
Holiday & Touring Park
Alford Road, Mablethorpe
LN12 1NE
t (01507) 427814

Holivans Ltd ★★★
Touring Park
Dept G, Quebec Road,
Mablethorpe LN12 1QH
t (01507) 473327
e holivans@enterprise.net
w holivans.co.uk

MARKET BOSWORTH
Leicestershire

Bosworth Water Trust ★★★
Touring & Camping Park
Wellesborough Road, Market
Bosworth CV13 6PD
t (01455) 291876
e info@bosworthwatertrust.co.uk
w bosworthwatertrust.co.uk

MARKET HARBOROUGH
Leicestershire

Brook Meadow ★★
Holiday & Camping Park
Welford Road, Sibbertoft
LE16 9UJ
t (01858) 880886
e brookmeadow@farmline.com
w brookmeadow.co.uk

MOIRA
Derbyshire

Conkers, National Forest Camping and Caravanning Club Site
Rating Applied For
Holiday, Touring & Camping Park
Enterprise Glade, Bath Lane,
Swadlincote DE12 6BD
t 0845 130 7631

MUMBY
Lincolnshire

Inglenook Caravan Park ★★★
Touring Park
Hogsthorpe Road, Mumby
LN13 9SE
t (01507) 490365
e pulse@lincolnshiretourism.com

NEWARK
Nottinghamshire

Milestone Caravan Park ★★★★★
Touring Park
Great North Road, Cromwell
NG23 6JE
t (01636) 821244

NORMANBY
Lincolnshire

Normanby Hall Country Park ★★★
Touring Park
Scunthorpe DN15 9HU
t (01724) 720588
e normanby.hall@northlincs.gov.uk
w northlincs.gov.uk/normanby

RIPLEY
Derbyshire

Golden Valley Caravan & Camping ★★★★
Touring & Camping Park
The Tanyard, Coach Road,
Golden Valley, Ripley
DE55 4ES
t (01773) 513881
e enquiries@goldenvalleycaravanpark.co.uk
w goldenvalleycaravanpark.co.uk

RUFFORD
Nottinghamshire

Sherwood Forest, Center Parcs ★★★★★
Forest Holiday Village
Sherwood Forest, Newark
NG22 9DN
t 0870 067 3030
w centerparcs.co.uk

SALTFLEET
Lincolnshire

Sunnydale Holiday Park ★★★★
Holiday Park
Sea Lane, Saltfleet, Louth
LN11 7RP
t (01507) 338100
w gbholidayparks.co.uk

SCUNTHORPE
Lincolnshire

Brookside Caravan Park ★★★★★
Touring Park
Stather Road, Burton upon
Stather, Scunthorpe
DN15 9DH
t (01724) 721369
e brooksidecp@aol.com
w brooksidecaravanpark.co.uk

SKEGNESS
Lincolnshire

Butlins at Skegness Butlins Limited ★★★★
Roman Bank, Skegness
PE25 1NJ
t (01754) 762311

Manor Farm Caravan Park
★★
Touring & Camping Park
Sea Road, Anderby PE24 5YB
t (01507) 490372
e skegnessinfo@e-lindsey.
gov.uk

Richmond Holiday Centre
★★★
Holiday & Touring Park
Richmond Drive, Skegness
PE25 3TQ
t (01754) 762097
e sales@richmondholidays.
com
w richmondholidays.com

Skegness Water Leisure
Park ★★★
*Holiday, Touring & Camping
Park*
Walls Lane, Ingoldmells,
Skegness PE25 1JF
t (01754) 899400
e enquiries@
skegnesswaterleisurepark.co.
uk
w skegnesswaterleisurepark.
co.uk

Walsh's Holiday Park ★★★
Holiday Park
Roman Bank, Skegness
PE25 1QP
t (01754) 764485

SUTTON IN ASHFIELD
Nottinghamshire

Shardaroba Caravan Park
Rating Applied For
Touring & Camping Park
Silverhill Lane, Teversal,
Sutton-in-Ashfield NG17 3JJ
t (01623) 551838
e stay@shardaroba.co.uk
w shardaroba.co.uk

SUTTON-ON-SEA
Lincolnshire

Cherry Tree Site ★★★★
Touring Park
Huttoft Road, Sutton-on-Sea
LN12 2RU
t (01507) 441626
e info@cherrytreesite.co.uk
w cherrytreesite.co.uk

SUTTON ST EDMUND
Lincolnshire

Orchard View Caravan &
Camping Park ★★★
*Holiday, Touring & Camping
Park*
102 Broadgate, Sutton St
Edmund, Spalding PE12 0LT
t (01945) 700482
e raymariaorchardview@
btinternet.com

SWADLINCOTE
Derbyshire

Beehive Farm Woodland
Lakes ★★★
Touring & Camping Park
Rosliston, Swadlincote
DE12 8HZ
t (01283) 763981
e info@beehivefarm-
woodlandlakes.co.uk
w beehivefarm-
woodlandlakes.co.uk

TANSLEY
Derbyshire

Lickpenny Caravan Park
★★★★
Touring Park
Lickpenny Lane, Tansley,
Matlock DE4 5GF
t (01629) 583040
e lickpenny@btinternet.com
w lickpennycaravanpark.co.uk

Packhorse Farm Bungalow
C&C ★★★
Touring Park
Packhorse Farm, Foxholes
Lane, Matlock DE4 5LF
t (01629) 580950

TRUSTHORPE
Lincolnshire

Seacroft Holiday Estate Ltd
★★★★ ROSE AWARD
Holiday & Touring Park
Sutton Road, Trusthorpe,
Mablethorpe LN12 2PN
t (01507) 472421
e info@seacroftcaravanpark.
co.uk
w seacroftcaravanpark.co.uk

Sutton Springs Holiday
Estate ★★★
Holiday Park
Sutton Road, Trusthorpe,
Mablethorpe LN12 2PZ
t (01507) 441333
e d.brailsford@ukonline.co.uk

WHATSTANDWELL
Derbyshire

Birchwood Farm Caravan
Park ★★
*Holiday, Touring & Camping
Park*
Wirksworth Road,
Whatstandwell, Matlock
DE4 5HS
t (01629) 822280
w birchwoodfcp.co.uk

WHISSENDINE
Rutland

Greendale Farm Caravan &
Camping Park ★★★★
Touring & Camping Park
Pickwell Lane, Whissendine,
Oakham LE15 7LB
t (01664) 474516
e enq@rutlandgreendale.co.
uk
w rutlandgreendale.co.uk

WOODHALL SPA
Lincolnshire

Bainland Country Park Ltd
★★★★★
*Holiday, Touring & Camping
Park*
Horncastle Road, Roughton
Moor, Woodhall Spa LN10 6UX
t (01526) 352903
e bookings@bainland.co.uk
w bainland.co.uk

WORKSOP
Nottinghamshire

Clumber Park Caravan Club
Site ★★★★
Touring Park
Lime Tree Avenue, Clumber
Park, Worksop S80 3AE
t (01909) 484758
w caravanclub.co.uk

YOULGREAVE
Derbyshire

Camping and Caravanning
Club Site ★★★
Touring & Camping Park
c/o Hopping Farm, Youlgrave,
Bakewell DE45 1NA
t (01629) 636555

EAST OF ENGLAND

ATTLEBOROUGH
Norfolk

Oak Tree Park ★★★★
Touring Park
Norwich Road, Attleborough
NR17 2JX
t (01953) 455565
e oaktree.cp@virgin.net

BACTON
Norfolk

The Red House Chalet and
Caravan Park ★★★
Holiday Park
Paston Road, Norwich
NR12 0JB
t (01692) 650815

BACTON-ON-SEA
Norfolk

Cable Gap Holiday Park
★★★★★ ROSE AWARD
Holiday Park
Coast Road, Bacton, Norwich
NR12 0EW
t (01692) 650667
e holiday@cablegap.co.uk
w cablegap.co.uk

BANHAM
Norfolk

Applewood Caravan and
Camping Park ★★★★
Touring Park
The Grove, Kenninghall Road,
Banham NR16 2HE
t (01953) 888370

BAWBURGH
Norfolk

Norfolk Showground
Caravan Club Site ★★★★
Touring Park
Royal Norfolk Agricultural
Association Showground, Long
Lane, Bawburgh, Norwich
NR9 3LX
t (01603) 742708

BELTON
Norfolk

Wild Duck Holiday Park
★★★★
Holiday Park
Howards Common, Belton,
Great Yarmouth NR31 9NE
t (01493) 780268

BENHALL
Suffolk

Whitearch (Touring
Caravan) Park ★★★
Holiday Park
Main Road, Benhall IP17 1NA
t (01728) 604646

BRENTWOOD
Essex

Kelvedon Hatch Camping
and Caravanning Club Site
★★★★
Touring & Camping Park
Warren Lane, Doddinghurst
CM15 0JG
t (01277) 372773

BUCKLESHAM
Suffolk

The Oaks Caravan Park
★★★★
Holiday & Touring Park
Chapel Road, Bucklesham,
Ipswich IP10 0BT
t (01394) 448837

BUNGAY
Suffolk

Outney Meadow Caravan
Park ★★★
Touring & Camping Park
Outney Meadow, Bungay
NR35 1HG
t (01986) 892338
e c.r.hancy@ukgateway.net
w outneymeadow.co.uk

BURGH CASTLE
Norfolk

Burgh Castle Marina and
Caravan Park ★★★
*Holiday, Touring & Camping
Park*
Butt Lane, Burgh Castle, Great
Yarmouth NR31 9PZ
t (01493) 780331
e info@burghcastlemarina.co.
uk
w burghcastlemarina.co.uk

BURGH ST PETER
Norfolk

Waveney River Centre ★★★★
Holiday Park
Staithe Road, Burgh St Peter
NR34 0BT
t (01502) 677343
e info@waveneyrivercentre.
co.uk
w waveneyrivercentre.co.uk

BURNHAM DEEPDALE
Norfolk

Deepdale Camping ★★★★
Camping Park
Deepdale Farms, Burnham
Deepdale, King's Lynn
PE31 8DD
t (01485) 210256
🖼🖼

CAISTER-ON-SEA
Norfolk

Caister Holiday Park ★★★
Holiday Park
Ormesby Road, Caister-on-Sea,
Great Yarmouth NR30 5NQ
t (01493) 728931

**Eastern Beach Caravan Park
★★★★**
Holiday Park
Manor Road, Caister-on-Sea,
Great Yarmouth NR30 5HH
t (01493) 720367

**Elm Beach Caravan Park
★★★★**
Holiday Park
Manor Road, Caister-on-Sea,
Great Yarmouth NR30 5HG
t (01493) 721630
e enquiries@
elmbeachcaravanpark.com
w elmbeachcaravanpark.com

Wentworth Holidays ★★★
Holiday Park
9 Bultitudes Loke, Caister-on-
Sea, Great Yarmouth
NR30 5DH
t (01493) 720382

CALIFORNIA
Norfolk

**Wakefield Court Beach T/A
Beachside Holidays ★★★★**
Holiday Park
California, Scratby, Great
Yarmouth NR29 3QT
t (01493) 730279
e holidays@theseaside.org
w beachside-holidays.co.uk

CAMBRIDGE
Cambridgeshire

Appleacre Park ★★
Touring Park
London Road, Fowlmere
SG8 7RU
t (01763) 208354
e ajbearpark@aol.com
w appleacrepark.co.uk

Cherry Hinton Caravan Club Site ★★★★★
Touring & Camping Park
Lime Kiln Road, Cherry Hinton,
Cambridge CB1 8NQ
t (01223) 244088
w caravanclub.co.uk
🖼

**Highfield Farm Touring Park
★★★★★**
Touring & Camping Park
Long Road, Comberton,
Cambridge CB23 7DG
t (01223) 262308
e enquiries@
highfieldfarmtouringpark.co.uk
w highfieldfarmtouringpark.co.
uk

CLACTON-ON-SEA
Essex

**Highfield Holiday Park
★★★**
Holiday Park
London Road, Clacton-on-Sea
CO16 9QY
t (01255) 424244

**Valley Farm Holiday Park
★★★★**
Holiday Park
Valley Road, Clacton-on-Sea
CO15 6LY
t (01255) 422484

CLIPPESBY
Norfolk

Clippesby Hall ★★★★
Holiday Park
Hall Lane, Clippesby, Great
Yarmouth NR29 3BL
t (01493) 367800

CORTON
Suffolk

**Broadland Sands Holiday
Park ★★★★**
Holiday Park
Coast Road, Corton NR32 5LG
t (01502) 730939
e admin@broadlandsands.co.
uk
w broadlandsands.co.uk

CROMER
Norfolk

**Forest Park Caravan Site
★★★★**
Touring & Camping Park
Northrepps Road, Northrepps,
Cromer NR27 0JR
t (01263) 513290

**Seacroft Camping Park
★★★★**
Touring & Camping Park
Runton Road, Cromer
NR27 9NH
t (01263) 514938
w caravanclub.co.uk

DUNWICH
Suffolk

**Cliff House Holiday Park
★★★★**
Holiday Park
Minsmere Road, Dunwich,
Saxmundham IP17 3DQ
t (01728) 648282
e info@cliffhouseholidays.co.
uk
w cliffhouseholidays.co.uk

EAST HARLING
Norfolk

**The Dower House Touring
Park ★★★★**
Touring & Camping Park
Thetford Forest, East Harling
NR16 2SE
t (01953) 717314

EAST MERSEA
Essex

**Coopers Beach Holiday Park
★★★★**
Holiday Park
East Mersea, Colchester
CO5 8TN
t (01206) 383236

**Cosway Holiday Home Park
★★★★★**
Holiday Park
Fen Lane, East Mersea,
Colchester CO5 8UA
t (01206) 383252

**Fen Farm Caravan and
Camping Site ★★★★**
Holiday Park
East Mersea, Colchester
CO5 8UA
t (01206) 383275
e fenfarm@talk21.com

EAST RUNTON
Norfolk

Woodhill Park ★★★★
*Holiday, Touring & Camping
Park*
Cromer Road, East Runton,
Cromer NR27 9PX
t (01263) 512242
e info@woodhill-park.com

ELVEDEN
Suffolk

**Center Parcs Elveden Forest
★★★★★**
Forest Holiday Village
Elveden Forest Holiday Village,
Brandon IP27 0YZ
t 0870 067 3030
w centerparcs.co.uk

FAKENHAM
Norfolk

Fakenham Racecourse ★★★
Touring Park
The Racecourse, Fakenham
NR21 7NY
t (01328) 862388
e caravan@
fakenhamracecourse.co.uk
w fakenhamracecourse.co.uk

The Old Brick Kilns
★★★★★
Touring & Camping Park
Little Barney Lane, Barney
NR21 0NL
t (01328) 878305
e enquiries@old-brick-kilns.co.
uk
w old-brick-kilns.co.uk
🖼🖼

FELIXSTOWE
Suffolk

**Peewit Caravan Park
★★★★**
Touring & Camping Park
Walton Avenue, Felixstowe
IP11 2HB
t (01394) 284511
🖼

FOXHALL
Suffolk

**Low House Touring Caravan
Centre ★★★**
Holiday Park
Low House, Bucklesham Road,
Foxhall IP10 0AU
t (01473) 659437

GOLDHANGER
Essex

Osea Leisure Park ★★★★
Holiday Park
Goldhanger Road, Heybridge
CM9 4SA
t (01621) 854695

GREAT HOCKHAM
Norfolk

**Thetford Forest Camping &
Caravan Club ★★★★**
*Holiday, Touring & Camping
Park*
Wretham Road, Thetford
IP24 1PA
t (01953) 498455

GREAT SHELFORD
Cambridgeshire

**Cambridge Camping and
Caravanning Club Site
★★★★**
Touring Park
19 Cabbage Moor, Great
Shelford CB2 5NB
t (01223) 841185
w campingandcaravanning
club.co.uk

GREAT YARMOUTH
Norfolk

**Breydon Water Holiday Park
(Bure Village) ★★★★**
*Holiday, Touring & Camping
Park*
Butt Lane, Burgh Castle, Great
Yarmouth NR31 9PY
t (01493) 780481

**Cherry Tree Holiday Park
★★★★**
Holiday Park
Mill Road, Great Yarmouth
NR31 9QR
t (01493) 780229
w parkdeanholidays.co.uk

The Grange Touring Park
★★★★
Holiday Park
Yarmouth Road, Ormesby St
Margaret, Great Yarmouth
NR29 3QG
t (01493) 730306
e info@grangetouring.co.uk
w grangetouring.co.uk

Grasmere Caravan Park
★★★
Touring Park
Bultitudes Loke, Yarmouth
Road, Caister-on-Sea, Great
Yarmouth NR30 5DH
t (01493) 720382
w grasmere-wentworth.co.uk

**Great Yarmouth Caravan
Club Site** ★★★★
Touring Park
Great Yarmouth Racecourse,
Jellicoe Road, Great Yarmouth
NR30 4AU
t (01493) 855223
w caravanclub.co.uk

Hopton Holiday Village
★★★★
Holiday Park
Warren Lane, Hopton, Great
Yarmouth NR31 9BW
t (01502) 730214

Potters Leisure Resort
★★★★★
Coast Road, Hopton-on-Sea,
Great Yarmouth NR31 9BX
t (01502) 730345
e potters@pottersholidays.
com
w pottersholidays.com

**Seacroft (Hemsby) Ltd
Summerfields Holiday
Village** ★★★★
Holiday Park
Beach Road, Scratby, Great
Yarmouth NR29 3NW
t (01493) 731419

Seashore Holiday Park ★★★
Holiday Park
North Denes, Great Yarmouth
NR30 4HG
t (01493) 851131

Vauxhall Holiday Park
★★★★★
Holiday & Touring Park
Acle New Road, Great
Yarmouth NR30 1TB
t (01493) 857231

HANWORTH
Norfolk

**Deer's Glade Caravan &
Camping Park** ★★★★★
Touring & Camping Park
White Post Road, Hanworth,
Norwich NR11 7HN
t (01263) 768633

HEACHAM
Norfolk

**Heacham Beach Holiday
Park** ★★★★
Holiday Park
South Beach Road, Heacham,
King's Lynn PE31 7BD
t (01485) 570270

HEMINGFORD ABBOTS
Cambridgeshire

Quiet Waters Caravan Park
★★★★
*Holiday, Touring & Camping
Park*
Hemingford Abbots,
Huntingdon PE28 9AJ
t (01480) 463405
e quietwaters.park@
btopenworld.com
w quietwaterscaravanpark.co.
uk

HEMSBY
Norfolk

**Newport Caravan Park
(Norfolk) Ltd** ★★★★
*Holiday, Touring & Camping
Park*
Newport Road, Hemsby, Great
Yarmouth NR29 4NW
t (01493) 730405

HERTFORD
Hertfordshire

**Hertford Camping and
Caravanning Club Site**
★★★★
Touring & Camping Park
Mangrove Road, Hertford
SG13 8AJ
t (01992) 586696
w campingandcaravanning
club.co.uk

HUNSTANTON
Norfolk

Manor Park Holiday Village
★★★★
Holiday & Touring Park
Manor Road, Hunstanton
PE36 5AZ
t (01485) 532300

Searles Leisure Resort
★★★★★ ROSE AWARD
*Holiday, Touring & Camping
Park*
South Beach Road, Hunstanton
PE36 5BB
t (01485) 534211
e bookings@searles.co.uk
w searles.co.uk

HUNTINGDON
Cambridgeshire

**Grafham Water Caravan
Club Site** ★★★★
Holiday & Touring Park
Church Road, Grafham,
Huntingdon PE28 0BB
t (01480) 810264
w caravanclub.co.uk

**Houghton Mill Caravan Club
Site** ★★★★
Touring Park
Mill Street, Houghton,
Huntingdon PE28 2AZ
t (01480) 466716

JAYWICK
Essex

Martello Beach Holiday Park
★★★★
Holiday & Touring Park
Belsize Avenue, Jaywick
CO15 2LF
t (01255) 820372
w park-resorts.com

KESSINGLAND
Suffolk

Alandale Park ★★
Holiday Park
Bethel Drive, Kessingland,
Lowestoft NR33 7SD
t (01502) 740610

**Heathland Beach Caravan
Park** ★★★★★
*Holiday, Touring & Camping
Park*
London Road, Kessingland
NR33 7PJ
t (01502) 740337

**Kessingland Beach Holiday
Park** ★★★
*Holiday, Touring & Camping
Park*
Beach Road, Kessingland
NR33 7RW
t (01502) 740636

**Kessingland Camping and
Caravanning Club Site**
★★★★
Touring & Camping Park
Whites Lane, Kessingland,
Lowestoft NR33 7TF
t (01502) 742040
w campingandcaravanning
club.co.uk

LITTLE CORNARD
Suffolk

Willowmere Caravan Park
★★★
Touring & Camping Park
Bures Road, Little Cornard
CO10 0NN
t (01787) 375559

LOUGHTON
Essex

Debden House Camp Site
★★
Touring & Camping Park
Debden Green, Loughton
IG10 2NZ
t (020) 8508 3008

LOWESTOFT
Suffolk

**Beach Farm Residential and
Holiday Park Limited** ★★★
Holiday Park
Arbor Lane, Pakefield
NR33 7BD
t (01502) 572794
e beachfarmpark@aol.com

MERSEA ISLAND
Essex

Waldegraves Holiday Park
★★★★
*Holiday, Touring & Camping
Park*
Waldegraves Lane, Mersea
Island, Colchester CO5 8SE
t (01206) 382898
e holidays@waldegraves.co.uk
w waldegraves.co.uk

MILDENHALL
Suffolk

**Round Plantation Caravan
Club Site** ★★★★
Touring Park
Brandon Road, Bury St
Edmunds IP28 7JE
t (01638) 713089

MUNDESLEY
Norfolk

**Sandy Gulls Cliff Top
Touring Park** ★★★
Holiday & Touring Park
Cromer Road, Mundesley,
Norwich NR11 8DF
t (01263) 720513

MUTFORD
Suffolk

Beulah Hall Caravan Park
★★★
Touring & Camping Park
Beulah Hall, Dairy Lane,
Beccles NR34 7QJ
t (01502) 476609
e beulah.hall@btinternet.com

NORTH RUNCTON
Norfolk

**Kings Lynn Caravan &
Camping Park** ★★★
Touring Park
New Road, North Runcton,
King's Lynn PE33 0RA
t (01553) 840004

NORTH WALSHAM
Norfolk

Two Mills Touring Park
★★★★★
Touring Park
Yarmouth Road, North
Walsham NR28 9NA
t (01692) 405829

NORWICH
Norfolk

**Norwich Camping and
Caravanning Club Site** ★★★
Holiday Park
Martineau Lane, Norwich
NR1 2HX
t (01603) 620060
w campingandcaravanning
club.co.uk

**Reedham Ferry Touring and
Camping Park** ★★★
*Holiday, Touring & Camping
Park*
Ferry Road, Reedham, Norwich
NR13 3HA
t (01493) 700999

OULTON BROAD
Suffolk

Broadland Holiday Village
★★★★★ ROSE AWARD
Holiday Park
Marsh Road, Oulton Broad,
Lowestoft NR33 9JY
t (01502) 573033

OVERSTRAND
Norfolk

Ivy Farm Holiday Park
★★★★
Holiday, Touring & Camping Park
Overstrand, Cromer NR27 0AB
t (01263) 579239

PAKEFIELD
Suffolk

Pakefield Caravan Park
★★★
Holiday Park
Arbor Lane, Pakefield,
Lowestoft NR33 7BQ
t (01502) 561136

PENTNEY
Norfolk

Pentney Park Caravan Site
★★★★
Touring & Camping Park
Main Road, Pentney, King's
Lynn PE32 1HU
t (01760) 337479
e holidays@pentney.demon.
co.uk
w pentney-park.co.uk

PETERBOROUGH
Cambridgeshire

**Ferry Meadows Caravan
Club Site** ★★★★★
Holiday Park
Ham Lane, Peterborough
PE2 5UU
t (01733) 233526
w caravanclub.co.uk

SAHAM HILLS
Norfolk

Lowe Caravan Park ★★★★
Touring & Camping Park
Ashdale, Hills Road, Saham
Hills, Thetford IP25 7EZ
t (01953) 881051
w lowecaravanpark.co.uk

ST NEOTS
Cambridgeshire

**St Neots Camping and
Caravanning Club Site**
★★★★
Touring Park
Hardwick Road, Eynesbury
PE19 2PR
t (01480) 474404
w campingandcaravanning
club.co.uk

ST OSYTH
Essex

**The Orchards Holiday
Village** ★★★
Holiday Park
Point Clear, Clacton-on-Sea
CO16 8LJ
t (01255) 820651

SANDRINGHAM
Norfolk

**Sandringham Camping and
Caravanning Club Site**
★★★★★
Touring Park
The Sandringham Estate,
Double Lodges, Hunstanton
PE36 6EA
t (01485) 542555
w campingandcaravanning
club.co.uk

**The Sandringham Estate
Caravan Club Site** ★★★★★
Touring Park
Glucksburgh Woods,
Sandringham PE35 6EZ
t (01553) 631614

SCRATBY
Norfolk

**California Cliffs Holiday
Park** ★★★★
Holiday Park
Rottenstone Lane, Scratby,
Great Yarmouth NR29 3QU
t (01493) 730584

Green Farm Caravan Park
★★★★★
Holiday & Touring Park
Beach Road, Scratby, Great
Yarmouth NR29 3NW
t (01493) 730440

Scratby Hall Caravan Park
★★★★
Touring & Camping Park
Thoroughfare Lane, Scratby,
Great Yarmouth NR29 3PH
t (01493) 730283

SNETTISHAM
Norfolk

**Diglea Caravan and
Camping Park** ★★★
*Holiday, Touring & Camping
Park*
Beach Road, Snettisham, King's
Lynn PE31 7RA
t (01485) 541367

SOUTHMINSTER
Essex

**Eastland Meadows Country
Park** ★★★
Holiday Park
East End Road, Bradwell-on-
Sea CM0 7PP
t (01621) 776800
e enquiries@
eastlandmeadows.co.uk

Waterside Holiday Park
★★★
Holiday & Touring Park
Main Road, St Lawrence Bay,
Southminster CM0 7LY
t (01621) 779248

STANHOE
Norfolk

**The Rickels Caravan and
Camping Park** ★★★★
Touring Park
Bircham Road, Stanhoe, King's
Lynn PE31 8PU
t (01485) 518671

SWAFFHAM
Norfolk

**The Covert Caravan Club
Site** ★★★★
Touring Park
High Ash, Thetford IP26 5BZ
t (01842) 878356

TATTERSETT
Norfolk

Greenwoods Campsite
★★★
Touring Park
Old Fakenham Road,
Tattersett, King's Lynn
PE31 8RS
t (01485) 528310
e webmaster@
greenwoodscampsite.co.uk

UPPER SHERINGHAM
Norfolk

Woodlands Caravan Park
★★★★
Holiday & Touring Park
Holt Road, Upper Sheringham,
Sheringham NR26 8TU
t (01263) 823802

WALTHAM CROSS
Hertfordshire

**Theobalds Park Camping
and Caravanning Club Site**
★★★
Holiday Park
Bulls Cross Ride, Waltham
Cross EN7 5HS
t (01992) 620604
w campingandcaravanning
club.co.uk

WALTON-ON-THE-NAZE
Essex

Naze Marine Holiday Park
★★
Holiday Park
Hall Lane, Walton-on-the-Naze
CO14 8HL
t 0870 442 9292

WEELEY
Essex

Homestead Lake Park
★★★★
*Holiday, Touring & Camping
Park*
Thorpe Road, Weeley, Clacton-
on-Sea CO16 9JN
t (01255) 833492

Weeley Bridge Holiday Park
★★★★
Holiday Park
Clacton Road, Weeley,
Clacton-on-Sea CO16 9DH
t (01255) 830403

WELLS-NEXT-THE-SEA
Norfolk

Pinewoods Holiday Park
★★★★
Holiday Park
Beach Road, Wells-next-the-
Sea NR23 1DR
t (01328) 710439

WEST ROW
Suffolk

The Willows ★★★
Touring & Camping Park
Hurdle Drove, West Row, Bury
St Edmunds IP28 8RB
t (01638) 715963
e tedandsue@hotmail.co.uk

WEST RUNTON
Norfolk

**West Runton Camping and
Caravanning Club Site**
★★★★
Touring & Camping Park
Holgate Lane, West Runton,
Cromer NR27 9NW
t (01263) 837544
w campingandcaravanning
club.co.uk

WEYBOURNE
Norfolk

Kelling Heath Holiday Park
★★★★★
*Holiday, Touring & Camping
Park*
Sandy Hill Lane, Weybourne,
Holt NR25 7HW
t (01263) 588181
e info@kellingheath.co.uk

WISBECH
Cambridgeshire

Virginia Lake Caravan Park
★★★★
Holiday Park
Smeeth Road, St Johns Fen End
PE14 8JF
t (01945) 430167
e louise@virginlake.co.uk
w virginlake.co.uk

WOODBRIDGE
Suffolk

Forest Camping ★★★
Touring & Camping Park
Tangham Campsite,
Rendlesham Forest Centre,
Woodbridge IP12 3NF
t (01394) 450707
e admin@forestcamping.co.uk
w forestcamping.co.uk

WORTWELL
Norfolk

Little Lakeland Caravan Park
★★★★
Holiday & Touring Park
Wortwell, Harleston IP20 0EL
t (01986) 788646

WYTON
Cambridgeshire

Wyton Lakes Holiday Park
★★★★
Holiday Park
Banks End, Wyton,
Huntingdon PE28 2AA
t (01480) 412715
e loupeter@supanet.com
w wytonlakes.com

LONDON

INNER LONDON

E4

Lee Valley Campsite ★★★★
Touring & Camping Park
Sewardstone Road, Chingford,
London E4 7RA
t (020) 8529 5689
e scs@leevalleypark.org.uk
w leevalleypark.org.uk

N9

Lee Valley Leisure Centre Camping and Caravan Park ★★★★
Touring & Camping Park
Picketts Lock Lane, London
N9 0AS
t (020) 8803 6900
e leisurecentre@leevalleypark.org.uk
w leevalleypark.com

SE2

Abbey Wood Caravan Club Site ★★★★★
Touring & Camping Park
Federation Road, Abbey
Wood, London SE2 0LS
t (020) 8311 7708
w caravanclub.co.uk

SE19

Crystal Palace Caravan Club Site ★★★★★
Touring & Camping Park
Crystal Palace Parade, London
SE19 1UF
t (020) 8778 7155
w caravanclub.co.uk

SOUTH EAST ENGLAND

ALBURY
Surrey

Edgeley Holiday Park ★★★
Touring Park
Farley Green, Albury, Guildford
GU5 9DW
t (01483) 202129
e edgeley@haulfryn.co.uk

ANDOVER
Hampshire

Wyke Down Touring Caravan & Camping Park ★★★
Touring & Camping Park
Picket Piece, Andover
SP11 6LX
t (01264) 352048
e info2008@wykedown.co.uk
w wykedown.co.uk

APSE HEATH
Isle of Wight

Old Barn Touring Park ★★★★
Touring & Camping Park
Cheverton Farm, Newport
Road, Sandown PO36 9PJ
t (01983) 866414
e oldbarn@weltinet.com
w oldbarntouring.co.uk

Village Way Caravan & Camping Site ★★★
Holiday, Touring & Camping Park
Newport Road, Apse Heath
PO36 9PJ
t (01983) 863279

ARRETON
Isle of Wight

Perreton Farm ★★
Holiday Park
East Lane, Arreton, Newport
PO30 3DL
t (01983) 865218
e roger.perreton@virgin.net
w islandbreaks.co.uk

ASHFORD
Kent

Broadhembury Holiday Park ★★★★★
Holiday, Touring & Camping Park
Steeds Lane, Kingsnorth,
Ashford TN26 1NQ
t (01233) 620859
e holidaypark@broadhembury.co.uk
w broadhembury.co.uk

ATHERFIELD BAY
Isle of Wight

Chine Farm Camping Site ★★
Touring & Camping Park
Military Road, Atherfield Bay,
Ventnor PO38 2JH
t (01983) 740228
e info@chine-farm.co.uk
w chine-farm.co.uk

BANBURY
Oxfordshire

Bo-Peep Caravan Park ★★★★
Holiday & Touring Park
Aynho Road, Adderbury,
Banbury OX17 3NP
t (01295) 810605
e warden@bo-peep.co.uk
w bo-peep.co.uk

BATTLE
East Sussex

**Crowhurst Park ★★★★★
ROSE AWARD**
Holiday Park
Telham Lane, Battle TN33 0SL
t (01424) 773344
e enquiries@crowhurstpark.co.uk
w crowhurstpark.co.uk

Normanhurst Court Caravan Club Site ★★★★★
Touring Park
Stevens Crouch, Battle
TN33 9LR
t (01424) 773808
w caravanclub.co.uk

BEACONSFIELD
Buckinghamshire

Highclere Farm Country Touring Park ★★★★
Touring & Camping Park
Newbarn Lane, Seer Green,
Beaconsfield HP9 2QZ
t (01494) 874505
e highclerepark@aol.com
w highclerepark.co.uk

BEMBRIDGE
Isle of Wight

Sandhills Holiday Park ★★★
Holiday Park
Whitecliff Bay, Bembridge
PO35 5QB
t (01983) 872277
e enquiries@sandhillsholidaypark.com
w sandhillspark.com

Whitecliff Bay Holiday Park ★★★★
Holiday Park
Hillway Road, Bembridge
PO35 5PL
t (01983) 872671
e holiday@whitecliff-bay.com
w whitecliff-bay.com

BEXHILL-ON-SEA
East Sussex

Cobbs Hill Farm Caravan & Camping Park ★★★★
Holiday, Touring & Camping Park
Watermill Lane, Sidley, Bexhill-on-Sea TN39 5JA
t (01424) 213460
e cobbshillfarmuk@hotmail.com
w cobbshillfarm.co.uk

Kloofs Caravan Park ★★★★
Touring & Camping Park
Sandhurst Lane, Bexhill-on-Sea
TN39 4RG
t (01424) 842839
e camping@kloofs.com
w kloofs.com

BIDDENDEN
Kent

Woodlands Park ★★★★
Touring & Camping Park
Tenterden Road, Biddenden
TN27 8BT
t (01580) 291216
e woodlandsp@aol.com
w campingsite.co.uk

BIRCHINGTON
Kent

Quex Caravan Park ★★★★★
Holiday & Touring Park
Park Road, Birchington
CT7 0BL
t (01843) 841273
e info@keatfarm.co.uk
w keatfarm.co.uk

Two Chimneys Holiday Park ★★★★★
Holiday, Touring & Camping Park
Shottendane Road, Birchington
CT7 0HD
t (01843) 841068
e info@twochimneys.co.uk
w twochimneys.co.uk

BOGNOR REGIS
West Sussex

Copthorne Caravans ★★★★
Holiday Park
Rose Green Road, Bognor
Regis PO21 3ER
t (01243) 262408
e copthornecaravans@dsl.pipex.com

Riverside Caravan Centre (Bognor) Ltd ★★★★★
Holiday Park
Shripney Road, Bognor Regis
PO22 9NE
t (01243) 865823
e info@rivcentre.co.uk
w rivcentre.co.uk

Rowan Park Caravan Club Site ★★★★★
Touring & Camping Park
Rowan Way, Bognor Regis
PO22 9RP
t (01243) 828515
w caravanclub.co.uk

BRIGHSTONE
Isle of Wight

Grange Farm Brighstone Bay ★★★
Holiday & Touring Park
Grange Chine, Military Road,
Brighstone PO30 4DA
t (01983) 740296
e grangefarm@brighstonebay.fsnet.co.uk
w brighstonebay.fsnet.co.uk

Lower Sutton Farm ★★★
Holiday Park
Military Road, Brighstone
PO30 4PG
t (01983) 740401
e info@dinosaur-farm-holidays.co.uk
w dinosaur-farm-holidays.co.uk

Sheepcote Valley Caravan Club Site ★★★★★
Touring & Camping Park
East Brighton Park, Brighton
BN2 5TS
t (01273) 626546
w caravanclub.co.uk

Compton Farm ★★
Holiday Park
Brook, Newport PO30 4HF
t (01983) 740215

Burford Caravan Club Site ★★★★★
Touring Park
Bradwell Grove, Burford
OX18 4JJ
t (01993) 823080
w caravanclub.co.uk

Camber Sands Holiday Park ★★★★
Holiday Park
New Lydd Road, Camber, Rye
TN31 7RT
t 0871 664 9718
e holidaysales.cambersands@park-resorts.com
w park-resorts.com

Camping & Caravanning Club Site Canterbury ★★★★
Touring & Camping Park
Bekesbourne Lane, Canterbury
CT3 4AB
t (01227) 463216
w campingandcaravanning club.co.uk

Yew Tree Park ★★★★
Holiday, Touring & Camping Park
Stone Street, Petham,
Canterbury CT4 5PL
t (01227) 700306
e info@yewtreepark.com
w yewtreepark.com

Little Satmar Holiday Park ★★★★
Holiday, Touring & Camping Park
Winehouse Lane, Capel-le-Ferne, Folkestone CT18 7JF
t (01303) 251188
w katefarm.co.uk

Varne Ridge Holiday Park ★★★★★
Holiday & Touring Park
Old Dover Road, Capel-le-Ferne, Folkestone CT18 7HX
t (01303) 251765
e vrcp@varne-ridge.freeserve.co.uk
w varne-ridge.co.uk

Camping & Caravanning Club Site Chipping Norton ★★★★
Touring & Camping Park
Chipping Norton Road,
Chadlington, Chipping Norton
OX7 3PE
t (01608) 641993
w campingandcaravanning club.co.uk

Chertsey Camping and Caravanning Club Site ★★★★
Touring & Camping Park
Bridge Road, Chertsey
KT16 8JX
t (01932) 562405
w campingandcaravanning club.co.uk

Bell Caravan Park ★★
Holiday & Touring Park
Bell Lane, Birdham, Chichester
PO20 7HY
t (01243) 512264

Wicks Farm Holiday Park ★★★★★
Holiday & Camping Park
Redlands Lane, West
Wittering, Chichester
PO20 8QE
t (01243) 513116
e wicks.farm@virgin.net
w wicksfarm.co.uk

Colwell Bay Caravan Park ★★★★
Holiday Park
Madeira Lane, Colwell
PO40 9SR
t (01983) 752403
e james.bishop1@tinyworld.co.uk
w isleofwight-colwellbay.co.uk

Sunnycott Caravan Park ★★★★
Holiday Park
Rew Street, Gurnard
PO31 8NN
t (01983) 292859
e info@sunnycottcaravanpark.co.uk
w sunnycottcaravanpark.co.uk

Pevensey Camping & Caravanning Club ★★★★
Touring & Camping Park
Pevensey BN24 6PR
t 0845 130 7633
w campingandcaravanning club.co.uk

Bridge Villa Caravan & Camping Park ★★★★
Touring & Camping Park
The Street, Crowmarsh Gifford,
Wallingford OX10 8HB
t (01491) 836860
e bridge.villa@btinternet.com

Amerden Caravan & Camping Park ★★★★
Touring & Camping Park
Old Marsh Lane, Dorney
Reach, Maidenhead SL6 0EE
t (01628) 627461
e beverly@amerdencaravanpark.co.uk

Sutton Vale Country Club & Caravan Park ★★★★
Holiday & Touring Park
Vale Road, Sutton-by-Dover,
Dover CT15 5DH
t (01304) 374155
e office@sutton-vale.co.uk
w sutton-vale.co.uk

Dymchurch Caravan Park ★★★★
Holiday Park
St Marys Road, Dymchurch,
Romney Marsh TN29 0PW
t (01303) 872303

E & J Piper Caravan Park ★★★★
Holiday Park
St Marys Road, Dymchurch,
Romney Marsh TN29 0PN
t (01303) 872103

Waverley Park Holiday Centre ★★★★
Holiday, Touring & Camping Park
51 Old Road, East Cowes
PO32 6AW
t (01983) 293452
e holidays@waverley-park.co.uk
w waverley-park.co.uk

Camping and Caravanning Club Site, Horsley ★★★★
Touring & Camping Park
Ockham Road North, East
Horsley KT24 6PE
t (01483) 283273
w campingandcaravanning club.co.uk

Fairfields Farm Caravan & Camping Park ★★★★
Touring & Camping Park
Eastbourne Road, Westham,
Pevensey BN24 5NG
t (01323) 763165
e enquiries@fairfieldsfarm.com
w fairfieldsfarm.com

Ashcroft Coast Holiday Park ★★★★
Holiday Park
Plough Road, Eastchurch,
Sheerness ME12 4JH
t 0871 664 9701
e holidaysales.ashcroftcoast@park-resorts.com
w park-resorts.com

Shurland Dale Holiday Park ★★★★
Holiday Park
Warden Road, Eastchurch,
Sheerness ME12 4EN
t 0871 664 9769
e holidaysales.shurland@park-resorts.com
w park-resorts.com

Warden Springs Holiday Park ★★★★
Holiday, Touring & Camping Park
Thorn Hill Road, Eastchurch,
Sheerness ME12 4HF
t 0871 664 9790
e holidayparks.wardensprings@park-resorts.com
w park-resorts.com

Black Horse Farm Caravan Club Site ★★★★★
Touring & Camping Park
385 Canterbury Road, Densole,
Folkestone CT18 7BG
t (01303) 892665
w caravanclub.co.uk

Camping & Caravanning Club Site Folkestone
★★★★★
Touring & Camping Park
The Warren, Folkestone
CT19 6NQ
t (01303) 255093
w campingandcaravanning
club.co.uk

Sandy Balls Holiday Centre
★★★★★ **ROSE AWARD**
Holiday Park
Godshill, Fordingbridge
SP6 2JY
t (01425) 653042
w sandy-balls.co.uk

Heathfield Farm Camping Site ★★★★
Touring & Camping Park
Heathfield Road, Freshwater
PO40 9SH
t (01983) 756756
e web@heathfieldcamping.co.
uk
w heathfieldcamping.co.uk

Kingfisher Caravan Park
★★★
Holiday, Touring & Camping Park
Browndown Road, Stokes
Road, Gosport PO13 9BG
t (023) 9250 2611
e info@kingfisher-caravan-
park.co.uk
w kingfisher-caravan-park.co.
uk

Graffham Camping & Caravanning Club Site
★★★★
Touring & Camping Park
Great Bury, Graffham,
Petworth GU28 0QJ
t 0845 130 7633
w campingandcaravanning
club.co.uk

Peel House Farm Caravan Park (Touring) ★★★★
Holiday, Touring & Camping Park
Sayerland Lane, Polegate,
Hailsham BN26 6QX
t (01323) 845629
e peelhocp@tesco.net

Riverside Holidays ★★★
Holiday, Touring & Camping Park
Satchell Lane, Hamble
SO31 4HR
t (023) 8045 3220
e enquiries@riversideholidays.
co.uk
w riversideholidays.co.uk

Combe Haven Holiday Park
★★★★
Holiday Park
Harley Shute Road, St
Leonards-on-Sea TN38 8BZ
t (01424) 427891

Rocklands Holiday Park
★★★★
Holiday Park
Rocklands Lane, East Hill,
Hastings TN35 5DY
t (01424) 423097

Shear Barn Holiday Park
★★★★
Holiday, Touring & Camping Park
Barley Lane, Hastings
TN35 5DX
t (01424) 423583

Stalkhurst Camping & Caravan Park ★★★
Holiday, Touring & Camping Park
Ivyhouse Lane, Hastings
TN35 4NN
t (01424) 439015
e stalkhurstpark@btinternet.
com

Fishery Creek Caravan & Camping Park ★★★★
Touring & Camping Park
Fishery Lane, Hayling Island
PO11 9NR
t (023) 9246 2164
e camping@fisherycreek.
fsnet.co.uk
w keyparks.co.uk

Hayling Island Holiday
★★★★
Holiday Park
Manor Road, Hayling Island
PO11 0QS
t 0870 777 6754
e hayling@weststarholidays.
co.uk
w weststarholidays.co.uk

Orchard View Park
★★★★★
Holiday Park
Victoria Road, Herstmonceux,
Hailsham BN27 4SY
t (01323) 832335
e managers@orchard-view-
park.co.uk
w orchard-view-park.com

Horam Manor Touring Park
★★★★
Touring & Camping Park
Horam, Heathfield TN21 0YD
t (01435) 813662
e camp@horam-manor.co.uk
w horam-manor.co.uk

Honeybridge Park ★★★★
Holiday Park
Honeybridge Lane, Dial Post,
Nr Horsham RH13 8NX
t (01403) 710923
e enquiries@
honeybridgepark.co.uk
w honeybridgepark.co.uk

Sumners Ponds Fishery & Campsite ★★★★
Touring Park
Slaughterford Farm, Chapel
Road, Barns Green, Horsham
RH13 0PR
t (01403) 732539
e sumnersponds@dsl.pipex.
com
w sumnersponds.co.uk

Hurley Riverside Park
★★★★
Holiday Park
Hurley, Maidenhead SL6 5NE
t (01628) 824493
e info@hurleyriversidepark.co.
uk
w hurleyriversidepark.co.uk

Hurleyford Farm Ltd ★★★★
Holiday Park
Mill Lane, Hurley, Maidenhead
SL6 5ND
t (01628) 829009

Bluewood Park ★★★★
ROSE AWARD
Holiday Park
Kingham, Chipping Norton
OX7 6UJ
t (01608) 659946
e rachel@bluewoodpark.com
w bluewoodpark.com

Kingsdown Park Holiday Village ★★★★★
Holiday Park
Upper Street, Kingsdown, Deal
CT14 8AU
t (01304) 361205
e info@kingsdownpark.co.uk
w kingsdownpark.net

Brookside Caravan Park
★★★
Holiday Park
Lyminster Road, Lyminster
BN17 7QE
t (01903) 713292
e mark@brooksideuk.com
w brooksideuk.com

Tanner Farm Touring Caravan & Camping Park
★★★★★
Touring & Camping Park
Goudhurst Road, Tonbridge
TN12 9ND
t (01622) 832399
e enquiries@tannerfarmpark.
co.uk
w tannerfarmpark.co.uk

Carrington Park ★★★★★
Holiday Park
New Lane, Milford-on-Sea,
Lymington SO41 0UQ
t (01590) 642654

Downton Holiday Park Ltd
★★★★
Holiday Park
Shorefield Road, Milford-on-
Sea, Lymington SO41 0LH
t (01425) 476131 &
(01590) 642515

Lytton Lawn Touring Park
★★★★
Touring & Camping Park
Lymore Lane, Milford-on-Sea,
Lymington SO41 0TX
t (01590) 648331
e holidays@shorefield.co.uk
w shorefield.co.uk

Shorefield Country Park
★★★★★
Holiday Park
Shorefield Road, Milford-on-
Sea, Lymington SO41 0LH
t (01590) 648331

Wayside Caravan Park
★★★★★
Holiday Park
Way Hill, Minster, Ramsgate
CT12 4HW
t (01843) 821272
e lydia@scott9330.freeserve.
co.uk

Anita's Touring Caravan Park ★★★★
Touring & Camping Park
Church Farm, Mollington,
Banbury OX17 1AZ
t (01295) 750731
e anitagail@btopenworld.com
w caravancampingsites.co.uk

The Foxhunter Park
★★★★★
Holiday Park
Monkton Street, Monkton,
Ramsgate CT12 4JG
t (01843) 821311
e foxhunterpark@aol.com
w thefoxhunterpark.co.uk

NEW MILTON
Hampshire

Glen Orchard Holiday Park ★★★★
Holiday Park
Walkford Lane, New Milton
BH25 5NH
t (01425) 616463

Hoburne Bashley ★★★★
Holiday Park
Sway Road, New Milton
BH25 5QR
t (01425) 612340
e enquiries@hoburne.com
w hoburne.com

Hoburne Naish ★★★★★
Holiday Park
Christchurch Road, New Milton
BH25 7RE
t (01425) 273586
e enquiries@hoburne.com
w hoburne.com

NEW ROMNEY
Kent

Romney Sands Holiday Park ★★★★
Holiday Park
The Parade, Greatstone, New
Romney TN28 8RN
t 0871 664 9760
e holidaysales.romneysands@
park-resorts.com
w park-resorts.com

NEWCHURCH
Isle of Wight

Southland Camping Park ★★★★★
Touring & Camping Park
Winford Road, Sandown
PO36 0LZ
t (01983) 865385
e info@southland.co.uk
w southland.co.uk

NEWCHURCH
Kent

Norwood Farm Caravan & Camping Park Ltd ★★★★
Touring & Camping Park
Newchurch, Romney Marsh
TN29 0DU
t (01303) 873659
e jameswimble@farming.co.uk

NITON
Isle of Wight

Meadow View Caravan Site ★
Holiday Park
Newport Road, Ventnor
PO38 2NS
t (01983) 730015

NORTON
Isle of Wight

Warners Norton Grange Classic Resort ★★★
Warners Holiday Centre,
Norton Grange, Norton
PO41 0SD
t (01983) 760323
e melanie.cox@bourne-
leisure.co.uk
w nortongrange.co.uk

OLNEY
Buckinghamshire

Emberton Country Park ★★
Touring & Camping Park
Emberton, Olney MK46 5FJ
t (01234) 711575
e embertonpark@milton-
keynes.gov.uk
w mkweb.co.uk/embertonpark

OWER
Hampshire

Green Pastures Caravan Park ★★★
Touring Park
Whitemoor Lane, Ower,
Romsey SO51 6AJ
t (023) 8081 4444
e enquiries@
greenpasturesfarm.com
w greenpasturesfarm.com

PAGHAM
West Sussex

Church Farm Holiday Village ★★★★
Holiday Park
Church Lane, Bognor Regis
PO21 4NR
t 0870 405 0151
e churchfarm@bourne-leisure.
co.uk
w churchfarm-park.co.uk

PEVENSEY
East Sussex

Camping and Caravanning Club Site Normans Bay ★★★★
Touring & Camping Park
Normans Bay, Pevensey
BN24 6PR
t (01323) 761190

PEVENSEY BAY
East Sussex

Bay View Park Ltd ★★★
Holiday, Touring & Camping Park
Old Martello Road, Pevensey
Bay BN24 6DX
t (01323) 768688
e holidays@bay-view.co.uk
w bay-view.co.uk

Martello Beach Park ★★★★★
Holiday Park
Eastbourne Road, Pevensey
Bay, Pevensey BN24 6DH
t (01323) 761424
e m.smart@
martellobeachpark.fsbusiness.
co.uk
w ukparks.co.uk/martello

RAMSGATE
Kent

Manston Caravan & Camping Park ★★★★
Holiday, Touring & Camping Park
Manston Court Road, Manston,
Ramsgate CT12 5AU
t (01843) 823442

Nethercourt Touring Park ★★★
Touring & Camping Park
Nethercourt Hill, Ramsgate
CT11 0RX
t (01843) 595485

READING
Berkshire

Wellington Country Park ★★★★
Touring & Camping Park
Odiham Road, Riseley, Reading
RG7 1SP
t (0118) 932 6444
e info@wellington-country-
park.co.uk
w wellington-country-park.co.
uk

REDHILL
Surrey

Alderstead Heath Caravan Club Site ★★★★
Touring Park
Dean Lane, Redhill RH1 3AH
t (01737) 644629
w caravanclub.co.uk

RINGWOOD
Hampshire

Shamba Holidays ★★★★
Touring & Camping Park
230 Ringwood Road, St
Leonards, Ringwood BH24 2SB
t (01202) 873302
e enquiries@shambaholidays.
co.uk
w shambaholidays.co.uk

ROCHESTER
Kent

Allhallows Leisure Park ★★★★
Holiday Park
Allhallows-on-Sea, Rochester
ME3 9QD
t (01634) 270385
e enquiries@british-holidays.
co.uk
w allhallows-park.co.uk

ROMSEY
Hampshire

Hill Farm Caravan Park ★★★★
Holiday, Touring & Camping Park
Branches Lane, Sherfield
English, Romsey SO51 6FH
t (01794) 340402
e gib@hillfarmpark.com
w hillfarmpark.com

ROOKLEY
Isle of Wight

Rookley Country Park ★★★★
Holiday Park
Main Road, Rookley PO38 3LU
t (01983) 721606
e info@islandviewhols.co.uk
w islandviewhols.co.uk

RYDE
Isle of Wight

Beaper Farm ★★★
Touring & Camping Park
Brading Road, Ryde PO33 1QJ
t (01983) 615210
e beaper@btinternet.com
w beaperfarm.com

Isle of Wight Self Catering – Pondwell Bungalows ★★★
Holiday Park
Salterns Road, Seaview
PO34 5AQ
t (01983) 612330
e info@isleofwightselfcatering.
co.uk
w isleofwightselfcatering.co.uk

Roebeck Camping and Caravan Park ★★
Touring & Camping Park
Gatehouse Road, Upton Cross,
Ryde PO33 4BS
t (01983) 611475
e andrew.cross@roebeck-
farm.co.uk
w roebeck-farm.co.uk

ST HELENS
Isle of Wight

Carpenters Farm Campsite ★★★
Touring & Camping Park
Carpenters Road, St Helens,
Ryde PO33 1YL
t (01983) 874557
e info@carpentersfarm.co.uk
w carpentersfarm.co.uk

Field Lane Holiday Park ★★★★★
Holiday Park
Field Lane, St Helens
PO33 1UX
t (01983) 872779
e alison@fieldlane.com
w fieldlane.com

Hillgrove Park ★★★★★
ROSE AWARD
Holiday Park
Field Lane, St Helens
PO33 1UT
t (01983) 872802
e holidays@hillgrove.co.uk
w hillgrove.co.uk

Nodes Point Holiday Park ★★★★
Holiday, Touring & Camping Park
Nodes Road, Ryde PO33 1YA
t 0871 664 9758
e holidaysales.nodespoint@
park-resorts.com
w park-resorts.com

Old Mill Holiday Park ★★★★★
Holiday Park
Mill Road, Ryde, St Helens
PO33 1UE
t (01983) 872507
e web@oldmill.co.uk
w oldmill.co.uk

ST LAWRENCE
Isle of Wight

Undercliff Glen Caravan Park ★★★★★
Holiday Park
Undercliff Drive, St Lawrence
PO38 1XY
t (01983) 730261
e lee@morrisl9.freeserve.co.
uk

ST-MARGARETS-AT-CLIFFE
Kent

St Margarets Holiday Park ★★★★★
Holiday Park
Reach Road, St Margarets-at-
Cliffe, Dover CT15 6AE
t 0871 664 9772
e holidaysales.
stmargaretsbay@park-resorts.
com
w park-resorts.com

ST NICHOLAS AT WADE
Kent

St Nicholas Camping Site ★★
Touring & Camping Park
Court Road, St Nicholas at
Wade, Birchington CT7 0NH
t (01843) 847245

SANDOWN
Isle of Wight

Adgestone Camping & Caravanning Club Site ★★★★
Holiday Park
Lower Adgestone Road,
Adgestone, Sandown
PO36 0HL
t (01983) 403432
w campingandcaravanning
club.co.uk

Cheverton Copse Holiday Park Ltd ★★★★
Holiday Park
Scotchells Brook Lane,
Sandown PO36 0JP
t (01983) 403161
e holidays@chevertoncopse.
com
w chevertoncopse.com

Fairway Holiday Park ★★★
Holiday Park
The Fairway, Sandown
PO36 9PS
t (01983) 403462
e enquiries@
fairwayholidaypark.co.uk
w fairwayholidaypark.co.uk

Fort Holiday Park ★★★
Holiday Park
Avenue Road, Sandown
PO36 8BD
t (01983) 402858
e bookings@fortholidaypark.
co.uk
w fortholidaypark.co.uk

Fort Spinney Holiday Chalets ★★★★★
Holiday Park
Yaverland Road, Sandown
PO36 8QB
t (01983) 402360
e fortspinney@iowight.com
w iowight.com/spinney

Sandown Holiday Chalets ★★★
Holiday Park
Avenue Road, Sandown
PO36 9AP
t (01983) 404025
e chalets@iowight.com
w iowight.com/chalets

SANDWICH
Kent

Sandwich Leisure Park ★★★★★
Holiday, Touring & Camping Park
Woodnesborough Road,
Sandwich CT13 0AA
t (01304) 612681
e info@
coastandcountryleisure.com
w coastandcountryleisure.com

SEAFORD
East Sussex

Sunnyside Caravan Park ★★★★
Holiday Park
Marine Parade, Seaford
BN25 2QW
t (01323) 892825
e managers@sunnyside-
caravan-park.co.uk
w sunnyside-caravan-park.co.
uk

SEAL
Kent

Camping & Caravanning Club Site Oldbury Hill ★★★★
Touring & Camping Park
Styants Bottom, Seal,
Sevenoaks TN15 0ET
t (01732) 762728
w campingandcaravanning
club.co.uk

SEASALTER
Kent

Homing Leisure Park ★★★★
Holiday, Touring & Camping Park
Church Lane, Seasalter,
Whitstable CT5 4BU
t (01227) 771777
e info@
coastandcountryleisure.com
w coastandcountryleisure.com

SEAVIEW
Isle of Wight

Isle of Wight Self Catering – Salterns ★★★
Holiday Park
Salterns Road, Seaview
PO34 5AQ
t (01983) 612330
e info@isleofwightselfcatering.
co.uk
w isleofwightselfcatering.co.uk

Isle of Wight Self Catering – Tollgate ★★★
Holiday Park
Salterns Road, Seaview
PO34 5AQ
t (01983) 612330
e info@isleofwightselfcatering.
co.uk
w isleofwightselfcatering.co.uk

SELSEY
West Sussex

Bunn Leisure – Green Lawns Holiday Park ★★★★★
Holiday Park
Paddock Lane, Selsey,
Chichester PO20 9EJ
t (01243) 604121
e holidays@bunnleisure.co.uk
w bunnleisure.co.uk

Warner Farm Touring Park ★★★★★
Touring Park
Warners Lane, Selsey,
Chichester PO20 9EL
t (01243) 604499 &
(01243) 606080
e touring@bunnleisure.co.uk
w bunnleisure.co.uk

West Sands Holiday Park ★★★★ ROSE AWARD
Holiday Park
Mill Lane, Selsey, Chichester
PO20 9BH
t (01243) 606080
e holidays@bunnleisure.co.uk
w bunnleisure.co.uk

White Horse Caravan Park ★★★★ ROSE AWARD
Holiday Park
Paddock Lane, Selsey,
Chichester PO20 9EJ
t (01243) 606080
e holidays@bunnleisure.co.uk
w bunnleisure.co.uk

SHANKLIN
Isle of Wight

Landguard Camping Park ★★★★
Touring & Camping Park
Landguard Manor Road,
Shanklin PO37 7PH
t (01983) 867028
e landguard@weltnet.com
w landguard-camping.co.uk

Landguard Holidays – Davidson Leisure Resorts Ltd ★★★★
Holiday Park
Landguard Manor Road,
Shanklin PO37 7PJ
t (01983) 863100
e enquiries@
landguardholidays.co.uk
w landguardholidays.co.uk

Lower Hyde Holiday Park ★★★★
Holiday, Touring & Camping Park
Landguard Road, Shanklin
PO37 7LL
t 0871 664 9752
e holidaysales.lowerhyde@
park-resorts.com
w park-resorts.com

Ninham Country Holidays ★★★★
Holiday & Touring Park
Ninham Farm, Shanklin
PO37 7PL
t (01983) 864243
e info@ninham.fsnet.co.uk
w ninham-holidays.co.uk

SLINDON
West Sussex

Camping & Caravanning Club Site, Slindon ★★
Touring Park
Slindon Park, Arundel
BN18 0RG
t (01243) 814387
w campingandcaravanning
club.co.uk

SMALL DOLE
West Sussex

Southdown Caravan Park ★★★
Holiday & Touring Park
Henfield Road, Small Dole,
Henfield BN5 9XH
t (01903) 814323

SOUTHBOURNE
West Sussex

Chichester Camping & Caravan Club ★★★
Touring & Camping Park
Main Road, Southbourne,
Chichester PO10 8JH
t 0845 130 7633
w campingandcaravanning
club.co.uk

SOUTHWATER
West Sussex

Raylands Park ★★★
Holiday, Touring & Camping Park
Jackrells Lane, Southwater,
Horsham RH13 9DH
t (01403) 730218
e raylands@
roundstonecaravans.com
w roundstonecaravans.com

STANDLAKE
Oxfordshire

Hardwick Parks ★★★
Holiday, Touring & Camping Park
The Downs, Standlake, Witney
OX29 7PZ
t (01865) 300501
e info@hardwickparks.co.uk
w hardwickparks.co.uk

Lincoln Farm Park Limited ★★★★★
Touring Park
High Street, Standlake, Witney
OX29 7RH
t (01865) 300239
e info@lincolnfarm.touristnet.
uk.com
w lincolnfarmpark.uk.com

THORNESS BAY
Isle of Wight

Thorness Bay Holiday Park
★★★★
Holiday, Touring & Camping Park
Thorness Lane, Cowes
PO31 8NJ
t 0871 664 9779
e holidaysales.thornessbay@
park-resorts.com
w park-resorts.com

UCKFIELD
East Sussex

Honeys Green Caravan Park
★★
Holiday, Touring & Camping Park
Easons Green, Framfield,
Uckfield TN22 5RE
t (01732) 860205

WALTON-ON-THAMES
Surrey

Camping and Caravanning Club Site (Walton on Thames) ★★★
Camping Park
Fieldcommon Lane, Walton-on-Thames KT12 3QG
t (01932) 220392
w campingandcaravanning
club.co.uk

WARSASH
Hampshire

Dibles Park Company Ltd
★★★★
Touring Park
Dibles Park, Dibles Road,
Warsash SO31 9SA
t (01489) 575232
e dibles.park@btconnect.com

WASHINGTON
West Sussex

Washington Caravan & Camping Park ★★★★
Touring & Camping Park
London Road, Washington,
Pulborough RH20 4AJ
t (01903) 892869
e washcamp@amserve.com
w washcamp.com

WINCHESTER
Hampshire

Morn Hill Caravan Club Site
★★★★
Touring & Camping Park
Morn Hill, Winchester
SO21 2PH
t (01962) 869877
w caravanclub.co.uk

WORTHING
West Sussex

Northbrook Farm Caravan Club Site ★★★★
Touring Park
Titnore Way, Worthing
BN13 3RT
t (01903) 502962
w caravanclub.co.uk

WROTHAM HEATH
Kent

Gate House Wood Touring Park ★★★★★
Touring Park
Ford Road, Wrotham Heath,
Sevenoaks TN15 7SD
t (01732) 843062
e gatehousewood@btinternet.com

WROXALL
Isle of Wight

Appuldurcombe Gardens Holiday Park ★★★★
Holiday, Touring & Camping Park
Appuldurcombe Road, Ventnor
PO38 3EP
t (01983) 852597
e info@
appuldurcombegardens.co.uk
w appuldurcombegardens.co.uk

YARMOUTH
Isle of Wight

The Orchards Holiday Caravan & Camping Park ★★★★★ ROSE AWARD
Holiday & Touring Park
Main Road, Newbridge
PO41 0TS
t (01983) 531331
e info@orchards-holiday-park.co.uk
w orchards-holiday-park.co.uk

Silver Glades Caravan Park
★★★★
Holiday Park
Solent Road, Cranmore
PO41 0XZ
t (01983) 760172
e holiday@silvergladesiow.co.uk
w silvergladesiow.co.uk

SOUTH WEST ENGLAND

ALDERHOLT
Dorset

Hill Cottage Farm Camping & Caravan Park ★★★★
Touring & Camping Park
Sandleheath Road, Alderholt,
Fordingbridge SP6 3EG
t (01425) 650513
e hillcottagefarmcaravansite@
supanet.com
w hillcottagefarm.co.uk

ASHBURTON
Devon

Parkers Farm Holiday Park
★★★★
Holiday, Touring & Camping Park
Higher Mead Farm, Alston Cross, Ashburton, Newton Abbot TQ13 7LJ
t (01364) 652598
e parkersfarm@btconnect.com
w parkersfarm.co.uk

River Dart Adventures
★★★★
Touring & Camping Park
Holne Park, Ashburton,
Newton Abbot TQ13 7NP
t (01364) 652511
e info@riverdart.co.uk
w riverdart.co.uk

AXMINSTER
Devon

Andrewshayes Caravan Park
★★★★
Holiday Park
Dalwood, Axminster EX13 7DY
t (01404) 831225
e enquiries@andrewshayes.co.uk
w andrewshayes.co.uk

Hunters Moon Country Estate ★★★★
Holiday, Touring & Camping Park
Hawkchurch, Axminster
EX13 5UL
t (01297) 678402
w ukparks.co.uk/huntersmoon

BARNSTAPLE
Devon

Kentisbury Grange Country Park ★★★★
Holiday, Touring & Camping Park
Kentisbury, Barnstaple
EX31 4NL
t (01271) 883454
e info@kentisburygrange.co.uk
w kentisburygrange.co.uk

BATH
Somerset

Newton Mill Camping
★★★★
Touring & Camping Park
Twaebrook Ltd, Newton Mill
Camping Park, Newton Road,
Bath BA2 9JF
t (01225) 333909
e newtonmill@hotmail.com
w campinginbath.co.uk

BEETHAM
Somerset

Five Acres Caravan Club Site
★★★★
Touring Park
Giants Grave Road, Chard
TA20 3QA
t (01460) 234519

BERE REGIS
Dorset

Rowlands Wait Touring Park
★★★
Touring & Camping Park
Rye Hill, Bere Regis, Wareham
BH20 7LP
t (01929) 472727
e enquiries@rowlandswait.co.uk
w rowlandswait.co.uk

BERRY HEAD
Devon

Landscove Holiday Village
★★★★
Holiday Park
Gillard Road, Brixham TQ5 9EP
t 0870 442 9750
e bookings@landscove.biz
w southdevonholidays.biz

BERRYNARBOR
Devon

Sandaway Beach Holiday Park ★★★★
Holiday Park
Berrynarbor, Ilfracombe
EX34 9ST
t (01271) 866766
e stay@johnfowlerholidays.com
w johnfowlerholidays.com

BIDEFORD
Devon

Bideford Bay Holiday Park
★★★★
Holiday Park
Bucks Cross, Bideford
EX39 5DU
t (01237) 431331
e gm.bidefordbay@park-resorts.com
w park-resorts.com

BISHOP SUTTON
Somerset

Bath Chew Valley Caravan Park ★★★★★
Touring Park
Ham Lane, Bishop Sutton,
Bristol BS39 5TZ
t (01275) 332127

BLACKWATER
Cornwall

Trevarth Holiday Park ★★★★ ROSE AWARD
Touring & Camping Park
Blackwater, Truro TR4 8HR
t (01872) 560266
e trevarth@lineone.net
w trevarth.co.uk

BLANDFORD FORUM
Dorset

The Inside Park ★★★★
Touring & Camping Park
Down House Estate, Blandford
St Mary, Blandford Forum
DT11 9AD
t (01258) 453719
e inspark@aol.com
w members.aol.com/inspark/
inspark

BLUE ANCHOR
Somerset

Hoburne Blue Anchor ★★★★
Holiday & Touring Park
Carhampton Road, Blue
Anchor TA24 6JT
t (01643) 821360
e enquiries@hoburne.co.uk
w hoburne.co.uk

BODMIN
Cornwall

Camping & Caravanning Club (Bodmin) ★★★★
Touring & Camping Park
Old Callywith Road, Bodmin
PL31 2DZ
t (01872) 501658
w campingandcaravanning
club.co.uk

Ruthern Valley Holidays ★★★★
Holiday, Touring & Camping Park
Ruthern Bridge, Bodmin
PL30 5LU
t (01208) 831395

BOSSINEY
Cornwall

Ocean Cove Caravan Park ★★★★★
Holiday Park
Old Borough Farm, Bossiney,
Tintagel PL34 0AZ
t (01840) 770325
e gavin.hobbs@haulfryn.co.uk
w ocean-cove.co.uk

BOURNEMOUTH
Dorset

Meadow Bank Holidays ★★★★★
Holiday, Touring & Camping Park
Stour Way, Christchurch
BH23 2PQ
t (01202) 483597
e enquiries@meadowbank-
holidays.co.uk
w meadowbank-holidays.co.uk

BOVISAND
Devon

Bovisand Lodge Estate Ltd ★★★★
Holiday Park
Bovisand Lodge, Bovisand,
Plymouth PL9 0AA
t (01752) 403554
e stay@bovisand.com
w bovisand.com

BRATTON CLOVELLY
Devon

South Breazle Holidays ★★★★
Holiday, Touring & Camping Park
Okehampton EX20 4JS
t (01837) 871752
e louise@
southbreazleholidays.co.uk
w southbreazleholidays.co.uk

BRATTON FLEMING
Devon

Greenacres Farm Touring Caravan Park ★★★★
Touring Park
Bratton Fleming, Barnstaple
EX31 4SG
t (01598) 763334

BRAUNTON
Devon

Lobb Fields Caravan and Camping Park ★★★★
Touring & Camping Park
Saunton Road, Braunton
EX33 1EB
t (01271) 812090
e info@lobbfields.com
w lobbfields.com

BREAN
Somerset

Diamond Farm ★★★
Touring & Camping Park
Weston Road, Brean,
Burnham-on-Sea TA8 2RL
t (01278) 751263
e trevor@diamondfarm42.
freeserve.co.uk
w diamondfarm.co.uk

Dolphin Caravan Park ★★★★★
Holiday Park
Coast Road, Burnham-on-Sea
TA8 2QY
t (01278) 751258
w dolphincaravanpark.co.uk

Golden Sands Caravan Park ★★★
Holiday Park
South Road, Brean Sands
TA8 2RF
t (01278) 752100
e admin@brean.com
w brean.com

Holiday Resort Unity ★★★
Coast Road, Brean Sands
TA8 2RB
t (01278) 751235
e admin@hru.co.uk
w hru.co.uk

Isis and Wyndham Park ★★★★
Holiday Park
Warren Road, Brean Sands,
Burnham-on-Sea TA8 2RP
t (01278) 751227
e enquiries@warren-farm.co.
uk
w warren-farm.co.uk

Northam Farm Touring Park ★★★★
Holiday, Touring & Camping Park
Brean Sands, Burnham-on-Sea
TA8 2SE
t (01278) 751244
e enquiries@northamfarm.co.
uk
w northamfarm.co.uk

Warren Farm Holiday Centre ★★★★
Holiday, Touring & Camping Park
Warren Road, Brean Sands,
Burnham-on-Sea TA8 2RP
t (01278) 751227
e enquiries@warren-farm.co.
uk
w warren-farm.co.uk

BRIDESTOWE
Devon

Glebe Park ★★★
Holiday & Touring Park
Bridestowe, Okehampton
EX20 4ER
t (01837) 861261

BRIDGWATER
Somerset

Fairways International Touring Caravan and Camping Park ★★★
Touring & Camping Park
Bath Road, Bawdrip,
Bridgwater TA7 8PP
t (01278) 685569
e holiday@
fairwaysinternational.co.uk
w fairwaysinternational.co.uk

BRIDPORT
Dorset

Binghams Farm Touring Caravan Park ★★★★
Touring & Camping Park
Binghams Farm, Melplash,
Bridport DT6 3TT
t (01308) 488234
e enquiries@binghamsfarm.
co.uk
w binghamsfarm.co.uk

Eype House Caravan Park Ltd ★★★
Holiday, Touring & Camping Park
Eype, Bridport DT6 6AL
t (01308) 424903
e enquiries@eypehouse.co.uk
w eypehouse.co.uk

Freshwater Beach Holiday Park ★★★★
Holiday, Touring & Camping Park
Burton Bradstock, Bridport
DT6 4PT
t (01308) 897317
e office@freshwaterbeach.co.
uk
w freshwaterbeach.co.uk

Golden Cap Holiday Park ★★★★★ ROSE AWARD
Holiday, Touring & Camping Park
Seatown, Chideock, Bridport
DT6 6JX
t (01308) 422139
e holidays@wdlh.co.uk
w wdlh.co.uk

Highlands End Holiday Park ★★★★★ ROSE AWARD
Holiday, Touring & Camping Park
Eype, Bridport DT6 6AR
t (01308) 422139
e holidays@wdlh.co.uk
w wdlh.co.uk

BRISTOL
City of Bristol

Baltic Wharf Caravan Club Site ★★★★
Touring Park
Cumberland Road, Bristol
BS1 6XG
t (0117) 926 8030
w caravanclub.co.uk

BRIXHAM
Devon

Brixham Holiday Park ★★★★
Holiday Park
Fishcombe Road, Brixham
TQ5 8RB
t (01803) 853324
e enquiries@brixhamholpk.
fsnet.co.uk
w brixhamholidaypark.co.uk

Galmpton Touring Park ★★★★
Touring & Camping Park
Greenway Road, Galmpton,
Brixham TQ5 0EP
t (01803) 842066
e galmptontouringpark@
hotmail.com
w galmptontouringpark.co.uk

Hillhead Holiday Park Caravan Club Site ★★★★★
Touring & Camping Park
Hillhead, Brixham TQ5 0HH
t (01803) 853204
w caravanclub.co.uk

Riviera Bay Holiday Centre
★★★★
Holiday Park
Mudstone Lane, Brixham
TQ5 9EJ
t (01803) 856335
e info@rivierabay.biz
w rivierabay.biz

BUDE
Cornwall

Bude Holiday Park (Cranstar Holidays) ★★★
Holiday, Touring & Camping Park
Maer Lane, Bude EX23 9EE
t (01288) 355955
e wendy.bude@btconnect.com
w budeholidaypark.com

Budemeadows Park
★★★★★
Touring Park
Budemeadows, Bude
EX23 0NA
t (01288) 361646
e infootb@budemeadows.com
w budemeadows.com

Penhalt Farm Holiday Park
★★★
Touring & Camping Park
Poundstock, Bude EX23 0DG
t (01288) 361210
e denandjennie@penhaltfarm.fsnet.co.uk
w penhaltfarm.co.uk

Sandymouth Bay Holiday Park ★★★★
Holiday & Touring Park
Sandymouth Bay, Bude
EX23 9HW
t (01288) 352563
e reception@sandymouthbay.co.uk
w sandymouthbay.co.uk

Upper Lynstone Caravan and Camping Site ★★★★
Holiday, Touring & Camping Park
Upton, Bude EX23 0LP
t (01288) 352017
e reception@upperlynstone.co.uk
w upperlynstone.co.uk

Wooda Farm Park ★★★★★
Holiday & Touring Park
Poughill, Bude EX23 9HJ
t (01288) 352069
e enquiries@wooda.co.uk
w wooda.co.uk

BURNHAM-ON-SEA
Somerset

Burnham-on-Sea Holiday Village ★★★★
Holiday, Touring & Camping Park
Marine Drive, Burnham-on-Sea TA8 1LA
t (01278) 783391
e enquiries@british-holidays.co.uk
w british-holidays.co.uk

Home Farm Holiday Park
★★★★★
Holiday & Touring Park
Edithmead, Highbridge
TA9 4HD
t (01278) 788888
e office@homefarmholidaypark.co.uk
w homefarmholidaypark.co.uk

Lakeside Holiday Park
★★★★
Holiday Park
Westfield Road, Burnham-on-Sea TA8 2AE
t (01278) 792222
e margaret.difford@btconnect.com
w lakesideholidays.co.uk

The Retreat Caravan Park
★★★★★
Holiday Park
Berrow Road, Burnham-on-Sea TA8 2ES
t 0700 7387328
e roger@retreat.uk.com
w retreatcaravanpark.co.uk

BURTON BRADSTOCK
Dorset

Coastal Caravan Park ★★★
Holiday, Touring & Camping Park
Annings Lane, Burton Bradstock, Bridport DT6 4QP
t (01308) 897361
e holidays@wdlh.co.uk
w wdlh.co.uk

CAMELFORD
Cornwall

Juliots Well Holiday Park
★★★
Holiday, Touring & Camping Park
Camelford PL32 9RF
t (01840) 213302
e juliotswell@breaksincornwall.com
w juliotswell.com

Lanteglos Hotel & Villas Ltd
★★★
Holiday Park
Camelford PL32 9RF
t (01840) 213551

CARDINHAM
Cornwall

Gwel-An-Nans ★★★
Touring & Camping Park
Cardinham, Bodmin PL30 4EF
t (01208) 821359
e shelia.worden@btopenworld.com

CARNON DOWNS
Cornwall

Carnon Downs Caravan and Camping Park ★★★★★
Touring & Camping Park
Carnon Downs, Truro TR3 6JJ
t (01872) 862283
e info@carnon-downs-caravanpark.co.uk
w carnon-downs-caravanpark.co.uk

CHACEWATER
Cornwall

Chacewater Park ★★★★
Touring & Camping Park
Cox Hill, Chacewater, Truro TR4 8LY
t (01209) 820762
e enquiries@chacewaterpark.co.uk
w chacewaterpark.co.uk

Killiwerris Touring Park
★★★★
Touring Park
Penstraze, Chacewater, Truro TR4 8PF
t (01872) 561356
e killiwerris@tiscali.co.uk
w killiwerris.co.uk

CHARD
Somerset

Alpine Grove Touring Park
★★★★
Touring Park
Chard TA20 4HD
t (01460) 63479
e stay@alpinegrovetouringpark.com
w alpinegrovetouringpark.com

CHARMOUTH
Dorset

The Camping and Caravanning Club Site Charmouth ★★★★★
Touring & Camping Park
Monkton Wyld, Bridport DT6 6DB
t (01297) 32965
w campingandcaravanningclub.co.uk

Dolphins River Park ★★★★
Holiday Park
Berne Lane, Charmouth, Bridport DT6 6RD
t 0800 074 6375
w dolphinsriverpark.co.uk

Manor Farm Holiday Centre
★★★
Holiday, Touring & Camping Park
The Street, Charmouth, Bridport DT6 6QL
t (01297) 560226
e enq@manorfarmholidaycentre.co.uk
w manorfarmholidaycentre.co.uk

Monkton Wyld Farm Caravan & Camping Park
★★★★
Touring & Camping Park
Monkton Wyld, Bridport DT6 6DB
t (01297) 631131
e simonkewley@mac.com
w monktonwyld.co.uk

Newlands Holidays
★★★★★
Holiday, Touring & Camping Park
Newlands Holiday Park, Charmouth DT6 6RB
t (01297) 560259
e enq@newlandsholidays.co.uk
w newlandsholidays.co.uk

Seadown Holiday Park
★★★★★
Holiday, Touring & Camping Park
Bridge Road, Charmouth, Bridport DT6 6QS
t (01297) 560154
w seadowncaravanpark.co.uk

Wood Farm Caravan and Camping Park ★★★★★
Holiday, Touring & Camping Park
Charmouth, Bridport DT6 6BT
t (01297) 560697
e holidays@woodfarm.co.uk
w woodfarm.co.uk

CHEDDAR
Somerset

Broadway House Holiday Touring and Camping Park ★★★★
ROSE AWARD
Holiday, Touring & Camping Park
Axbridge Road, Cheddar BS27 3DB
t (01934) 742610
e info@broadwayhouse.uk.com
w broadwayhouse.uk.com

Cheddar Bridge Touring Park ★★★★
Holiday & Touring Park
Draycott Road, Cheddar BS27 3RJ
t (01934) 743048

Mendip Heights Camping and Caravan Park ★★★★
Touring & Camping Park
Townsend, Wells BA5 3BP
t (01749) 870241
e bta@mendipheights.co.uk
w mendipheights.co.uk

CHELTENHAM
Gloucestershire

Cheltenham Racecourse Caravan Club Site ★★★
Touring & Camping Park
Prestbury Park, Evesham Road, Cheltenham GL50 4SH
t (01242) 523102
e debby.towers@caravanclub.co.uk

CHICKERELL
Dorset

Bagwell Farm Touring Park
★★★★
Touring & Camping Park
Knights in the Bottom,
Chickerell, Weymouth
DT3 4EA
t (01305) 782575
e enquiries@bagwellfarm.co.
uk
w bagwellfarm.co.uk

CHRISTCHURCH
Dorset

Beaulieu Gardens Holiday Park ★★★★★
ROSE AWARD
Holiday Park
Beaulieu Avenue, Christchurch
BH23 2EB
t (01202) 486215
e enquiries@meadowbank-holidays.co.uk
w meadowbank-holidays.co.uk

Harrow Wood Farm Caravan Park ★★★
Camping Park
Poplar Lane, Bransgore,
Christchurch BH23 8JE
t (01425) 672487
e harrowwood@caravan-sites.
co.uk
w caravan-sites.co.uk

Hoburne Park ★★★★★
Holiday Park
Hoburne Caravan Park,
Hoburne Lane, Christchurch
BH23 4HU
t (01425) 273379
e enquiries@hoburne.com
w hoburne.com

CHUDLEIGH
Devon

Finlake Holiday Park
★★★★★
Holiday Park
Chudleigh, Newton Abbot
TQ13 0EJ
t (01626) 853833
e finlake@haulfryn.co.uk
w finlake.co.uk

Holmans Wood Holiday Park
★★★★
Holiday, Touring & Camping Park
Harcombe Cross, Chudleigh,
Newton Abbot TQ13 0DZ
t (01626) 853785
e enquiries@holmanswood.co.
uk
w holmanswood.co.uk

COLEFORD
Gloucestershire

Rushmere Farm ★★
Camping Park
Crossways, Coleford GL16 8QP
t (01594) 835319

COMBE MARTIN
Devon

Newberry Farm Touring and Camping Site ★★★★
Touring & Camping Park
Newberry Farm, Woodlands,
Combe Martin, Ilfracombe
EX34 0AT
t (01271) 882334
e enq@newberrycampsite.co.
uk
w newberrycampsite.co.uk

Stowford Farm Meadows
★★★★
Touring & Camping Park
Combe Martin, Ilfracombe
EX34 0PW
t (01271) 882476
e enquiries@stowford.co.uk
w stowford.co.uk

CONNOR DOWNS
Cornwall

Higher Trevaskis Park
★★★★
Touring & Camping Park
Gwinear Road, Connor Downs,
Hayle TR27 5JQ
t (01209) 831736

COOMBE BISSETT
Wiltshire

Summerlands Caravan Park
★★★
Touring & Camping Park
College Farm, Rockbourne
Road, Coombe Bissett,
Salisbury SP5 4LP
t (01722) 718259
w summerlands-park.com

CORFE CASTLE
Dorset

Norden Farm Campsite ★★
Holiday, Touring & Camping Park
Norden Farm, Wareham
BH20 5DS
t (01929) 480098
e nordenfarm@fsmail.net
w nordenfarm.com

Woodyhyde Farm Camping Park ★★
Camping Park
Afflington, Corfe Castle,
Wareham BH20 5HT
t (01929) 480274
e camp@woodyhyde.fsnet.co.
uk
w woodyhyde.co.uk

CRACKINGTON HAVEN
Cornwall

Hentervene Caravan & Camping Park ★★★
Holiday, Touring & Camping Park
Crackington Haven, Bude
EX23 0LF
t (01840) 230365
e contact@hentervene.co.uk
w hentervene.co.uk

CROWCOMBE
Somerset

Quantock Orchard Caravan Park ★★★★★
Holiday, Touring & Camping Park
Crowcombe TA4 4AW
t (01984) 618618
e qocp@flaxpool.freeserve.co.
uk
w quantockorchard.co.uk

CROYDE
Devon

Croyde Bay Holiday Village (Unison) ★★★★
Croyde, Braunton EX33 1QB
t (01271) 890890
e s.willis@unison.co.uk
w croydeholidays.co.uk

CROYDE BAY
Devon

Ruda Holiday Park ★★★★
Holiday, Touring & Camping Park
Croyde Bay, Braunton
EX33 1NY
t 0871 641 0191
e enquiries@
parkdeanholidays.co.uk
w parkdeanholidays.co.uk

CUBERT
Cornwall

Treworgans Holiday Park
Rating Applied For
Holiday Park
Cubert, Newquay TR8 5HH
t (01637) 830200
e treworganshp@tiscali.co.uk
w treworgansholidaypark.co.
uk

DAWLISH
Devon

Cofton Country Holidays
★★★★ ROSE AWARD
Holiday, Touring & Camping Park
Cofton, Starcross, Exeter
EX6 8RP
t (01626) 890111
e info@coftonholidays.co.uk
w coftonholidays.co.uk

Dawlish Sands Holiday Park
★★★★
Holiday Park
Warren Road, Dawlish Warren,
Dawlish EX7 0PG
t (01626) 862038

Golden Sands Holiday Park
★★★★
Holiday, Touring & Camping Park
Week Lane, Dawlish Warren,
Dawlish EX7 0LZ
t (01626) 863099
e info@goldensands.co.uk
w goldensands.co.uk

Ladys Mile Touring and Camping Park ★★★★
ROSE AWARD
Holiday Park
Exeter Road, Dawlish EX7 0LX
t (01626) 863411
e info@ladysmile.co.uk
w ladysmile.co.uk

Leadstone Camping ★★★
Touring & Camping Park
Warren Road, Dawlish
EX7 0NG
t (01626) 864411
e info@leadstonecamping.co.
uk
w leadstonecamping.co.uk

Oakcliff Holiday Park
★★★★
Holiday Park
Mount Pleasant Road, Dawlish
Warren, Dawlish EX7 0ND
t (01626) 863347
e info@oakcliff.co.uk
w oakcliff.co.uk

Peppermint Park ★★★★
Holiday, Touring & Camping Park
Warren Road, Dawlish Warren
Dawlish EX7 0PQ
t (01626) 863436
e info@peppermintpark.co.uk
w peppermintpark.co.uk

Welcome Family Holiday Park ★★★★ ROSE AWARD
Holiday Park
Warren Road, Dawlish Warren
Dawlish EX7 0PH
t (01626) 862070
e fun@welcomefamily.co.uk
w welcomefamily.co.uk

DOBWALLS
Cornwall

Hoburne Doublebois
★★★★
Holiday Park
Doublebois, Dobwalls, Liskeard
PL14 6LD
t (01579) 320049

DONIFORD
Somerset

Doniford Bay Holiday Park
★★★★
Holiday Park
Sea Lane, Watchet TA23 0TJ
t (01984) 632423
e doniford.bay@bourne-leisure.co.uk
w donifordbay-park.co.uk

Sunnybank Caravan Park
★★★★★
Holiday Park
Doniford Camp, Watchet
TA23 0UD
t (01984) 632237
e mail@sunnybankcp.co.uk
w sunnybankcp.co.uk

DORCHESTER
Dorset

Giants Head Caravan & Camping Park ★★
Touring & Camping Park
Old Sherborne Road,
Dorchester DT2 7TR
t (01300) 341242
e holidays@giantshead.co.uk
w giantshead.co.uk

Morn Gate Caravan Park ★★★★
Holiday Park
Bridport Road, Dorchester
DT2 9DS
t (01305) 889284
e morngate@ukonline.co.uk
w morngate.co.uk

DOUBLEBOIS
Cornwall

Pine Green Caravan Park ★★★★
Touring & Camping Park
Doublebois, Dobwalls, Liskeard
PL14 6LE
t (01579) 320183
e mary.ruhleman@btinternet.com
w pinegreenpark.co.uk

DREWSTEIGNTON
Devon

Woodland Springs Touring Park ★★★★
Touring & Camping Park
Venton, Drewsteignton, Exeter
EX6 6PG
t (01647) 231695
e enquiries@woodlandsprings.co.uk
w woodlandsprings.co.uk

DRYBROOK
Gloucestershire

Greenway Farm Caravan & Camping Park ★★★★
Holiday, Touring & Camping Park
Puddlebrook Road, Hawthorns,
Drybrook GL17 9HW
t (01594) 543737
e greenwayfarm@aic.co.uk
w greenwayfarm.org

DULVERTON
Somerset

Exmoor House Caravan Club Site ★★★★
Touring Park
Dulverton TA22 9HL
t (01398) 323268
w caravanclub.co.uk

Lakeside Caravan Club Site ★★★★★
Touring Park
Higher Grants, Exebridge,
Dulverton TA22 9BE
t (01398) 324068
w caravanclub.co.uk

EAST STOKE
Dorset

Luckford Wood Farm Caravan & Camping Park
Rating Applied For
Holiday, Touring & Camping Park
Luckford Wood House,
Wareham BH20 6AW
t (01929) 463098
e johnbarnes@ukipemail.com

EAST WORLINGTON
Devon

Yeatheridge Farm Caravan Park ★★★★
Touring & Camping Park
East Worlington, Crediton
EX17 4TN
t (01884) 860330

EXFORD
Somerset

Westermill Farm ★★
Camping Park
Exford, Minehead TA24 7NJ
t (01643) 831238
e holidays@westermill-exmoor.co.uk
w exmoorcamping.co.uk

EXMOUTH
Devon

Webbers Caravan & Camping Park ★★★★★
Touring Park
Castle Lane, Woodbury, Exeter
EX5 1EA
t (01395) 232276
e reception@webberspark.co.uk
w webberspark.co.uk

FALMOUTH
Cornwall

Pennance Mill Farm ★★★
Holiday, Touring & Camping Park
Maenporth, Falmouth
TR11 5HJ
t (01326) 317431
w pennancemill.co.uk

FOWEY
Cornwall

Penhale Caravan & Camping Park ★★★
Holiday, Touring & Camping Park
Fowey PL23 1JU
t (01726) 833425
e info@penhale-fowey.co.uk
w penhale-fowey.co.uk

Penmarlam Caravan & Camping Park ★★★★
Touring & Camping Park
Bodinnick by Fowey, Fowey
PL23 1LZ
t (01726) 870088
e info@penmarlampark.co.uk
w penmarlampark.co.uk

GLASTONBURY
Somerset

The Old Oaks Touring Park ★★★★★
Holiday Park
Wick, Glastonbury BA6 8JS
t (01458) 831437
e info@theoldoaks.co.uk
w theoldoaks.co.uk

GOONHAVERN
Cornwall

Perran Springs Holiday Park ★★★
Holiday, Touring & Camping Park
Goonhavern, Truro TR4 9QG
t (01872) 540568
e info@perransprings.co.uk
w perransprings.co.uk

Silverbow Park ★★★★★
Holiday Park
Perranwell, Goonhavern, Truro
TR4 9NX
t (01872) 572347

GREAT TORRINGTON
Devon

Greenways Valley Holiday Park ★★★★
Holiday Park
Caddywell Lane, Torrington
EX38 7EW
t (01805) 622153
e enquiries@greenwaysvalley.co.uk
w greenwaysvalley.co.uk

Smytham Manor Holiday Park ★★★★
Holiday & Touring Park
Little Torrington, Torrington
EX38 8PU
t (01805) 622110
e info@smytham.co.uk
w smytham.co.uk

HAMWORTHY
Dorset

Rockley Park Holiday Park ★★★★★ ROSE AWARD
Holiday, Touring & Camping Park
Napier Road, Poole BH15 4LZ
t (01202) 679393
e enquiries@british-holidays.co.uk
w british-holidays.co.uk

HAYLE
Cornwall

Atlantic Coast Caravan Park ★★★★
Holiday & Touring Park
53 Upton Towans, Hayle
TR27 5BL
t (01736) 752071
e enquiries@atlanticcoast-caravanpark.co.uk
w atlanticcoast-caravanpark.co.uk

Beachside Holiday Park ★★★★
Holiday, Touring & Camping Park
Lethlean Lane, Phillack, Hayle
TR27 5AW
t (01736) 753080
e reception@beachside.demon.co.uk
w beachside.co.uk

Churchtown Farm Caravan and Camping ★★★
Touring & Camping Park
Gwithian, Hayle TR27 5BX
t (01736) 753219
e caravanning@churchtownfarmgwithian.fsnet.co.uk
w churchtownfarm.org.uk

Riviere Sands Holiday Park ★★★★
Holiday Park
Riviere Towans, Hayle
TR27 5AX
t (01736) 752132

St Ives Bay Holiday Park ★★★★
Holiday, Touring & Camping Park
73 Loggans Road, Upton
Towans, Hayle TR27 5BH
t (01736) 752274
e stivesbay@dial.pipex.com
w stivesbay.co.uk

HELSTON
Cornwall

Poldown Camping & Caravan Park ★★★★
Holiday, Touring & Camping Park
Carleen, Breage, Helston
TR13 9NN
t (01326) 574560
e info@poldown.co.uk
w poldown.co.uk

Sea Acres Holiday Park ★★★★
Holiday Park
Kennack Sands, Ruan Minor,
Helston TR12 7LT
t 0871 641 0191
e enquiries@parkdeanholidays.co.uk
w parkdeanholidays.co.uk

Seaview Holiday Park ★★★
Holiday & Touring Park
Gwendreath, Ruan Minor,
Helston TR12 7LZ
t (01326) 290635
e reception@seaviewcaravanpark.com
w seaviewcaravanpark.com

HIGHBRIDGE
Somerset

Greenacre Place Touring Caravan Park and Holiday Cottage ★★★★
Touring Park
Bristol Road, Highbridge
TA9 4HA
t (01278) 785227
e info@greenacreplace.com
w greenacreplace.com

HIGHCLIFFE
Dorset

Cobb's Holiday Park ★★★★
Holiday Park
32 Gordon Road, Highcliffe-on-Sea, Christchurch BH23 5HN
t (01425) 273301
e enquiries@
cobbsholidaypark.co.uk

HOLTON HEATH
Dorset

Sandford Holiday Park ★★★★
Holiday, Touring & Camping Park
Organford Road, Holton Heath, Poole BH16 6JZ
t 0870 444 7774
e bookings@weststarholidays.co.uk
w weststarholidays.co.uk

Tanglewood Holiday Park Ltd ★★★★★
Holiday Park
Organford Road, Holton Heath, Poole BH16 6JY
t (01202) 632618

HOLYWELL BAY
Cornwall

The Meadow ★★★
Holiday, Touring & Camping Park
Newquay TR8 5PP
t (01872) 572752
w holywellbeachholidays.co.uk

HORN'S CROSS
Devon

Steart Farm Touring Park ★★★
Touring & Camping Park
Horns Cross, Bideford EX39 5DW
t (01237) 431836
e steart@tiscali.co.uk

ILFRACOMBE
Devon

Beachside Holiday Park ★★★★★
Holiday Park
33 Beach Road, Hele, Ilfracombe EX34 9QZ
t (01271) 863006
e enquiries@beachsidepark.co.uk
w beachsidepark.co.uk

Hele Valley Holiday Park ★★★★ ROSE AWARD
Holiday, Touring & Camping Park
Hele Bay, Ilfracombe EX34 9RD
t (01271) 862460
e holidays@helevalley.co.uk
w helevalley.co.uk

Hidden Valley Touring & Camping Park ★★★★
Touring & Camping Park
West Down, Ilfracombe EX34 8NU
t (01271) 813837
e relax@hiddenvalleypark.com
w hiddenvalleypark.com

MULLACOTT PARK ★★★★
Holiday Park
Mullacott Cross, Ilfracombe EX34 8NB
t (01271) 862212
e info@mullacottpark.co.uk
w mullacottpark.co.uk

IPPLEPEN
Devon

Ross Park ★★★★★
Touring Park
Moor Road, Ipplepen, Newton Abbot TQ12 5TT
t (01803) 812983
e enquiries@
rossparkcaravanpark.co.uk
w rossparkcaravanpark.co.uk

Woodville Touring Caravan Park ★★★★
Touring Park
Totnes Road, Ipplepen, Newton Abbot TQ12 5TN
t (01803) 812240
e jo@woodvillepark.co.uk
w caravan-sitefinder.co.uk/sthwest/devon/woodville.html

ISLES OF SCILLY
Isles of Scilly

St Martin's Campsite ★★★★
Camping Park
Middle Town, St Martin's TR25 0QN
t (01720) 422888
e chris@stmartinscampsite.freeserve.co.uk
w stmartinscampsite.co.uk

Troytown Farm Campsite ★★★
Camping Park
St Agnes TR22 0PL
t (01720) 422360
e troytown@talk21.com
w st-agnes-scilly.org

KENNFORD
Devon

Exeter Racecourse Caravan Club Site ★★★
Touring & Camping Park
Kennford, Exeter EX6 7XS
t (01392) 832107
w caravanclub.co.uk

KENTISBEARE
Devon

Forest Glade Holiday Park ★★★★ ROSE AWARD
Holiday & Touring Park
Kentisbeare, Cullompton EX15 2DT
t (01404) 841381
e nwellard@forest-glade.co.uk
w forest-glade.co.uk

KEWSTOKE
Somerset

Ardnave Holiday Park ★★★
Holiday & Touring Park
Crookes Lane, Kewstoke BS22 9XJ
t (01934) 622319

Kewside Caravans ★★
Holiday Park
Crookes Lane, Weston-super-Mare BS22 9XF
t (01934) 521486

KILKHAMPTON
Cornwall

Penstowe Park Holiday Village ★★★★
Penstowe Holiday Village, Bude EX23 9QY
t (01288) 321354
e info@penstoweholidays.co.uk
w penstoweholidays.co.uk

KINGSBRIDGE
Devon

Challaborough Bay Holiday Park ★★★★
Holiday Park
Challaborough Beach, Kingsbridge TQ7 4HU
t 0871 641 0191
e enquiries@
parkdeanholidays.co.uk
w parkdeanholidays.co.uk

KINGTON LANGLEY
Wiltshire

Plough Lane Caravan Site ★★★★★
Touring Park
Plough Lane, Kington Langley SN15 5PS
t (01249) 750146
e ploughlane@lineone.net
w ploughlane.co.uk

LACOCK
Wiltshire

Piccadilly Caravan Park Ltd ★★★★★
Touring & Camping Park
Folly Lane (West), Lacock, Chippenham SN15 2LP
t (01249) 730260
e piccadillylacock@aol.com

LANDRAKE
Cornwall

Dolbeare Caravan & Camping Park
Rating Applied For
Touring & Camping Park
St Ive Road, Landrake, Saltash PL12 5AF
t (01752) 851332
e reception@dolbeare.co.uk
w dolbeare.co.uk

LAND'S END
Cornwall

Cardinney Caravan & Camping Park ★★★
Touring & Camping Park
Penberth Valley, St Buryan, Penzance TR19 6HJ
t (01736) 810880
e cardinney@btinternet.com
w cardinney-camping-park.co.uk

LANGPORT
Somerset

Bowdens Crest Caravan and Camping Park ★★★★
Holiday, Touring & Camping Park
Bowdens, Langport TA10 0DD
t (01458) 250553
e bowcrest@btconnect.com
w Bowdenscrest.co.uk

LANIVET
Cornwall

Kernow Caravan Park ★★★
Holiday Park
Clann Lane, Lanivet, Bodmin PL30 5HD
t (01208) 831343

LONGLEAT
Wiltshire

Center Parcs Longleat Forest ★★★★★
Forest Holiday Village
Longleat Forest, Warminster BA12 7PU
t 0870 067 3030
w centerparcs.co.uk

LOOE
Cornwall

Looe Bay Holiday Park ★★★★
Holiday Park
St Martins, Looe PL13 1NX
t 0870 444 7774
e bookings@weststarholidays.co.uk
w weststarholidays.co.uk/ic

Seaview Holiday Village ★★★★
Holiday Park
Polperro, Looe PL13 2JE
t (01503) 272335
e reception@
seaviewholidayvillage.co.uk
w seaviewholidayvillage.co.uk

Tencreek Caravan Park ★★★★
Holiday, Touring & Camping Park
Polperro Road, Looe PL13 2JR
t (01503) 262447
e reception@tencreek.co.uk
w dolphinholidays.co.uk

LOWER METHERELL
Cornwall

Trehorner Farm Holiday Park ★★★★
Holiday Park
Lower Metherell, Callington PL17 8BJ
t (01579) 351122
w trehorner.co.uk

LYDFORD
Devon

Camping & Caravanning Club Site – Lydford ★★★★
Touring & Camping Park
Lydford, Okehampton EX20 4BE
t (01822) 820275
w campingandcaravanningclub.co.uk

LYME REGIS
Dorset

Shrubbery Caravan Park
★★★★
Touring & Camping Park
Rousdon, Lyme Regis
DT7 3XW
t (01297) 442227
w ukparks.co.uk/shrubbery

LYNTON
Devon

Camping & Caravanning Club Site – Lynton ★★★★
Touring & Camping Park
Caffyn's Cross, Lynton
EX35 6JS
t (01598) 752379
w campingandcaravanning club.co.uk

Channel View Caravan and Camping Park ★★★★
ROSE AWARD
Holiday & Touring Park
Manor Farm, Lynton EX35 6LD
t (01598) 753349
e relax@channel-view.co.uk
w channel-view.co.uk

MALMESBURY
Wiltshire

Burton Hill Caravan and Camping Park ★★★
Touring & Camping Park
Burton Hill Caravan Park,
Arches Lane, Malmesbury
SN16 0EH
t (01666) 826880
e info@burtonhill.co.uk
w burtonhill.co.uk

MARAZION
Cornwall

Mounts Bay Caravan Park
★★★★★
Holiday Park
Green Lane, Marazion
TR17 0HQ
t (01736) 710307
e mountsbay@onetel.net
w mountsbay-caravanpark.co.uk

Wayfarers Caravan Park
★★★★
Touring & Camping Park
Relubbus Lane, St Hilary,
Penzance TR20 9EF
t (01736) 763326
e elaine@wayfarerspark.co.uk
w wayfarerspark.co.uk

MARLDON
Devon

Widend Touring Park
★★★★
Holiday, Touring & Camping Park
Totnes Road, Marldon,
Paignton TQ3 1RT
t (01803) 550116

MARTOCK
Somerset

Southfork Caravan Park
★★★★★
Holiday, Touring & Camping Park
Parrett Works, Martock
TA12 6AE
t (01935) 825661
e southforkcaravans@ btconnect.com
w southforkcaravans.co.uk

MAWGAN PORTH
Cornwall

Marver Holiday Park ★★★
Holiday, Touring & Camping Park
Marver Chalets, Mawgan
Porth, Newquay TR8 4BB
t (01637) 860493
e familyholidays@aol.com
w marverholidaypark.co.uk

Sun Haven Valley Holiday Park
Rating Applied For
Holiday, Touring & Camping Park
Mawgan Porth, Newquay
TR8 4BQ
t (01637) 860373
e sunhaven@sunhavenvalley. com
w sunhavenvalley.com

MEVAGISSEY
Cornwall

Sea View International
★★★★★ ROSE AWARD
Holiday, Touring & Camping Park
Boswinger, Gorran, St Austell
PL26 6LL
t (01726) 843425
e holidays@ seaviewinternational.com
w seaviewinternational.com

MINEHEAD
Somerset

Beeches Holiday Park
★★★★
Holiday Park
Blue Anchor Bay, Minehead
TA24 6JW
t (01984) 640391
e info@beeches-park.co.uk
w beeches-park.co.uk

Butlins Skyline Ltd ★★★★
Warren Road, Minehead
TA24 5SH
t (01643) 703331
e minehead.hbs@bourne-leisure.co.uk
w butlins.com

Minehead Camping and Caravanning Club ★★★★
Camping Park
Hill Road, North Hill, Minehead
TA24 5LB
t (01643) 704138
w campingandcaravanning club.co.uk

MODBURY
Devon

Broad Park Caravan Club Site ★★★★
Touring Park
Higher East Leigh, Modbury,
Ivybridge PL21 0SH
t (01548) 830714
w caravanclub.co.uk

Camping & Caravanning Club Site – California Cross
★★★★
Touring & Camping Park
Modbury, Ivybridge PL21 0SG
t (01548) 821297
w campingandcaravanning club.co.uk

Moor View Touring Park
★★★★
Touring & Camping Park
Modbury, Ivybridge PL21 0SG
t (01548) 821485
e info@moorviewtouringpark. co.uk
w moorviewtouringpark.co.uk

Pennymoor Camping and Caravan Park ★★★★
Holiday, Touring & Camping Park
Modbury, Ivybridge PL21 0SB
t (01548) 830542
e enquiries@pennymoor-camping.co.uk
w pennymoor-camping.co.uk

MOORSHOP
Devon

Higher Longford Caravan & Camping Park ★★★★
Touring & Camping Park
Moorshop, Tavistock PL19 9LQ
t (01822) 613360
e stay@higherlongford.co.uk
w higherlongford.co.uk

MORETON
Dorset

Moreton Camping & Caravanning Club Site
★★★★
Touring & Camping Park
Station Road, Moreton,
Dorchester DT2 8BB
t (01305) 853801

MORETON-IN-MARSH
Gloucestershire

Moreton-in-Marsh Caravan Club Site ★★★★★
Touring Park
Bourton Road, Moreton-in-Marsh GL56 0BT
t (01608) 650519
w caravanclub.co.uk

MORTEHOE
Devon

Easewell Farm Holiday Park & Golf Club ★★★
Holiday, Touring & Camping Park
Mortehoe, Woolacombe
EX34 7EH
t (01271) 870343
w woolacombe.com

North Morte Farm Caravan and Camping Park ★★★★
Holiday, Touring & Camping Park
North Morte Road, Mortehoe,
Woolacombe EX34 7EG
t (01271) 870381
e info@northmortefarm.co.uk
w northmortefarm.co.uk

Twitchen House Holiday Parc ★★★★
Holiday, Touring & Camping Park
Mortehoe Station Road,
Mortehoe EX34 7ES
t (01271) 870343
e goodtimes@woolacombe. com
w woolacombe.com

Warcombe Farm Camping Park ★★★★
Touring & Camping Park
Station Road, Woolacombe
EX34 7EJ
t (01271) 870690
e info@warcombefarm.co.uk
w warcombefarm.co.uk/ devon-campsite.html

MUCHELNEY
Somerset

Thorney Lakes and Caravan Park ★★★
Touring & Camping Park
Thorney Lakes, Langport
TA10 0DW
t (01458) 250811
e enquiries@thorneylakes.co. uk
w thorneylakes.co.uk

MULLION
Cornwall

Mullion Holiday Park
★★★★
Holiday, Touring & Camping Park
Ruan Minor, Helston TR12 7LJ
t 0870 444 5344

NANCLEDRA
Cornwall

Higher Chellew Camp Site
★★★★
Touring & Camping Park
Nancledra, Penzance
TR20 8BD
t (01736) 364532
e camping@higherchellew.co. uk
w higherchellewcamping.co.uk

NEWQUAY
Cornwall

Crantock Beach Holiday Park ★★★★
Holiday Park
Crantock, Newquay TR8 5RH
t 0871 641 0191
e enquiries@
parkdeanholidays.co.uk
w parkdeanholidays.co.uk

Headland Cottages ★★★★★
Headland Road, Fistral Beach, Newquay TR7 1EW
t (01637) 872211
e reception@headlandhotel.co.uk
w headlandhotel.co.uk

Hendra Holiday Park ★★★★
Holiday, Touring & Camping Park
Newquay TR8 4NY
t (01637) 875778
e enquiries@hendra-holidays.com
w hendra-holidays.com

Holywell Bay Holiday Park ★★★★
Holiday Park
Holywell Bay, Newquay TR8 5PR
t 0871 641 0191
e enquiries@
parkdeanholidays.co.uk
w parkdeanholidays.co.uk

Mawgan Porth Holiday Park ★★★★★
Holiday Park
Mawgan Porth, Newquay TR8 4BD
t (01637) 860322

Nancolleth Caravan Gardens ★★★★
Holiday Park
Summercourt, Newquay TR8 4PN
t (01872) 510236
e nancolleth@summercourt.freeserve.co.uk
w nancolleth.co.uk

Newperran Holiday Park ★★★★ ROSE AWARD
Holiday Park
Rejerrah, Newquay TR8 5QJ
t (01872) 572407
e holidays@newperran.co.uk
w newperran.co.uk

Newquay Holiday Park ★★★★
Holiday Park
Newquay TR8 4HS
t 0871 641 0191
e enquiries@
parkdeanholidays.co.uk
w parkdeanholidays.co.uk

Porth Beach Tourist Park ★★★★ ROSE AWARD
Holiday, Touring & Camping Park
Porth, Newquay TR7 3NH
t (01637) 876531
e info@porthbeach.co.uk
w porthbeach.co.uk

Riverside Holiday Park ★★★★
Holiday, Touring & Camping Park
Gwills Lane, Newquay TR8 4PE
t (01637) 873617
e info@riversideholidaypark.co.uk
w riversideholidaypark.co.uk

Trekenning Tourist Park ★★★
Holiday, Touring & Camping Park
Newquay TR8 4JF
t (01637) 880462
e holidays@trekenning.co.uk
w trekenning.co.uk

Treloy Touring Park ★★★★
Touring & Camping Park
Newquay TR8 4JN
t (01637) 872063 & (01637) 876279
e treloy.tp@btconnect.com
w treloy.co.uk

Trethiggey Touring Park ★★★★
Holiday, Touring & Camping Park
Quintrell Downs, Newquay TR8 4QR
t (01637) 877672
e enquiries@trethiggey.co.uk
w trethiggey.co.uk

Trevella Caravan & Camping Pk ★★★★★
Holiday, Touring & Camping Park
Crantock, Newquay TR8 5EW
t (01637) 830308
e holidays@trevella.co.uk
w trevella.co.uk

Trevornick Holiday Park ★★★★★
Holiday Park
Holywell Bay, Newquay TR8 5PW
t (01637) 832906
e paul@trevornick.co.uk
w trevornick.co.uk

NEWTON ABBOT
Devon

Dornafield ★★★★★
Touring & Camping Park
Two Mile Oak, Newton Abbot TQ12 6DD
t (01803) 812732
e enquiries@dornafield.com
w dornafield.com

NORTH MOLTON
Devon

Riverside Caravan & Camping ★★★★
Touring & Camping Park
South Molton EX36 3HQ
t (01769) 579269
e relax@exmoorriverside.co.uk
w exmoorriverside.co.uk

NORTH PETHERTON
Somerset

Somerset View Caravan Park ★★★
Touring Park
Taunton Road, North Petherton TA6 6NW
t (01278) 661294 & 07767 032687
e qcs@somersetview.co.uk
w somersetview.co.uk

OARE
Wiltshire

Hill-View Park ★★★
Touring & Camping Park
Sunnyhill Lane, Oare, Marlborough SN8 4JG
t (01672) 563151

ORCHESTON
Wiltshire

Stonehenge Touring Park ★★★
Touring & Camping Park
Stonehenge Park, Orcheston, Salisbury SP3 4SH
t (01980) 620304
e stay@
stonehengetouringpark.com
w stonehengetouringpark.com

OSMINGTON
Dorset

White Horse Holiday Park ★★★
Holiday Park
Osmington Hill, Osmington, Weymouth DT3 6ED
t (01305) 832164
e enquiries@whitehorsepark.co.uk
w whitehorsepark.co.uk

OWERMOIGNE
Dorset

Sandyholme Holiday Park ★★★★
Holiday, Touring & Camping Park
Moreton Road, Owermoigne, Dorchester DT2 8HZ
t (01305) 852677
e smeatons@sandyholme.co.uk
w sandyholme.co.uk

PADSTOW
Cornwall

Carnevas Farm Holiday Park (Camping) ★★★★
Holiday, Touring & Camping Park
Carnevas Farm, St Merryn, Padstow PL28 8PN
t (01841) 520230
e carnevascampsite@aol.com
w carnevasholidaypark.co.uk

The Laurels ★★★★
Touring & Camping Park
Padstow Road, Whitecross, Wadebridge PL27 7JQ
t (01209) 313474
e jamierielly@btconnect.com
w thelaurelsholidaypark.co.uk

Mother Iveys Bay Caravan Park ★★★★★ ROSE AWARD
Holiday, Touring & Camping Park
Trevose Head, Padstow PL28 8SL
t (01841) 520990
e info@motheriveysbay.com
w motheriveysbay.com

Padstow Touring Park ★★★
Touring & Camping Park
Padstow PL28 8LE
t (01841) 532061
e mail@padstowtouringpark.co.uk
w padstowtouringpark.co.uk

PAIGNTON
Devon

Ashvale Holiday Park ★★★★
Holiday Park
Goodrington Road, Paignton TQ4 7JD
t (01803) 843887
e info@beverley-holidays.co.uk
w beverley-holidays.co.uk

Beverley Park ★★★★★ ROSE AWARD
Holiday, Touring & Camping Park
Goodrington Road, Paignton TQ4 7JE
t (01803) 843887
e info@beverley-holidays.co.uk
w beverley-holidays.co.uk

Byslades International Touring & Camping Park ★★★★
Touring & Camping Park
Totnes Road, Paignton TQ4 7PY
t (01803) 555072
e info@byslades.co.uk
w byslades.co.uk

Higher Well Farm Holiday Park ★★★★
Holiday, Touring & Camping Park
Waddeton Road, Stoke Gabriel, Totnes TQ9 6RN
t (01803) 782289
e higherwell@talk21.com
w higherwellfarmholidaypark.co.uk

Hoburne Torbay ★★★★
Holiday & Touring Park
Grange Road, Paignton TQ4 7JP
t (01803) 558010
e enquiries@hoburne.com
w hoburne.com

Marine Park Holiday Centre ★★★★
Holiday & Touring Park
Grange Road, Paignton
TQ4 7JR
t (01803) 843887
e info@beverley-holidays.co.
uk
w beverley-holidays.co.uk

Paignton Holiday Park ★★★★
Holiday Park
Totnes Road, Paignton
TQ4 7PW
t (01803) 550504

Waterside Holiday Park ★★★★
Holiday Park
Three Beaches, Dartmouth
Road, Paignton TQ4 6NS
t (01803) 842400
w watersidepark.co.uk

Whitehill Country Park ★★★★
Holiday, Touring & Camping Park
Stoke Road, Paignton TQ4 7PF
t (01803) 782338
e info@whitehill-park.co.uk
w whitehill-park.co.uk

PAR
Cornwall

Par Sands Holiday Park ★★★★
Holiday, Touring & Camping Park
Par Beach, Par PL24 2AS
t (01726) 812868
e holiday@parsands.co.uk
w parsands.co.uk

PENTEWAN
Cornwall

Pentewan Sands Holiday Park ★★★★
Holiday, Touring & Camping Park
Mevagissey, St Austell
PL26 6BT
t (01726) 843485
e info@pentewan.co.uk
w pentewan.co.uk

PENZANCE
Cornwall

Tower Park Caravans & Camping ★★★
Holiday, Touring & Camping Park
St Buryan, Penzance TR19 6BZ
t (01736) 810286
e enquiries@
towerparkcamping.co.uk
w towerparkcamping.co.uk

PERRANPORTH
Cornwall

Haven Perran Sands Holiday Park ★★★★
Holiday, Touring & Camping Park
Perran Sands Holiday Park,
Perranporth TR6 0AQ
t 0870 405 0144
e lisa.spickett@bourne-leisure.
co.uk
w perransands-park.co.uk

Perranporth Caravan Holidays ★★★
Holiday Park
1 Crow Hill, Bolingey,
Perranporth TR6 0DG
t (01872) 572385
w caravanscornwall.co.uk

PERROTTS BROOK
Gloucestershire

Mayfield Touring Park ★★★★
Touring Park
Cheltenham Road, Bagendon
GL7 7BH
t (01285) 831301
e mayfield-park@cirencester.
fsbusiness.co.uk
w mayfieldpark.co.uk

PLYMOUTH
Devon

Plymouth Sound Caravan Club Site ★★★★
Touring Park
Bovisand Lane, Down Thomas,
Plymouth PL9 0AE
t (01752) 862325
w caravanclub.co.uk

POLGOOTH
Cornwall

Saint Margaret's Holiday Bungalows ★★★★★
Holiday Park
Tregongeeves Lane, St Austell
PL26 7AX
t (01726) 74283

POLRUAN-BY-FOWEY
Cornwall

Polruan Holidays (Camping & Caravanning) ★★★★
Holiday, Touring & Camping Park
Townsend, Polruan PL23 1QH
t (01726) 870263
e polholiday@aol.com

POLZEATH
Cornwall

Polzeath Beach Holiday Park ★★★★
Holiday Park
Trenant Nook, Polzeath,
Wadebridge PL27 6ST
t (01208) 863320
e info@
polzeathbeachholidaypark.com
w polzeathbeachholidaypark.
com

Valley Caravan Park ★★
Holiday, Touring & Camping Park
Polzeath, Wadebridge
PL27 6SS
t (01208) 862391
e martin@valleycaravanpark.
co.uk
w valleycaravanpark.co.uk

POOLE
Somerset

Cadeside Caravan Club Site ★★★★
Touring Park
Nynehead Road, Wellington
TA21 9HN
t (01823) 663103
e enquiries@caravanclub.co.
uk
w caravanclub.co.uk

PORLOCK
Somerset

Burrowhayes Farm Caravan and Camping Site and Riding Stables ★★★★
Holiday, Touring & Camping Park
West Luccombe, Porlock,
Minehead TA24 8HT
t (01643) 862463
e info@burrowhayes.co.uk
w burrowhayes.co.uk

Porlock Caravan Park ★★★★
Holiday, Touring & Camping Park
Highbank, Porlock TA24 8ND
t (01643) 862269
e info@porlockcaravanpark.
co.uk
w porlockcaravanpark.co.uk

PORTH
Cornwall

Trevelgue Holiday Park ★★★
Holiday, Touring & Camping Park
Trevelgue Road, Porth,
Newquay TR8 4AS
t (01637) 851850

PORTHTOWAN
Cornwall

Porthtowan Tourist Park ★★★★
Touring & Camping Park
Mile Hill, Porthtowan, Truro
TR4 8TY
t (01209) 890256
e admin@
porthtowantouristpark.co.uk
w porthtowantouristpark.co.uk

PORTLAND
Dorset

Cove Holiday Park ★★★★★
Holiday Park
Pennsylvania Road, Portland
DT5 1HU
t (01305) 821286
e enquiries@coveholidaypark.
co.uk
w coveholidaypark.co.uk

PORTREATH
Cornwall

Cambrose Touring Park ★★★
Touring & Camping Park
Portreath Road, Cambrose,
Redruth TR16 4HT
t (01209) 890747
e cambrosetouringpark@
supanet.com
w cambrosetouringpark.co.uk

Tehidy Holiday Park ★★★★
Holiday, Touring & Camping Park
Harris Mill, Illogan, Redruth
TR16 4JQ
t (01209) 216489
e holiday@tehidy.co.uk
w tehidy.co.uk

PRAA SANDS
Cornwall

Lower Pentreath Caravan & Campsite ★★★
Holiday, Touring & Camping Park
The Old Farm, Lower
Pentreath, Penzance TR20 9TL
t (01736) 763221
e andrew.wearne1@
btinternet.com
w theoldfarmpraasands.co.uk

PRESTON
Dorset

Weymouth Bay Holiday Park ★★★★
Holiday Park
Preston Road, Preston,
Weymouth DT3 6BQ
t (01305) 832271
w havenholidays.com

RATTERY
Devon

Edeswell Farm ★★★
Holiday Park
Rattery, South Brent TQ10 9LN
t (01364) 72177
e welcome@edeswellfarm.co.
uk
w edeswellfarm.co.uk

REDHILL
Somerset

Brook Lodge Farm Touring Caravan and Tent Park ★★★
Touring & Camping Park
Brook Lodge Farm, Cowslip
Green BS40 5RB
t (01934) 862311
e brooklodgefarm@aol.com
w brooklodgefarm.com

REDRUTH
Cornwall

Lanyon Caravan & Camping Park ★★★★
Holiday, Touring & Camping Park
Loscombe Lane, Four Lanes,
Redruth TR16 6LP
t (01209) 313474
e jamierielly@btconnect.com
w lanyonholidaypark.co.uk

RELUBBUS
Cornwall

River Valley Country Park ★★★★★
Holiday Park
Relubbus, Penzance TR20 9ER
t (01736) 763398
e rivervalley@surfbay.dircon.
co.uk
w surfbayholidays.co.uk

RODNEY STOKE
Somerset

Bucklegrove Caravan & Camping Park ★★★★
Holiday, Touring & Camping Park
Wells Road, Cheddar
BS27 3UZ
t (01749) 870261

ROSUDGEON
Cornwall

Kenneggy Cove Holiday Park ★★★★ **ROSE AWARD**
Holiday, Touring & Camping Park
Higher Kenneggy, Rosudgeon, Penzance TR20 9AU
t (01736) 763453
e enquiries@kenneggycove.co.uk
w kenneggycove.co.uk

ROUSDON
Devon

Pinewood Homes ★★★★★
Holiday Park
Sidmouth Road, Rousdon, Lyme Regis DT7 3RD
t (01297) 22055
e info@pinewood.uk.net
w pinewood.uk.net

RUAN MINOR
Cornwall

Silver Sands Holiday Park ★★★★
Holiday, Touring & Camping Park
Gwendreath, Nr Kennack Sands, Ruan Minor, Helston TR12 7LZ
t (01326) 290631
e enquiries@silversandsholidaypark.co.uk
w silversandsholidaypark.co.uk

ST AGNES
Cornwall

Beacon Cottage Farm Touring Park ★★★★
Touring Park
Beacon Drive, St Agnes TR5 0NU
t (01872) 552347
e beaconcottagefarm@lineone.net
w beaconcottagefarmholidays.co.uk

ST AUSTELL
Cornwall

Carlyon Bay Caravan & Camping ★★★★★
Touring & Camping Park
Cypress Avenue, Carlyon Bay, St Austell PL25 3RE
t (01726) 812735
e holidays@carlyonbay.net
w carlyonbay.net

River Valley Holiday Park ★★★★★ **ROSE AWARD**
Holiday, Touring & Camping Park
Pentewan Road, London Apprentice, St Austell PL26 7AP
t (01726) 73533
w cornwall-holidays.co.uk

Sun Valley Holiday Park ★★★★★
Holiday, Touring & Camping Park
Pentewan Road, St Austell PL26 6DJ
t (01726) 843266

Trencreek Farm Holiday Park ★★★
Holiday, Touring & Camping Park
Hewaswater, St Austell PL26 7JG
t (01726) 882540
e bookings@trencreek.co.uk
w trencreek.co.uk

ST BURYAN
Cornwall

Camping & Caravanning Club (Sennen Cove) ★★★★
Touring & Camping Park
Higher Tregiffian Farm, St Buryan, Penzance TR19 6JB
t (01736) 871588
w campingandcaravanningclub.co.uk

ST EWE
Cornwall

Heligan Woods Camping & Caravan Park ★★★★
Holiday, Touring & Camping Park
Mevagissey, St Austell PL26 6BT
t (01726) 843485
e info@pentewan.co.uk
w pentewan.co.uk

ST GENNYS
Cornwall

Camping & Caravanning Club (Bude) ★★★★
Touring & Camping Park
Gillards Moor, St Gennys, Bude EX23 0BG
t (01840) 230650
w campingandcaravanningclub.co.uk

ST IVES
Cornwall

Ayr Camping & Touring Park ★★★★
Holiday, Touring & Camping Park
Higher Ayr, St Ives TR26 1EJ
t (01736) 795855
e recept@ayrholidaypark.co.uk
w ayrholidaypark.co.uk

Little Trevarrack Holiday Park ★★★★
Touring & Camping Park
Laity Lane, Carbis Bay, St Ives TR26 3HW
t (01736) 797580
e info@littletrevarrack.co.uk
w littletrevarrack.co.uk

Polmanter Tourist Park ★★★★★
Touring & Camping Park
St Ives TR26 3LX
t (01736) 795640
e reception@polmanter.com
w polmanter.com

Trevalgan Touring Park, St Ives ★★★★
Touring & Camping Park
Trevalgan Touring Park, St Ives TR26 3BJ
t (01736) 795855
w trevalgantouringpark.co.uk

ST JUST-IN-PENWITH
Cornwall

Roselands Caravan Park ★★★★
Holiday, Touring & Camping Park
Dowran, St Just, Penzance TR19 7RS
t (01736) 788571
e info@roselands.co.uk
w roselands.co.uk

ST JUST IN ROSELAND
Cornwall

Trethem Mill Touring Park ★★★★★
Touring & Camping Park
Trethem, St Just in Roseland TR2 5JF
t (01872) 580504
e reception@trethem.com
w trethem.com

ST LEONARDS
Dorset

Back-of-Beyond Touring Park ★★★★
Touring & Camping Park
Ringwood Road, St Leonards BH24 2SB
t (01202) 876968
e melandsuepike@aol.com
w backofbeyondtouringpark.co.uk

Forest Edge Holiday Park ★★★
Touring & Camping Park
229 Ringwood Road, St Leonards, Ringwood BH24 2SD
t (01590) 648331
e holidays@shorefield.co.uk
w shorefield.co.uk

Oakdene Forest Park ★★★★
Holiday Park
St Leonards BH24 2RZ
t (01590) 648331
e holidays@shorefield.co.uk
w shorefield.co.uk

ST MERRYN
Cornwall

Trethias Farm Caravan Park ★★★
Touring Park
Trethias, St Merryn, Padstow PL28 8PL
t (01841) 520323

Trevean Farm ★★★★
Holiday, Touring & Camping Park
St Merryn, Padstow PL28 8PR
t (01841) 520772
e trevean.info@virgin.net

ST MINVER
Cornwall

Dinham Farm Family Cvn & Cmp Park ★★★★
Holiday, Touring & Camping Park
St Minver, Wadebridge PL27 6RH
t (01208) 812878
e info@dinhamfarm.co.uk
w dinhamfarm.co.uk

Little Dinham Woodland Caravan Park ★★★★
Holiday Park
St Minver, Rock, Wadebridge PL27 6RH
t (01208) 812538
e littledinham@hotmail.com
w littledinham.co.uk

St Minver Holiday Park ★★★★
Holiday, Touring & Camping Park
St Minver, Wadebridge PL27 6RR
t 0871 641 0191
e enquiries@parkdeanholidays.co.uk
w parkdeanholidays.co.uk

ST TUDY
Cornwall

Hengar Manor Country Park ★★★★★
Holiday Park
St Tudy, Bodmin PL30 3PL
t (01208) 850382
e holidays@hengarmanor.co.uk
w hengarmanor.co.uk

Michaelstow Manor Holiday Park ★★★★
Holiday Park
Michaelstow, St Tudy, Bodmin PL30 3PB
t (01208) 850244
e michaelstow@eclipse.co.uk
w michaelstow-holidays.co.uk

SALCOMBE
Devon

Bolberry House Farm Caravan & Camping ★★★
Holiday, Touring & Camping Park
Bolberry, Malborough, Kingsbridge TQ7 3DY
t (01548) 561251
e bolberry.house@virgin.net
w bolberryparks.co.uk

Higher Rew Touring Caravan & Camping Park ★★★★
Touring & Camping Park
Higher Rew, Malborough,
Kingsbridge TQ7 3DW
t (01548) 842681
e enquiries@higherrew.co.uk
w higherrew.co.uk

SALCOMBE REGIS
Devon

Kings Down Tail Caravan & Camping Park ★★★★
Touring & Camping Park
Salcombe Regis, Sidmouth
EX10 0PD
t (01297) 680313
e info@kingsdowntail.co.uk
w kingsdowntail.co.uk

SALISBURY
Wiltshire

Camping And Caravanning Club Site Salisbury ★★★★
Touring & Camping Park
Hudson's Field, Castle Road,
Salisbury SP1 3RR
t (01722) 320713
w campingandcaravanning
club.co.uk

SANDY BAY
Devon

Devon Cliffs Holiday Park ★★★★
Holiday Park
Sandy Bay, Exmouth EX8 5BT
t (01395) 226226
w havenholiday.co.uk

SEATON
Devon

Axe Vale Caravan Park ★★★★
Holiday Park
Colyford Road, Seaton
EX12 2DF
t (01297) 21342
e info@axevale.co.uk
w axevale.co.uk

Lyme Bay Holiday Village ★★★
Holiday Park
7 Harbour Road, Seaton
EX12 2NE
t (01297) 626800
w lymebayholidayvillage.co.uk

SEEND
Wiltshire

Camping and Caravanning Club Site Devizes ★★★★
Touring & Camping Park
Spout Lane, Seend, Melksham
SN12 6RN
t (01380) 828839
w campingandcaravanning
club.co.uk

SENNEN
Cornwall

Sea View Holiday Park ★★★
Holiday, Touring & Camping Park
Sennen, Penzance TR19 7AD
t (01736) 871266

SHALDON
Devon

Coast View Holiday Park ★★★
Holiday, Touring & Camping Park
Torquay Road, Shaldon,
Teignmouth TQ14 0BG
t (01626) 872392
e info@coast-view.co.uk
w coast-view.co.uk

Devon Valley Holiday Village ★★★★
Holiday Park
Coombe Road, Ringmore,
Teignmouth TQ14 0EY
t 0870 442 9750
e info@devonvalley.biz
w southdevonholidays.biz

SIDBURY
Devon

Putts Corner Caravan Club Site ★★★★★
Touring Park
Sidbury, Sidmouth EX10 0QQ
t (01404) 42875
w caravanclub.co.uk

SIDMOUTH
Devon

Salcombe Regis Camping and Caravan Park ★★★★★ ROSE AWARD
Holiday, Touring & Camping Park
Salcombe Regis, Sidmouth
EX10 0JH
t (01395) 514303
e contact@salcombe-regis.co.uk
w salcombe-regis.co.uk

SIXPENNY HANDLEY
Dorset

Church Farm Caravan & Camping Park ★★★
Touring & Camping Park
High Street, Sixpenny Handley,
Salisbury SP5 5ND
t (01725) 552563
e churchfarmcandcpark@
yahoo.co.uk
w churchfarmcandcpark.co.uk

SLAPTON
Devon

Camping & Caravanning Club Site – Slapton Sands ★★★★
Touring & Camping Park
Middle Grounds, Slapton,
Kingsbridge TQ7 2QW
t (01548) 580538
w campingandcaravanning
club.co.uk

SOUTH CERNEY
Gloucestershire

Hoburne Cotswold ★★★★
Holiday Park
Broadway Lane, South Cerney,
Cirencester GL7 5UQ
t (01285) 860216
e cotswold@hoburne.com
w hoburne.com

SWANAGE
Dorset

Cauldron Barn Farm Caravan Park ★★★★
Holiday, Touring & Camping Park
Cauldron Barn Road, Swanage
BH19 1QQ
t (01929) 422080
e info@
cauldronbarncaravanpark.co.uk
w cauldronbarncaravanpark.
co.uk

Haycraft Caravan Club Site ★★★★★
Touring Park
Haycrafts Lane, Swanage
BH19 3EB
t (01929) 480572
w caravanclub.co.uk

Swanage Caravan Park ★★★★
Holiday Park
Panorama Road, Swanage
BH19 2QS
t (01929) 422130

Swanage Coastal Park ★★★
Holiday, Touring & Camping Park
Priests Way, Swanage
BH19 2RS
t (01590) 648331
e holidays@shorefield.co.uk
w shorefield.co.uk

Ulwell Cottage Caravan Park ★★★★
Holiday, Touring & Camping Park
Ulwell BH19 3DG
t (01929) 422823
e enq@ulwellcottagepark.co.
uk
w ulwellcottagepark.co.uk

Ulwell Farm Caravan Park ★★★
Holiday Park
Ulwell, Swanage BH19 3DG
t (01929) 422825
e ulwell.farm@virgin.net
w ukparks.co.uk/ulwellfarm

TAUNTON
Somerset

Ashe Farm Caravan and Campsite ★★★
Holiday, Touring & Camping Park
Thornfalcon, Taunton
TA3 5NW
t (01823) 442567
e camping@ashe-farm.fsnet.
co.uk

Holly Bush Park ★★★★
Touring & Camping Park
Culmhead, Taunton TA3 7EA
t (01823) 421515
e info@hollybushpark.com
w hollybushpark.com

TAVISTOCK
Devon

Harford Bridge Holiday Park ★★★★ ROSE AWARD
Holiday, Touring & Camping Park
Peter Tavy, Tavistock PL19 9LS
t (01822) 810349
e enquiry@harfordbridge.co.
uk
w harfordbridge.co.uk

Langstone Manor Caravan and Camping Park ★★★★ ROSE AWARD
Holiday, Touring & Camping Park
Moortown, Tavistock PL19 9JZ
t (01822) 613371
e jane@langstone-manor.co.
uk
w langstone-manor.co.uk

Woodovis Park ★★★★★
Holiday, Touring & Camping Park
Gulworthy, Tavistock PL19 8NY
t (01822) 832968
e info@woodovis.com
w woodovis.com

TEDBURN ST MARY
Devon

Springfield Holiday Park ★★★
Holiday, Touring & Camping Park
Tedburn St Mary, Exeter
EX6 6EW
t (01647) 24242
e enquiries@
springfieldholidaypark.co.uk
w springfieldholidaypark.co.uk

TEIGNGRACE
Devon

Twelve Oaks Farm Caravan Park ★★★★
Touring & Camping Park
Teigngrace, Newton Abbot
TQ12 6QT
t (01626) 352769
e info@twelveoaksfarm.co.uk
w twelveoaksfarm.co.uk

TEWKESBURY
Gloucestershire

Croft Farm Waterpark ★★★
Holiday & Touring Park
Croft Farm, Bredons Hardwick,
Nr Tewkesbury GL20 7EE
t (01684) 772321
e enquiries@croftfarmleisure.
co.uk

Tewkesbury Abbey Caravan Club Site ★★★★
Touring & Camping Park
Gander Lane, Tewkesbury
GL20 5PG
t (01684) 294035
w caravanclub.co.uk

TINTAGEL
Cornwall

Trewethett Farm Caravan Club Site ★★★★★
Touring & Camping Park
Trethevy, Tintagel PL34 0BQ
t (01840) 770222
w caravanclub.co.uk

TORQUAY
Devon

TLH Leisure Resort ★★★★
Derwent Hotel, 22-28 Belgrave Road, Torquay TQ2 5HT
t (01803) 400500
e rooms@tlh.co.uk
w tlh.co.uk

Torquay Holiday Park ★★★★
Holiday Park
Kingskerswell Road, Torquay TQ2 8JU
t 0871 641 0191
e enquiries@
parkdeanholidays.co.uk
w parkdeanholidays.co.uk

Widdicombe Farm Touring Park ★★★★
Holiday, Touring & Camping Park
Marldon, Paignton TQ3 1ST
t (01803) 558325
e info@widdicombefarm.co.uk
w torquaytouring.co.uk

TOTNES
Devon

Broadleigh Farm Park ★★★★
Touring & Camping Park
Coombe House Lane, Aish, Stoke Gabriel, Totnes TQ9 6PU
t (01803) 782309
e enquiries@broadleighfarm.co.uk
w gotorbay.com/accommodation

Steamer Quay Caravan Club Site ★★★
Touring Park
Steamer Quay Road, Totnes TQ9 5AL
t (01803) 862738

TREGURRIAN
Cornwall

Camping and Caravanning Club Site Tregurrian ★★★★
Touring & Camping Park
Newquay TR8 4AE
t (01637) 860448

TRURO
Cornwall

Summer Valley Touring Park ★★★★
Touring Park
Shortlanesend, Truro TR4 9DW
t (01872) 277878
e res@summervalley.co.uk
w summervalley.co.uk

UMBERLEIGH
Devon

Camping & Caravanning Club Site Umberleigh ★★★★
Touring & Camping Park
Over Weir, Umberleigh EX37 9DU
t (01769) 560009
w campingandcaravanningclub.co.uk

UPTON
Somerset

Lowtrow Cross Caravan & Camping Site ★★★★
Holiday, Touring & Camping Park
Lowtrow Cross, Wiveliscombe TA4 2DB
t (01398) 371199
e info@lowtrowcross.co.uk
w lowtrowcross.co.uk

VERYAN
Cornwall

Camping & Caravanning Club (Veryan) ★★★★
Touring & Camping Park
Tretheake Manor, Veryan, Truro TR2 5PP
t (01872) 501658
w campingandcaravanningclub.co.uk

WADEBRIDGE
Cornwall

Little Bodieve Holiday Park (Camping) ★★★★
Holiday, Touring & Camping Park
Bodieve Road, Wadebridge PL27 6EG
t (01208) 812323
e berry@littlebodieveholidaypark.fsnet.co.uk
w littlebodieve.co.uk

WAREHAM
Dorset

Birchwood Tourist Park ★★★★
Touring & Camping Park
Bere Road, Coldharbour, Wareham BH20 7PA
t (01929) 554763
e birchwoodtouristpark@hotmail.com

The Lookout Holiday Park ★★★★ ROSE AWARD
Holiday, Touring & Camping Park
Corfe Road, Stoborough, Wareham BH20 5AZ
t (01929) 552546
e enquiries@caravan-sites.co.uk
w caravan-sites.co.uk

Wareham Forest Tourist Park Ltd ★★★★★
Touring & Camping Park
Bere Road, North Trigon, Wareham BH20 7NZ
t (01929) 551393
e holiday@wareham-forest.co.uk
w wareham-forest.co.uk

WARMINSTER
Wiltshire

Longleat Caravan Club Site ★★★★★
Touring Park
Longleat, Warminster BA12 7NL
t (01985) 844663
w caravanclub.co.uk

WARMWELL
Dorset

Warmwell Caravan Park ★★★★
Holiday, Touring & Camping Park
Warmwell, Dorchester DT2 8JD
t (01305) 852313
e stay@warmwellcaravanpark.co.uk
w warmwellcaravanpark.co.uk

Warmwell Leisure Resort ★★★★
Holiday Park
Warmwell, Dorchester DT2 8JE
t 0871 641 0191
e enquiries@parkdeanholidays.co.uk
w parkdeanholidays.co.uk

WATERROW
Somerset

Waterrow Touring Park ★★★★★ ROSE AWARD
Touring & Camping Park
Waterrow, Taunton TA4 2AZ
t (01984) 623464
w waterrowpark.co.uk

WEMBURY
Devon

Churchwood Valley Holiday Cabins ★★★★
Holiday Park
Churchwood Valley, Wembury Bay, Plymouth PL9 0DZ
t (01752) 862382
e churchwoodvalley@btinternet.com
w churchwoodvalley.com

WEST BAY
Dorset

West Bay Holiday Park ★★★★
Holiday, Touring & Camping Park
West Bay, Bridport DT6 4HB
t 0871 641 0191
e enquiries@parkdeanholidays.co.uk
w parkdeanholidays.co.uk

WEST BEXINGTON
Dorset

Gorselands Caravan Park ★★★★
Holiday Park
West Bexington Road, West Bexington, Dorchester DT2 9DJ
t (01308) 897232
w gorselands.co.uk

WEST DOWN
Devon

Brook Lea ★★★★
Touring Park
Brooklea Caravan Club Site, Ilfracombe EX34 8NE
t (01271) 862848
e debby.towers@caravanclub.co.uk

WEST LULWORTH
Dorset

Durdle Door Holiday Park ★★★
Holiday, Touring & Camping Park
West Lulworth, Wareham BH20 5PU
t (01929) 400200
e durdle.door@lulworth.com
w lulworth.com

WEST QUANTOXHEAD
Somerset

St Audries Bay ★★★★
Holiday & Touring Park
West Quantoxhead, Williton TA4 4DY
t (01984) 632515
e info@staudriesbay.co.uk
w staudriesbay.co.uk

WESTON
Devon

Oakdown Touring and Holiday Caravan Park ★★★★★
Holiday & Touring Park
Weston, Sidmouth EX10 0PH
t (01297) 680387
e enquiries@oakdown.co.uk
w oakdown.co.uk

Stoneleigh Holiday and Leisure Village ★★★★
Weston, Sidmouth EX10 0PJ
t (01395) 513619
w stoneleighholidays.co.uk

WESTON-SUPER-MARE
Somerset

Carefree Holiday Park ★★★★★
Holiday Park
12 Beach Road, Kewstoke BS22 9UZ
t (01934) 624541
e crichardson@hotmail.co.uk

Country View Holiday Park ★★★★
Holiday, Touring & Camping Park
29 Sand Road, Sand Bay, Weston-super-Mare BS22 9U
t (01934) 627595
w cvhp.co.uk

Dulhorn Farm Camping Site ★★★
Touring & Camping Park
Weston Road, Lympsham, Weston-super-Mare BS24 0JO
t (01934) 750298

Sand Bay Holiday Village
★★★
57 Beach Road, Kewstoke
BS22 9UR
t (01934) 428200
w sandbayholidayvillage.co.uk

**Weston-super-Mare
Camping and Caravanning
Club Site ★★★**
Touring Park
West End Farm, Locking
BS24 8RH
(01934) 822548

WESTWARD HO!
Devon

Beachside Holiday Park
★★★★
Holiday Park
Merley Road, Westward Ho!,
Bideford EX39 1JX
0845 601 2541 &
845 601 2541
e beachside@surfbay.dircon.
o.uk
w beachsideholidays.co.uk

Surf Bay Holiday Park
★★★
Holiday Park
Golf Links Road, Westward
Ho!, Bideford EX39 1HD
0845 601132 &
845 601 1132
surfbayholidaypark@
urfbay.dircon.co.uk
w surfbay.co.uk

WEYMOUTH
Dorset

Chesil Beach Holiday Park
★★★★
Holiday Park
Chesil Beach, Portland Road,
Weymouth DT4 9AG
(01305) 773233
info@chesilholidays.co.uk
chesilholidays.co.uk

**Crossways Caravan Club
Site ★★★★**
Touring Park
Crossways, Dorchester
DT2 8BE
(01305) 852032
caravanclub.co.uk

East Fleet Farm Touring Park
★★★
Touring & Camping Park
Fleet Lane, Chickerell,
Weymouth DT3 4DW
(01305) 785768
enquiries@eastfleet.co.uk
eastfleet.co.uk

Littlesea Holiday Park
★★★★★
*Holiday, Touring & Camping
Park*
Lynch Lane, Weymouth
DT4 9DT
t (01305) 774414
e david.bennett@bourne-
leisure.co.uk

Pebble Bank Caravan Park
★★★
*Holiday, Touring & Camping
Park*
90 Camp Road, Wyke Regis,
Weymouth DT4 9HF
t (01305) 774844
e info@pebblebank.co.uk
w pebblebank.co.uk

Seaview Holiday Park ★★★
*Holiday, Touring & Camping
Park*
Preston, Weymouth DT3 6DZ
t (01305) 833037
w havenholidays.com

Waterside Holiday Park
★★★★★
Holiday & Touring Park
Bowleaze Coveway,
Weymouth DT3 6PP
t (01305) 833103
e info@watersideholidays.co.
uk
w watersideholidays.co.uk

WHITE CROSS
Cornwall

White Acres Country Park
★★★★★
*Holiday, Touring & Camping
Park*
Whitecross, Newquay
TR8 4LW
t 0871 641 0191
e enquiries@
parkdeanholidays.co.uk
w parkdeanholidays.co.uk

WIMBORNE MINSTER
Dorset

Merley Court Touring Park
★★★★★
Touring Park
Merley Court, Merley,
Wimborne BH21 3AA
t (01590) 648331
e holidays@shorefield.co.uk
w shorefield.co.uk

**Wilksworth Farm Caravan
Park ★★★★★**
Touring & Camping Park
Cranborne Road, Furzehill,
Wimborne BH21 4HW
t (01202) 885467
e rayandwendy@
wilksworthfarmcaravanpark.co.
uk
w wilksworthfarmcaravanpark.
co.uk

WINCANTON
Somerset

**Wincanton Racecourse
Campsite ★★★**
Touring & Camping Park
Old Hill, Wincanton BA9 8BJ
t (01963) 34276
e enquiries@caravanclub.co.
uk
w caravanclub.co.uk

WINCHCOMBE
Gloucestershire

**Camping and Caravanning
Club Site Winchcombe**
★★★★
Touring & Camping Park
Brooklands Farm, Alderton,
Tewkesbury GL20 8NX
t (01242) 620259
w campingandcaravanning
club.co.uk

WINSFORD
Somerset

**Halse Farm Caravan & Tent
Park ★★★★**
Touring & Camping Park
Winsford, Minehead TA24 7JL
t (01643) 851259
e brit@halsefarm.co.uk
w halsefarm.co.uk

WOODLANDS
Dorset

**Camping & Caravanning
Club Site Verwood, New
Forest ★★★**
Touring & Camping Park
Sutton Hill, Woodlands,
Wimborne BH21 8NQ
t (01202) 822763
w campingandcaravanning
club.co.uk

WOOL
Dorset

Whitemead Caravan Park
★★★★
Touring & Camping Park
East Burton Road, Wool,
Wareham BH20 6HG
t (01929) 462241
e whitemeadcp@aol.com
w whitemeadcaravanpark.co.
uk

WOOLACOMBE
Devon

**Golden Coast Holiday
Village ★★★★**
Holiday Park
Station Road, Woolacombe
EX34 7HW
t (01271) 870343
e goodtimes@woolacombe.
com
w woolacombe.com

**Woolacombe Bay Holiday
Parcs (Cleavewood House)**
★★★★
*Holiday, Touring & Camping
Park*
Woolacombe EX34 7HW
t (01271) 870343

**Woolacombe Bay Holiday
Village ★★★★**
*Holiday, Touring & Camping
Park*
Seymour, Sandy Lane,
Woolacombe EX34 7AH
t (01271) 870343
e goodtimes@woolacombe.
com
w woolacombe.com

**Woolacombe Sands Holiday
Park ★★★★**
*Holiday, Touring & Camping
Park*
Beach Road, Woolacombe
EX34 7AF
t (01271) 870569
e lifesabeach@woolacombe-
sands.co.uk
w woolacombe-sands.co.uk

YEOVIL
Somerset

Long Hazel Park ★★★★
*Holiday, Touring & Camping
Park*
High Street, Sparkford, Yeovil
BA22 7JH
t (01963) 440002
e longhazelpark@hotmail.com
w sparkford.f9.co.uk/lhi.htm

Help before you go

When it comes to your next British break, the first stage of your journey could be closer than you think.

You've probably got a Tourist Information Centre nearby which is there to serve the local community – as well as visitors. Knowledgeable staff will be happy to help you, wherever you're heading.

Many Tourist Information Centres can provide you with maps and guides, and it's often possible to book accommodation and travel tickets too.

You'll find the address of your nearest centre in your local phone book, or look at the beginning of each regional section in this guide for a list of Official Partner Tourist Information Centres.

Further information

Views from Nottingham Castle,
Nottingham

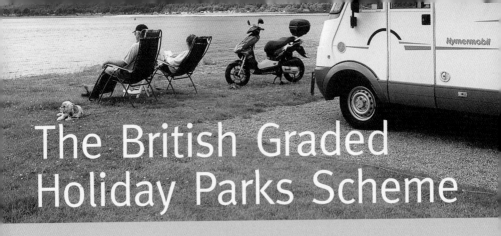

The British Graded Holiday Parks Scheme

When you're looking for a place to stay, you need a rating system you can trust. The British Graded Holiday Parks Scheme, operated jointly by the national tourist boards for England, Scotland, Wales and Northern Ireland, was devised in association with the British Holiday and Home Parks Association and the National Caravan Council. It gives you a clear guide of what to expect in an easy-to-understand form.

The process to arrive at a star rating is very thorough to ensure that when you make a booking you can be confident it will meet your expectations. Professional assessors visit parks annually and take into account over 50 separate aspects, from landscaping and layout to maintenance, customer care and, most importantly, cleanliness.

Strict guidelines are in place to ensure that every park is assessed to the same criteria. A random check is made of a sample of accommodation provided for hire (caravans, chalets etc) but the quality of the accommodation itself is not included in the grading assessment.

In addition to The British Graded Holiday Parks Scheme, VisitBritain operates a rating scheme for Holiday Villages. The assessor stays on the site overnight and grades the overall quality of the visitor experience, including accommodation, facilities, cleanliness, service and food.

So you can rest assured that when you choose a star-rated park or holiday village you won't be disappointed.

Holiday, touring and camping parks

Parks are required to meet progressively higher standards of quality as they move up the scale from one to five stars:

ONE STAR Acceptable
To achieve this grade, the park must be clean with good standards of maintenance and customer care.

TWO STAR Good
All the above points plus an improved level of landscaping, lighting, refuse disposal and maintenance. May be less expensive than more highly rated parks.

THREE STAR Very good
Most parks fall within this category; three stars represent the industry standard. The range of facilities provided may vary from park to park, but they will be of a very good standard and will be well maintained.

FOUR STAR Excellent
You can expect careful attention to detail in the provision of all services and facilities. Four star parks rank among the industry's best.

FIVE STAR Exceptional
Highest levels of customer care will be provided. All facilities will be maintained in pristine condition in attractive surroundings.

Holiday villages

Holiday Villages are assessed under a separate rating scheme and are awarded one to five stars based on both the quality of facilities and the range of services provided. The option to include breakfast and dinner is normally available. A variety of accommodation if offered, mostly in custom-built rooms such as chalets.

★ Simple, practical, no frills

★★ Well presented and well run

★★★ Good level of quality and comfort

★★★★ Excellent standard throughout

★★★★★ Exceptional with a degree of luxury

Advice and information

Making a booking

When enquiring about a place to stay, make sure you check prices, the quality rating, and other important details. You will also need to state your requirements clearly and precisely.

Booking by letter or email
Misunderstandings can easily happen over the telephone, so do request a written confirmation together with details of any terms and conditions.

Deposits and advance payments
In the case of caravan, camping and touring parks, and holiday villages the full charge often has to be paid in advance. This may be in two instalments – a deposit at the time of booking and the balance by, say, two weeks before the start of the booked period.

Cancellations

Legal contract
When you accept a booking that is offered to you, by telephone or in writing, you enter a legally binding contract with the proprietor. This means that if you cancel or fail to take up your booking or leave early, the proprietor may be entitled to compensation if he or she cannot re-let for all or a good part of the booked period. You will probably forfeit any deposit you have paid and may well be asked for an additional payment.

At the time of booking you should be advised of what charges would be made in the event of cancelling the accommodation or leaving early. If this is not mentioned you should ask so that future disputes can be avoided. The proprietor cannot make a claim until after the booked period, and during that time he or she should make every effort to re-let the accommodation. If there is a dispute it is sensible for both sides to seek legal advice on the matter. If you do have to change your travel plans, it is in your own interests to let the proprietor know in writing as soon as possible, to give them a chance to re-let your accommodation.

And remember, if you book by telephone and are asked for your credit card number, you should check whether the proprietor intends charging your credit card account should you later cancel your booking. A proprietor should not be able to charge your credit card account with a cancellation fee unless he or she has made this clear at the time of your booking and you have agreed. However, to avoid later disputes, we suggest you check whether this is the intention.

Insurance
A travel or holiday insurance policy will safeguard you if you have to cancel or change your holiday plans. You can arrange a policy quite cheaply through your insurance company or travel agent.

Finding a park

Tourist signs similar to the one shown here are designed to help visitors find their park. They clearly show whether the park is for tents or caravans or both.

Tourist information centres throughout Britain are able to give campers and caravanners information about parks in their areas. Some tourist information centres have camping and caravanning advisory services that provide details of park availability and often assist with park booking.

Electric hook-up points

Most parks now have electric hook-up points for caravans and tents. Voltage is generally 240v AC, 50 cycles. Parks may charge extra for this facility, and it is advisable to check rates when making a booking.

Avoiding peak season

In the summer months of June to September, parks in popular areas such as North Wales, Cumbria, the West Country or the New Forest in Hampshire may become full. Campers should aim to arrive at parks early in the day or, where possible, should book in advance. Some parks have overnight holding areas for visitors who arrive late. This helps to prevent disturbing other campers and caravanners late at night and means that fewer visitors are turned away. Caravans or tents are directed to a pitch the following morning.

Other caravan and camping places

If you enjoy making your own route through Britain's countryside, it may interest you to know that the Forestry Commission operates campsites in Britain's Forest Parks as well as in the New Forest. Some offer reduced charges for youth organisations on organised camping trips, and all enquiries about them should be made, well in advance of your intended stay, to the Forestry Commission.

Bringing pets to Britain

Dogs, cats, ferrets and some other pet mammals can be brought into the UK from certain countries without having to undertake six months' quarantine on arrival provided they meet all the rules of the Pet Travel Scheme (PETS).

For full details, visit the PETS website at
w defra.gov.uk/animalh/quarantine/index.htm
or contact the PETS Helpline
t +44 (0)870 241 1710
e pets.helpline@defra.gsi.gov.uk
Ask for fact sheets which cover dogs and cats, ferrets or domestic rabbits and rodents.

What to expect at holiday, touring and camping parks

In addition to fulfilling its statutory obligations, including having applied for a certificate under the Fire Precautions Act 1971 (if applicable) and holding public liability insurance, and ensuring that all caravan holiday homes/chalets for hire and the park and all buildings and facilities thereon, the fixtures, furnishings, fittings and decor are maintained in sound and clean condition and are fit for the purposes intended, the management is required to undertake the following:

- To ensure high standards of courtesy, cleanliness, catering and service appropriate to the type of park;

- To describe to all visitors and prospective visitors the amenities, facilities and services provided by the park and/or caravan holiday homes/chalets whether by advertisement, brochure, word of mouth or other means;

- To allow visitors to see the park or caravan holiday homes/chalets for hire, if requested, before booking;

- To present grading awards and/or any other national tourist board awards unambiguously;

- To make clear to visitors exactly what is included in prices quoted for the park or caravan holiday homes/chalets, meals and refreshments, including service charge, taxes and other surcharges. Details of charges, if any, for heating or for additional services or facilities available should also be made clear;

- To adhere to, and not to exceed, prices current at time of occupation for caravan holiday homes/chalets or other services;

- To advise visitors at the time of booking, and subsequently if any change, if the caravan holiday home/chalet or pitch offered is in a different location or on another park, and to indicate the location of this and any difference in comfort and amenities;

- To give each visitor, on request, details of payments due and a receipt if required;

- To advise visitors at the time of booking of the charges that might be incurred if the booking is subsequently cancelled;

- To register all guests on arrival;

- To deal promptly and courteously with all visitors and prospective visitors, including enquiries, requests, reservations, correspondence and complaints;

- To allow a national tourist board representative reasonable access to the park and/or caravan holiday homes/chalet whether by prior appointment or on an unannounced assessment, to confirm that the VisitBritain Code of Conduct is being observed and that the appropriate quality standard is being maintained;

- The operator must comply with the provision of the caravan industry Codes of Practice.

What to expect at holiday villages

The operator/manager is required to undertake the following:

- To maintain standards of guest care, cleanliness, and service appropriate to the type of establishment;

- To describe accurately in any advertisement, brochure, or other printed or electronic media, the facilities and services provided;

- To make clear to visitors exactly what is included in all prices quoted for accommodation, including taxes, and any other surcharges. Details of charges for additional services/facilities should also be made clear;

- To give a clear statement of the policy on cancellations to guests at the time of booking ie by telephone, fax, email as well as information given in a printed format;

- To adhere to, and not to exceed prices quoted at the time of booking for accommodation and other services;

- To advise visitors at the time of booking, and subsequently of any change, if the accommodation offered is in an unconnected annexe or similar, and to indicate the location of such accommodation and any difference in comfort and/or amenities from accommodation in the establishment;

- To give each visitor, on request, details of payments due and a receipt, if required;

- To register all guests on arrival;

- To deal promptly and courteously with all enquiries, requests, bookings and correspondence from visitors;

- Ensure complaint handling procedures are in place and that complaints received are investigated promptly and courteously and that the outcome is communicated to the visitor;

- To give due consideration to the requirements of visitors with special needs, and to make suitable provision where applicable;

- To provide public liability insurance or comparable arrangement and to comply with applicable planning, safety and other statutory requirements;

- To allow a national tourist board representative reasonable access to the establishment, on request, to confirm the VisitBritain Code of Conduct is being observed.

Comments and complaints

Information

The proprietors themselves supply the descriptions of their establishments and other information for the entries (except ratings). They have all signed a declaration that their information conforms to the Trade Description Acts 1968 and 1972. VisitBritain cannot guarantee the accuracy of information in this guide, and accepts no responsibility for any error or misrepresentation.

All liability for loss, disappointment, negligence or other damage caused by reliance on the information contained in this guide, or in the event of bankruptcy or liquidation or cessation of trade of any company, individual or firm mentioned, is hereby excluded. We strongly recommend that you carefully check prices and other details when you book your accommodation.

Problems

Of course, we hope you will not have cause for complaint, but problems do occur from time to time.

If you are dissatisfied with anything, make your complaint to the management immediately. Then the management can take action at once to investigate the matter and put things right. The longer you leave a complaint, the harder it is to deal with it effectively.

In certain circumstances, VisitBritain may look into complaints. However, VisitBritain has no statutory control over establishments or their methods of operating. VisitBritain cannot become involved in legal or contractual matters or in seeking financial compensation.

If you do have problems that have not been resolved by the proprietor and which you would like to bring to our attention, please write to:

England
Quality in Tourism, Farncombe House, Broadway, Worcestershire WR12 7LJ

Scotland
Quality and Standards, VisitScotland, Thistle House, Beechwood Park North, Inverness IV2 3ED

Wales
VisitWales, Ty Glyndwr, Treowain Enterprise Park, Machynlleth, Powys SY20 8WW

Useful contacts

British Holiday & Home Parks Association

Chichester House, 6 Pullman Court,
Great Western Road, Gloucester GL1 3ND
t   (01452) 526911 (enquiries and brochure requests)
w parkholidayengland.org.uk

Professional UK park owners are represented by the British Holiday and Home Parks Association. Over 3,000 parks are in membership, and each year welcome millions of visitors seeking quality surroundings in which to enjoy a good value stay.

Parks provide caravan holiday homes and lodges for hire, and pitches for your own touring caravan, motor home or tent. On many, you can opt to buy your own holiday home.

A major strength of the UK's park industry is its diversity. Whatever your idea of holiday pleasure, there's sure to be a park which can provide it. If your preference is for a quiet, peaceful holiday in tranquil rural surroundings, you'll find many idyllic locations.

Alternatively, many parks are to be found at our most popular resorts – and reflect the holiday atmosphere with plenty of entertainment and leisure facilities. And for more adventurous families, parks often provide excellent bases from which to enjoy outdoor activities.

Literature available from BH&HPA includes a guide to over 600 parks which have this year achieved the David Bellamy Conservation Award for environmental excellence.

The Camping and Caravanning Club

Greenfields House, Westwood Way,
Coventry CV4 8JH
t   0845 130 7631
t   0845 130 7633 (advance bookings)
w campingandcaravanningclub.co.uk

Discover the peace and quiet of 100 award-winning Club Sites. Experience a different backdrop to your holiday every time you go away, with a choice of sites in the lakes and mountains, coastal and woodland glades or cultural and heritage locations.

The Club is proud of its prestigious pedigree and regularly achieves awards for spotless campsites, friendly service and caring for the environment – a guarantee that you will enjoy your holiday.

Non-members are welcome at the majority of our sites and we offer special deals for families, backpackers, overseas visitors and members aged 55 and over.

For more details please refer to our entries listed at the back of this publication or telephone 0845 130 7632 to request a free guide to the club.

The Caravan Club

East Grinstead House,
East Grinstead,
West Sussex RH19 1UA
t   (01342) 326944
w caravanclub.co.uk

The Caravan Club offers around 200 sites in the UK and Ireland. These include city locations such as London, Edinburgh, York and Chester, plus sites near leading heritage attractions such as Longleat, Sandringham, Chatsworth and Blenheim Palace. A further 20 sites are in National Parks.

Virtually all pitches have an electric hook-up point. The toilet blocks and play areas are of the highest quality. Friendly, knowledgeable site wardens are on hand too.

Most Caravan Club Sites are graded four or five stars according to The British Graded Holiday Parks Scheme, run by VisitBritain, so that you can be assured of quality at all times. Over 130 sites are open to non-members, but why not become a member and gain access to all sites, plus a further 2,500 Certificated Locations, rural sites for no more than five vans. Tent campers are welcome at over 60 sites.

Join The Club and you can save the cost of your subscription fee in just five nights with member discounts on site fees!

Forestry Commission

Heart of the National Forest, Bath Yard, Moira, Derbyshire DE12 6BD
t 0845 130 8223 (cabins)
t 0845 130 8224 (campsites)
w forestholidays.co.uk

Forest Holidays, a new partnership between the Forestry Commission and the Camping and Caravanning Club, have over 20 camping and caravan sites in stunning forest locations throughout Great Britain in addition to three cabins. Choose from locations such as the Scottish Highlands, the New Forest, Snowdonia National Park, the Forest of Dean, or the banks of Loch Lomond. Some sites are open all year and dogs are welcome at most. Advance bookings are accepted for many sites.

For a unique forest experience, call Forest Holidays for a brochure on 0845 130 8224 or visit our website.

The Motor Caravanners' Club Ltd

FREEPOST (TK 1292), Twickenham TW2 5BR
t (020) 8893 3883
f (020) 8893 8324
e info@motorcaravanners.eu
w motorcaravanners.eu

The Motor Caravanners' Club is authorised to issue the Camping Card International (CCI). It also produces a monthly magazine, Motor Caravanner, for all members. Member of The Federation Internationale de Camping et de Caravanning (FICC).

The National Caravan Council

The National Caravan Council, Catherine House, Victoria Road, Aldershot, Hampshire GU11 1SS
t (01252) 318251
w thecaravan.net

The National Caravan Council (NCC) is the trade body for the British caravan industry – not just touring caravans and motorhomes but also caravan holiday homes. It has in its membership parks, manufacturers, dealers and suppliers to the industry – all NCC member companies are committed continually to raise standards of technical and commercial excellence.

So, if you want to know where to buy a caravan, where to find a caravan holiday park or simply need advice on caravans and caravanning, see the website thecaravan.net where there is lots of helpful advice including:

- How to check whether the caravan, motorhome or caravan holiday home you are buying complies with European Standards and essential UK health and safety regulations (through the Certification scheme that the NCC operates).
- Where to find quality parks to visit on holiday.
- Where to find approved caravan and motorhome workshops for servicing and repair.

Caravan holidays are one of the most popular choices for holidaymakers in Britain – the NCC works closely with VisitBritain to promote caravan holidays in all their forms and parks that are part of the British Graded Quality Parks Scheme.

Help before you go

i When it comes to your next British break, the first stage of your journey could be closer than you think.

You've probably got a Tourist Information Centre nearby which is there to serve the local community – as well as visitors. Knowledgeable staff will be happy to help you, wherever you're heading.

Many Tourist Information Centres can provide you with maps and guides, and it's often possible to book accommodation and travel tickets too.

You'll find the address of your nearest centre in your local phone book, or look at the beginning of each regional section in this guide for a list of Official Partner Tourist Information Centres.

About the guide entries

Entries

All the sites featured in this guide have been assessed or have applied for assessment under The British Graded Holiday Parks Scheme. Assessment automatically entitles sites to a listing in this guide. Start your search for a place to stay by looking in the regional sections of this guide where proprietors have paid to have their site featured in either a standard entry (includes description, facilities and prices) or an enhanced entry (photograph and extended details). If you can't find what you're looking for, turn to the listing section on the yellow pages for an even wider choice of sites in England.

Locations

Places to stay are listed under the town, city or village where they are located. If a place is in the countryside, you may find it listed under a nearby village or town (providing it is within a seven-mile radius). Place names are listed alphabetically within each regional section of the guide, along with the name of the ceremonial county they are in and their map reference.

Map references

These refer to the colour location maps at the front of the guide. The first figure shown is the map number, the following letter and figure indicate the grid reference on the map. Only place names under which standard or enhanced entries (see above) feature appear on the maps. Some entries were included just before the guide went to press, so they do not appear on the maps.

Addresses

County names, which appear in the place headings, are not repeated in the entries. When you are writing, you should of course make sure you use the full address and postcode.

Telephone numbers

Booking telephone numbers are listed below the contact address for each entry. Area codes are shown in brackets.

Prices

The prices shown are only a general guide and include VAT where applicable; they were supplied to us by proprietors in summer 2007. Remember, changes may occur after the guide goes to press, so we strongly advise you to check prices when you book your accommodation.

Touring pitch prices are based on the minimum and maximum charges for one night for two persons, car and either caravan or tent. (Some parks may charge separately for car, caravan or tent, and for each person and there may be an extra charge for caravan awnings.) Minimum and maximum prices for caravan holiday homes are given per week.

Prices often vary through the year, and may be significantly lower outside peak holiday weeks. You can get details of other bargain packages that may be available from the sites themselves, regional tourism organisations or your local tourist information centre (TIC). Your local travel agent may also have information, and can help you make bookings.

Opening period

If an entry does not indicate an opening period, please check directly with the site.

Symbols

The at-a-glance symbols included at the end of each entry show many of the services and facilities available at each site. You will find the key to these symbols on the back-cover flap. Open out the flap and you can check the meanings of the symbols as you go.

Pets

Many places accept visitors with dogs, but we do advise that you check this when you book, and ask if there are any extra charges or rules about exactly where your pet is allowed. The acceptance of dogs is not always extended to cats, and it is strongly advised that cat owners contact the site well in advance. Some sites do not accept pets at all. Pets are welcome where you see this symbol 🐕.

The quarantine laws have changed in England, and dogs, cats and ferrets are able to come into Britain from over 50 countries. For details of the Pet Travel Scheme (PETS) please turn to page 312.

Chalets/villas for hire

Where a site has chalets or villas for hire this is indicated by this symbol ⬛. Please note that this type of accommodation is not necessarily included within the official quality rating for the park and it is advisable to contact the proprietor directly if you require further information.

Payment accepted

The types of payment accepted by a site are listed in the payment accepted section. If you plan to pay by card, check that your particular card is acceptable before you book. Some proprietors will charge you a higher rate if you pay by credit card rather than cash or cheque. The difference is to cover the percentage paid by the proprietor to the credit card company. When you book by telephone, you may be asked for your credit card number as confirmation. But remember, the proprietor may then charge your credit card account if you cancel your booking. See under Cancellations on page 311.

Awaiting confirmation of rating

At the time of going to press some parks featured in this guide had not yet been assessed for their rating for the year 2008 and so their new rating could not be included. Rating Applied For indicates this.

Country ways

The Countryside Rights of Way Act gives people new rights to walk on areas of open countryside and registered common land.

To find out where you can go and what you can do, as well as information about taking your dog to the countryside, go online at countrysideaccess.gov.uk.

And when you're out and about…

Always follow the Country Code

- Be safe – plan ahead and follow any signs
- Leave gates and property as you find them
- Protect plants and animals, and take your litter home
- Keep dogs under close control
- Consider other people

Getting around Britain

Britain is a place of perfect proportions – big enough to find a new place to discover, yet small enough to guarantee it's within easy reach. Getting from A to B can be easier than you think...

Planning your journey

Make transportdirect.info your first portal of call! It's the ultimate journey-planning tool to help you find the best way from your home to your destination by car or public transport. Decide on the quickest way to travel by comparing end-to-end journey times and routes. You can even buy train and coach tickets and find out about flights from a selection of airports.

With so many low-cost domestic flights, flying really is an option. Just imagine, you could finish work in Bishop's Stortford and be in Newquay just three hours later for a fun-packed weekend!

You can island hop too, to the Isle of Wight or the Isles of Scilly for a relaxing break. No worries.

If you're travelling by car and want an idea of distances check out the mileage chart overleaf. Or let the train take the strain – the National Rail network is also shown overleaf.

Think green

If you'd rather leave your car behind and travel by 'green transport' when visiting some of the attractions highlighted in this guide you'll be helping to reduce congestion and pollution as well as supporting conservation charities in their commitment to green travel.

The National Trust encourages visits made by non-car travellers. It offers admission discounts or a voucher for the tea room at a selection of its properties if you arrive on foot, cycle or public transport. (You'll need to produce a valid bus or train ticket if travelling by public transport.)

More information about The National Trust's work to encourage car-free days out can be found at nationaltrust.org.uk. Refer to the section entitled Information for Visitors.

To help you on your way you'll find a list of useful contacts at the end of this section.

Counties and regions at-a-glance

If you know what English county you wish to visit you'll find it in the regional section shown below.

County	Region
Bedfordshire	East of England
Berkshire	South East England
Bristol	South West England
Buckinghamshire	South East England
Cambridgeshire	East of England
Cheshire	England's Northwest
Cornwall	South West England
County Durham	North East England
Cumbria	England's Northwest
Derbyshire	East Midlands
Devon	South West England
Dorset	South West England
East Riding of Yorkshire	Yorkshire
East Sussex	South East England
Essex	East of England
Gloucestershire	South West England
Greater Manchester	England's Northwest
Hampshire	South East England
Herefordshire	Heart of England
Hertfordshire	East of England
Isle of Wight	South East England
Isles of Scilly	South West England
Kent	South East England
Lancashire	England's Northwest

County	Region
Leicestershire	East Midlands
Lincolnshire	East Midlands
Merseyside	England's Northwest
Norfolk	East of England
North Yorkshire	Yorkshire
Northamptonshire	East Midlands
Northumberland	North East England
Nottinghamshire	East Midlands
Oxfordshire	South East England
Rutland	East Midlands
Shropshire	Heart of England
Somerset	South West England
South Yorkshire	Yorkshire
Staffordshire	Heart of England
Suffolk	East of England
Surrey	South East England
Tees Valley	North East England
Tyne and Wear	North East England
Warwickshire	Heart of England
West Midlands	Heart of England
West Sussex	South East England
West Yorkshire	Yorkshire
Wiltshire	South West England
Worcestershire	Heart of England

To help readers we do not refer to unitary authorities in this guide.

By car and by train

Distance chart

The distances between towns on the chart below are given to the nearest mile, and are measured along routes based on the quickest travelling time, making maximum use of motorways or dual-carriageway roads. The chart is based upon information supplied by the Automobile Association.

To calculate the distance in kilometres multiply the mileage by 1.6

For example: Brighton to Dover
82 miles x 1.6 =131.2 kilometres

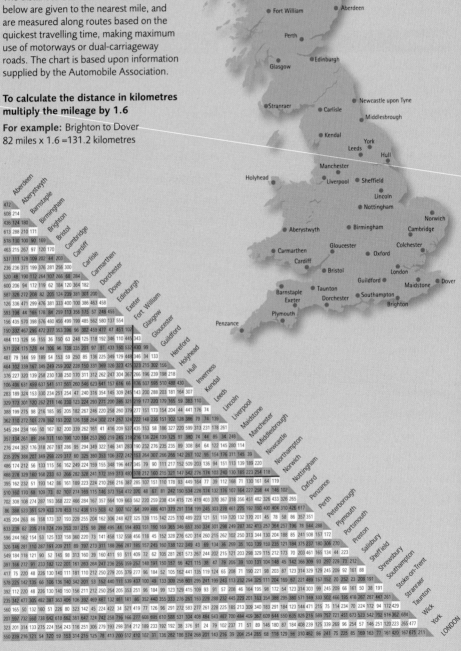

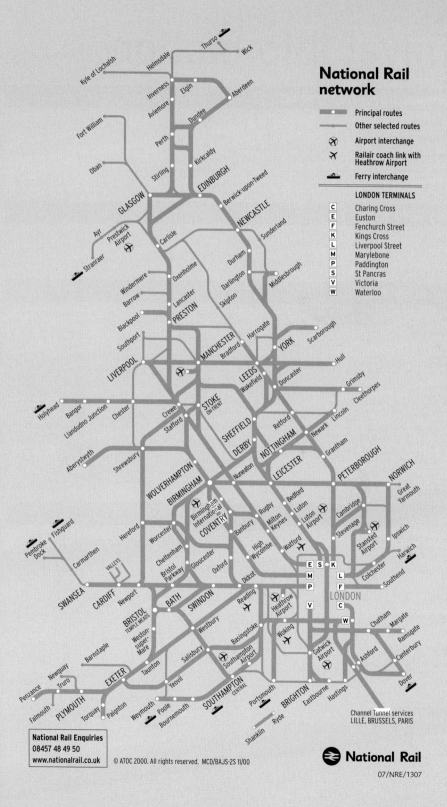

National Rail network

Principal routes

Other selected routes

Airport interchange

Railair coach link with Heathrow Airport

Ferry interchange

LONDON TERMINALS

C — Charing Cross
E — Euston
F — Fenchurch Street
K — Kings Cross
L — Liverpool Street
M — Marylebone
P — Paddington
S — St Pancras
V — Victoria
W — Waterloo

National Rail Enquiries
08457 48 49 50
www.nationalrail.co.uk

© ATOC 2000. All rights reserved. MCD/BAJS-2S 11/00

National Rail

07/NRE/1307

Channel Tunnel services
LILLE, BRUSSELS, PARIS

Travel information

General travel information

Streetmap	streetmap.co.uk	
Transport Direct	transportdirect.info	
Transport for London	tfl.gov.uk	(020) 7222 1234
Travel Services	departures-arrivals.com	
Traveline	traveline.org.uk	0870 200 2233

Bus & coach

Megabus	megabus.com	0901 331 0031
National Express	nationalexpress.com	0870 580 8080
WA Shearings	washearings.com	(01942) 824824

Car & car hire

AA	theaa.com	0870 600 0371
Green Flag	greenflag.co.uk	0845 246 1557
RAC	rac.co.uk	0870 572 2722
Alamo	alamo.co.uk	0870 400 4562*
Avis	avis.co.uk	0844 581 0147
Budget	budget.co.uk	0844 581 2231
Easycar	easycar.com	0906 333 3333
Enterprise	enterprise.com	0870 350 3000*
Hertz	hertz.co.uk	0870 844 8844*
Holiday Autos	holidayautos.co.uk	0870 400 4461
National	nationalcar.co.uk	0870 400 4581
Thrifty	thrifty.co.uk	(01494) 751500

Air

Airport information	a2btravel.com/airports	0870 888 1710
Air Southwest	airsouthwest.com	0870 043 4553
Blue Islands (Channel Islands)	blueislands.com	0845 620 2122
BMI	flybmi.com	0870 607 0555
BMI Baby	bmibaby.com	0871 224 0224
British Airways	ba.com	0870 850 9850
British International (Isles of Scilly to Penzance)	islesofscillyhelicopter.com	(01736) 363871*
Eastern Airways	easternairways.com	0870 366 9100*
Easyjet	easyjet.com	0871 244 2366
Flybe	flybe.com	0871 522 6100
Jet2.com	jet2.com	0871 226 1737*
Ryanair	ryanair.com	0871 246 0000
Skybus (Isles of Scilly)	islesofscilly-travel.com	0845 710 5555
VLM	flyvlm.com	0871 666 5050

Train

National Rail Enquiries	nationalrail.co.uk	0845 748 4950
The Trainline	trainline.co.uk	
UK train operating companies	rail.co.uk	
Arriva Trains	arriva.co.uk	0845 748 4950
c2c	c2c-online.co.uk	0845 601 4873
Chiltern Railways	chilternrailways.co.uk	0845 600 5165
CrossCountry	crosscountrytrains.co.uk	0845 748 4950
East Midlands Trains	eastmidlandstrains.co.uk	0845 748 4950
First Capital Connect	firstcapitalconnect.co.uk	0845 748 4950
First Great Western	firstgreatwestern.co.uk	0845 700 0125
Gatwick Express	gatwickexpress.co.uk	0845 850 1530
Heathrow Express	heathrowexpress.com	0845 600 1515
Hull Trains	hulltrains.co.uk	0845 071 0222
Island Line	island-line.co.uk	0845 748 4950
London Midland	londonmidland.com	0845 748 4950
Merseyrail	merseyrail.org	0845 748 4950
Northern Rail	northernrail.org	0845 748 4950
One Railway	onerailway.com	0845 600 7245
South Eastern Trains	southeasternrailway.co.uk	0845 000 2222
South West Trains	southwesttrains.co.uk	0845 600 0650
Southern	southernrailway.com	0845 127 2920
Stansted Express	stanstedexpress.com	0845 600 7245
Transpennine Express	tpexpress.co.uk	0845 600 1671
Virgin Trains	virgintrains.co.uk	0845 722 2333*

Ferry

Ferry information	sailanddrive.com	
Condor Ferries (Channel Islands)	condorferries.co.uk	0870 243 5140*
Steam Packet Company (Isle of Man)	steam-packet.com	0871 222 1333
Isles of Scilly Travel	islesofscilly-travel.co.uk	0845 710 5555
Red Funnel (Isle of Wight)	redfunnel.co.uk	0870 444 8898
Wight Link (Isle of Wight)	wightlink.co.uk	0870 582 0202

Phone numbers listed are for general enquiries unless otherwise stated.

* Booking line only

David Bellamy Conservation Award

"These well-deserved awards are a signpost to parks which are making real achievements in protecting our environment. Go there and experience wrap-around nature....you could be amazed at what you find!" says Professor David Bellamy.

Many of Britain's holiday parks have become 'green champions' of conservation in the countryside, according to leading conservationist David Bellamy. More than 600 gold, silver and bronze parks were this year named in the David Bellamy Conservation Awards, organised in conjunction with the British Holiday and Home Parks Association. These parks are recognised for their commitment to conservation and the environment through their management of landscaping, recycling policies, waste management, the cultivation of flora and fauna and the creation of habitats designed to encourage a variety of wildlife onto the park. Links with the local community and the use of local materials are also important considerations.

Parks participating in the scheme are assessed for the awards by holidaymakers who complete postcards to be returned to David Bellamy, an inspection by a local, independent Environmental Consultant and David Bellamy's own study of the parks' environmental audit completed when joining the scheme. Parks with Bellamy Awards offer a variety of accommodation from pitches for touring caravans, motor homes and tents, to caravan holiday homes, holiday lodges and cottages for rent or to buy. Holiday parks with these awards are not just those in quiet corners of the countryside. Amongst the winners are much larger centres in popular holiday areas that offer a wide range of entertainments and attractions.

The parks listed overleaf all have a detailed entry in this guide and have received a Gold, Silver or Bronze David Bellamy Conservation Award. Use the park index to find the page number.

For a free brochure featuring a full list of award-winning parks please contact:
BH&HPA,
6 Pullman Court,
Great Western Road,
Gloucester GL1 3ND
t (01452) 526911
e enquiries@bhhpa.org.uk
w davidbellamyconservation.org.uk

Castlerigg Hall Caravan & Camping Park	GOLD	Keswick	Northwest
Church Stile Holiday Park	GOLD	Wasdale	Northwest
Crake Valley Holiday Park	GOLD	Coniston	Northwest
Gelder Wood Country Park	GOLD	Heywood	Northwest
Hill of Oaks and Blakeholme Caravans	GOLD	Windermere	Northwest
Limefitt Park	GOLD	Windermere	Northwest
Waterfoot Caravan Park	GOLD	Ullswater	Northwest
White Cross Bay Holiday Park and Marina	GOLD	Windermere	Northwest
Wild Rose Park	GOLD	Appleby-in-Westmorland	Northwest
Woodclose Caravan Park	GOLD	Kirkby Lonsdale	Northwest
Finchale Abbey Caravan Park	SILVER	Durham	North East
Seafield Caravan Park	GOLD	Seahouses	North East
Allerton Park Caravan Park	GOLD	York	Yorkshire
Cayton Village Caravan Park	GOLD	Scarborough	Yorkshire
Golden Square Caravan and Camping Park	GOLD	Helmsley	Yorkshire
Ladycross Plantation Caravan Park	GOLD	Whitby	Yorkshire
Lebberston Touring Park	GOLD	Scarborough	Yorkshire
Middlewood Farm Holiday Park	GOLD	Whitby	Yorkshire
Rudding Holiday Park	GOLD	Harrogate	Yorkshire
St Helena's Caravan Site	GOLD	Leeds	Yorkshire
Sleningford Watermill Caravan & Camping Park	GOLD	Ripon	Yorkshire
Upwood Holiday Park	GOLD	Haworth	Yorkshire
Fernwood Caravan Park	GOLD	Ellesmere	Heart of England
Island Meadow Caravan Park	GOLD	Aston Cantlow	Heart of England
The Ranch Caravan Park	GOLD	Evesham	Heart of England
Ashby Park	GOLD	Horncastle	East Midlands
Golden Valley Caravan & Camping	GOLD	Ripley	East Midlands
Rivendale Caravan and Leisure Park	GOLD	Alsop-en-le-Dale	East Midlands
Cable Gap Holiday Park	SILVER	Bacton-on-Sea	East of England
Fen Farm Caravan and Camping Site	GOLD	East Mersea	East of England
Grasmere Caravan Park	BRONZE	Great Yarmouth	East of England
Searles Leisure Resort	GOLD	Hunstanton	East of England
Waldegraves Holiday Park	GOLD	Mersea Island	East of England
Wyton Lakes Holiday Park	SILVER	Wyton	East of England
Bay View Park Ltd	GOLD	Pevensey Bay	South East
Crowhurst Park	GOLD	Battle	South East
Highclere Farm Country Touring Park	BRONZE	Beaconsfield	South East
Hillgrove Park	GOLD	St Helens	South East
Honeybridge Park	GOLD	Horsham	South East
Hurley Riverside Park	GOLD	Hurley	South East
Landguard Camping Park	GOLD	Shanklin	South East
Sandy Balls Holiday Centre	GOLD	Fordingbridge	South East
Sumners Ponds Fishery & Campsite	GOLD	Horsham	South East
Tanner Farm Touring Caravan & Camping Park	GOLD	Marden	South East
Whitecliff Bay Holiday Park	GOLD	Bembridge	South East
Beverley Park	GOLD	Paignton	South West
Broadway House Holiday Touring Caravan and Camping Park	GOLD	Cheddar	South West
Coastal Caravan Park	GOLD	Burton Bradstock	South West

Cofton Country Holidays	GOLD	Dawlish	South West
Dornafield	GOLD	Newton Abbot	South West
Fairways International Touring Caravan and Camping Park	SILVER	Bridgwater	South West
Forest Glade Holiday Park	GOLD	Kentisbeare	South West
Freshwater Beach Holiday Park	BRONZE	Bridport	South West
Golden Cap Holiday Park	GOLD	Bridport	South West
Halse Farm Caravan & Tent Park	GOLD	Winsford	South West
Harford Bridge Holiday Park	GOLD	Tavistock	South West
Higher Longford Caravan & Camping Park	GOLD	Moorshop	South West
Highlands End Holiday Park	GOLD	Bridport	South West
Monkton Wyld Farm Caravan & Camping Park	GOLD	Charmouth	South West
Mother Ivey's Bay Caravan Park	GOLD	Padstow	South West
Newton Mill Camping	GOLD	Bath	South West
The Old Oaks Touring Park	GOLD	Glastonbury	South West
PadstowTouring Park	SILVER	Padstow	South West
Parkers Farm Holiday Park	SILVER	Ashburton	South West
Polruan Holidays (Camping & Caravanning)	SILVER	Polruan-by-Fowey	South West
Porthtowan Tourist Park	SILVER	Porthtowan	South West
Rowlands Wait Touring Park	GOLD	Bere Regis	South West
Silver Sands Holiday Park	GOLD	Ruan Minor	South West
Stowford Farm Meadows	GOLD	Combe Martin	South West
Summer Valley Touring Park	SILVER	Truro	South West
Treloy Touring Park	SILVER	Newquay	South West
Warmwell Caravan Park	SILVER	Warmwell	South West
Whitehill Country Park	GOLD	Paignton	South West
Wilksworth Farm Caravan Park	GOLD	Wimborne Minster	South West
Wooda Farm Park	GOLD	Bude	South West
Belhaven Bay Caravan and Camping Park	GOLD	Dunbar	Scotland
Dovecot Caravan Park	SILVER	Laurencekirk	Scotland
Glen Nevis Caravan & Camping Park	GOLD	Fort William	Scotland
Linnhe Lochside Holidays	GOLD	Fort William	Scotland
Linwater Caravan Park	GOLD	Edinburgh	Scotland
Loch Ken Holiday Park	GOLD	Parton	Scotland
Lomond Woods Holiday Park	GOLD	Balloch	Scotland
Three Lochs Estate	GOLD	Kirkcowan	Scotland
Witches Craig Caravan Park	GOLD	Stirling	Scotland
Silver Birch Caravan Park	SILVER	Prestatyn	Wales
Tan y Don Caravan Park	SILVER	Prestatyn	Wales

National Accessible Scheme index

Parks participating in the National Accessible Scheme are listed below. At the front of the guide you can find information about the scheme. Parks in colour have a detailed entry in this guide. Place names are listed alphabetically within their region.

♿ Mobility level 1

Armathwaite England's Northwest	Englethwaite Hall Caravan Club Site ★★★★	273
Bury England's Northwest	Burrs Country Park Caravan Club Site ★★★★★	57
Coniston England's Northwest	Park Coppice Caravan Club Site ★★★★	58
Grange-over-Sands England's Northwest	Meathop Fell Caravan Club Site ★★★★★	59
Kendal England's Northwest	Low Park Wood Caravan Club Site ★★★★	60
Lamplugh England's Northwest	Dockray Meadow Caravan Club Site ★★★★	62
Newlands England's Northwest	Low Manesty Caravan Club Site ★★★★	275
Penrith England's Northwest	Troutbeck Head Caravan Club Site ★★★★★	62
Thurstaston England's Northwest	Wirral Country Park Caravan Club Site ★★★★	276
Windermere England's Northwest	Braithwaite Fold Caravan Club Site ★★★★	64
Berwick-upon-Tweed North East England	Seaview Caravan Club Site ★★★★	277
Durham North East England	Grange Caravan Club Site ★★★★★	78
Powburn North East England	River Breamish Caravan Club Site ★★★★★	79
Rothbury North East England	Nunnykirk Caravan Club Site ★★★★	278
Stockton-on-Tees North East England	White Water Caravan Club Park ★★★★★	80
Bolton Abbey Yorkshire	Strid Wood Caravan Club Site ★★★★★	95
Gilling West Yorkshire	Hargill House Caravan Club Site ★★★★	279
Harmby Yorkshire	Lower Wensleydale Caravan Club Site ★★★	279
Hebden Bridge Yorkshire	Lower Clough Foot Caravan Club Site ★★★★★	97
Knaresborough Yorkshire	Knaresborough Caravan Club Site ★★★★★	97
Sneaton Yorkshire	Low Moor Caravan Club Site ★★★★	281
York Yorkshire	Beechwood Grange Caravan Club Site ★★★★★	102
York Yorkshire	Rowntree Park Caravan Club Site ★★★★★	103
Birmingham Heart of England	Chapel Lane Caravan Park ★★★★★	114
Blackshaw Moor Heart of England	Blackshaw Moor Caravan Club Site ★★★★★	115
Little Tarrington Heart of England	The Millpond ★★★★★	283
Presthope Heart of England	Presthope Caravan Club Site ★★★	116
Ashbourne East Midlands	Blackwall Plantation Caravan Club Site ★★★★	284
Bakewell East Midlands	Chatsworth Park Caravan Club Site ★★★★★	128
Buxton East Midlands	Grin Low Caravan Club Site ★★★★★	129

⃛ Mobility level 1 continued

⃛ Mobility level 2

⃛ Category 2 (Scotland)

Parks in colour have a detailed entry in this guide.

Quick reference index

If you're looking for a specific facility use this index to see at-a-glance parks that match your requirement. Establishments are listed alphabetically by place name within each region.

🏊 Indoor pool

Quick reference index

⇄ Outdoor pool

Parks listed here have a detailed entry in this guide.

Index by park name

All parks with a detailed entry in this guide are listed below.

Parks listed here have a detailed entry in this guide.

Index by place name

The following places all have detailed park entries in this guide. If the place where you wish to stay is not shown, the location maps (starting on page 28) will help you to find somewhere to stay in the area.

Turn to the pages indicated for detailed park entries in these places.

Index to display advertisers

Published by: VisitBritain, Thames Tower, Blacks Road, London W6 9EL in partnership with Britain's tourism industry
visitbritain.com
Publishing Manager: Tess Lugos
Production Manager: Iris Buckley
Compilation, design, copywriting, production and advertisement sales: Jackson Lowe Marketing, 3 St Andrews Place, Southover Road, Lewes, East Sussex BN7 1UP
t (01273) 487487 jacksonlowe.com
Typesetting: Marlinzo Services, Somerset and Jackson Lowe Marketing
Accommodation maps: Based on digital map data © ESR Cartography, 2007
Touring maps: © VisitBritain 2005. National Parks, Areas of Outstanding Natural Beauty, National Trails and Heritage Coast based on information supplied by Natural England Licence No. 1000 46223, the Countryside Council for Wales Licence No. 1000 18813 and Scottish National Heritage. Cycle Networks provided by Sustrans
Printing and binding: Emirates Printing Press, Dubai, United Arab Emirates

Front cover: Three Cliffs Bay Caravan Park, Penmaen, Gower, Swansea (britainonview.com/Rod Edwards)
Back cover (top): Clumber Park, Bassetlaw; britainonview/Rod Edwards/McCormick-McAdam

Photography credits: britainonview/ANPA/Daniel Bosworth/Martin Brent/brightononview /Coventry Cathedral/East Midlands Tourism/East of England Tourism/Jakob Ebrey /Rod Edwards/Damir Fabijanic/FCO/Dennis Hardley/Adrian Houston/Kent Tourism Alliance/Simon Kreitem/Leicester Shire Pr/Pawel Libera/James McCormick/McCormick-McAdam/Eric Nathan/NWDA/Tony Pleavin/Grant Pritchard/Ingrid Rasmussen/Ian Shaw/Jon Spaull/Visit Chester & Cheshire/Visit London/Wales Tourist Board Photo Library/Jenny Woodcock; Caravan Club; Matt Cardy; The Deep; East Midlands Development Agency; Four Seasons Teesside White Water Centre; Johnny Haddock; Herefordshire Council; Imperial War Museum North; Michael Jackson; Marketing Birmingham; One NorthEast Tourism; Joan Russell; Trentham Leisure; Visit London; visitlondonimages/britainonview

A VisitBritain Publishing guide